TWO STEPS FORWARD

Housing policy into
the new millennium

Edited by Dave Cowan and Alex Marsh

The POLICY
P ≈ P
P R E S S

First published in Great Britain in July 2001 by

The Policy Press
34 Tyndall's Park Road
Bristol BS8 1PY
UK

Tel +44 (0)117 954 6800
Fax +44 (0)117 973 7308
e-mail tpp@bristol.ac.uk
www.policypress.org.uk

© The Policy Press 2001

British Library Cataloguing in Publication Data

A catalogue record for this book is available from the British Library

ISBN 1 86134 229 2 paperback

A hardcover version of this book is also available

Dave Cowan is a Lecturer and **Alex Marsh** is a Senior Research Fellow, both at
the University of Bristol.

Cover design by Qube Design Associates, Bristol.

Front cover: Photograph supplied by kind permission of Helen Cowan

Printed and bound in Great Britain by Hobbs the Printers Ltd, Southampton.

Contents

Notes on contributors

Sarah Blandy qualified as a solicitor in 1978 and worked as a housing lawyer in private practice in London and Sheffield, and at Tower Hamlets Law Centre. She was the Landlord and Tenant Relations Officer for Sheffield City Council and subsequently Principal Officer for Hostels and Homelessness. She has been a Senior Lecturer in Housing Law at Sheffield Hallam University since 1993, teaching, researching and writing on housing law.

Pauline Card (formerly Pauline Papps) is a Research Associate at the Centre for Housing Management and Development, Department of City and Regional Planning, Cardiff University. Her doctoral research is on the management of anti-social behaviour by local housing authorities in England and Wales.

Helen Carr qualified as a solicitor in 1982 and practised at Bradford Law Centre for 10 years, specialising in housing law. Since joining the University of North London she has taught housing law on a variety of professional and academic courses. Her research interests include the relationship between housing law and housing policy and citizenship. She has published 'The sorting of the forks from the spades: an unnecessary distraction in Housing Law' in D. Cowan (ed) *Housing: Participation and exclusion* (Dartmouth, 1998).

Dave Cowan is Lecturer in Law at the University of Bristol. His publications include *Homelessness:The (In-)appropriate applicant* (Dartmouth, 1997) and *Housing law and policy* (Macmillan, 1999) and he edited *Housing: Participation and exclusion* (Dartmouth, 1998). With various colleagues he has completed work on the rehousing of sex offenders as well as harassment and unlawful eviction in the private rented sector. Current research projects include joint work on internal reviews in homelessness cases, the private rented sector in Northern Ireland, and unauthorised encampments.

Kenneth Gibb is a Senior Lecturer in the Department of Urban Studies at the University of Glasgow. He is primarily interested in using housing economics to analyse housing market, policy and financial questions. He has published widely in the area of the design of housing subsidies for low-income households.

Robina Goodlad is Professor of Housing and Urban Studies at the University of Glasgow. Prior to working at the University she directed the (Scottish) Tenant Participation Advisory Service during its first five years. She has carried out a number of research projects on tenant and citizen participation.

Caroline Hunter is a barrister and Senior Lecturer in Housing Law at Sheffield Hallam University. She is deputy general editor of *the Encyclopedia of Housing Law and Practice*, the *Housing Law Reports* and the *Journal of Housing Law*. With colleagues at Sheffield Hallam University she has been involved in a number of research projects on legal aspects of housing management, most recently on the use of legal remedies to deal with anti-social behaviour. The final report of the research, *Neighbour nuisance, social landlords and the law*, was published by the Chartered Institute of Housing in July 2000.

Philip Leather is Professor of Housing and Urban Renewal, and Director of the Centre for Urban and Regional Studies, at the University of Birmingham. He is an experienced housing researcher with particular interests in poor housing conditions and housing renewal policies, sustainable home ownership, private rented housing, and the housing needs of older people. He is adviser to the Joseph Rowntree Foundation on housing renewal policy.

Alex Marsh is currently Senior Research Fellow at the School for Policy Studies, the University of Bristol. His research interests include rent setting policy in the social housing sector and the changing organisation and regulation of social housing management. His publications include *Housing and public policy* (edited with David Mullins, Open University Press, 1998) and *Homelessness: Exploring the new terrain* (edited with Patricia Kennett, The Policy Press, 1999).

Barbara Mauthe is a Lecturer in Law at the University of Lancaster. Her specialist interests are the central–local relationship and Public Law theory.

Tom Mullen is Senior Lecturer in Law at the School of Law, University of Glasgow. His main teaching and research interests are in constitutional law, administrative law, and housing law. He was for several years convener of the board of a community controlled law centre, and was in 1995/96 a special advisor to the Select Committee on Scottish Affairs on their inquiry into housing and anti-social behaviour. Publications include *Tenancy rights and repossession rates: In theory and practice* (with Suzie Scott, Suzanne Fitzpatrick and Robina Goodlad, Scottish Homes, 1997) and *Legal remedies for neighbour nuisance* (with Caroline Hunter and Suzie Scott, Scottish Homes, 1998).

Alan Murie is Professor of Urban and Regional Studies at the Centre for Urban and Regional Studies, University of Birmingham. He has carried out a wide range of research and published widely on housing and related issues.

Brendan Nevin is a Lecturer in Urban and Regional Studies at the Centre for Urban and Regional Studies, University of Birmingham. His main research activities include work on changing housing markets in England and on different aspects of housing stock transfers.

Peter Robson is Professor of Social Welfare Law at the University of Strathclyde. He is also part-time judge in the Appeals Service dealing with social security and child support issues. He is Chair of the Board of Trustees of Shelter and Shelter (Scotland). He is author of a number of books including *Homeless people and the law* (Butterworths, 1996), *Residential tenancies* (W. Green & Son, 1998) and *Property* (W. Green & Son, 1998) and joint editor of the *Journal of Law and Society* Special Issue on Law and Film (2001).

Dorothy Sefton-Green is a former Senior Lecturer in Economics at the University of North London where she specialised in social economics, particularly in the field of housing. She directed courses in Policy Studies and Public Administration and has collaborated with Helen Carr on several interdisciplinary projects in the area of rented housing.

Peter Somerville is Professor of Social Policy and Head of the Policy Studies Research Centre at the University of Lincolnshire and Humberside. He has a background in housing practice and in research on housing and social policy. He has published widely on resident participation, empowerment and social exclusion. His latest book, entitled *Social relations and social exclusion*, is published by Routledge (2000).

Damien Tissier is the Managing Director of Strategic Urban Futures. He has 17 years of community development and urban regeneration experience in the public and voluntary sectors. He has substantial senior management experience and in 1997 was a gold medal winner of the Local Government Chronicle Management Challenge. Among his main areas of expertise are: capacity building, community consultation, project initiation and partnership development. Currently, he is leading on the community development aspects of the Finsbury Park Single Regeneration Budget 5 Programme.

Peter Vincent-Jones is Professor of Law and Director of Research at Lancashire Law School, University of Central Lancashire. He has published extensively on contract, housing and public management issues from a socio-legal perspective. He was director of a recently completed research project funded by the ESRC, 'Conflict and Cooperation in Contracting for Professional Services: A Comparative Study'. Most recently his work has focused on the UK government's abolition of Compulsory Competitive Tendering and its replacement by a statutory framework of Best Value under the 1999 Local Government Act.

Bruce Walker is Senior Lecturer in the Economics of Public Policy in the School of Public Policy at the University of Birmingham. His current research interests include rent restructuring in social housing, the implications of the Best Value regime for Registered Social Landlords and the impact of contracting on public service provision.

Acknowledgements

Early work on this book took place while Alex Marsh was a visitor at the Centre for Analysis of Social Exclusion (CASE), London School of Economics, during Spring 2000. He would like to thank CASE for its hospitality and for providing the ideal environment within which to develop the idea.

ONE

Analysing New Labour housing policy

Dave Cowan and Alex Marsh

There has been an exponential growth in policy debate and development related to, and concerning, housing since the New Labour administration came to power in 1997. Testament to this are the various reports from the Social Exclusion Unit and its Policy Action Teams, Consultation Papers on topics ranging from cowboy builders through to reforms to local authority housing finance, requirements to set up Tenant Participation Compacts, and the publication in 2000 of the first English Green Paper on housing for 23 years. Following a period in which housing academics had been relatively negative regarding the prospects for housing policy – some were even asking whether it had a future – it has moved closer to the heart of policy. This higher priority has been accompanied by a modest increase in central government funding.

This book examines some of the central themes of this panoply of reports and policy statements. We focus on eight issues of contemporary policy concern: housing transfers; housing standards; social housing allocation; tenant participation; anti-social behaviour; Best Value; social sector rent policies; and Housing Benefit and personal subsidy. This is our first aim. Our second aim is to bring an extra dimension to the discussion by pairing writers from the field of housing studies, on the one hand, and socio-legal studies, on the other, and asking them to provide a perspective on a particular policy theme. Not only does this provide two different interpretations of the relevant developments, but we believe that it also highlights the potential for greater collaboration and cross-boundary exchange between the two subject areas. There is great potential for cross-fertilisation of ideas, guiding precepts, and theoretical understandings between these areas – a point to which we return in our concluding chapter. The pairing of contributions enables a richer account of each theme to emerge, while simultaneously illustrating that there is both commonality and diversity of interest between the two subject areas. We hope that it will also encourage the reader to ask basic questions – such as whether law *is* the answer and what shapes the values underlying the development of law and policy – that would perhaps have passed without comment if the discussion did not encompass contributions from both subject bases.

The remainder of this first chapter seeks to elaborate on these themes and aims. The next section reviews the development of housing policy during the 20th century to provide a background for the discussion in the succeeding chapters. It then draws attention to the debates concerning the future of housing policy as a preface to our discussion of New Labour housing policy and, more specifically, our summary of the main proposals in the 2000 Housing Green Paper. Subsequent sections then engage with the second aim of the book by considering the character of housing and socio-legal studies and some of the issues arising from collaboration between the two fields. The chapter concludes by outlining briefly the content of the rest of the volume.

Evolution and revolution in housing

In the UK, as in most other western industrialised countries, the stability brought to the early post Second World War period by government commitment to full employment and the development of the Keynesian welfare state was accompanied by rising real incomes and increased affluence. The economic crises of the 1970s saw a re-emergence of a belief in the prescriptions of classical economics – free trade, free markets, minimal government intervention – and ushered in a period of market liberalisation and welfare state retrenchment. The 'decommodification' of the post-war period gave way to a recommodifying impulse as a variety of privatisation initiatives – affecting many areas of the economy – were implemented in countries across the globe.

These social and economic changes were reflected in and refracted through the housing system in the UK. The starkest, and most well-known, change is the tenure shift from a system dominated by private renting at the start of the century to a system dominated by owner-occupation at the century's end. Equally significant is the general improvement in the condition and amenity of the housing stock, with the implications that this carries for improved public health.

Several factors influenced the replacement of private renting by owner-occupation and social rented housing. Rising real incomes brought home ownership within the reach of a greater number of households and an extensive programme of local authority construction offered private tenants better housing options. The rise of alternative investment vehicles and the existence of rent control made other investments more attractive than private landlordism. Consequently private renting declined rapidly until the late 1980s. Yet a feature of the current housing system is the rehabilitation of the image of the private rented sector. Twenty years ago it was viewed as an anachronistic remnant of a previous age, but there is now near consensus among politicians and commentators that a healthy private rented sector is essential if the UK economy is to compete in the contemporary global economy. Nonetheless, there continue to be problems with the standard both of properties and of housing management in parts of the private rented sector.

With the arrival of the Conservative governments of the 1980s the key dimension of tenure restructuring was not the move out of private renting but the transfer of stock from the local authority sector to the owner-occupied sector and, more recently, to the Registered Social Landlord (RSL) sector. The Right to Buy policy saw 1.4 million dwellings transfer from the local authority sector between 1980 and 1999 (Wilcox, 2000, p 113). After 20 years the Right to Buy continues to play a role in reshaping the structure of housing provision at local level. In addition, since the first transfer in 1988 more than 450,000 dwellings have left the local authority sector for the RSL sector through large-scale voluntary transfer. The properties are now managed by not-for-profit landlords. Most properties have been transferred to housing associations, but latterly local housing companies (LHCs) have emerged as a new type of landlord organisation. After a relatively tentative start this transfer programme has picked up speed and promises a revolution in the way that the housing needs of low-income households are met.

The Right to Buy policy had its origins in the government's antipathy to council housing and desire to create a property-owning democracy. But, as with the longer-term decline in the private rented sector, financial concerns and mechanisms have been a key driver behind these more recent changes. The deregulation of the mortgage market during the 1980s meant that more households could access mortgage finance, while the discounts offered to local authority tenants made purchase more appealing. In the local authority sector the financial regime effected a switch from price subsidies which reduce rents towards higher rents and a reliance on Housing Benefit to assist those on lower incomes. Increased

rents made the switch from renting to owning more appealing for many
of those tenants in a position to exercise their Right to Buy.

Not only did local authority tenants face progressively higher rents,
tight control on capital spending in order to restrict overall public
expenditure meant the properties in which they lived were deteriorating.
In contrast, RSLs are able to access private funds to finance repairs,
improvement and development without it counting towards public
spending totals and hence incurring central government displeasure. This
combination of factors persuaded many local authority officers and tenants
that transfer to the RSL sector was desirable. The implications of such
change for local democratic accountability and the delivery of policy
objectives are less well explored.

The purchase of property under the Right to Buy was selective. Those
who purchased tended to have relatively high incomes and the stock
purchased tended to be of better quality. The social housing building
programme since the 1980s has been concentrated in the RSL sector and
has not been of a scale sufficient to compensate for the loss of stock
through the Right to Buy. As a consequence, a shrinking social housing
stock has increasingly been allocated to those in the most urgent housing
need, although the last Conservative government sought to curtail the
access of homeless households, who had previously been considered in
urgent need, to public sector housing using the 1996 Housing Act.

A process of progressive residualisation of the social rented sector was
under way more than quarter of a century ago (Murie, 1983), but changes
in socio-economic circumstances and in policy have clearly accelerated
this process. Moreover, the process of residualisation has become
exacerbated in many areas by the increasingly poor image of social housing,
which has become intimately linked in the minds of many with issues of
anti-social behaviour and crime, poor schools and amenities. The problems
– both real and perceived – of the social housing sector are dramatically
illustrated by high turnover and high void rates in the social sector. In
the 1990s the apparently declining popularity of certain parts of the
housing stock has led to concern with so-called 'low demand'. Low
demand has its origins in a number of social and economic processes, but
some part of it is associated with low-income households exercising choice.
Where the pressure on the local social housing stock is not so great that
the stock is heavily rationed, tenants and prospective tenants are presented
with a choice of properties. Indeed, in some areas they face a choice of
tenures and, perhaps for the first time, some are choosing to be rehoused
in the private rented sector in preference to accepting an offer of social

housing. This is seen as a way of avoiding the problems and stigma that has come to be attached to the status of being a social housing tenant in particular locations.

While much attention has been focused on the issues and problems emerging in the social housing sector, the situation of some living in the owner-occupied sector is also a cause for concern. The increased reliance on the owner-occupied sector means, inevitably, that the sector has to accommodate households in a wider range of circumstances, including those on low or insecure incomes. Low-income and marginal owner-occupiers can face difficulties both in maintaining their position by keeping up with their mortgage payments and keeping up their property to ensure that it is maintained as a healthy and safe living environment.

The private housing market in Britain is characterised by considerable volatility in terms of both prices and affordability. The causes of this volatility are disputed. What is not in dispute is that since the mid-1980s the deregulated housing finance market in Britain has allowed house purchasers to become heavily indebted and the extensive use of variable rate mortgages has meant that changes in interest rates are passed on rapidly to existing borrowers. High levels of borrowing against the value of housing led, in the early 1990s, to the widespread emergence of 'negative equity'. Adverse economic trends, high interest rates and rising unemployment led to rising mortgage arrears and repossessions. Further retrenchment on the part of the government in the early 1990s saw a reduction in the availability of state support for those who find themselves in difficulty. This reduction in support was accompanied by central government's exhortation that households should arrange private cover to insure against income instability and unemployment. An emphasis on developing an increased role for private welfare provision is perhaps to be expected from a Conservative administration. Less predictable is the way in which the Labour government of the late 1990s continued to accept the legitimacy of the role of the private sector in providing welfare services. However, government now sees itself as concerned with forging a 'Third Way' between state and market: the talk is of public–private partnership, rather than of greater private provision being desirable in itself.

The production and consumption of housing is shaped by the complex interaction between a range of social, economic and policy changes. Consequently it is possible to identify elements of evolution – such as the decline of private renting – in the way the housing system developed during the last century. Overlaid on these longer-term changes are periods of change which are little short of revolutionary: the early phase of the implementation of the Right to Buy policy is a good example. The net result of change is that the housing circumstances of many have improved over time, but there remains a range of problems – some long-standing, some relatively new – that policy could potentially seek to address. Yet, the early and mid-1990s were a time of relatively limited active housing policy.

The end or a new beginning for housing policy?

The 'end of housing policy' debate

The thrust of central government policy over the 1980s and 1990s led commentators to debate whether the end of the millennium may be an appropriate time to accept that talk of a distinctive housing policy is no longer meaningful (eg Kleinman, 1996; Bramley, 1997; Malpass, 1999). There is an increased reliance on market forms of provision, while support for owner-occupiers – assistance when unemployed, subsidies to mortgage payments, improvement grants – has been curtailed or withdrawn. As a consequence a large proportion of housing consumers are not directly affected by active housing policies.

In the social housing sector, the decline of public funding for new construction and the transfer of stock to RSLs means that what Bramley (1997) terms 'formal' housing policy has declined markedly in significance. Where publicly funded investment in the existing stock occurs on any substantial scale, it is likely to be part of a package of measures implemented under the auspices of regeneration, rather than housing, policy. Rent increases in the social housing sector and the deregulation of rents in the private rented sector mean that the burden of assisting low-income renters rests with personal subsidy through Housing Benefit, which is largely an income support measure. Hence some have been tempted to view housing policy as a branch of either regeneration or social security policy, rather than as a separate policy field in its own right. Equally there are dimensions to housing policy that could be thought of as primarily a component of social care or health policy. Such a view would be underlined by the reorientation of government thinking towards prevention rather than cure and the recognition, in documents such as *Our healthier nation* (DoH, 1998), that housing is one of the key determinants of ill-health.

Whether this is an appropriate interpretation of the current state of policy development remains unclear. It depends in part on current policy and, in particular, on the fate of the proposals contained in the housing Green Paper (DETR/DSS, 2000). An equally important question is whether it matters. The current government underlines the importance of 'joined-up thinking' and holistic approaches to dealing with complex social problems, as exemplified in the approach to addressing the problems of disadvantaged areas adopted by the Social Exclusion Unit (eg SEU, 2000). Most would consider this development an advance over previous departmentalised and compartmentalised approaches to policy making: the fact that 'housing policy' might cease to be an identifiable entity is surely of lesser importance.

In part, the question as to whether we should mourn or celebrate the potential disappearance of an identifiable housing policy cannot be answered in the abstract. It depends crucially on our view of the aims and scope of housing policy. Arguably, a lack of a coherent and widely accepted vision for the role of government in the housing system has impaired the ability to evaluate contemporary policy developments. Unless we are clear what we think housing policy is trying to achieve we are not well placed to judge whether allowing housing concerns to be subsumed within a variety of other policy areas represents an effective strategy.

In any event, housing policy has for the moment returned to the central government policy agenda. The early years of the New Labour administration witnessed a number of relatively modest housing initiatives (see Kemp, 1999, for a review). There were also broader policy developments – such as the replacement of Compulsory Competitive Tendering by the Best Value regime or the formulation of policy towards 'anti-social behaviour' – which carried substantial implications for housing. It was, however, the Green Paper on housing policy in England, promised since the General Election in May 1997 and eventually published on 4 April 2000, which can be seen as signalling the re-emergence of housing as an issue worthy of sustained central government attention.

The Green Paper – a summary

Quality and choice are the key themes of the Housing Green Paper, although they do not exhaust its scope. The concern with quality encompasses all tenures and is directed variously at the standard of existing and new build stock, housing management, construction and building industries, and financial products. The Green Paper's discussion of choice is more focused on the social rented sector and, in particular, on the issues of allocations and transfers. The key principles for housing policy are set out as follows:

- Offering everyone opportunity, choice and a stake in their home, whether rented or owned.
- Ensuring an adequate supply of decent housing to meet needs.
- Giving responsibility to individuals to provide for their own homes where they can, providing help for those who cannot.
- Improving the quality and design of the housing stock, new housing and residential environments, helping to achieve an urban renaissance and protecting the countryside.
- Delivering modern, efficient, secure, customer-focused public services and empowering individuals to influence them.
- Reducing barriers to work, particularly in relation to benefit and rent policy.
- Supporting vulnerable people and tackling all forms of social exclusion, including bad housing, homelessness, poverty, crime and poor health.
- Promoting sustainable development that supports thriving, balanced communities and a high quality of life in urban and rural areas. (DETR/DSS, 2000, para 1.5)

For an extended period there has been substantial underinvestment in the housing stock across the major tenures. This has led to problems of disrepair and the need for extensive improvement and modernisation. A key current policy question is how to ensure that the standard of the existing stock is raised. An early move by the current government was to make available £800 million in capital receipts for re-investment in the council stock over the period 1997-99 (DETR, 1997). This was followed by an increase in planned spending for housing for the period 1999-2002 of £3.9 billion (see Wilcox, 1999). While this injection of funds has been welcomed, the Green Paper envisages that in order to generate a sufficient increase in the quality of the stock alternative routes will need to be pursued. Specifically, the government sees a major role for the continuation of the programme of transferring stock from the local authority to the RSL sector that began under the Conservative government. There is also a proposal for the creation of a new type of organisational arrangement – the local authority-owned arm's-length management company. If the government's vision were to be realised then, by 2004, RSLs would become the majority providers of social housing.

The process of maintaining and upgrading the fabric of owner-occupied properties is a topic which the previous government largely neglected. It is an area that the Green Paper addresses directly and canvasses opinion on a proposed new approach to the improvement grant system (paras 4.46-4.55). The government's concern for standards in the private rented sector has already led to a commitment to introduce a licensing system covering 'houses in multiple occupation', although it is not clear when that will be implemented. Licensing in the wider private rented sector is rejected in the Green Paper as being unnecessarily burdensome (para 5.31). Relatively modest proposals to replace the housing fitness standard with a health and safety rating scale and to overhaul local authorities' powers to intervene where housing is unfit are presented. As alternative approaches to raising standards, the Green Paper raises the possibility that direct payments of Housing Benefit might be denied to landlords who provide unacceptable housing and that the Housing Benefit available to tenants in poor quality properties might be restricted in areas of over-supply/low demand. Little appears to be directed at poor quality properties in high demand areas.

Not only the quality of the existing stock, but also the quality of rental housing management is regarded as in need of improvement. In the private rented sector there are a range of modest suggestions, differentiated between those designed to assist 'good and well intentioned landlords' – such as supporting local landlord accreditation schemes and a 'kitemark' for letting agents – and those designed to 'make the worst landlords better' (paras 5.8-5.25 and 5.26-5.49 respectively). In the latter category are the denial of Housing Benefit payments direct and limited licensing focused on defined local areas of declining demand. A range of more specific suggestions are directed at raising the quality of processes and products in various parts of the housing market. Many of these proposals fall under the broad heading of consumer protection, which the government sees as one of its key contributions to facilitating the operation of the housing market (para 4.4).

While choice occupies a prominent position in the Green Paper, it is focused more narrowly. There are some specific issues relating to the private sector – such as the government's drive to increase the intelligibility of mortgage products to allow consumers to make better informed choices – but the main concern, as it was for the previous government, is to facilitate choice in the social rented sector (ch 9). The discussion is predicated on the notion of tenant as consumer. Choice – between housing providers as well as within the stock of a single provider – is seen not just as desirable but as fundamental to reducing the stigmatisation and reversing the residualisation of social housing. In terms of choice between the dwellings in a social landlord's stock, the key routes are through potentially far-reaching reforms of the allocations and transfer systems – represented by a shift from 'allocation' to 'letting' – and through restructuring rents to create 'fairer' patterns of rents. On choice between landlords there is a desire to see a range of social housing providers in a locality 'competing for tenants' custom' (para 6.14). Another important, but perhaps more indirect, means of facilitating choice between landlords is the proposal that there should be convergence in rents between neighbouring local authorities and the RSLs operating within their area.

A theme which vies with quality and choice for prominence in the Green Paper is the role of the local authority in local housing markets. The government indicates its desire to see local authorities take a stronger strategic role which encompasses concern for all tenures (ch 3). The strategic role starts with identifying need and then encompasses a number of strands including facilitating, often through partnership working, the various routes through which needs can be met. Authorities are also in a position to link housing needs to wider social, economic and environmental concerns. Much of the subsequent discussion about improvement in quality contains reference back to the strategic role of local authorities in effecting change.

In the light of existing documents on neighbourhoods and social exclusion originating from the Social Exclusion Unit, the Green Paper addresses issues of the sustainability of communities and of low demand or unpopular housing. These broader debates encompass issues of local economic, crime and regeneration policy rather than simply being housing policy issues, but they clearly inform policy proposals in the social and private rented sector. In the social sector, the reform of allocations policies will not only be about facilitating choice for individuals but also about 'local lettings' policies that aim to change the social composition of areas in order to bring stability and build sustainable communities. The Green Paper also signals existing policies and powers on anti-social behaviour as being a key element in the process of creating and supporting sustainable communities (paras 12.27-12.31). In the private rented sector the Green Paper recognises that it is not simply anti-social behaviour by tenants but the "large-scale operations of some unscrupulous landlords" (para 5.32) that are undermining the social fabric of particular localities. Despite these selective discussions, anti-social behaviour is a theme of New Labour housing policy which does not receive prominence in the Green Paper.

Partly, this is because it had received attention in earlier policy documents emanating from the Social Exclusion Unit, and partly also perhaps because policy in this area is being driven by the agenda of the Home Office.

Many commentators were looking for, and expecting, the Green Paper to signal major changes in the way the Housing Benefit system operates. Its current form is seen as embodying a whole range of perverse incentives and inefficiencies (para 11.4 and see Kemp, 1998). While the Green Paper raises the novel possibility of using Housing Benefit to improve quality in the private rented sector, it does not propose its fundamental restructuring. Instead, at this stage, the government seems content to focus on improving the administration of the system, reducing the complexity of the rules, tackling fraud and error, and improving work incentives. It signals that longer-term fundamental reform is needed, but that the way forward needs to be debated. While some of the initiatives in the Green Paper are to be welcomed, they are at best incremental and there must be concern regarding how existing measures to eradicate fraud are affecting innocent tenants. Proceeding with more comprehensive or extensive anti-fraud measures needs to be considered carefully. Not only could they have potentially damaging effects on people's lives, but by underlining the fact that welfare recipients are viewed as actual or potential 'knaves' (terminology used by Le Grand, 1997) they could contribute to the further stigmatisation of those who seek assistance.

Socio-legal studies, housing studies and interdisciplinarity

There is a need to examine critically this increased level of policy activity. We need to consider how current housing policy developments relate to previous policy: are we looking at continuity or change, evolution or revolution? How do they relate to broader policy agendas or changing conceptualisations of the role of government, society and the individual? In making sense of developments we need to draw on the full range of conceptual and theoretical resources within the social sciences.

A central purpose of this book is to bring together two subject areas – housing studies and housing law. They are both subjects which are concerned with, among other issues, assessing the outputs of government which shape the housing system, but they have often been separated, both within institutions and in research. Yet, while such physical and intellectual separation exists, there are signs of convergence. This book is intended to provide a further stimulus in this direction.

In this section, we seek to provide an introduction to socio-legal studies and housing studies, briefly setting out some of the key characteristics of each area. This will identify the broad parameters within which each subject operates. Our position is that there is plenty of scope for collaboration between authors from the two areas, but this can and should only be done once there is a level of appreciation of the aims and objectives within each subject. To put it another way, each subject must be 'cognitively open' to the strengths and weaknesses of the other.

Our rationale for pairing these two subject areas can be summarised as follows: the substance of much of housing studies is influenced by housing law – yet this aspect is rarely explored by authors from the housing studies tradition; the substance of housing law is influenced by broader social, economic and housing policy changes – yet this aspect is rarely explored by authors from the housing law tradition. Despite the fact that there is a considerable overlap between the two subjects, they have rarely come into contact with each other. Here, then, we take the opportunity to provide a brief overview of two subject areas.

Before doing so, we should reflect on what we perceive the benefits of collaboration to be, as well as on the pitfalls of such a joint approach. The benefits of collaboration mean that one can draw on a wider body of literature –which is otherwise missed – in order to provide a broader, more rounded critique of aspects of housing policy. Being sensitised to activities and developments in another field means that not only can inadvertent replication of the work of others be avoided, but a range of different understandings and approaches can be incorporated into the analysis. Our joint research into harassment and unlawful eviction required the insights from both housing studies and housing law to be integrated within our understanding of the macro- and micro-processes involved in the policing of the landlord–tenant relation (Marsh et al, 2000). Similar processes have infused the collaboration of colleagues at Sheffield Hallam and Glasgow Universities (respectively Nixon et al, 1996; Mullen et al, 1997). These studies have all broadly concerned the way in which due process rights have been translated into the housing system and the success in doing so.

The collaborative approach we advocate is not without pitfalls. Most significant is that researchers may be 'semi-literate' in other subjects, which may confuse discussion and serve to obfuscate the necessary connections. Indeed, as Teubner suggests (1983, p 300), "when the actions of black boxes must be co-ordinated, each focuses not on the unseen internal workings of the other but on the interrelations between them".

Collaborative research needs to be rooted in a firm understanding of the 'home' subject area and be approached critically.

While we can see great potential in collaborative work, the ambitions of the current volume are more modest. The authors provide their own perspective on a particular theme. They were not required to draw on or incorporate insights from the literature generated within the 'other' subject. It is through the juxtaposition of the contributions that the differences of perspective and potential for cross-fertilisation and synthesis emerge. We reflect further on this potential in the conclusion. This volume presents contributions that are valuable in their own right, but it represents only the beginning of the process of fostering collaboration.

About socio-legal studies

University law schools have, for most of their lifespan, concentrated on the production of doctrinal research which feeds into and, hopefully, influences legal practice. Doctrinal research might be characterised as positivistic, value neutral production of research which informs the reader what the law is, or should be, on any particular topic. In many law schools, this provides the dominant mode not only of research but also teaching.

Since the 1970s, however, socio-legal studies has developed within university law schools to the extent that some authors have regarded it as a paradigm "that will affect and alter the world of all academic lawyers" (Thomas, 1996, p 19). Indeed, one author has, perhaps with some exaggeration, suggested that most academic research into law is now socio-legal (Bradney, 1998). While it has increased in prominence, socio-legal studies has none the less been criticised as being theoretically underdeveloped (Campbell and Wiles, 1976), concentrating too much on the "pull of the policy audience" (Sarat and Silbey, 1988), and attempting the impossible (for discussion, see Cotterell, 1998).

Although there is no overarching definition of what socio-legal studies actually *is* – nor should there be – what one can say is that it involves a commitment to interdisciplinarity: "The 'socio' in socio-legal studies means to us an interface with a context within which law exists, be that a sociological, historical, economic, geographical or other context" (Thomas and Wheeler, 2000, p 271). In addition, there is increasing interest between law and humanities.

On one level, the debate is about the place and importance of context(s) within legal studies. The *Law in Context* series provide one arm of socio-legal studies. Partington's text on landlord and tenant (1975) provides an example of this germane to housing, and also highlights a problem that derives from within such studies. This text was the first landlord and tenant law book to incorporate references to social policy and sociological material – that is what marks it out as the genesis of socio-legal work in housing. Yet, at the same time, it gives prominence to doctrinal law, thus "providing us with a frame of reference for the legal model from within law itself" (Wheeler, 1997, p 285). Subsequent studies have sought to generate theoretical and methodological understandings beyond this, through a commitment to interdisciplinarity that does not place law as the predominant controlling value.

Despite that commitment to interdisciplinarity, there is also an 'uncertainty of identity' inherent within socio-legal studies – as to whether it is social, legal, or a mixture of the two (Fitzpatrick, 1995). On this perspective, it is said that law provides a view of society in which it is "manifested and affirmed as general authority predominant over any particular or 'lesser' authority" (p 110). It is then said that social science is, or can only be, 'on tap, but not on top' within socio-legal research (for discussion and rejection of this point, see Cotterell, 1998; cf Nelken, 1998). Thus, drawing on systems theory, it is suggested that law provides its own set of truths and explanations, which are impervious to sociological understanding.

Although it is not the intention of the chapters that follow to engage with these issues, they present problems for future researchers seeking to engage in interdisciplinary or, as Cotterell suggests (1998, p 183), "transdisciplinary" understandings. Our mission in this book is to bring the two subject areas closer together, but researchers will need to be aware of, and respond to, these issues.

While housing research and teaching within university law schools has traditionally tended to follow the model of doctrinal law, we can acknowledge the development of socio-legal research into housing, which, it can be asserted, has now become the predominant approach. From the mid-1980s, socio-legal research into housing came of age (as can be demonstrated by the collection of papers from the Socio-Legal Studies Association annual conference in 1997: Cowan, 1998). One particular focus has been the administration of social housing allocation and homelessness, following up the enquiries of Lewis (1976). Particular attention has been given to the role and 'impact' of judicial review on such administration, leading to the rich and important work of Loveland (1988, 1995) and Halliday (1998, 2000). Secondly, a school of work has been developed by those at Sheffield Hallam University drawing socio-legal insights generated from the use of discourse analysis to identify prejudices about tenure (see, for example, Hunter and Nixon, 1999; Blandy and Goodchild, 1999). Thirdly, after Partington's groundbreaking text on landlord and tenant law (1975), the subsequent work of Mullen et al (1999) has shown the relevance of different tenancy agreements given by different social landlords on the repossession process. Fourthly, there have been important studies concerning regulation of the housing system, such as mortgage lenders (Whitehouse, 1999) and Compulsory Competitive Tendering (Vincent-Jones, 1999). Fifthly, there has been a series of reflective concerns about housing law itself, developing analytical and structural frameworks for understanding the role and values of law (Stewart, 1996; Cowan, 1999).

About housing studies

Housing has been the subject of social research since the start of systematic social inquiry. Early work on low incomes, housing conditions and health was a foundation stone of empirical social research in Britain (eg Chadwick, 1842; Booth, 1892). Yet, with the notable exception of studies such as Bowley (1945), housing did not receive sustained academic attention in the UK until the 1960s. It was then that research centres with a specialist focus on housing were established and innovative theoretical work focusing on housing, but carrying implications for wider social scientific debates, emerged.

Much housing research is research *for* policy. This has led critics to suggest that housing studies as a subject is theoretically underdeveloped and dominated by agendas set by policy makers (Kemeny, 1988, 1992). However, the subject is arguably no more dominated by the current policy agenda than other applied fields. It is also the case that policy-driven research can be the springboard to addressing broader theoretical questions (eg Cameron and Field, 2000). There has been a consistent component to the housing studies literature that has sought to relate components of, and developments within, the housing system to broader theoretical concerns.

The theoretical base for housing studies is broad. Researchers draw on theoretical and conceptual resources from the full range of social scientific disciplines in order to explore the social, economic and political dimensions to housing. The flow of ideas and analysis should not, however, be seen as all one way. The seminal study by Rex and Moore (1967), for example, sought to conceptualise the link between housing and social stratification. The 1980s debate around the role of housing in consumption sector cleavages (eg Saunders, 1984, 1986) sought to question dominant accounts which placed class relations, defined with reference to production, at the centre of social analysis. A concern with the way in which housing markets create or reinforce social division is a recurrent theme of housing studies. The analysis is both cross-sectional – examining spatial and social differentiation resulting from the operation of housing markets, policy change and bureaucratic processes (eg Lee and Murie, 1999; Forrest and Murie, 1990; Henderson and Karn, 1987) – and longitudinal – examining the impacts of, for example, the spread of home ownership on capital accumulation and intergenerational wealth transfers (eg Hamnett et al, 1991; Hamnett, 1998; Forrest and Murie, 1994). Authors within housing studies have demonstrated a willingness to engage with a range of contemporary theoretical debates and methodological developments. This includes work utilising discourse analysis (Jacobs and Manzi, 1996, 2000; Gurney, 1999a, 1999b; Haworth and Manzi, 1999) or social constructionism (Franklin and Clapham, 1997; Jacobs et al, 1999), work linking housing market change to the debate about the risk society (Forrest, 1999; Perri 6, 1998; Nettleton and Burrows, 1998) or citizenship (Kennett, 1998, 1999), and work considering key developments in policy such as the rise of the 'new public management' (Walker, 1998) or the nature and growth of regulation (Mullins, 1997).

Not only is there a strong element of research for policy within housing studies but there is also a concern to provide external evaluations of policy development and impacts, with a view to influencing subsequent policy directions. A good example of this type of work is the critique of the social rent policies pursued by the Conservative governments of the early 1990s. Work by Wilcox and Meen (1995), among others, which highlighted the implications of rising rents for poverty traps and index-linked benefits, contributed to the government's change of direction and increased emphasis on affordability from 1995. It is in this tradition of commentary and appraisal of contemporary policy directions that the contributions to this book can be located.

The scope of the book

This book is structured around eight key themes of New Labour housing policy selected by the editors. The primary criterion for the inclusion of a theme was the belief that it was a key contemporary policy issue. Yet the themes can be differentiated further. Some are issues of perennial or recurrent concern in the housing field (allocations policy, housing standards, and tenant participation), while others connect with the broader policy agendas and innovations set out by New Labour (anti-social behaviour, Best Value). Themes also address policies which have had a major impact on the way the housing system is structured (stock transfer), and areas of policy in which reform is felt to be long overdue (social housing rent policy, Housing Benefit).

Other themes undoubtedly compete for attention. The strategic role of local authorities or the question of sustaining low-income home ownership are just two important areas to which it would be desirable to devote more space. The themes finally selected are those that were felt to have potential for drawing out some of the points of connection and contrast between the two contributing subject areas.

For each theme, one author from housing studies and one from socio-legal studies was asked to provide a critique of current policy and, if it were felt appropriate, to explore possible alternative directions. As noted above, authors were asked to provide a perspective from either housing studies or socio-legal studies, with no necessity to attempt to draw on the literature from the 'other' subject area. The editors did not attempt to constrain authors either in terms of the breadth or focus of their coverage of a particular theme. The objective was in part to see the nature of the contributions that emerged from this relatively broad brief. Paired authors were not expected to compare notes in preparing their chapters, although in one or two cases authors chose to do so. This approach offers the potential for paired chapters to contain considerable duplication and repetition. However, the paired authors generally offered perspectives that diverged to the extent that overlap was relatively limited. There are some instances in which, for example, authors review similar policy developments or summarise the provisions of the Housing Green Paper. While in such instances there was editorial direction to reduce overlap, we took the view that it was more important to maintain the integrity of individual contributions and preserve them as free-standing contributions.

For ease of reference, each themed pair of chapters is prefaced by a short introduction which sets out some of the key differences in approach and substance between the two contributions. The ordering of the subject perspectives alternates between themes, so as not to suggest inadvertently the privileging of one or other subject area.

The first theme examined is the policy that is perhaps having the most significant effect on the contemporary housing system: stock transfer.

Alan Murie and Brendan Nevin reflect on the origins of the policy and the fact that, perhaps contrary to expectations, New Labour has adopted and extended the stock transfer programme relatively uncritically. Tom Mullen offers a socio-legal perspective on a range of dimensions to stock transfer, with a particular focus on tenants' rights. The second theme – housing standards in the private sector – throws up a clear contrast in focus. Sarah Blandy addresses the private rented sector and considers issues of security of tenure, management, harassment and eviction, physical standards and the role of Housing Benefit. Her analysis focuses on the three Rs: regulation, responsibility and rights. Philip Leather's contribution, in contrast, encompasses the problems of both low-income owner-occupiers and the lower end of the private rented sector. The discussion contained in the Green Paper suggests that assistance to low-income owners is one area in which a significant change of policy direction is a possibility. Leather offers some important observations regarding the degree to which renewal policies can sensibly be expected to address the problems facing the sector.

The third pair of authors are concerned with perhaps the most radical of all the suggestions in the Green Paper – that concerning the allocation of social housing. The approach in these chapters diverge considerably. Dave Cowan draws attention to five problems identified by socio-legal researchers which need to be addressed: the motivations behind the legislation; the application process; the shift away from need towards risk-based policies; interagency working; and adjudication. He is essentially sceptical about the concept of housing need. Peter Somerville, by contrast, seeks to provide an alternative set of proposals to give meaning to the concept of housing need. He argues that the managerialism of New Labour policies has not been linked with changes on the ground; that it is difficult to see how increased choice can be facilitated without increasing inequality; and that thought needs to be given to how individual need is to be balanced against community need.

Both of the authors addressing the fourth theme – tenant participation – suggest that this cross-party policy aim lacks any definition. That is, however, their only similarity. Their approaches to the issues are rather different. On the socio-legal side, Helen Carr, Dorothy Sefton-Green and Damien Tissier argue that tenant participation "cannot be separated from the contemporaneous reduction in political, economic and legal accountability". By way of contrast to the Right to Buy, which gives tenants considerable powers to exit the tenure, tenant participation creates little in the way of collective rights. Robina Goodlad, on the housing studies side, draws on three separate social theoretical perspectives in her analysis – theories of democracy and citizenship; theories of the state; and power. She suggests that a new citizenship right of tenant participation is now emerging.

The fifth pair of contributors were asked to consider anti-social behaviour and, once again, both suggest that there are definitional problems. Pauline Card argues that prevailing political discourses have caused the focus of responses to anti-social behaviour to be on the occupants of social housing. Caroline Hunter, on the other hand, draws attention to different approaches adopted by social housing managers and notes that their reasons for using their powers may relate to extraneous factors. Both chapters then consider alternative approaches to the policing of anti-social behaviour.

The sixth theme is the organisation and provision of housing management in the context of Best Value. Here again the perspective adopted by the two authors diverged considerably. Peter Vincent-Jones focuses on the local authority sector and central–local relations, while Bruce Walker largely restricts his discussion to the application of Best Value to the RSL sector. Vincent-Jones examines the range of regulatory mechanisms and strategies and seeks to locate Best Value within a broader current of policy leading to the 'responsibilisation' of local authorities. Walker, in contrast, takes an explicitly economic approach that, while also concerned with issues of regulation, is more narrowly focused on incentives, performance measurement and the role of the regulator.

The seventh pair of authors address the issue of rent policy in the social rented sector. Both authors focus on the local authority sector, but approach the topic from a very different angle. Alex Marsh provides an overview of policy development leading up to New Labour's restructuring of rent policy. He then examines the options that featured in current discussions. He argues that, while most commentators are in broad agreement regarding the future direction for policy, there are fundamental questions, assumptions and value positions that have not been explored as fully as might be desirable. Barbara Mauthe, in contrast, relates the issue of rent setting more firmly to changing central–local relations. She locates rent policy more explicitly within the context of other contemporary policy changes. She explores the utility of two concepts from the socio-legal literature – juridification and governance – in understanding the evolution of rent policies, before developing the case for an alternative approach: politicalisation.

The final pair of chapters address the thorny issue of Housing Benefit and personal subsidy. This is an area which has been seen as ripe for reform for many years and many had expected New Labour to grapple with systems which were seen as failing to deliver on just about every level. Peter Robson examines Housing Benefit policy in the context of the development of broader welfare policies and provides a discussion that encompasses a number of the more detailed questions about the way in which policy is administered and about adjudication. In contrast, Kenneth Gibb writes from an economic perspective and examines the effectiveness of both the Housing Benefit and Income Support for Mortgage Interest system. His contribution is particularly concerned with the incentives embodied in each system. He reflects briefly on why the Housing Benefit system has thus far proved relatively immune to reform and reviews some of the possible directions for future change. Neither author feels that current policy proposals have gone far enough, although for very different reasons.

Conclusion

The contributions to this volume offer a range of perspectives on contemporary developments in housing policy. By bringing authors working within different traditions together the volume also seeks to highlight the potential for further cross-subject collaboration. We believe that the following chapters represent a valuable contribution to ongoing policy debates and to the broader search for satisfactory understandings of the complex social phenomena that are the subject of housing policy and law. They could undoubtedly contribute to shaping the thinking that underpins housing policy in this new millennium. We hope they also act as a stimulus for future work seeking to cross the boundary between housing studies and housing law.

References

6, Perri (1998) 'Housing policy in the risk archipelago: towards anticipatory and holistic government', *Housing Studies*, vol 13, no 3, pp 347-76.

Blandy, S. and Goodchild, B. (1999) 'From tenure to rights: conceptualising the changing focus of housing law in England', *Housing, Theory and Society*, vol 16, no 1, pp 31-42.

Booth, C. (1892) *Life and labour of the people of London*, London: Macmillan.

Bowley, M. (1945) *Housing and the state, 1919-1944*, London: George Allen and Unwin.

Bradney, A. (1998) 'Law as a parasitic discipline', *Journal of Law and Society*, vol 25, pp 71-85.

Bramley, G. (1997) 'Housing policy: a case of terminal decline?', *Policy & Politics*, vol 25, no 4, pp 387-408.

Cameron, S. and Field, A. (2000) 'Community, ethnicity and neighbourhood', *Housing Studies*, vol 15, no 6, pp 827-44.

Campbell, C. and Wiles, P. (1976) 'The study of law and society in Britain', *Law and Society Review*, vol 11, pp 547-86.

Chadwick, E. (1942) *Report on the sanitary conditions of the labouring population of Great Britain*, London: HMSO.

Cotterell, R. (1998) 'Why must legal ideas be interpreted sociologically?', *Journal of Law and Society*, vol 25, no 2, pp 171-92.

Cowan, D. (ed) (1998) *Housing: Participation and exclusion*, Aldershot: Dartmouth.

Cowan, D. (1999) *Housing law and policy*, Basingstoke: Macmillan.

DETR (Department of the Environment, Transport and the Regions) (1997) *Capital receipts initiative: Guidance to local authorities*, London: DETR.

DETR/DSS (Department of Social Security) (2000) *Quality and choice: A decent home for all*, Housing Green Paper, London: DETR/DSS.

DoH (Department of Health) (1998) *Our healthier nation: A contract for health*, Cm 3852, London: The Stationery Office.

Fitzpatrick, P. (1995) 'Being social in socio-legal studies', *Journal of Law and Society*, vol 22, pp 105-12.

Forrest, R. (1999) 'The new landscape of precariousness', in P. Kennett and A. Marsh (eds) *Homelessness: Exploring the new terrain*, Bristol: The Policy Press.

Forrest, R. and Murie, A. (1990) *Selling the welfare state: The privatisation of public housing*, London: Routledge.

Forrest, R. and Murie, A. (eds) (1994) *Housing and family wealth*, London: Routledge.

Franklin, B. and Clapham, D. (1997) 'The social construction of housing management', *Housing Studies*, vol 12, pp 7-25.

Gurney, C. (1999a) 'Lowering the drawbridge: a case study of analogy and metaphor in the social construction of home-ownership', *Urban Studies*, vol 36, pp 1705-22.

Gurney, C. (1999b) 'Pride and prejudice: discourses of normalisation in public and private accounts of home ownership', *Housing Studies*, vol 14, pp 163-85.

Halliday, S. (1998) 'Researching the "impact" of judicial review on routine administrative decision-making', in D. Cowan (ed) *Housing: Participation and exclusion*, Aldershot: Ashgate.

Halliday, S. (2000) 'Institutional racism in bureaucratic decision-making: a case study in the administration of homelessness law', *Journal of Law and Society*, vol 27, pp 449-72.

Hamnett, C. (1998) *Winners and losers*, London: UCL Press.

Hamnett, C., Harmer, M. and Williams, P. (1991) *Safe as houses: Housing inheritance in Britain*, London: Paul Chapman Publishing.

Haworth, A. and Manzi, T. (1999) 'Managing the "underclass": interpreting the moral discourse of housing management', *Urban Studies*, vol 36, pp 153-65.

Henderson, J. and Karn, V. (1987) *Race, class and the allocation of state housing*, Aldershot: Gower.

Hunter, C. and Nixon, J. (1999) 'Tenure preference, discourse and housing debt: language's role in tenure stigmatisation', *Habitat International*, vol 23, pp 79-92.

Jacobs, K. and Manzi, T. (1996) 'Discourse and policy change: the significance of language for housing research', *Housing Studies*, vol 11, pp 543-60.

Jacobs, K. and Manzi, T. (2000) 'Performance indicators and social constructivism: conflict and control in housing management', *Critical Social Policy*, vol 20, no 1, pp 85-103.

Jacobs, K., Kemeny, J. and Manzi, T. (1999) 'The struggle to define homelessness: a constructivist approach', in S. Hutson and D. Clapham (eds) *Homelessness: Public policies and private troubles*, London: Cassell.

Kemeny, J. (1988) 'Defining housing reality: ideological hegemony and power in housing research', *Housing Studies*, vol 3, no 4, pp 205-18.

Kemeny, J. (1992) *Housing and social theory*, London: Routledge.

Kemp, P. (1998) *Housing Benefit: Time for reform*, York: Joseph Rowntree Foundation.

Kemp, P. (1999) 'Housing policy under New Labour', in M. Powell (ed) *New Labour, New welfare state? The 'third way' in British social policy*, Bristol: The Policy Press.

Kennett, P. (1998) 'Differential citizenship and housing experience', in A. Marsh and D. Mullins (eds) *Housing and public policy*, Buckingham: Open University Press.

Kennett, P. (1999) 'Homelessness, citizenship and social exclusion', in P. Kennett and A. Marsh (eds) *Homelessness: Exploring the new terrain*, Bristol: The Policy Press.

Kleinman, M. (1996) *Housing, welfare and the state in Europe*, Cheltenham: Edward Elgar.

Le Grand, J. (1997) 'Knights, knaves or pawns? Human behaviour and social policy', *Journal of Social Policy*, vol 26, pp 149-69.

Lee, P. and Murie, A. (1999) 'Spatial and social divisions within British cities: beyond Residualisation', *Housing Studies*, vol 14 no 5, pp 625-40.

Lewis, N. (1976) 'Council housing allocation: problems of discretion and control', *Public Administration*, vol 54, pp 147-60.

Loveland, I. (1988) 'Housing Benefit, administrative law and administrative practice', *Public Administration*, vol 66, pp 57-76.

Loveland, I. (1995) *Housing homeless persons*, Oxford: Oxford University Press.

Malpass, P. (1999) 'Housing policy: does it have a future?', *Policy & Politics*, vol 27, no 2, pp 217-28.

Marsh, A., Niner, P., Cowan, D., Forrest, R. and Kennett, P. (2000) *Harassment and unlawful eviction of private rented sector tenants and park home residents*, London: DETR.

Mullen, T., Scott, S., Fitzpatrick, S. and Goodlad, R. (1997) *Tenancy rights and repossession rates in theory and practice*, Edinburgh: Scottish Homes.

Mullen, T., Scott, S., Fitzpatrick, S. and Goodlad, R. (1999) 'Rights and security in housing: the repossession process in the social rented sector', *Modern Law Review*, vol 62, pp 11-32.

Mullins, D. (1997) 'From regulatory capture to regulated competition: an interest group analysis of the regulation of housing associations in England', *Housing Studies*, vol 12, pp 301-19.

Murie, A. (1983) *Housing inequality and deprivation*, London: Heinemann.

Nelken, D. (1998) 'Blinding insights? The limits of a reflexive sociology of law', *Journal of Law and Society*, vol 25, 407-26.

Nettleton, S. and Burrows, R. (1998) 'Individualisation processes and social policy: insecurity, reflexivity and risk in the restructuring of contemporary British health and social policies', in J. Carter (ed) *Postmodernity and the fragmentation of welfare*, London: Routledge.

Nixon, J., Hunter, C., Smith, Y. and Wishart, B. (1996) *Housing cases in county courts*, Bristol/York: The Policy Press/Joseph Rowntree Foundation.

Partington, M. (1975) *Landlord and tenant*, London: Weidenfeld & Nicolson.

Rex, J. and Moore, R. (1967) *Race, community and conflict*, Oxford: Oxford University Press.

Sarat, A. and Silbey, S. (1988) 'The pull of the policy audience', *Law and Policy*, vol 10, pp 98-120.

Saunders, P. (1984) 'Beyond housing classes', *International Journal of Urban and Regional Research*, vol 8, pp 202-27.

Saunders, P. (1986) *Social theory and the urban question* (2nd edn), London: Hutchinson.

SEU (Social Exclusion Unit) (2000) *National strategy for neighbourhood renewal: A framework for consultation*, London: SEU.

Stewart, A. (1996) *Rethinking housing law,* London: Sweet and Maxwell.

Teubner, G. (1983) 'Substantive and reflexive elements in modern law', *Law and Society Review*, vol 17, pp 239-85.

Thomas, P. (1996) 'Socio-legal studies: the case of disappearing fleas and bustards', in P. Thomas (ed) *Socio-legal studies*, Aldershot: Dartmouth.

Thomas, P. and Wheeler, S. (2000) 'Socio-legal studies', in D. Hayton (ed) *Law's future(s)*, Oxford: Hart.

Vincent-Jones, P. (1999) 'The regulation of contractualisation in quasi-markets for public services', *Public Law*, pp 304-27.

Walker, R. (1998) 'New public management and housing associations: from comfort to competition', *Policy & Politics*, vol 26, pp 71-86.

Wheeler, S. (1997) 'Company law', in P. Thomas (ed) *Socio-legal studies*, Aldershot: Dartmouth.

Whitehouse, L. (1999) 'The home-owner: citizen or consumer?', in S. Bright and J. Dewer (eds) *Land law: Themes and perspectives*, Oxford: Oxford University Press.

Wilcox, S. (1999) *Housing finance review 1999/2000*, York: Joseph Rowntree Foundation.

Wilcox, S. (2000) *Housing finance review 2000/2001*, York: Joseph Rowntree Foundation/Chartered Institute of Housing/Council of Mortgage Lenders.

Wilcox, S. and Meen, G. (1995) *The cost of higher rents*, London: National Federation of Housing Associations.

Stock transfer in the social rented sector

Introduction

The transfer of local authority owned stock to the Registered Social Landlord (RSL) sector is currently the major factor reshaping the structure of housing provision in England. The stock transfer process is also getting underway in Scotland. It is therefore an appropriate theme for our first pair of contributions.

The origins of the policy lie, as Alan Murie and Brendan Nevin discuss, in the reaction of local authorities to the constraints that they faced under the Conservative adminstrations of the 1980s and 1990s. Any expectations that the arrival of New Labour would represent the end of the stock transfer process and the revalorisation of council housing have been disappointed. In their contribution Murie and Nevin trace the change in Labour thinking on transfers from antipathy to acceptance. They consider whether – and how – New Labour transfers thinking, as set out in the Housing Green Paper, differs from the approach of the previous administrations. They query the seemingly uncritical acceptance of the desirability of stock transfer that characterises much current policy thinking. In their concluding discussion of future prospects they raise a wide range of questions and issues which it would be wise to address before accepting that stock transfer is the most appropriate way forward in all cases. These include questions about area regeneration, low demand, and the compatibility of stock transfer with other current policy goals. Implicit in their discussion is the view that current policy lacks the degree of 'joined-up thinking' that is both desirable and necessary for it to be effective.

While Murie and Nevin devote much of their discussion to changes in political thought at the national level, Tom Mullen is more concerned to examine central–local relations and, in particular, to examine the transfer process from the perspective of the collective and individual rights of tenants. He notes that tenants are typically presented with a very limited choice when balloted regarding transfer: either transfer and have your home repaired/improved or do not transfer and remain in substandard accommodation. He argues that this process does not allow tenants to exercise their collective rights effectively: important options that are likely to meet with tenant approval are not available. The legal framework governing stock transfer is highly discretionary which leads Mullen to highlight the difficulties facing those who are unhappy with the outcome of the transfer process and who might wish to mount a legal challenge. There has been only one legal case seeking to question a transfer decision and the outcome of that case was such that it decreased the likelihood of future challenges.

Transferring from the local authority sector to the RSL sector sees tenants moving from secure to assured tenancies. Mullen explains why in principle this represents a diminution of tenants' rights. In particular, it makes eviction for rent arrears easier. He notes that research has highlighted differences in the way and extent to which social landlords make use of the 'additional' possession grounds associated with assured tenancies. The differences were, however, better understood as a result of differences in policy and tenant profile than arising from differences in the legal relationship between landlord and tenant. Nonetheless, given that the government sees local authorities and RSLs as pursuing similar objectives, the fact that their tenants have a different legal relationship with their landlord is anomalous. Current discussions about a single form of tenure for residents in the social rented sector should be seen therefore not just as something of specialist interest but as fundamental to realising future visions for social housing.

TWO

New Labour transfers

Alan Murie and Brendan Nevin

Introduction

In spite of the active privatisation strategies of the 1980s and 1990s over
3 million council houses remained in England in 2000 and they formed
some 15% of all dwellings. By the late 1990s the backlog of under-
maintenance and the effects of a prolonged residualisation process were
no longer denied but were key considerations in the future of housing
policy. Against this background proposals for the transfer of ownership
and control of council housing were an important element in the Housing
Green Paper (DETR/DSS, 2000). What was regarded by many as a policy
inherited from the Conservatives was not only endorsed by New Labour
but the scale of anticipated transfer represented a considerable increase
when compared with the achievements of the previous government. With
little evidence of strong support either from local government or council
tenants the strength of commitment to this policy may be regarded as
surprising. At the same time the increase in activity, if it is achieved, will
further change the housing market in England and the impacts of such
changes are uncertain.

This chapter outlines the origins of stock transfer policies before setting
out the key proposals in this area. It argues that the continuity in policy,
while surprising in some respects, can be explained especially in relation
to public expenditure considerations. It also argues that, in view of the
significance of the planned change, there is a striking failure to discuss a
range of potentially important issues.

Thatcherite origins

The widest background to stock transfer policy is a continuing political debate about the merits of different tenures and about the failings (alleged and actual) of state housing. The Conservative party's antipathy to state housing was deep rooted and, in the post-war period, became more vehement as the market was deemed more capable of responding to outstanding housing needs. Critiques of the waiting list society and lack of choice were not just voiced by Conservatives and, over time, as the council stock aged and included more dilapidated properties, alternatives to council ownership became more attractive.

Historical examples of stock transfers between public sector landlords, acquisitions by them and disposals can be identified (see, for example, Murie, 1999). However, in the modern era, stock transfers have been associated with the privatisation, demunicipalisation and devalorisation strategies developed by the Conservative governments in the period after 1980. There are a number of discussions of these developments (see, for example, Malpass and Murie, 1999; Cole and Furbey, 1994; Forrest and Murie, 1990). The flagship policy of the government was the Right to Buy and the motivations for privatisation were as much associated with electoral and political judgements as with housing or financial considerations. Breaking the municipal stranglehold on large sections of the population was seen to be a key way of breaking the political solidarity of council estates.

The early years of the Right to Buy were seen as a success in terms of the scale of impact of the policy. Yet peak sales were achieved in 1982. By 1985 sales were only half the figure for 1982. It was also evident that the policy was having an uneven impact, with proportionately fewer sales of flats and of properties in the North and in the major urban centres. Adjustments were made to the Right to Buy to remedy this, but with only limited effect. It was against this background that government began to look at new ways of achieving the same effect – of breaking up municipal monopoly and municipal ownership. It is important to recognise that throughout this period there were continuing disposals of individual vacant properties. The notorious Westminster sales campaign was carried out with the approval of the Secretary of State and can be seen to be a precursor of attempts to widen the demunicipalisation process beyond the Right to Buy. One further major initiative merits reference. In 1983 the 3,000-unit Cantril Farm Estate in Knowsley was transferred to the Stockbridge Village Trust which had been created for this purpose.

The Trust was charged with raising finance to improve and remodel the area. Legislation in 1986 provided local authorities with powers to dispose of block holdings of properties. Although some local authorities began to dispose of properties in order to escape the capital expenditure restrictions which prevented them from upgrading estates (Usher, 1987), the numbers of such disposals remained low.

The key developments in the new phase of stock transfer emerged in the lead up to the 1987 General Election. The Conservative party identified the 'right to rent' and an agenda which was concerned with providing a choice of landlord. New legislation passed in 1988 provided a Tenants' Choice procedure and enabled the setting up of Housing Action Trusts (HATs). HATs involved stock transfer for estate improvement and came with a large public expenditure commitment based on the experience of what had been required for Stockbridge Village Trust. Additionally, and also because of the reluctance of private sector financial institutions to lend in difficult areas, reforms to tenancies and the ability to raise finance against housing association rental streams were introduced. It would appear that government was seeking a new weapon to break municipal monopolies. The opportunity to choose and change landlord was expected to be too great to be resisted by the dissatisfied council tenantry. Giving them to the right to change landlord was expected to lead to a major flow of stock transfers.

This assumption proved to be incorrect and Tenants' Choice remained an almost wholly unused provision. At the same time the areas that government had selected for HATs uniformly rejected this development. Much as with the transfers referred to earlier, what actually happened was that local authority landlords began to see opportunities in the legislation associated with HATs and with Tenants' Choice to achieve things that they couldn't achieve otherwise. They began to see stock transfer as a way of generating capital receipts and escaping from responsibilities that they could not deliver and they took the lead in seeking transfers (Mullins et al, 1993, 1995). Rather than dissatisfied tenants driving a transfer process it was disabled landlords who sought to resolve their dilemmas through transfer.

For government, perhaps bruised by the rejection of its preferred option, the opportunity to adjust its stance but achieve demunicipalisation was an attractive one. HATs were negotiated in six places and a programme of large-scale voluntary transfers (LSVTs) began to take shape in rural and suburban locations.

The framework for these transfers was initially linked to the Tenants'

Choice model and matured into a managed programme. Throughout the life of this LSVT programme there have been concerns about not approving very large transfers that were inconsistent with the language of breaking up monopoly landlordism. Early on in the process concern also began to emerge about the Housing Benefit consequences of stock transfers. The lack of joined-up thinking in government meant that at the outset the impact of housing transfers (and higher rents) on the social security (Housing Benefit) budget had not been taken into account. Once noted a more managed process of transfer and some financial adjustment within government were put in place.

The LSVT programme worked in the shire counties and areas where positive asset values meant that stock transfers generated a windfall gain for the local authority – a gain that could be used to develop other policy priorities. The programme did not offer incentives and arguably could not work where there were negative values associated with the stock – in urban areas of the North and Midlands and in Inner London. The policy innovation designed to respond to this was the creation of an Estates Renewal Challenge Fund (ERCF) in 1995. This Challenge Fund was introduced to provide a mechanism to enable the transfer of negative value estates by providing a dowry through the Challenge Fund to enable transfers to take place with private sector funding. The ERCF had a limited budget and only achieved a limited number of transfers in urban areas. By March 1999 32,000 properties had been approved for transfer under ERCF compared with the 323,000 transferred under LSVT. The LSVT programme had achieved a lot more, but with very little activity in urban areas and none in areas with negative value. After three rounds of allocations the ERCF was discontinued and there has been a shift of emphasis in larger urban areas towards whole stock transfer.

Labour transfers thinking

Throughout the early Thatcherite period, the Labour Party's position in relation to housing privatisation was one of resignation and division. From an initial categorical rejection of the Right to Buy, electoral defeat had led Labour into a categorical support for it. Similarly, after an initial position of opposing Tenants' Choice and the legislation which was seen as seeking to dismantle a successful and effective housing policy, Labour developed a much more pragmatic stance at the national level. In the lead up to the General Election of 1997 it began to identify with a stock transfer agenda. Nick Raynsford, as the spokesperson in opposition, had been involved in the development of proposals about the formation of local housing companies (LHCs) and had sought to identify a distinctive approach to stock transfers which would be acceptable to Labour supporters.

Much of the Labour Party continued to be unimpressed by arguments and policies for stock transfer. Of the 68 transfers (of 260,000 properties) during the decade to 1998 only two (containing 2,900 properties) were in disadvantaged urban areas. The reasons for the refusal of Labour local authorities to cooperate with the transfer process are complex but can be summarised as flowing from a perceived democratic deficit within the housing association movement and from the fact that much of the council housing stock had a negative value and the failure to raise sufficient in capital receipts would leave the local authority servicing a residual housing debt.

These concerns had been partly addressed by the 1996 Housing Act which made it possible for local authorities to nominate councillors to the Boards of new LHCs and by the introduction of the dowry fund administered through the ERCF. These changes resulted in considerably more interest in transfer being shown by Labour and Liberal Democrat local authorities in the Midlands, London and the North West. However, comparatively little interest has been shown in the North East, Yorkshire and Humberside and the East Midlands.

The Labour Party's view of stock transfers has changed over recent years but has continued to reflect differences within the party. As the recognition of the need for additional resources to modernise and improve council housing strengthened, outright opposition to transfers gave way to a more pragmatic position at the national level. If they represented the only way to access the resources needed then transfer had to be contemplated. While some in the Party had become enthusiastic about the LHC model others were reluctant but resigned. A considerable number of powerful local authorities remained opposed. A view held by opponents of transfer was that it was only needed because of the way that the Treasury defined and operated the public expenditure system. While council housing is in the public sector it is subject to Treasury controls on borrowing and in this framework there was no likelihood of sufficient funding being provided, given the lack of priority afforded to housing. Transfer to organisations which were defined as being in the private sector meant escape from these constraints and the possibility of accessing the resources needed.

At the time of its election in 1997 the tensions within the Labour Party at local and national levels were apparent. Some thought that the new government would redefine public expenditure to bring it more into line with the rest of Europe and to release local authorities from the capital restraints that they were working under. There were also expectations that levels of public expenditure would be increased sufficiently to make transfer unnecessary. It is clear that some people expected to hear very little more about stock transfers.

This view was fuelled by the early decision to release over a three-year period the £5 billion of accumulated receipts from the sale of council housing. Although the capital receipts initiative would not be sufficient to deal with the backlog of disrepair in the council housing stock, there was a hope that government would come up with other proposals. The study of the feasibility of whole stock transfers, as one of the options favoured within the Labour Party, also raised questions about whether this would work. A key concern was financial: the negative values associated with the urban housing stock were particularly difficult to overcome (LGA, 1997).

It became increasingly apparent that government was neither going to alter definitions of public expenditure nor was it going to find the funds to revalorise council housing when education and health were the priorities. The outstanding question then was: where would government go next? Given the refusal to contemplate the much higher public expenditure levels required to bring council housing up to standard, there appeared to be two options. One related to stock transfer and the second to continuing to manage a declining and deteriorating housing sector. Perhaps this left government with exactly the same dilemma as faced by local authorities 20 years earlier. In the absence of capacity to deliver what their supporters felt was needed, it was better to transfer ownership and achieve the improvement than continue to be associated with the management of a deteriorating product. This was facilitated by a relaxation of the transfer rules to allow the Treasury to write off debt in whole stock transfers with a negative or marginal value. This has been estimated as costing over £1 billion in urban areas considering transfer (*Housing Today*, 2000).

By the time the Housing Green Paper (DETR/DSS, 2000) emerged it was clear that while steady but slow progress was being made in improving council housing, transfers remained the one viable option to rapidly improve the quality of the housing stock for many urban authorities. Yet, at the same time the government's own initiatives are perhaps reducing the pressures which encourage local authorities to opt for transfer. The capital receipts initiative and the increased housing expenditures indicated following the Comprehensive Spending Review announced in 2000 began to alter the prospects for council housing in urban areas where the levels of disrepair were not so high. Greater expenditure and increased maintenance allocations offer the prospect of adequate finance without transfer and without altering the arrangements governing the control of public expenditure. The uncertainty over the need to transfer remains and, in the light of the debate about the future rent regimes for Registered Social Landlords (RSLs), is likely to have increased.

All of this suggests a pragmatic policy response which would not achieve uniform support throughout the Labour Party, but which would be seen as unavoidable. For many in local and central government it may also have been seen as a way of escaping one of the embarrassments associated with Labour's tradition of direct public service provision. Although tenants were not enthusiastic about other landlords, the criticism of local authorities' performance in relation to housing was a consistent source of difficulty for Labour councils and others in government. For those who were concerned with the modernisation agenda, the legacy of municipal housing was an embarrassment. Offloading embarrassments is a long established part of central government's traditions. Its tendency has often been to distance itself by passing administrative responsibility – but not policy responsibility – to local government (as with Housing Benefit). In this case, it could pass responsibility to independent, autonomous bodies – RSLs. At the same time, the formula adopted by the New Labour government did not simply reflect the older Conservative models.

The Green Paper proposals

The Green Paper reflects these tensions and develops the approach to stock transfer in tandem with a number of alternatives. Chapter 7 is entitled 'Raising the quality of social housing'. Its first eight paragraphs relate to investment in the social rented sector. The next 36 paragraphs refer to stock transfer, its contribution to regeneration, and alternatives to stock transfer including Private Finance Initiative (PFI) and the introduction of arm's-length management companies. This is followed by six paragraphs on better management and tenant empowerment and a single paragraph conclusion which states: "We want to see a step change in the performance of all social landlords and in the quality of social housing" (para 7.5 1).

However, the chapter states that the government recognises:

> ... that public investment will not be enough to bring about the marked improvements in quality and management that we seek. Other approaches must be pursued if we are to make the difference that is needed. (para 7.8)

The three main approaches are then identified as stock transfer, the creation of arm's-length management companies and the PFI.

While the origins of stock transfer are undoubtedly associated with previous Conservative administrations, as we noted above, the Labour Party in opposition had begun to accept the transfer agenda. Consequently the inclusion of stock transfers in the Green Paper is hardly surprising. Nevertheless there are surprises. The scale of the proposed transfer programme is planned to accelerate, while the proposals for arm's-length management organisations for council housing represent a major innovation. In other respects the models for the process of transfer and resulting arrangements reflect a very uncritical view of previous policy in this area. More importantly there is very little reflection on the interaction between these proposals and other parts of the Green Paper – especially those associated with rents, maintenance and the Right to Buy. There is a striking silence on where transfers are expected to be implemented and what impact they would have on patterns of residential segregation, the local housing market and RSLs. As a result any speculations about the pattern and likely effect of transfers cannot be tested against the assumptions made by the authors of the Green Paper.

The debates carried out in opposition and those about whole stock transfers are reflected in the options emerging in the Green Paper. The ERCF had already been discarded – the first Comprehensive Spending Review completed in 1998 shifted the future capital funding of negative value transfers to the main Housing Investment Programme (HIP). Government has maximised its identity with a new model stock transfer programme. This emphasises flexibility and responsiveness to local authority preferences and the significance of resident and tenant representation on boards. The Labour approach to transfers presented the possibility of companies with a high degree of accountability to tenants; with councillors represented on the boards; and managing very different portfolios with different kinds of group structures and federal arrangements. Additionally, the government has been far more flexible in relation to the number of properties to be transferred, allowing Coventry and Tameside to transfer nearly 20,000 units each to new parent companies.

It is certainly possible to see these developments as distinctive and not simply following the Conservative model, but in other respects the proposals for stock transfer involve continuity in systems. The same point could be made in relation to the development of the PFI in relation to public sector housing. It could be reasonably argued that the Labour government has shown a much greater enthusiasm for this programme than its predecessor (as it does not necessarily involve the transfer of ownership). The one thing that might not have been expected in a Conservative Party Green Paper was the new proposal that arm's-length management companies could be developed by local authorities. This would be a different type of company which continued to have a greater degree of municipal ownership and is more consistent with the historical debates within the Labour party. However, borrowing by such companies will remain constrained by the current public sector accounting conventions and the pilots will be funded by £400 million made available from within the Comprehensive Spending Review announced in 2000.

The Green Paper notes that since 1988, more than 400,000 homes had been transferred from around 100 local authorities to RSLs. The government is proposing that:

> From 2001–02 we will support the transfer of up to 200,000 dwellings each year. If local authorities submit transfer proposals at that level, and if tenants support them, registered social landlords will become the majority providers of social housing from 2004 onwards. If the demand for stock transfer from local authorities and tenants greatly exceeds 200,000 homes each year, we will consider supporting the higher level of transfer. (para 7.19)

The brakes were off and the discussion was of a 10-year programme transferring 2 million of the remaining council housing stock. At the end of this period and given the likelihood that the Right to Buy would continue to erode the stock, the residual council housing sector would be very small. It is plausible to contemplate the possibility that at that stage a final act in the execution of privatisation policies would develop. The strategy for stock transfer is effectively a strategy to remove, rethink, or recreate council housing – depending on which position you take.

Stock transfers would bring more investment into the housing sector, but the case for housing transfer does not rest solely on financial advantage.

The Green Paper refers to a more diverse pattern of dynamic and competitive organisations to run social housing in much the same way as did the previous government:

> Transfer presents an opportunity to move away from large monopoly providers of social housing to a greater number of smaller bodies that are based in or closer to the communities where the homes are transferred. (para 7.14)

> Transfer also helps to separate out local authorities strategic responsibilities from their landlord functions.... Increasingly, across the whole range of housing policy, there is a need for local authorities to play a more strategic role. (para 7.15)

In spite of these protestations the enthusiasm for stock transfers on this scale appears to be principally driven by financial considerations and to involve an uncritical view of stock transfers and the process involved. Theoretical propositions rather than experience or evidence of tenant demand underpin the argument. There is no discussion of alternative models of transfer or management and no discussion of whether the approach was equally appropriate in different market situations. Having perhaps taken a pragmatic view that transfers were the only way of achieving a quality social housing sector, the government's position was to emphasise the benefit of transfers while being seen not to force the issue on reluctant local politicians and tenants. The benefits identified include: improving the quality of housing by bringing in private investment; creating a wider range of bodies with higher levels of tenant involvement to run housing; improving services and matching them more closely to tenants needs and preferences; stressing the link between housing investment and community regeneration; and enabling local authorities to concentrate on their strategic responsibilities for social housing.

The Green Paper states:

> We are pleased with the success of the transfer programme to date and, against this background, we want to expand and modernise the transfer of housing stock. (para 7.16)

The Green Paper refers to a study of six transfers which concludes that they are successful and that the transfer programme has established a new type of dynamic landlord, developing a wider role for themselves than simply delivering housing in a single district. The transfer associations have actively sought out new opportunities in other districts in terms of new build development and care for older people and people needing support with their tenancies.

This account of benefits appears to avoid the obvious observations that the individual tenant still only has one landlord and the monopoly is unchanged; landlords that are dynamic and working outside their area are less easily perceived as local and community based; and that stock transfers have generally resulted in considerable increases in rents and were widely regarded as having reduced accountability. Although these issues are not explicitly referred to, some of the action proposed to make transfers more acceptable could be seen as a response to them.

The Green Paper states that the government believes that the transfer process can be improved so that it yields advantages for tenants, communities and local authorities, while protecting the interests of tax payers and lenders and continuing to attract private investment. The emphasis on tenant involvement in the process of making decisions is considerable, but, arguably, no greater than that which led John Patten in 1987 to seek the populist agenda of Tenants' Choice. The key criteria for approval of future stock transfers were set out as consistent with Best Value review criteria:

- evidence of support among tenants;
- part of a coherent local authority strategy designed to help meet the future needs of the area;
- providing value for money;
- contributing to achieving other housing, social and other economic objectives;
- delivering diversity and a better service to tenants;
- the relationship between the landlord and the local authority; and
- the long-term demand for social housing in the area.

This list is not so different than that adopted by the Department of the Environment, Transport and the Regions under its previous political leadership. The criteria also appear, as they are presented above, sufficiently vague to present little difficulty to the policy professional charged with drawing up proposals which would be acceptable.

The Green Paper asserts that these key criteria for future stock transfer proposals reflect wider objectives of providing choice and tackling social exclusion. They represent a change of emphasis from previous years in a number of respects:

- a greater emphasis on community regeneration, particularly as more urban authorities contemplate transfer;
- a more strategic approach to tackling changes in demand;
- greater competition within the transfer process;
- ensuring that the transfer of stock results in better services for tenants;
- wanting to move housing management away from large-scale monopoly landlords.

But, again, this list is not impressive. It is hard to believe that it was not already pencilled in in a previous government's thinking. Similarly, the consultation papers which government issued in August 1999 (DETR, 1999) and which framed proposals to deal with overhanging debt and altering the levy applied to LSVTs can be seen as likely to have emerged in any event. This is not to deny that these steps, or those relating to the timetable for transfer, are other than sensible. They are simply unsurprising.

The new element in the Green Paper relates to arm's-length management companies for local authority-owned housing. It is here that it would be easiest to suggest a concession to municipal supporters. The new option would mean that the best performing authorities would be able operate with higher levels of expenditure than received through the normal credit approvals through HIP. As with the stock transfer programme, a small number of authorities would be able to pursue this option in any year and only those authorities that were delivering high quality housing services, making effective use of resources and had put their housing management at arm's length would be eligible. The housing stock would remain in local authority ownership. In this sense, there is a new option that promises sufficient investment to deliver a quality service without an insistence on stock transfer. Although there is an insistence on establishing arm's-length management it may be difficult to persuade tenants and residents in areas where this takes place that anything has changed. There may also be a view that once an arm's-length management company has been set up it is easy to cut the arm off and convert it into a conventional RSL. Perhaps it would be cynical to suggest that this represents a perfect preparation for privatisation and subsequent stock transfer by a later government.

Looking forward

The fundamental question in all of this, it may be argued, is not whether the Housing Green Paper says the same as a Conservative Green Paper would have done or whether it is innovative. More important is whether it will achieve improvements for tenants and residents currently in the council housing sector and currently or subsequently in the RSL sector. In this context a crucial issue is how far the proposals anticipate changes, are forward looking (rather than reflecting the debates of two decades previously) and link with concerns about neighbourhood renewal and the concentration of disadvantage in towns and cities. In addition to the government's new policy agenda around social exclusion the contemporary debate in housing reflects concern about changing and low demand. There are concerns about the sustainability of areas with different tenure characteristics, but the future demand for parts of the council housing sector is addressed in this debate (see, for example, Cole et al, 1999; Murie et al, 1998). In the context of changing markets some of the debate is about the need for a profound restructuring and renewal of cities and parts of cities. The impact of growing affluence and obsolescence also raises questions about future strategies. There are external threats to the sustainability of areas, and transfer could weaken the capacity to respond to these – in some places enabling strategies could be weakened and a fragmentation of ownership and control could affect the ability to develop coherent policies. The nature of transfers and of the continuing relationship between the local authority and transfer RSLs may have a profound influence and require more attention.

These considerations are more important because of the planned scale of transfers. If the proposed programme of transfers is realised then council housing will quickly become a minority tenure and there will be large areas (especially those with buoyant markets and property values) with no council housing. The scale of transfers will transform the RSL sector as well as councils' roles: it will also have profound implications for regulation, regeneration, governance and community involvement. If these things have not been thought through effectively and the policies are designed to deal with the problems of the past rather than the future, it may prove very difficult to respond and remedy in the future.

In this discussion rents and rights are important – future tenants will have fewer rights than those who are balloted (if only because of the absence of the Right to Buy) and rents will be higher (depending on what happens in relation to linking rents to capital values). At the same time the process of transfers as developed from LSVT and ERCF is artificial and flawed (see, for example, Nevin, 1999) and does not provide the basis on which to build tenant-driven organisations.

Most of the research commentaries in this area and many of the political ones have arrived at a view that tenure is not the key factor determining the quality of service. RSLs do not uniformly deliver better services than local authorities. There are good performers and bad performers in each category of 'social landlord'. Stock transfer does not necessarily provide a guarantee of continuing good quality future service. None of the key considerations set out in the discussion of stock transfers actually provide such a guarantee. Will they ensure that landlords in the future will provide good quality services? The answer to this must be equivocal. Stock transfers do not occur in a vacuum. They are being carried out in the context of a rapidly changing housing market.

The role and quality of housing in the social rented sector is affected by a wide range of factors. As with the previous stock transfer programme, there are four key issues.

First, there is the question of anticipating future changes. The key selection criteria refer to the future housing needs of the area and future changes in the long-term demand for social housing. The capacity to assess and evaluate these changes is limited. Increasing affluence, the increasingly easy access to home ownership for many households, changing aspirations and changing patterns of demand are not so easily forecast and the inadequacy of planning and other methodologies in this respect are a serious problem.

Second, the proposals regarding support among tenants deny difficulties associated with other residents and, perhaps more importantly, with future residents. The deal for tenants includes a preserved Right to Buy and often more favourable rent treatment than the next generation of tenants. The next generation is not included in the ballot and doesn't have much say. This relates to the third issue.

Arguably tenants and future tenants will have power through representation on boards. However, again there is reason to question the assumptions here. First of all, how powerful will boards be in relation to their officers or their funders or the Housing Corporation as their regulator? Governments and the Housing Corporation emphasise the need for boards to drive organisations, but it is naive to believe that this will be easily achieved. Time, turnover, training, trust, differences in circumstances and attitudes may all make it very difficult to achieve.

The final concern relates to the issue of deprivation. A key selection criterion for future stock transfers will be how far transfer will contribute to achieving the government's other housing, social and economic objectives, greater involvement of the private sector and regeneration of the most deprived areas. Leaving aside the continuing question of our ability to anticipate future changes, this raises the question of how far government strategies in relation to social exclusion and housing will make social rented housing attractive to live in. The argument goes full circle, stock transfers on their own will not achieve this. They are an element in contributing to regeneration, but if the other elements were inadequate will stock transfers make as much difference as the government appears to hope? What will be the attitude if what is needed is significant redevelopment and demolition in the context of major sub-regional and urban redevelopment and renewal? Where will the resources for such substantial redevelopment come from? Stock transfer itself does not necessarily imply a wider programme of social and economic regeneration, nor does it mean changes to the ways that decisions are made about new investment or the delivery of a wide range of services in neighbourhoods.

If the proposals in the Green Paper and in the parallel paper on neighbourhood decline are insufficient to alter significantly the future of the most deprived neighbourhoods then stock transfers affecting such neighbourhoods will merely mean that the most deprived people continue to have fewer opportunities but have a different landlord. Will it make any difference if there is a greater degree of self-management in these areas? It would be as easy to conclude that stock transfers were a new mechanism to manage and police deprived areas more effectively rather than to transform them. We must wait and see whether this is the case.

This leads on to a final issue – the extent to which the stock transfer proposals in the Green Paper are likely to be affected by other policy proposals within the Green Paper itself. Proposals in relation to rent levels and future rent increases are particularly important, as are those related to maintenance and demolitions. Where council housing has a high capital value rents linked to such values are more likely to mean positive value transfers and effective business plans. Transfers in the South and London should be easy to promote and fund – as long as the arm's-length option does not sap the political will for transfer. Will the additional resources available for maintenance be sufficient to enable local authorities to remedy the backlog of disrepair without transfer? Which local authorities will be left with incentives to transfer? Will it be only those with positive values and the prospect of generating capital receipts which they can use elsewhere under new single capital allocation arrangements? What about the North and Midlands and areas with low values and problems of low demand? What will be the impact of restrictions on future rent increases? Will some potential transfers founder because effective business plans require rents to rise? Or will such restrictions effectively be bypassed as cost-related increases are exempted? Will the 2 million transfers take place but cream off the high value properties and have a distinctive spatial pattern – much as has been the experience with all of the other privatisation and stock transfer policies so far? Will the process speed us even further towards a US style welfare housing system with different patterns of ownership and management practices in areas with different market circumstances? It would be valuable if the process of developing and consulting on policy included a sharing of assumptions and thinking on these issues.

References

Cole, I and Furbey, R. (1994) *The eclipse of council housing*, London: Routledge.

Cole, I., Kane, S. and Robinson, D. (1999) *Changing demand, changing neighbourhoods: The response of social landlords*, Sheffield: Sheffield Hallam University.

DETR (Department of the Environment, Transport and the Regions) (1999) *Dealing with overhanging debt and altering the LSVT levy*, Consultation Paper, London: DETR.

DETR/DSS (Department of Social Security) (2000) *Quality and choice: A decent home for all*, Housing Green Paper, London: DETR/DSS.

Forrest, R. and Murie, A. (1990) *Selling the welfare state: The privatisation of public housing*, London: Routledge.

Housing Today (2000) 'Housing debt write off close to £1 billion', 27 January.

LGA (Local Government Association) (1997) *A new financial framework for local authority housing*, London: LGA.

Malpass, P. and Murie, A. (1999) *Housing policy and practice* (5th edn), Basingstoke: Macmillan.

Mullins, D, Niner, P. and Riseborough, M. (1993) 'Large scale voluntary transfers', in P. Malpass and R. Means (eds) *Implementing housing policy*, Buckingham: Open University Press.

Mullins, D, Niner, P. and Riseborough, M. (1995) *Evaluating large scale voluntary transfers of local authority housing*, London: HMSO.

Murie, A. (1999) 'The acquisition and sale of properties by social landlords: justifications and consequences', *Netherlands Journal of Housing and the Built Environment*, vol 14, no 3, pp 293-308.

Murie A., Nevin B. and Leather P. (1998) *Changing demand and unpopular housing*, London: The Housing Corporation.

Nevin, B. (1999) *Local housing companies: Progress and problems*, Coventry: Chartered Institute of Housing.

Usher, D. (1987) *Housing privatisation: The sale of council estates*, SAUS Working Paper 67, Bristol: SAUS Publications.

THREE

Stock transfer

Tom Mullen

Introduction

The transfer of local authority housing stock to other landlords has been an important and controversial aspect of housing policy since the late 1980s. This chapter concentrates on the role of law in stock transfer including its effect on tenants' individual and collective rights. The origins and development of stock transfer policy have been described by Murie and Nevin in Chapter Two. It is not my intention to repeat that discussion, but it is important to highlight a few points as a prelude to what follows. The Thatcher government was committed to 'rolling back the frontiers of the state'. Among other things this entailed drastically reducing the role of local authorities in providing housing. The Right to Buy was one vehicle deployed for this purpose and stock transfer another.

Both of the 1987 Housing White Papers (DoE/Welsh Office, 1987; Scottish Office, 1987), therefore, encouraged the transfer of ownership of houses with sitting tenants to new non-local authority landlords. The 1988 Housing Act ('the 1988 Act'), and 1988 Housing (Scotland) Act introduced new legal mechanisms to implement the policy. The encouragement of stock transfer was presented as part of a new vision of the local authority's housing role as a strategic or enabling housing authority rather than a direct provider of housing on a large scale. The future role of local authorities was stated to be essentially a strategic one, identifying housing needs and demands, encouraging innovative methods of provision by other bodies to meet such needs, maximising the use of private finance, and encouraging the revival of non-local authority rented housing (DoE/Welsh Office, 1987).

New funding for social rented housing was to be concentrated on the housing association movement which was expected to expand greatly as a consequence of stock transfer and continued grant support for new building. Housing associations were also expected to make much more use of private capital for investment in housing. One consequence of the greater reliance on private capital was the switch from letting on secure tenancies to letting on the new private sector model – the assured tenancy – for all new tenants. This change was presented as being necessary to encourage private sector finance. But there was clearly also an ideological element to the change: the government wished to emphasise the dissimilarity between local authority and housing associations and letting on assured tenancies provided symbolic confirmation that the housing association movement should not be seen as part of the public sector. Differences between the rights of secure and assured tenants have emerged as a significant issue in stock transfers.

As Murie and Nevin point out, Labour thinking on stock transfer shifted during its opposition years and following its election in 1997 the policy of encouraging stock transfer has been maintained. Indeed the rate of transfer under Labour has accelerated. Over the whole period between 1988 and Spring 2000 about 450,000 houses were transferred from local authorities to registered social landlords (RSLs) (www.housing.detr.gov.uk/transfers/index.htm) under the large-scale voluntary transfer (LSVT) programme, an average of fewer than 40,000 houses per year. But the housing transfer programme announced for 1999/2000 involved 140,000 houses, and the two largest municipal landlords in the UK – Glasgow and Birmingham (each having around 90,000 council properties) – both announced that they were investigating the possibility of transfer the whole of their stock (should tenants agree) to new landlords. The 2000 Housing Green Paper (DETR/DSS, 2000) confirmed that this increase in the pace of disposal is intended to be long term by stating that the government will support the transfer of up to 200,000 homes each year to RSLs. As in the 1987 White Paper, encouragement of stock transfer is linked to the need for local authorities to play a more strategic role in housing. It is assumed that the strategic or enabling role of the local authority cannot successfully be combined with a substantial provider role (para 7.15).

One problem facing the stock transfer programme has been the marked differences in the quality of stock as between different local authorities. Stock transfer was much more attractive to (principally rural) local authorities managing stock with a positive transfer value, than to (mainly urban) authorities for whom the poor quality of stock resulted in a negative transfer value which would leave the authority still servicing debt after the sale of its stock. The recent conversion of large Labour-controlled authorities to stock transfer reflects a perception that there is no alternative method for obtaining the investment necessary to improve stock, coupled with indications that the government is willing to fund the debt write-offs necessary to make transfers economically feasible.

The promotion of the stock transfer programme led to changes to legal framework for the authorisation of transfers, and to tenants' collective and individual rights.

This chapter attempts to analyse those changes and to consider briefly relevant aspects of the Green Paper proposals. The order of treatment will be:

- the legal framework
- stock transfer, tenants' preferences and tenants' collective rights
- the role of law in stock transfer
- tenants' individual rights
- the Green Paper proposals.

The legal framework

Local authorities were never obliged to have any housing stock. As in many other areas of local government, the statutory framework was permissive and discretionary. The enormous growth of council housing in the 20th century was to a considerable extent a product of the availability of subsidy and central government encouragement. Housing legislation provided the framework for this, including the authority for councils to provide additional subsidy from their rate funds. However, there was no compulsion to have any council stock even after the 1977 Housing (Homeless Persons) Act imposed specific duties to find accommodation for the homeless. Nonetheless, it was a working assumption of housing policy for much of the 20th century, shared (admittedly with differences of emphasis) by the two main political parties, that councils should have a major role as housing providers.

This largely permissive framework also applied to the sale of stock with sitting tenants. Such sales required the consent of the Secretary of State but the initiative in proposing stock transfers lay with the local authority. While many local authorities had, by the late 1980s, begun to consider disposing of their stock, many other councils (especially Labour-controlled authorities) remained keen to hang on to their stock. The

1988 Act introduced two new methods of forcing a transfer on unwilling local authorities: Tenants' Choice and Housing Action Trusts (HATs). The former was a procedure which allowed tenants to force the transfer of their houses to a new landlord approved by the Housing Corporation. The latter allowed the Secretary of State to set up a quango to take over local authority housing in an area. Both policies proved to be failures, essentially because of lack of tenant enthusiasm. The Tenants' Choice provisions were repealed by the 1996 Housing Act and, although the HAT provisions remain in force, it is not expected that any more HATs will be designated.

In practice the only important vehicle for stock transfer has been LSVT under Section 32 of the 1985 Housing Act. These transfers are voluntary in the sense that local authorities are empowered rather than required to dispose of council houses and land held for housing purposes. The LSVT rules were amended by section 6 of the 1986 Housing and Planning Act which added a new section 106A and Schedule 3A to the 1985 Act. Briefly, the requirements for a planned voluntary transfer to go ahead are that affected secure tenants have been consulted on the proposal, given the opportunity to make representations to the local authority, and that the Secretary of State must have given consent. The information that must be given includes the identity of the proposed purchaser, the likely consequences for the tenants of disposal, the fact that the secure tenants' Right to Buy is preserved (1985 Act, sections 171A–171H), and the effect of the consultation requirements. Although there is no express requirement for a ballot, in practice one must be held because the Secretary of State may not give consent if a majority of the relevant tenants are against the disposal, and a ballot is the best evidence of this.

Judicial guidance on the interpretation of the consultation provisions was given in *R v Secretary of State for the Environment, ex parte Walters (1997) 30 HLR 328*. Despite the more detailed regulation imposed by the 1988 Act there remains a large measure of discretion on the part of both the local authority and the Secretary of State. The decision to sell is essentially voluntary: neither tenants (as in Tenants' Choice) nor the Secretary of State can force a sale of stock. The statute does not state in any detail the criteria according to which the decision of the Secretary of State to grant or withhold consent should be made, although it does require the Secretary of State to have regard to the extent to which the transferee is likely to be subject to influence from the authority.

The policy on approval has always been contained in non-statutory guidelines (DoE, 1988, 1993) which suggest that consent will not be given unless the intended transferee is suitable (which, among other things, means being independent of the local authority) and the transfers do not exceed size limits.

There have been a number of changes to the approval framework since 1988. Section 135 of the 1993 Leasehold Reform, Housing and Urban Development Act introduced the notion of an annual programme, whereby a qualifying stock transfer could not take place unless included in a programme for that year approved by the Secretary of State. Section 136 of the same Act introduced the LSVT levy (to date this has been 20% of the transfer receipt net of any Housing Revenue Account debt) designed to compensate central government for the increase in Housing Benefit subsidy likely to be caused by stock transfer. There have also been adjustments to the non-statutory guidelines, for example, the maximum permitted size for a transfer to a single landlord has increased from 5,000 to 12,000 houses.

Stock transfer, tenants' preferences and tenants' collective rights

As explained in the preceding section, tenants' collective rights in the stock transfer process were enhanced by the 1986 Housing and Planning Act. As a matter of legal form the framework appears to leave the initiative in proposing transfers largely with the local authority, and the final decision with the tenants. The legal rules for authorising transfers are ostensibly designed to guarantee groups of tenants collectively a free choice as to their future landlords. But it can be argued that the way the policy has developed has shown a lack of respect for the principle that tenants collectively should be able to choose their future landlord, because consent to transfers has been obtained despite limited tenant support for the strategy of demunicipalisation, by limiting the choices available to tenants.

The results of the ballots that have taken place may, of course, be used as an indicator of tenant support. A clear majority of ballots conducted have favoured transfer: Mullins et al (1995) reported that up to 1995 about two thirds of ballots conducted under LSVT rules were in favour of transfer. However, this may overestimate support for stock transfer. The outcomes of ballots in other stock transfer contexts – the creation of Housing Action Trusts, and those on the winding up of the Scottish new town development corporations (Goodlad and Scott, 1996) – provided powerful evidence of tenant antipathy towards proposals to change to new landlords. Nor should the successful ballots under LSVT rules necessarily be seen as an indication that tenants were happy to leave the local authority sector. From the outset the choice of landlord in LSVT proposals has been heavily influenced by economic constraints and incentives.

Since the late 1980s new capital investment in social rented housing has been heavily skewed towards housing associations and other RSLs. Proposals for stock transfer were invariably worked out along with a financial package for investment in the stock to be transferred. In the case of transfers to housing associations this would have been a mixture of Housing Association Grant (now Social Housing Grant) and private capital. Local authorities were subject to tight capital allocations which often meant that they were unable to promote plans to improve and modernise the same stock themselves.

In effect tenants whose houses were in poor condition and in need of catch-up repairs and/or modernisation (which was true of many houses transferred under LSVT) were faced with a simple choice. They could accept a definite offer of major investment in their homes in the short term on condition that they chose a new landlord, or they could stay with the local authority in the knowledge that they might face many more years in substandard accommodation. Two further economic incentives that were given to existing secure tenants were rent guarantees which usually limited rent increases in the first five years and the preservation of the Right to Buy. For those who might be able to finance a purchase in future this was a major benefit, as after the development programme was complete their houses would be much more valuable assets. Similarly, where stock was already in good condition, as in many of the earlier transfers, the preserved Right to Buy removed one of the most obvious potential disadvantages of transfer.

It would of course have been entirely possible to allow local authorities to make the necessary investment in their stock, but predicating investment on transfer was attractive to the Thatcher and Major governments for two reasons. First, it furthered the ideological aim of shrinking the size of the public sector housing stock. Second, it allowed for substantial investment in rented housing which would not count as public expenditure or show up in the public sector borrowing requirement. As the importance of simple ideological preferences for private sector provision has declined, so arguments about the level and definition of public expenditure have become more prominent. Housing professionals have argued that the conventions defining the public sector borrowing requirement should be redefined so as to exclude investment in social housing (Hawksworth and Wilcox, 1995). This would allow funds to be raised without their counting towards the public expenditure total. The current Labour government has, however, strongly resisted such suggestions. Acceptance that the government is not likely to be persuaded on this point has been one of the factors encouraging large Labour-controlled authorities who wish to make up for years of under-investment to propose selling their entire stock.

This is not an argument against stock transfer as such. There is a respectable argument that providing social housing on a large scale should not be a local authority function, and the argument has been made from the Left (Clapham, 1989) and from a 'non-political' perspective (Inquiry into British Housing, 1991) as well as from the Right. But it is important to be clear that the drive to transfer stock to non-local authority landlords should not be seen as a product of tenants' desires. Neither the general drive towards transfer nor the specific proposals brought forward for particular transfers have been tenant-led. More than that, tenants involved in stock transfer proposals have been presented with choice within very narrow constraints: the choice between a change of landlord with major new investment in their homes, and keeping the same landlord without the same scale of investment. The option of substantial investment within the public sector has not been on the table, nor will it be for the future if the Green Paper proposals are accepted. The rhetoric of choice used in, for example, the 1987 White Paper, tends to obscure this. The policy of stock transfer has been pursued in spite of the wishes of many citizens to remain as council tenants.

Why is this important? If the rights of tenants collectively to make choices about their future housing is really valued then the 'choices' made available to tenants should not be artificially constrained. There is little point in using the rhetoric of choice if the only change from that status quo that is acceptable is the government's preferred option. To date, the formal legal framework for securing tenant consent to transfer has operated as a legitimating device in a descriptive rather than a normative sense. As we shall see, the lack of genuine respect for tenants' preferences continues to manifest itself in the Green Paper proposals.

However, before considering that, we should consider the role law has played in the implementation of the stock transfer programme and issues arising from tenants' individual rights.

The role of law in stock transfer

One of the interesting features of all this from a lawyer's perspective is how the stock transfer programme has developed over more than a decade largely free from legal challenge despite its high political profile, the interests involved, and evidence that the policy of demunicipalisation was unpopular with local authority tenants. Moreover, it developed in a period when litigation has been increasingly resorted to in disputes between central and local government (Loughlin, 1996, 2000). There has been only one reported case, *ex parte Walters* (above), which concerned a challenge to a proposed transfer in the London Borough of Brent. One might have expected applications for judicial review of local authority actions or of ministerial consent to be brought by or on behalf of disappointed tenants and tenants' groups who wanted to remain with the council, or by or on behalf of other interested parties such as affected public sector workers. Apart from the *Walters* case this has not occurred.

Does stock transfer, therefore, form an exception to the juridification thesis that has been used to explain developments in central–local relations over the last two decades? The concept of juridification was developed primarily by German theorists such as Teubner (1987) to describe a process whereby social relations are increasingly formalised in juridical terms. Loughlin (2000) has applied this general theory to central–local relations in the United Kingdom and suggested that juridification of the relationship has taken two forms. The first form of juridification is the product of a normative gulf. Before the upheavals of the 1980s the role of law in central–local relations was essentially facilitative rather than regulatory. Central–local relations were structured more by conventional understandings and practices than by law. One consequence of the politicisation of central–local relations in the 1980s was that the conventional understandings lost their authority as determinants of the relationship, and both central government and local authorities turned to the legal framework to determine their rights and duties. Thus, law filled the normative gulf left by the breakdown of the traditional relationship. Specific consequences included an increased role for lawyers in the policy-making process and an increased tendency for disputes to end up in the courts.

The second form of juridification is the product of restructuring which envisages that local authorities will much more than formerly be rule-bound agencies, subject to a greater degree of judicial supervision, and that the central–local relationship assumes an authoritative hierarchical form. This form of juridification is associated with the changes government has sought to force on the provision of local services which have eroded local discretion in a variety of ways, including the reliance on performance indicators for service provision, contracting out of service provision, additional supervisory powers for government departments, and a stronger role for the Audit Commission.

However, it is not just the relationship between the centre and local authorities which has been juridified in recent years, but also the relationship between local government and citizens, including local authority tenants. In the field of housing the Right to Buy, the introduction of security of tenure, enhanced rights of consultation, and the now repealed Tenants' Choice provisions are all examples of rules which have cut down the discretion local authorities formerly had in dealing with citizens. As these examples indicate, the formalisation of social relationships in juridical terms is not necessarily to be deplored: more rights in a field previously left to discretion may be a good thing. A later section of this chapter advocates enhancing the statutory rights of tenants in the social rented sector. What juridification theorists have done is to emphasise the pathological consequences that such formalisation can produce under certain conditions.

In the specific context of stock transfer it is clear that there is certainly a greater *quantity* of legislation as a result of the various amendments made to the LSVT rules. This has not led to greater resort to the courts because of the particular features of the LSVT process. Most importantly, the interests of the centre and of those local authorities who have promoted stock transfers have coincided. Both shared the objective of achieving the sale of the housing stock. The process of balloting also ensures that those transfer proposals to which there is the greatest tenant opposition do not proceed. Thus, any challenge was only likely to come from minority groups on the council or tenants who voted against transfer, or perhaps public sector unions. Importantly, these groups would not have had access to council funds to finance legal action, and would (with the possible exception of public sector unions) have had difficulty in financing it in any other way given the nature of the eligibility criteria for legal aid.

It is also important to note that despite the various additional rules introduced into the LSVT process the legal framework remains highly discretionary; so much so that it would be very difficult to mount a challenge to either a local authority decision to approve a proposal for transfer or the Secretary of State's consent on substantive grounds. The scope for procedural challenge is also limited by the provision in paragraph

6 of Schedule 3A which states that the Secretary of State's consent is not invalidated by his failure to comply with any of the requirements of the schedule (including the requirement that the majority of the relevant tenants are against the disposal). This does not prevent, although it does limit the scope for judicial review (see *Walters*). The *Walters* case itself is unlikely to encourage challenges. Schiemann LJ found clear defects in Brent's consultation and a misunderstanding of the law on the part of the Secretary of State, but exercised his discretion not to grant relief taking into account all the interests involved, including those of tenants who wished the transfer to go ahead, and the likely adverse effects of starting the consultation process anew.

Despite the injection of additional rules, the framework of stock transfer remains essentially facilitative rather than regulatory: the driving forces behind the policy are the economic incentives, and the experiment with compulsory mechanisms for transfer of stock to new landlords (Tenants' Choice and HATs) were unsuccessful. This not only means that the whole process is less rule-bound than other central interventions aimed at changing the way local services are provided, for example, Compulsive Competitive Tendering, but also that the process has largely escaped legal challenge and obstruction.

Tenants' individual rights

We have already considered the role played by tenants' collective rights in the stock transfer process. But the individual rights of tenants have also been an important and at times controversial issue in stock transfers. Because transfers have generally been to non-local authority landlords, and because housing associations began to let on assured tenancies from 15 January 1989 onwards, tenants have experienced a change of status from secure tenants under the 1985 Act to assured tenants under the 1988 Act as a result of a stock transfer. We need to consider individual rights both because of their possible impact on the development of the stock transfer programme, and to evaluate the appropriateness of the variations in tenants' rights which now exist in the social rented sector.

Transferring from a secure to an assured tenancy is arguably to the disadvantage of the tenant because the bundle of rights that goes with an assured tenancy is less attractive than the bundle of rights that goes with a secure tenancy. There are several respects in which the assured tenancy gives relatively less protection to the tenant's interest as compared to the secure tenancy. The potential loss of rights fuelled the controversy over stock transfer, and added a further issue for tenants to consider in deciding whether to consent to a proposed transfer.

The most important disadvantages of the assured tenancy are in relation to recovery of possession, and succession. There are additional grounds for possession available to the landlord in an assured tenancy, of which the most significant are those relating to rent arrears because rent arrears are the basis of the vast majority of possession actions. There is only one rent related ground in the secure tenancy: ground 1 provides that possession may be recovered where any rent lawfully due is in arrears, but it must be reasonable to award possession. This means the court always has discretion not to award possession. Ground 10 in the assured tenancy is broadly equivalent, but a landlord may also rely on ground 11 which allows possession to be awarded for persistent delay in paying rent even if there are no arrears outstanding at the date proceedings are begun, or on ground 8 under which possession is *mandatory* (ie the court cannot consider the reasonableness of eviction) where a minimum amount of arrears are owed (8 weeks to 3 months depending on how often rent is payable).

Ground 2 in assured tenancies which again has no counterpart in the secure tenancy has also caused concern in this context. It applies where the house is subject to a mortgage and the mortgagee is entitled to exercise a power of sale. This ground could be used by a bank or building society where the landlord defaulted on a loan. This ground is potentially of more significance than formerly because of the increased reliance on private capital to fund housing association building and refurbishment programmes.

Secure tenants also have better succession rights. In an assured tenancy, only the surviving spouse or cohabitee of the deceased tenant is entitled to succeed whereas a much larger group of family members may succeed in a secure tenancy. Secure tenants also have greater legal rights in a number of less important areas such as assignation and subletting, the statutory right to repair, and the statutory right to compensation for improvements. The most valuable right in economic terms is the Right to Buy. However, this is not an issue for tenants facing stock transfer because where the transfer takes place under LSVT rules the transferring tenants retain the Right to Buy.

Although there are marked differences between the rights of secure and assured tenants – and these have been given substantial publicity in the lead-up to many stock transfer ballots – they appear not to have been a major deterrent for tenants faced with transfer proposals. As discussed above, there is certainly ample evidence that many local authority tenants would prefer to remain in the sector. Yet, most transfer ballots have been successful. This is primarily because of the strong economic incentives to tenants to switch landlord: the prospects of repairs and improvements coupled with preservation of the Right to Buy.

It is also possible that efforts to counteract the differences in statutory rights helped to sweeten the pill of stock transfer. One of the ironies of the stock transfer process is that both the housing association movement and their regulators appear to have rejected the market-driven model of tenancy relations proposed in the 1987 White Paper and for which the 1988 Act created the legal framework. As a result the reduction in legal rights for secure tenants transferring to new landlords as assured tenants have not in practice necessarily been as great as the gap between the two statutory codes would have suggested.

This rejection of the market model was particularly marked in Scotland where the representative body for housing associations (the Scottish Federation of Housing Associations) promulgated a model assured tenancy agreement (SFHA, 1990) designed to ensure that assured housing association tenants should have the same rights by contract that secure tenants enjoyed under statute[1]. The great majority of members of the SFHA and, therefore, most housing associations in fact adopted the model agreement as the basis for their own leases (Mullen et al, 1997). There were imperfections in the execution of the aim because the model agreement did not precisely replicate secure tenants' rights, but the general intention of the movement to give assured tenants equivalent rights to secure tenants was clear. A revised version which more accurately reflected secure tenants' rights was published in 1997 (SFHA, 1997). The model assured tenancy agreement is not a formal requirement of the regulatory regime, but the document was endorsed by Scottish Homes, and forms part of their *Raising standards in housing*, which is used as a benchmark for performance monitoring. Scottish Office guidance also suggested that transferring tenants should receive tenancy agreements giving similar rights to secure tenants (SODD, 1996).

Developments in England and Wales also appeared to run counter to the market philosophy of the 1988 Act. The Tenants' Guarantee and statutory guidance to housing associations (now RSLs) issued by the Housing Corporation and Tai Cymru[2] indicated that tenants should be given the most secure form of tenancy compatible with the purpose of the housing (ie an assured periodic tenancy), and that "assured periodic tenants continue to have by contract most of the principal statutory rights of secure tenants". The current guidance for England contained in

Performance standards (Housing Corporation, 1997) indicates that assured tenants should be given contractual rights to exchange houses, to take lodgers, to be consulted on housing management, to carry out improvements and be compensated for them, and rights of succession for family members not covered by the Act. There is, however, no specific guidance on the use of possession grounds. There is also the model assured periodic tenancy agreement issued by the National Federation of Housing Associations (now the National Housing Federation) which gives assured tenants substantially greater rights than the 1988 Act.

It is not clear to what extent the guidance has been followed by RSLs in drafting their tenancy agreements, there having been no systematic research as in Scotland, although it does appear likely that secure tenants' rights have not been replicated by contract to the same extent as in Scotland. However, the important point is that the regulatory regime proceeds on the assumption that tenants of RSLs ought to have broadly similar rights to secure tenants.

Against this background, it is not surprising that reconsideration of the tenure split within social housing is taking place. The Chartered Institute of Housing (Hood, 1998) has proposed a single form of tenure for the whole of the social rented sector which "would reconcile the differences between secure and assured tenancies, combining the best features of both". The Green Paper gives qualified approval to this suggestion stating: "We believe there is merit in this proposal and will explore the benefits of, and options for, moving to a single form of tenure" (para 9.68). The Scottish White Paper (Scottish Executive, 2000) was less equivocal, making a specific commitment to introduce a single standard form of tenure for all tenants which has now been honoured in the Housing (Scotland) Bill introduced in the Scottish Parliament in December 2000.

It is perhaps surprising that a firmer commitment to a single tenure is not given in the Green Paper. The continued use of the assured tenancy in the social rented sector is inconsistent with the regulatory approach to the housing association sector, with the general drift of policy in this area, and with the assumptions about the future of social housing which structure the Green Paper. Both local authorities and housing associations are perceived by government as providing affordable housing to those in need. Similarities between the groups to which they let – for example, their income levels – have increased over time. For both, investment is to a large degree directed by central government priorities. The Green Paper consistently refers to common aims for the sector as a whole, for example, ensuring the consistent and rigorous application of Best Value and tenant participation compact principles across social housing, maintaining rents at affordable sub-market levels, and increasing personal choice in the allocation of social housing. If these aims are realised to a substantial extent, statutory tenure differences between local authority and RSL tenants will seem increasingly anomalous.

There are also more specific pragmatic arguments. The task of housing management is more complex where landlords have to operate multiple tenures (housing associations with secure and assured tenants). A single form of tenure simplifies the choice tenants have to make when considering stock transfer proposals and it may make it easier to increase social rented sector tenants' understanding of their rights. This, of course, presupposes that the new form of tenancy is introduced by the 'big bang' approach, whereby all existing tenancies are converted to the new form of tenancy on a given date (as in the Scottish Housing Bill), rather than a phased approach under which it applies only to new lets. The phased approach would not realise the principal aim of the proposal – harmonisation of rights – for many years.

The two most obvious sources of objection to the levelling up of rights would be lenders and individual housing associations themselves. However, most lenders interviewed for the Chartered Institute of Housing research on the single tenancy proposal stated that they would be equally happy to lend on secure tenancies as on assured tenancies (Hood, 1998), and this is consistent with the findings of earlier research on lenders' perceptions of risk (Chaplin et al, 1995).

As regards housing associations the Chartered Institute of Housing report suggested that some RSLs might object to the change, but there is both a theoretical and an empirical point to be made here. The theoretical point is that the changes made to the tenure of housing association tenants in 1989 were based on a false analogy with the private sector, and are inconsistent with current perceptions of the nature and functions of provision of social housing by housing associations. The empirical point is that there is no evidence that effective housing management would be impaired by the loss of the greater managerial discretion that goes with the assured tenancy. Take the case of possession proceedings for rent arrears. Studies of the possession process have repeatedly found that landlords find it relatively easy to obtain possession awards in rent arrears cases, and it does not appear as if the introduction of assured tenancies has made much difference (Leather and Jeffers, 1989; Nixon et al, 1996; Mullen et al, 1999).

The Scottish tenants' rights research (Mullen et al, 1999) compared the effect of the possession process on secure and assured tenants, and found that there was in practice substantial use of the 'additional' possession grounds by housing associations, and also that there were marked differences in the outcome of possession proceedings as between secure and assured tenants. However, the research also concluded, after detailed analysis of the outcomes of possession cases, that only a small part of those differences in outcomes could be explained by the differences in the statutory grounds for possession. The findings included that local authority tenants were much more likely to be taken to court and to have decrees of possession awarded against them than housing association assured tenants. However, the latter were more likely to be actually evicted from their homes than either housing association secure tenants or local authority secure tenants. Housing association secure tenants were the least likely of the three groups to be either taken to court, have decrees of possession awarded against them, or to be evicted.

The research identified two other sets of factors as important in influencing outcomes: differences in policies and practices for recovery of rent arrears between the housing association sector and the local authority sector; and differences in the profiles of different groups of tenants. As regards policies, local authorities were much readier to take tenants to court for arrears than housing associations, but much less likely to enforce any decree for possession obtained. As regards tenant profiles, housing association secure tenants had the lowest proportion of tenants in groups at high risk of accumulating rent arrears. It was the interaction of differences in policies and practices for rent arrears and differences in the tenant profiles which produced the pattern of results above.

However, while this research might be used to allay the fears of some housing associations that they would be losing a valuable managerial tool, it should not be used to suggest that differences in the statutory rights of different groups of tenants do not matter. The tenants' rights research offered an interpretation of security of tenure (in the material rather than the legal sense) based on tenant profiles and housing management policies in the mid-1990s. However, both of these factors are potentially subject to change, and the position of the legal floor of rights for different groups of tenants might become much more significant if, for example, social landlords changed their approaches to arrears control. Tenants in the social rented sector may in the future be very much in need of the additional protections that might be afforded to some or all by a new legal framework for tenancies of social housing.

The Green Paper proposals

To a large extent the proposals contained in the Green Paper can be seen as a continuation of policies put in place by the Conservatives and continued by Labour since 1997. The policy goal of demunicipalisation of social housing remains the same, as does the method of delivering it. Encouragement of stock transfer will continue to be through the provision of economic incentives both to tenants and landlords rather than through direct legal compulsion. Despite substantially increased provision for investment in housing by local authorities since the 1997 General Election the restrictions on public expenditure, and the refusal to reconsider conventions defining it, will continue to be an incentive to local authorities to look at stock transfer as the solution to needed investment in their housing stock. The Green Paper does suggest one route to increased investment in stock that remains in council ownership (paras 7.39-7.41). Local authorities may be given permission to retain more of their rental income to finance borrowing, but this is predicated on local authorities establishing arm's-length management companies to manage the stock and demonstrating a high level of performance against Best Value indicators.

Arguably, the most important change preceded the Green Paper: a change in approach to overhanging debt. In the past authorities whose debt on the housing stock exceeded the likely capital receipt were effectively excluded from the transfer programme. This meant that the councils with the poorest housing stock could not gain access to additional investment by this route. The new approach is for the government to make a one-off special payment to assist in clearing the debt. This has already happened in the case of Burnley, and it will be necessary to clear the debt in this way if the Birmingham and Glasgow[3] proposals are to go ahead.

The Green Paper suggests a number of specific proposals for 'modernising the stock transfer programme'. These are discussed by Murie and Nevin in Chapter Two. Apart from changing the way the LSVT levy would be calculated none of these changes would require legislation: they could all be implemented by reformulation of and/or different application of the non-statutory criteria for granting ministerial consent.

Reviewing the proposals suggests that the continuity of policy extends to the attitude towards tenants' preferences. What tenants actually want still does not seem to matter all that much. In fact the Green Paper suggests that the choices that tenants can realistically make, and their ability to influence the ultimate outcomes of the transfer process in the direction they want, may become even further constrained. This is apparent when one considers the likely interaction of three of the stated aims: accelerating the rate of transfer, greater competition within the transfer process, and moving housing management away from large-scale monopoly landlords.

There are clear tensions among these three aims, particularly squaring the accelerated rate of transfer with the aims of achieving greater competition and diversity. Thus, it is easy to state that "we do not believe it to be healthy that a single registered social landlord should be identified as the only route to transfer" (para 7.23), but much harder to deliver more competition given the costs imposed on small landlords by the bidding process. Similarly, the ceiling of 12,000 houses for transfers to a single landlord is cited as evidence of the intention to move away from large-scale monopoly landlords. This ignores the fact that the current ceiling is an increase on the previous one and is large enough to result in large estates continuing to be dominated by a single landlord. The Green Paper elides this difficulty by supporting "imaginative solutions" to the problem of separating stock into "manageable and sensible clusters" such as "allowing transfer initially to a single landlord in order to make possible a single ballot, followed immediately by onward transfer to sensible sized registered landlords" (para 7.24). Birmingham, the largest municipal landlord in England, is given as an example. But the Birmingham proposal, although it would break up the stock over the city as a whole, does not appear to involve any element of competition as to who the landlord will be at either stage.

Moreover, the possible implications for the exercise of tenants' collective rights are not considered at all. Two stage transfers will make it harder for tenants to use the consultation and consent requirements of existing law to exert leverage on the stock transfer process. Although ministerial consent for the subsequent transfer would be required under Section 133 of the 1985 Act, the requirements of tenant consultation in Schedule 3A do not apply to subsequent transfers. If the two stage transfer is a package, it does not seem entirely within the spirit of the current legislation for tenants not to be consulted on, and have equivalent information about, the second stage transfer. It is, of course, possible to consult tenants on both stages of the transfer before the whole stock ballot, and identify at that stage who the landlords after the second stage transfer will be. This is what is intended in the case of the Birmingham proposal (Birmingham City Council, 1999) which envisages the umbrella body that acquires the stock immediately transferring it to smaller locally based RSLs. But, if the onward transfer is not immediate then the consultation process would not have the same legitimacy.

No doubt issues of this nature can be considered when the Secretary of State is giving consent on the first transfer, but the Secretary of State is not in any way obliged to impose conditions on the second stage transfer when giving consent to the first. So, a great deal will depend in the larger transfers on the precise arrangements proposed for both first and second stage transfers. There is clearly potential for conflict among the various aims of moving stock swiftly out of the public sector, ensuring diversity in ownership and management of social housing stock, and ensuring full tenant consultation and participation. The important point of principle is that local authority tenants have a clear collective legal right of veto over a change in the identity of their landlords. After transfer to an RSL they no longer have such a right, and would be reliant on the Secretary of State's relatively unstructured discretion under Section 133 to ensure that adequate consultation had been carried out. This seems to be at odds with the general thrust of the Green Paper which is to promote convergence in many respects between the different parts of the social rented sector, and the stated vision of creating a sector in which "tenants are empowered in the decision-making processes which affect their homes" (para 6.15), suggesting that not enough thought has gone into considering the rights tenants of social housing should have after demunicipalisation.

Conclusion

As we have seen, there is essentially continuity of policy between the current Labour government and its Conservative predecessors: the core aim remains the replacement of local authorities by other bodies as social landlords. The pathological consequences of the juridification of central–local relations and of delivery of local services generally have not been experienced in this particular context. Whether changes in the nature of local authority involvement (large urban Labour-controlled authorities engaging in whole stock transfers) triggers more resort to law as a means of obstructing the process remains to be seen. We have also seen that the principal criticism of the stock transfer process – that local authority tenants are not given a meaningful choice of alternatives for increased investment in their housing – remains valid.

There are many issues arising from stock transfer which have not been discussed in any detail here, for example, the way rents are fixed, how tenant participation will be dealt with in future, and the future regulatory arrangements for social landlords. This chapter has emphasised, in particular, the questions of tenants' collective rights to influence decisions about who their landlords should be and the rights tenants should have as individuals. It has argued for harmonisation of both types of rights across the whole of the social rented sector. It has done so partly because of the importance of the issue to date in the stock transfer process and partly because it illustrates a failure to consider fully the implications of the convergence between different parts of the social rented sector on which recent trends in housing policy appear to be premised. Part of the process of clarifying the vision for the future of the social rented sector should be providing a common floor of rights for all social rented sector tenants, including extended rights of consultation and participation applying to all changes of landlord within the sector.

Notes

[1] The relevant Scottish legislation is Part III of the 1987 Housing (Scotland) Act, and Part II of the 1988 Housing (Scotland) Act.

[2] Tai Cymru was dissolved as part of the devolution settlement and its functions are now exercised by the National Assembly for Wales.

[3] The Glasgow proposal would have to be approved by the Scottish Executive under the 1987 Housing (Scotland) Act.

References

Birmingham City Council (1999) *Investing to regenerate: A future for Birmingham's housing*, Birmingham: Birmingham City Council.

Chaplin, R., Jones, M., Martin, S., Pryke, M., Royce, C., Saw, P., Whitehead, C. and Yang, J.H. (1995) *Rents and risks: Investing in housing associations*, York: Joseph Rowntree Foundation.

Clapham, D. (1989) *Goodbye council housing*, London: Unwin.

DETR (Department of the Environment, Transport and the Regions)/ DSS (Department of Social Security) (2000) *Quality and choice: A decent home for all*, Housing Green Paper, London: DETR/DSS.

DoE (Department of the Environment) (1988) *Circular 6/88*, London: DoE.

DoE (1993) *Large scale voluntary transfer: Guidelines*, London: DoE.

DoE/Welsh Office (1987) *Housing policy: The Government's proposals*, Cm 214, London: HMSO.

Goodlad, R. and Scott, S. (1996) 'Housing and the Scottish New Towns: a case study of policy termination and quasi-markets', *Urban Studies*, vol 33, pp 317-35.

Hawksworth, J. and Wilcox, S. (1995) *Challenging the conventions*, Coventry: Chartered Institute of Housing.

Hood, M. (1998) *One for all: A single tenancy for social housing*, Coventry: Chartered Institute of Housing.

Housing Corporation (1997) *Performance standards*, London: The Housing Corporation.

Inquiry into British Housing (Chairman HRH The Duke of Edinburgh) (1991) *Second Report*, York: Joseph Rowntree Foundation.

Leather, P. and Jeffers, S. (1989) *Taking tenants to court: A study of possession actions by local authorities*, London: DoE.

Loughlin, M. (1996) *Legality and locality: The role of law in central–local government relations*, Oxford: Oxford University Press.

Loughlin, M. (2000) 'The restructuring of central-local government relations', in J. Jowell and D. Oliver (eds) *The changing constitution* (4th edn), Oxford: Oxford University Press.

Mullen, T., Scott, S., Fitzpatrick, S. and Goodlad, R. (1997) *Tenancy rights and repossession rates: In theory and practice*, Edinburgh: Scottish Homes.

Mullen, T., Scott, S., Fitzpatrick, S. and Goodlad, R. (1999) 'Rights and security in housing: the repossession process in the social rented sector', *Modern Law Review*, vol 62, pp 11-31.

Mullins, D., Niner, P. and Riseborough, M. (1995) *Evaluating large scale voluntary transfers of local authority housing*, London: DoE.

Nixon, J., Hunter, C., Smith, Y. and Wishart B. (1996) *Housing cases in county courts*, Bristol/York: The Policy Press/Joseph Rowntree Foundation.

Scottish Executive (2000) *Better homes for Scotland's communities*, Edinburgh: Scottish Executive.

Scottish Homes (1999) *Raising standards in housing*, Edinburgh: Scottish Homes.

Scottish Office (1987) *Housing policy: The government's proposals*, Cm 242, Edinburgh: HMSO.

SFHA (Scottish Federation of Housing Associations) (1990) *Model assured tenancy agreement*, Edinburgh: SFHA.

SFHA (revised edn) (1997) *Model assured tenancy agreement*, Edinburgh: SFHA.

SODD (Scottish Office Development Department) (1996) *Transfers of local authority housing stock in Scotland*, Edinburgh: SODD.

Teubner, G. (1987) 'Juridification: concept, aspects, limits, solutions', in G. Teubner (ed) *Juridification of social spheres*, Berlin: Walter de Guyter.

Housing standards in the private sector

Introduction

Despite central government commitment to, and reliance on, the tenures of owner-occupation and the private rented sector, the delivery of better housing standards in each sector has assumed a relatively low profile in policy discussions. Nevertheless, it has always been assumed that housing standards are a legitimate interest of central government, and therefore that investment to maintain or raise standards is worth subsidising. But the thinking underlying the provision of subsidy has rarely been articulated clearly and, in any event, has probably shifted over time. In 1995, the Conservative government's White Paper suggested that "we are a nation of home improvers" (DoE, *Our future homes*, p 16) and appeared to place primary responsibility for the upkeep of property on its owners, subject to increasingly targeted (and declining) public grants. New Labour's Green Paper makes it crystal clear that responsibility for the state and condition of property rests with the owner – whether owner-occupier or landlord. Thus, in line with the broader retrenchment of the welfare state, the state appears to be seeking to withdraw from this area of activity.

In the private rented sector, there are additional questions beyond the standards of property provided. These questions relate to the limits of state regulation, particularly in the 'houses in multiple occupation' (HMOs) subsector. The Green Paper seeks to strike a balance between, on the one hand, excessive state regulation that might stifle growth in the sector and limit the willingness of institutional organisations to invest in it, and, on the other hand, under-regulation that does little to address the problem of 'bad' landlords and poor quality properties. In the latter case, the Green Paper advocates the possibility of withdrawing Housing Benefit, licensing of HMOs (a pre-election manifesto pledge), and consideration of changes to laws on unlawful eviction and harassment.

The two chapters concerned with housing standards consider different aspects and approach them differently. Sarah Blandy focuses on standards in the private rented sector. Drawing on a diverse literature concerning discourse analysis, three aspects of the private rented sector are identified as being either explicit or implicit in central government policy: regulation, responsibility and rights. Regulation and responsibility are discussed in some detail in the Green Paper, but discussion of rights is 'conspicuous by its absence'. Describing these concepts as the 'three Rs', their identification enables Blandy to link the discussion into broader socio-legal theoretical debates, in particular the shift towards legal pluralism. Arguing that the Green Paper's distinction between responsible and unscrupulous landlords is purposive, regulation is then justified in the latter sector but not in the former.

Blandy identifies three different rights for discussion: first, security of tenure, especially the right to quiet enjoyment; second, physical conditions of the property; and third, financial issues. The Green Paper's shift towards targeted regulation, at the local authority's discretion, and licensing is described as creating 'regulatory' rights for tenants – that is, rights which are only enforceable through a regulatory body, in this case the local authority. Discretionary models of regulation are rightly criticised for creating geographical variations. With respect to making Housing Benefit conditional on responsible behaviour by landlords and tenants, significant concerns are aroused in relation, first, to the exercise of local authority discretion in this complex area and, second, to the ability of landlords to seek possession for non-payment of rent.

Philip Leather's target is the broader issue of housing standards in the private sector. His chapter suggests that elements of the Green Paper are to be welcomed. He identifies, in particular, the policy focus on sustainability throughout the ownership of property, as opposed to original acquisition; the policy shift towards making owners responsible for the upkeep of their properties; and the 'major shift' away from local authority grants towards a more responsive system of grants or loans – with repayment of the latter being recycled into the system. However, the chapter also presents an acerbic critique of some of the policies outlined in the Green Paper. For example, Leather suggests that there is a "complete absence of any strategic thinking" about the future of the housing stock in a number of key areas. As regards the private rented sector, Leather regards the Green Paper's discussion of property standards as a little unreal in basing the rationale for its policy approach on "character rather than economics". As for attracting institutional investors to the sector, he considers the Green Paper to make no real contribution ("ideas on a postcard please").

Despite the differences in subject matter and approach between the two chapters, there are some areas of common concern. First, there is a broad concern with discretionary powers given to local authorities. This is an important area in which the interests of housing and socio-legal studies coincide, partly because of the geographical variation that is the inevitable result of the exercise of discretionary power and partly also because of an interest in the factors which influence individual decisions. Second, there is an engagement with the 'problems' of regulation and its focus on particular types of landlord. Third, although the chapters take a different approach to the issue, there is an acknowledgement that 'responsibility' and particular conceptions of citizenship underpin much of the debate and, indeed, have resonance for policy beyond this particular subject.

FOUR

Housing standards in the private rented sector and the three Rs: regulation, responsibility and rights

Sarah Blandy

Introduction

This chapter uses the technique of discourse analysis to examine the Labour government's policy and legislative proposals for the private rented sector in *Quality and choice: A decent home for all* (DETR/DSS, 2000 – hereafter 'the Green Paper'). These proposals are compared with the preceding government housing policy documents, *Housing: The government's proposals* (DoE, 1987a) and *Our future homes: Opportunity, choice, responsibility* (DoE, 1995) – hereafter 'the 1987 (or 1995) White Paper'.

The private rented sector is currently very diverse, both in respect of types of landlord and the markets which it serves. The focus of this chapter, and of the Green Paper, is the lower end of the private rented sector. Here tenants' main concerns are security of tenure and physical conditions; and issues which are fundamentally linked with the financial framework of the private rented sector, by which I mean rent levels, rates of return for landlords, availability of Housing Benefit for tenants, and the consequences of ability or failure to pay rent. Three alternative or overlapping policy approaches can be identified for maintaining and improving standards in the private rented sector: *regulation* by an outside agency; persuading private landlords and tenants to take *responsibility* by themselves; and/or giving tenants enforceable individual *rights* to use against defaulting landlords.

These three Rs raise important questions about the role of law in implementing policy, and law's relationship with administrative discretion.

These are central concerns of socio-legal studies which has produced many empirical studies exposing the gap between legal formalism and reality. In the first part of this chapter I draw on socio-legal theory, from a wider perspective as well as that which deals with housing law alone, and relate it to the Green Paper's attitude and assumptions about the three Rs, which are identified through discourse analysis. The following section then uses socio-legal research findings to evaluate the likely effectiveness of the Green Paper proposals for security of tenure, physical conditions and the financial framework for the private rented sector.

Discourse analysis and socio-legal theories

Discourse analysis, which involves "close scrutiny of the detail of grammar, lexis and narrative ... [to] reveal how discourses are reproduced and sustained in policy documents" (Hastings, 1998, p 94), shows how assumptions about the three Rs are woven into government policy and legislation. Discourse analysis discloses 'story-lines' (Hajer, 1995) in housing policy, continuing themes which provide a common-sense approach and a legitimising explanation for government policy. It also makes us aware of the significance of silence, both "things said and those concealed": policy makers can render problems invisible by denying a voice to powerless groups (Foucault, 1990, p 101; and see Hunter and Nixon, 1999, on indebted tenants of social landlords).

Discourse analysis reveals a striking, cross-party consensus on the place of the private rented sector, through similar – sometimes identical – wording in two key housing policy documents from governments of different political persuasion. In both the 1995 Conservative White Paper (DoE,1995, p 12), and Labour's Green Paper (DETR/DSS, 2000, p 16) 'sustainable home ownership' is emphasised, with the expectation that its share of the housing market will increase. In both documents ownership is presented as a major aim of housing policy, and as a perfectly normal aspiration for the majority of British households (see Gurney, 1999, on the normalising discourse process). The 1995 White Paper asserted that, alongside home ownership, a 'healthy private rented sector' assists young people, people whose personal circumstances have changed, and people who prefer to rent rather than buy, as well as helping mobility of labour (DoE, 1995, p 20). The same phrase is used for the title of Chapter 5 of the Green Paper – 'Promoting a healthy private rented sector' – which again stresses the provision of 'additional housing choices' for those who do not want to buy, and for younger households, as well as assisting the labour market (DETR/DSS, 2000, p 44).

The Green Paper's specific proposals for the private rented sector are now addressed through an examination of its underlying assumptions about and attitudes towards the three Rs. Relevant theoretical work in the socio-legal field is drawn on to illuminate this discussion.

Regulation and deregulation

The bogey of "excessive regulation, which can stifle growth to the detriment of tenants and responsible landlords" is raised early in the Green Paper (DETR/DSS, 2000, p 16). This echoes previous policy statements. For example in 1987 the Conservative government aimed to achieve a "better balance between the needs of tenants and landlords" by means of deregulating both rents and security of tenure (DoE, 1987b, ch 3). The 1988 Housing Act then deregulated the private rented sector by establishing assured and assured shorthold tenancies with market rents, an example of the second category of deregulation identified by Hancher and Moran: cancellation, substitution and systematisation (1989, pp 129-31). Subsequent 1995 White Paper proposals to make letting easier for non-professional landlords were included in the 1996 Housing Act, systematising the deregulation of assured shorthold tenancies as the 'default' tenancy type, requiring no additional paperwork.

The Green Paper assures landlords "that we intend no change in the present structure of assured and assured shorthold tenancies, which is working well. Nor is there any question of our re-introducing rent controls ..." as good landlords "need encouragement, support and education rather than further heavy regulation" (DETR/DSS, 2000, pp 44, 45). However, against this deregulated background, and commitment not to impose further regulation, there is concern about poor physical conditions and poor management at "the cheaper end of the market" in the private rented sector (p 21), especially in shared houses. Thus the proposed licensing scheme for houses in multiple occupation (HMOs) is justified as providing "a much more satisfactory framework ... incorporating the principles of better regulation", while avoiding "a more general and potentially counter-productive regulatory regime" (pp 48, 49). So there is tension between embracing deregulation and the need to "make sure that the worst landlords also improve their housing – or get out of the business altogether" (p 45).

Recent theoretical debates within and beyond the socio-legal studies movement have addressed the role of regulation and its relationship with formal law. Regulation has been defined as "a sustained control exercised by a public agency over an activity that is socially valued" (Harlow and Rawlings, 1997, p 141). Regulation is usually characterised as a new type of law, part of the development of legal pluralism associated with juridification. The process of juridification, according to Teubner, is as an inevitable product of modernity in the late 20th century in Europe. Its characteristics are "the emergence of new structures of law to keep pace with the growth of the welfare state" (Teubner, 1987, p 18). Legal theorists have recognised and discussed the growing phenomena of legal pluralism and informal justice over the last few decades. The pluralist view of law can be summarised as "a complex of overlapping, interpenetrating or intersecting normative systems or regimes, *amongst which relations of authority are unstable, unclear, contested or in course of negotiation*" (Cotterell, 1998, p 381, original emphasis). This chapter considers some of the problems experienced in the private rented sector as a result of the shift towards legal pluralism.

The growth of administrative regulation is sometimes posed as an alternative to law, which it is seen as having pushed aside. However, Veljanovski's argument is preferable. This suggests that regulation occurs in "the shadow of the law ... the law operates as the sanction of last resort against which compliance is sought through negotiation, bargaining and threats" (Veljanovski, 1991, p 13). The constitutive 'regulation approach' advocated by Hunt is also useful because it allows us to analyse the process of regulation while avoiding the dichotomy of 'law versus regulation' (Hunt, 1997, pp 73-5, 78). Hunt describes this process as including the creation of an object of regulation, because there are no ready-made or natural objects of regulation. This is inextricably linked with the formation of a mode of regulation (p 74). Regulatory agents must also be designated or created and have powers conferred on them. Regulatory knowledge has to be produced and regulatory strategies, involving rewards and/or sanctions, have to be formulated (p 75). The process of regulation as analysed by Hunt can be seen at work in the Green Paper, which constructs 'irresponsible' landlords and tenants as objects for regulation. The mode of regulation consists of the enforcement powers of the local authority, the regulatory agent. Information about poor physical standards, poor management of rented housing, and exploitation of the Housing Benefit system must be collected before a compliance strategy can be formulated.

Socio-legal theory has also addressed the effectiveness of regulation in meeting policy objectives. Cotterell (1992, pp 267-9) lists six factors which may undermine compliance strategies: inadequacy of resources, sanctions and support, lack of understanding from the courts, complexity of circumstances, and an insecure basis for the agent's authority. This analysis will be applied in analysing the difficulties or failures in regulating the private rented sector, as we examine the concerns of tenants in the following section of this chapter.

One further consequence of varying local enforcement strategies and success in enforcement is the development of 'local law'. This was identified by Stewart and Burridge (1989) in relation to conditions in the private rented sector:

> The cohesive framework of national norms and display of universal individual rights are crucial.... The process is inherently unstable, however, and the tenant ... is bound to suspect that the law is different down the road, or in the next town, or down south.... (p 82)

Van Kempen concludes that this unevenness is in part due to the fact that "[t]he organisations which deliver services, including rights, are made up of active, self-conscious individuals ... [who] reproduce their [ie the organisations'] structures and alter their outputs" (van Kempen, 1996, p 21). In the same vein, Lipsky (1980) has identified street-level bureaucrats as officials who have direct contact with the public and who have substantial discretion to develop techniques which they use to allocate resources between competing clients. The organisations they work for (in this case, local authorities) are described as 'negotiated orders' which develop their own cultures, assumptions and understanding of their environment (van Kempen, 1996, p 21). It is therefore not surprising that local law develops, and that landlords and tenants in the private rented sector experience differing levels of intervention and support from the regulatory agencies.

Rights and (ir-)responsibility

The Green Paper focuses on landlords rather than tenants. Unless they are causing problems tenants are deemed to be satisfactorily housed and in need of no advice or support. Because of this, the third 'R', rights, is conspicuous by its absence from the Green Paper. Similarly, the rights of private sector tenants have played no, or very little, part in previous government documents (see DoE, 1987a, 1995). Although the Green Paper specifically states that "the security of tenure enjoyed by *social* housing tenants" should not be reduced and that "the rights of existing tenants and new tenants who have a long term need for *social* housing" should not be diminished (DETR/DSS, 2000, p 91), restoring rights lost to private tenants through the 1988 and 1996 Housing Acts does not form part of the Green Paper's agenda.

The concept of rights has recently been increasingly linked to notions of responsibility and citizenship (see Papps, 1998), as indeed it is currently by a Labour government influenced by Etzioni's communitarianism and Giddens' Third Way politics. Cowan argues that in the field of housing we should now be concentrating on individual responsibility, rather than the protection of individual rights through the due process of law (Cowan, 1999, pp 364-6). However, the rhetoric of rights is still, or is perhaps becoming increasingly, powerful. As Simmonds (1998, p 212) observes, "[t]he very prestige attaching to 'rights' in modern culture guarantees that the word will be invoked more and more widely, leading to 'inflation' of the 'currency' of 'rights' in modern discourse".

In this sense, the Green Paper's silence on the issue of rights for private sector tenants can be seen as out of step with current developments, notably the introduction of the 1998 Human Rights Act. Rights in housing have traditionally been associated with tenure (but see Blandy and Goodchild, 1999). Housing rights "are essentially similar to other legally protected individual rights, albeit that ... they attach to a status rather than to a person" (Nelken, 1983, p 20). If private tenants were given rights then they could use them to achieve satisfactory standards in terms of security of tenure, physical conditions, and the financial aspects of their tenancies. But in the absence of individual rights, regulation by a third party must be the primary method of enforcing standards. Stewart (1996) has identified three 'spheres' of housing law: contractual, statutory and regulatory. Contract or statute can provide the basis for rights, whereas regulation can only lead to consumer rights which depend on external enforcement.

The second 'R' – responsibility – appeared in the sub-title of the 1995 White Paper. It also appears repeatedly in the Green Paper; for example, "As individuals, we all have responsibilities towards our homes"; "Landlords are in a position of immense importance and responsibility"; "Housing Benefit ... can be exploited by landlords and takes responsibility away from tenants" (DETR/DSS, 2000, pp 19, 23). The Green Paper has shifted concern about irresponsibility from the social rented sector to the private rented sector. In contrast, the 1995 White Paper noted that while the rights of social tenants had been increased in 1994 (the rights to manage, to repair, and to compensation for improvement) there was a growing problem of anti-social behaviour in that sector. It put forward a raft of proposals to "help local authorities to deal more effectively with their anti-social tenants" (DoE, 1995, p 43). In 2000, the focus is on identifying the wrongdoers in the private rented sector and encouraging the regulators to deal with them, rather than giving enforceable rights to tenants.

In general, Chapter 5 of the Green Paper classifies private landlords into two sharply differentiated categories: "Our many good landlords [who] deserve support and encouragement" as opposed to "A small minority of private landlords [who] set out to exploit their tenants and the community at large in flagrant disregard of the law" (p 44). The latter are worse than irresponsible. They are "unscrupulous" and can form an "unholy alliance [with] bad tenants" whose anti-social behaviour combines with Housing Benefit fraud in "destabilising local communities" (p 49). However, in some cases rather than allying with irresponsible tenants, "unscrupulous landlords ... resort to harassment and illegal eviction" (p 52). The opposing characterisations of landlords as 'responsible' and 'unscrupulous' is an example of a discourse pattern termed "division and rejection" by Foucault (1981, pp 52-6). In the Green Paper the technique is used to justify intervention in a sector which in general the government is concerned not to over-regulate.

Applying socio-legal research findings to the Green Paper proposals

This section of the chapter focuses on the areas identified as of most concern to tenants in the private rented sector. The theoretical framework for the three Rs has now been established, and their place in the Green Paper policy proposals has been analysed. Socio-legal research findings will be used to evaluate the effectiveness of those proposals.

Security of tenure

Private tenants with assured shorthold tenancies have minimal security of tenure. The 1987 White Paper (DoE, 1987a) proposed that this deregulation of the private rented sector should be accompanied by strengthened powers for local authorities to prosecute under the 1977 Protection from Eviction Act. This was accordingly included in the 1988 Housing Act (although some categories of occupiers, notably those with resident landlords, were removed from protection altogether). The issue of security of tenure for private tenants, and harassment and unlawful eviction by landlords, was not mentioned in the 1995 White Paper. The Green Paper includes only a brief paragraph on harassment and unlawful eviction, referring to research commissioned by the DETR (Marsh et al, 2000) and the good practice guide resulting from it (DETR, 2000), stating confidently that harassment and unlawful eviction affect only "an extremely small minority of tenants" (DETR/DSS, 2000, p 52).

The reluctance of the Green Paper to acknowledge this as a problem can be contrasted with the DETR research. Marsh et al surveyed 29 local authorities and conducted eight in-depth local case studies. They concluded that "it is not possible to construct a consistent picture of the number of cases which statutory and voluntary sector organisations deal with" (p 39). They point to a number of possible reasons for this, including failure to keep records, lack of publicity for tenancy relations services, tenants' awareness of their minimal security of tenure, or a combination of these. The research did find that more vulnerable tenants, with social problems, are the most likely to be on the receiving end of harassment or unlawful eviction, most likely from smaller or medium-sized landlords or smaller accommodation agencies. The key cause of harassment was ignorance of the law by landlords, with triggers being rent arrears or delay in Housing Benefit payments, and delays in court possession proceedings (Marsh et al, 2000).

The combination of few or no tenancy rights, and a shaky financial framework, leads to the need for action in Stewart's 'regulatory sphere'. The regulators under the Protection from Eviction Act are local authorities, and the ultimate sanction for such offences is prosecution. Home Office statistics show that there are around 100 prosecutions for harassment and unlawful eviction a year, with a conviction rate of just under 50 per cent. Marsh et al found that none of the members of the Association of Tenancy Relations Officers reported "a decrease in their workload.... However, the number of prosecutions brought annually has generally been decreasing, which is partly a product of a greater emphasis on the conciliation role of tenancy relations officers and partly due to financial constraints" (p 39). Thus, "the law operates as the sanction of last resort against which compliance is sought through negotiation, bargaining and threats" (Veljanovski, 1991, p 13). The DETR research noted that, despite the fact that "local authorities effectively have a duty to investigate allegations", some choose not even to investigate (Marsh et al, 2000, p 102). These findings bear out Cotterell's analysis of the factors which hinder compliance strategies, particularly inadequacy of resources, sanctions and support, while lack of understanding from the courts may well be a factor in the low conviction rate.

The DETR research considered whether local authorities should have a duty, rather than the current power, to prosecute, but concluded that this was "not likely to be practical or desirable..." . The good practice guide on harassment and unlawful eviction (DETR, 2000) makes a number of suggestions for improving performance of local authorities in this area, including monitoring the extent of local problems, and flexibility in response, from advice to prosecution. If tenants are not granted rights, and local authorities are free to adopt a range of strategies but have no duty to prosecute, then security of tenure together with the threat of harassment and unlawful eviction are likely to remain areas of concern in the private rented sector.

Physical conditions

The 1987 White Paper took a rights approach to this issue, and subsequently Section 11 of the 1985 Landlord and Tenant Act (which deals with repairing obligations of landlords) was extended to apply to all types of tenancies and to blocks of flats. However, the implementation gap applies here: tenants with little security are notoriously reluctant to risk asserting their rights to repair, for fear of their landlords' reaction. The 1995 White Paper made almost no mention of the poor state of repair in the private sector. Apart from a proposal to make grants to landlords discretionary and only available within renewal areas (DoE, 1995, p 17), the focus was on regenerating rundown local authority estates. The 1996 English House Condition Survey found an apparent reduction in unfitness: 18 per cent of privately rented dwellings (compared with 7.5 per cent of the total housing stock) were unfit in 1996, as against 31 per cent in 1986 (DETR, 1998a). However, this was probably due to the better-maintained formerly owner-occupied properties which entered the sector as a result of the property market downturn in the early 1990s. Those dwellings which were privately rented in both 1991 and in 1996 had a significantly higher level of disrepair than the new entrants, revealing that enforcement activity of local authorities had little effect (Crook et al, 1998).

Most local authorities are dissatisfied with the current regulatory regime, finding its complexity confusing. They take action on only around 5 out of every 100 substandard properties in each year (Randall, 1995).

As Leather (1999, p 12) concludes, "there is little point in having standards if they are not policed or if they can be ignored. The present fitness standard suffers greatly from this problem". The 1989 Local Government and Housing Act redefined the fitness criteria and made most grants discretionary, causing a fundamental change in the way that local authorities administer grants and assess private dwellings against the fitness standard. However, local variations in standards of fitness were already developing before this: "In spite of a legal duty to inspect their areas, lack of resources reduces [local authorities'] role to one of reaction, and this in turn adds further impetus to the definition of a local standard" (Stewart and Burridge, 1989, p 79).

In the Green Paper, the government proposes that the whole basis of local authority intervention should be changed from "the existing pass-or-fail fitness standard" to a "health and safety rating scale ... based directly on the actual hazards threatening the occupants". It argues that authorities' intervention can thus be better targeted, and on an appropriate scale to deal with the severity of the problem. This would address their "fear that the effect of strict enforcement will only be to reduce much-needed supply" of accommodation (DETR/DSS, 2000, p 48). The proposed rating scale comes from a consultation paper on the housing fitness standard (DETR, 1998b). The main question asked of respondents was: should there be a duty or a power to enforce standards? The Green Paper is clear that local authorities are expected to take a stronger strategic role, including "enforcing and raising standards" (DETR/DSS, 2000, p 25). However, no duty to prosecute in cases of unfitness, or where a dwelling comes dismally low on the new rating scale, is proposed.

The 1995 White Paper promoted the local authorities' "strategic and enabling role in supporting both landlords and tenants". It cited examples of good practice including a self-regulating landlord accreditation scheme, information and advice service to landlords, rent and deposit guarantee scheme, and Charter Marks for providing quality Housing Benefit services (DoE, 1995, p 23). The Green Paper advocates much the same approach, including professional self-regulation of landlords and agents: "we already encourage industry self-regulation" (DETR/DSS, 2000, p 46). Many associations of landlords and letting agents support self-regulation; for example the Association of Residential Letting Agents was instrumental in setting up the National Approved Letting Scheme. However, Crook et al (1998) found that landlords lack the knowledge and capacity to organise repair work. Thus self-regulation based on a concept of responsibility is not really a relevant consideration, and regulation by local authorities is an uphill task.

Local authorities have found the mixed diet of support, accreditation on a voluntary basis, and negotiation backed by the threat of prosecution, hard to manage successfully. Enforcement through law carries a high cost so most local authorities attempt to encourage compliance first (Leather, 1999). A clearer regulatory framework could provide the answer: "a licensing scheme covering all private rented homes offers the most effective way of ensuring minimum legal standards of health and safety are met" and would have the support of the majority of local authorities (Randall, 1995). However, the Green Paper rejects licensing the whole private rented sector because the "extra red tape involved" would be a deterrent to "some perfectly respectable landlords" who might leave the sector, or decide not to enter it (DETR/DSS, 2000, p 49). Selective licensing of "particularly problematic types of property, or neighbourhoods" is under consideration. *Inside Housing* (9 June 2000) reported on a survey of 75 local authorities about this proposal – only 4 per cent were in favour of selective licensing. It seems that central government is rejecting a proposal which is backed by the regulatory agencies, on the twin grounds of (avoidance of) regulation and encouragement of responsible landlords.

The subsector of the private rented sector with the worst physical and management standards, and the highest risk to the safety of occupiers, is HMOs. HMOs house over 3 million people, but 20 per cent of properties are unfit (DETR, 1998a). It is here that we see the only real change in policy resulting from the change in government. The Labour Party manifesto in 1997 promised "There will be a proper system of licensing by local authorities which will benefit tenants and responsible landlords alike". The proposal to license all HMOs, rather than rely on discretionary registration schemes run by local authorities as at present, had been canvassed in the 1994 consultation paper on licensing HMOs (DoE, 1994), but the 1995 White Paper plumped for "helping local authorities to develop their existing enforcement strategies ... while avoiding the dangers of bureaucracy and over-regulation inherent in a full scale licensing scheme" (DoE, 1995, p 24). In contrast, the Labour government's consultation paper on licensing HMOs (DETR, 1999a) noted that "the level of enforcement activity and standards applied have varied significantly around the country" because they are based on discretionary powers. The main proposals were that all shared houses should be included, and to issue licences to a single individual to ensure compliance.

The Green Paper repeats the government's commitment "to introducing, as soon as Parliamentary time allows, a compulsory licensing system for

HMOs, and to modernising and rationalising the confusing mass of controls in this area ... incorporating the principles of better regulation" (DETR/DSS, 2000, p 48). It seems that, in the case of HMOs, government objections to regulation have been overcome. Consistent and effective lobbying by groups such as the Campaign for Bedsit Rights has pointed out the high risk to tenants in such accommodation, who are among the most vulnerable groups in society and therefore least likely to enforce their rights. However, many of the arguments used by the government in justifying intervention into HMOs – local variations in standards, the problems of discretion, and over-complex regulations – can equally be applied to the other areas of the private rented sector under consideration here, where regulation has been rejected.

Financial issues in the private rented sector

This final area of concern links Housing Benefit with regulation of housing conditions and regulation of irresponsible tenants. A wider and more detailed view of Housing Benefit is dealt with in chapter 11 of the Green Paper, and discussed in Chapters Sixteen and Seventeen of this book. The concern here is with how tenants' rights to welfare benefits can become compromised through policy initiatives addressing other perceived problems. The government's problem is that a deregulated private rented sector has led to a soaring benefits bill. The consequent tightening up of Housing Benefit entitlement can be characterised (although not by central government) as further regulation. In 1995, proposals for amendments to the Housing Benefit system included "giving tenants an incentive to negotiate lower rents with their landlords and to choose less expensive accommodation when moving" (DoE, 1995, p 24). The system of rent officers fixing a local reference rent, which limits the Housing Benefit available for a particular tenancy to a notional 'reasonable rent', was introduced in January 1996. However, subsequent research has found that tenants still do not shop around for cheaper accommodation; it is bureaucracy rather than the market which limits rents at the lower end of the private rented sector (Kemp and Leather, 2000).

Research has found that only a very small minority of landlords (less than 1 per cent) actually prefer to let to tenants in receipt of Housing Benefit. The majority say they are put off by rent arrears and problems with local authority administration of benefits (DETR, 1999b). It is easy to understand why local authority administration gets into difficulties. The complex administration of Housing Benefit is a further example of legal pluralism with its consequent issues of unclear and contested relations of authority (Cotterell, 1998, p 381). Independent rent officers set local reference rents; in some areas there is an agency to which the local authority has contracted responsibility for administering the scheme; and claimants have a right of appeal to local authority Review Boards. A succession of cases has revealed the degree of confusion over a number of issues: do landlords have the right to challenge Housing Benefit payments and recovery of overpayments? What are the consequences of failure by a local authority to comply strictly with the Housing Benefit regulations? And do local authority decisions give rise to private law rights and duties, or are they public law decisions challengeable only by judicial review? (See, for example, *Warwick DC v Freeman (1995) 27 HLR 616*; *Plymouth CC v Gigg (1997) 30 HLR 284*; and *Haringey LBC v Awaritefe (1999) 32 HLR 517*.)

The Green Paper, far from recommending any simplification of the current system, contains proposals "to restrict Housing Benefit payments in respect of poor housing, but only in areas where the market is over-supplied and claimants have little difficulty in finding alternative homes" (DETR/DSS, 2000, p 49). There are two aspects to this proposal. The first is to allow local authorities running an 'approved' licensing or accreditation scheme the discretion to refuse Housing Benefit to a claimant in respect of a substandard dwelling. The second possibility is to "make the availability of direct payment of Housing Benefit to the landlord (rather than to the claimant) dependent on the landlord meeting acceptable standards of provision and management". It suggests that this would be particularly effective as "benefit is paid direct to the landlord in 70 per cent of cases" and could be extended more widely than in areas of low demand covered by an approved scheme (p 49). In a considered response to these proposals, Leather concludes that "tenants would be the most likely to suffer from this proposal", which would be highly bureaucratic, lengthen delays and serve as a deterrent to landlords to take claimants as tenants (Leather, 1999).

The Green Paper also links the concept of responsibility to the financial framework of the private rented sector, in addressing the problem of the "unholy alliance of bad landlords and bad tenants" in the private sector (p 49). It refers to the reports of the Policy Action Teams of the Social Exclusion Unit on unpopular housing (SEU, 1999) and anti-social behaviour (SEU, 2000). These include a tentative proposal to empower local authorities to take action against private tenants who are causing a nuisance, through the use of injunctions and evictions, and to charge the private landlords for the cost of such action. Local authorities already have the power to apply for anti-social behaviour orders against private tenants. The Green Paper proposal would significantly extend their role as regulator of the behaviour of local inhabitants, to intervene in the contractual relationship between private landlords and their tenants. Extensive recent research into the use of legal remedies for anti-social behaviour (Hunter et al, 2000) found considerable variation between social landlords themselves in their use of their powers to evict and obtain injunctions. Although the courts have become increasingly sympathetic to landlords in these circumstances, a number of housing officers felt that legal remedies failed to deal with the underlying causes of problem behaviour. Only a range of support services combined with improved housing management could tackle these issues (Hunter et al, 2000). The private rented sector is very unlikely to provide this.

The Green Paper itself proposes that the Housing Benefit rules "could be adapted to encourage both tenants and landlords to behave responsibly" (DETR/DSS, 2000, pp 51-2). Payment of Housing Benefit direct to landlords could be refused in circumstances where the tenant was causing a nuisance and the landlord refused to take action against the tenant, if this occurs in an area where the local authority operated an accreditation scheme requiring landlords to "take all appropriate steps to ensure that their tenants behaved in a responsible manner". It is also suggested that local authorities could be given the power to reduce Housing Benefit "and other housing related-benefits, to encourage responsible behaviour" by tenants instead of, or at the same time as, pursuing an anti-social behaviour order. The right to Housing Benefit is one of the few rights enjoyed by private sector tenants, and the Green Paper does acknowledge that this proposal "would mark a fundamental shift in the nature of Housing Benefit and we would need to proceed with great care". If implemented, local authorities, in their role as administrators of Housing Benefit, would have to exercise discretion in very complex circumstances, to withdraw welfare benefits from tenants or to refuse direct payments to landlords. The consequences could be extremely serious and would affect a large number of tenants. Seventy-eight per cent of landlords rent to at least one tenant in receipt of benefit (DETR, 1999b). Payment of Housing Benefit is vital to tenants on a low income, as rent arrears is a mandatory ground for possession under the 1988 Housing Act.

In respect of the financial framework for the private rented sector, the Green Paper contains radical proposals which would change what was previously a welfare right into a *conditional right*, dependent on "responsible behaviour" by landlord or tenant, or both.

Conclusion

What lessons can be learnt from the consequences of policy proposals, and subsequent legislation, in 1987/88 and 1995/96 designed to revitalise the private rented sector? Shorthold tenancies increased from 38 per cent of lettings in the private rented sector in 1993/94 to 52 per cent in 1997/ 98 (Wilcox, 1999, table 49). The private rented sector also increased its proportional share of the housing market following deregulation in 1988. The 1996 English House Condition Survey (DETR, 1998a) concluded that this increase was probably mainly due to deregulation, but that the property market downturn in the early 1990s also played a part, leading owner-occupiers to rent out homes they could not sell. Only 65 per cent of the properties in the sector had been privately rented in 1991 (DETR, 1998a).

Teubner's "emergence of new structures of law" (1987, p 18) can be seen throughout the private rented sector. This is because the withdrawal of legal provisions from some aspects of the private rented sector has led to the need for other forms of regulation. For example, in 1988 new tenants lost the rights and security which went with Rent Act tenancies, but landlords who harassed or unlawfully evicted their tenants were to be regulated by local authorities enforcing the strengthened 1977 Protection from Eviction Act. The fitness standard was changed in 1989, and grants to landlords became discretionary, but local authorities continued to regulate physical conditions and management in the sector. Rents were deregulated in 1988, but Housing Benefit reforms set up 'backdoor rent regulation' by rent officers and local authorities.

Turning now to the Green Paper, discourse analysis shows there is no change in the policy of avoiding further regulation (except in the case of HMOs). However, the emphasis on the concept of responsibility in the private rented sector represents a real shift in policy. In 2000, both landlords and tenants in the private rented sector are dichotomised: those on the irresponsible side of the line require regulating, and can have rights withdrawn. Local authorities are already responsible for regulating physical conditions, management of properties, and behaviour by landlords to tenants in the private rented sector. Socio-legal theories and research findings, as we have seen, can explain and illustrate the limitations of this type of regulation, and the complexities resulting from legal pluralism.

Nonetheless, the solution proposed in the Green Paper to problems caused by irresponsible landlords and tenants remains strategic intervention by local authorities. The lack of rights of private tenants is not problematised in the Green Paper. I am not suggesting that restoration of private tenants' rights would be in any way a panacea. The issue of enforcement of rights is also critical. The due process of law is affected by the length of time it takes to take a case through court, compared to the length of a short-term tenancy, and effectiveness of rights is dependent on the availability of advice and representation.

However, in my view, regulation of private landlords provides 'second-hand' rights for their tenants, as a means of enforcing central government's expectations of responsible landlord behaviour. This type of right – neither contractual nor statutory – but dependent on complaints to a regulatory body – can be described as a *regulatory right*. For tenants, this is not a satisfactory way of ensuring that standards in the private rented sector are maintained and improved. It falls far short of the 'consumerist' model of regulation which would bring together pressure to guarantee property standards and set up a Director-General of Fair Housing to maintain standards across all sectors of the housing market, proposed by Partington (1980, 1993).

Despite its emphasis on responsibility, the Green Paper does not explain how landlords or tenants in the private rented sector can be made to behave more responsibly, except by the threat of withdrawing Housing Benefit. It is left to local authorities to develop more effective strategic approaches from a wide range of options, including enforcement through law as a final and expensive resort, and thus to secure a "larger, better-quality, better-managed private rented sector" (DETR/DSS, 2000, p 45). However, the reliance on local authorities will inevitably lead to local variations in standards. It is very unlikely that sufficient resources will be made available to ensure that, in the words of the Green Paper, "the worst landlords perform better".

References

Blandy, S. and Goodchild, B. (1999) 'From tenure to rights: conceptualising the changing focus of housing law in England', *Housing Theory and Society*, vol 16, pp 31-42.

Cotterell, R. (1992) *The sociology of law*, London: Butterworths.

Cotterell, R. (1998) 'Law and community: a new relationship?', in M. Freeman (ed) *Current legal problems*, Oxford: Oxford University Press.

Cowan, D. (1999) *Housing law and policy*, Basingstoke: Macmillan.

Crook, T., Henneberry, J. and Hughes, J. (1998) *Repairs and improvements to private rented dwellings in the 1990s*, London: DETR.

DETR (Department of the Environment, Transport and the Regions) (1998a) *English House Condition Survey 1996*, London: DETR.

DETR (1998b) *Housing fitness standard: A consultation paper*, London: DETR.

DETR (1999a) *Licensing houses in multiple occupation – England: A consultation paper*, London: DETR.

DETR (1999b) *Housing Benefit and private landlords*, London: DETR.

DETR (2000) *Harassment and unlawful eviction of private sector tenants and park home residents: A good practice guide*, London: DETR.

DETR/DSS (2000) *Quality and choice: A decent home for all*, Housing Green Paper, London: DETR/DSS.

DoE (Department of the Environment) (1987a) *Housing: The government's proposals*, Cm 214, London: HMSO.

DoE (1987b) *The private rented sector: The government's legislative proposals*, London: DoE and Welsh Office.

DoE (1994) *Houses in multiple occupation – Consultation paper on the case for licensing*, London: DoE.

DoE (1995) *Our future homes: Opportunity, choice, responsibility*, Cm 2901, London: HMSO.

Foucault, M. (1981) 'The order of discourse', in R. Young (ed) *Untying the text: A post-structuralist reader*, Boston, MA/London: Routledge and Kegan Paul.

Foucault, M. (1990) *The history of sexuality. Volume 1: An introduction*, London: Penguin.

Gurney, C. (1999) 'Pride and prejudice: discourses of normalisation in public and private accounts of home ownership', *Housing Studies*, vol 14, pp 163-84.

Hajer, M. (1995) *The politics of environmental discourse*, Oxford: Clarendon Press.

Hancher, L. and Moran, M. (1989) 'Introduction: regulation and deregulation', *European Journal of Political Research*, vol 17, no 2, pp 129-36.

Harlow, C. and Rawlings, R. (1997) *Law and administration*, London: Butterworths.

Hastings, A. (1998) 'Connecting linguistic structures and social practices: a discursive approach to social policy analysis', *Journal of Social Policy*, vol 27, no 2, pp 191-211.

Hunt, A. (1997) 'The politics of law and the law of politics', in K. Tuori, Z. Bankowski and J. Uusitalo (eds) *Law and power*, Liverpool: Deborah Charles.

Hunter, C. and Nixon, J. (1999) 'Tenure preference, discourse and housing debt: language's role in tenure stigmatisation', *Habitat International*, vol 23, no 1, pp 79-92.

Hunter, C., Nixon, J. and Shayer, S. (2000) *Neighbour nuisance, social landlords and the law*, Coventry: Chartered Institute of Housing.

Kemp, P. and Leather, P. (2000) *Housing Benefit reform: Price incentives*, York: Joseph Rowntree Foundation.

Leather, P. (1999) *Housing Benefit, licensing and poor conditions in the private rented sector*, Unpublished mimeo, Birmingham: Centre for Urban and Regional Studies, University of Birmingham.

Lipsky, M. (1980) *Street-level bureaucracy: Dilemmas of the individual in the public service*, New York, NY: Russell Sage.

Marsh, A., Niner P., Cowan, D., Forrest, R. and Kennett, P. (2000) *Harassment and unlawful eviction of private rented sector tenants and park home residents*, London: DETR.

Nelken, D. (1983) *The limits of the legal process: A study of landlords, law and crime*, Edinburgh: Academic Press.

Papps, P. (1998) 'Anti-social behaviour strategies – individualistic or holistic?', *Housing Studies*, vol 13, no 5, pp 639-56.

Partington, M. (1980) 'Landlord and tenant: the British experience', in E. Kamenka and A. Erh-Soon Tay (eds) *Law and social control*, London: Edward Arnold.

Partington, M. (1993) 'Housing', in R. Blackburn (ed) *Rights of citizenship*, London: Mansell.

Randall, G. (1995) *Licensing private rented housing*, York: Joseph Rowntree Foundation.

SEU (Social Exclusion Unit) (1999) *Report of Policy Action Team 7: Unpopular housing*, London: SEU.

SEU (2000) *Report of Policy Action Team 8: Anti-social behaviour*, London: SEU.

Simmonds, N. (1998) 'Rights at the cutting edge', in M. Kramer, N. Simmonds, and H. Steiner (eds) *A debate over rights*, Oxford: Clarendon Press.

Stewart, A. (1996) *Rethinking housing law*, London: Sweet and Maxwell.

Stewart, A. and Burridge, R. (1989) 'Housing tales of law and space', *Journal of Law and Society*, vol 16, no 1, pp 65-82.

Teubner, G. (1987) 'Juridification – concepts, aspects, limits, solutions', in G. Teubner (ed) *Juridification of social spheres*, Berlin/New York: Walter de Gruyter.

van Kempen, E. (1996) 'Social citizenship rights, organisations and the locale', in J. Allen, I. Ambrose. and E. Kaltenberg-Kwiatkowska (eds) *Housing sociology and societal change: New challenges and new directions*, CIB-publication 189, Warsaw: Warsaw University of Technology Centre for Social Sciences.

Veljanovski, C. (1991) 'The regulation game', in C. Veljanowski (ed) *Regulators and the market*, London: Institute of Economic Affairs.

Wilcox, S. (1999) *Housing finance review 1999/2000*, Coventry: Chartered Institute of Housing/Council of Mortgage Lenders/Joseph Rowntree Foundation.

FIVE

Housing standards in the private sector

Philip Leather

Two chapters in the Green Paper cover the question of housing standards in the private sector. Standards in owner-occupied housing are considered under the broader heading of 'Encouraging sustainable home ownership'. Questions of quality and condition are presented primarily as financial issues and related to the ability of owners to afford to invest in their homes. The ability of households to sustain themselves in home ownership in housing of reasonable quality is linked to their ability to meet housing acquisition costs or to sustain themselves through unforeseen difficulties in meeting mortgage payments. This is potentially a welcome development and one which has been paralleled by organisational changes within the Department of the Environment, Transport and the Regions. It emphasises the point that the affordability of home ownership and problems associated with this are not simply linked to house acquisition costs but also with longer-term and ongoing repair and maintenance costs, a point which Right to Buy policies have never acknowledged.

Standards in the private rented sector are dealt with in a separate chapter of the Green Paper. The central thrust here is that the private rented sector is here to stay. It fulfils several important functions and indeed the government wishes to see it grow and prosper. Minor misunderstandings between landlords and the state such as rent control or security of tenure are a thing of the past. But there is disappointment that despite de-control and a massive input of public subsidy through Housing Benefit, private rented sector homes remain proportionately more likely to be in poor condition than other housing sectors and there are still many examples of incompetent or deliberately illegal management by private landlords. So the Green Paper puts forward twin proposals, on the one hand to support and encourage those landlords seeking to provide good quality accommodation and a good management service, but on the other to penalise those falling short of this.

Improving the quality of owner-occupied housing

The problem

Most owner-occupied housing is in good condition, as the regular five-yearly surveys in England reveal (see, for example, DETR, 1998). This is not surprising. Rising real incomes provide the resources for owners to spend around £16 billion a year in aggregate on repairing and renovating their homes. Although most investment is undertaken to enhance comfort, amenity and status, there is the consolation of rising house prices as a further encouragement to investment.

But as the national House Condition Surveys also reveal, not all owners and all properties participate in this upgrading process. The inability to afford repairs or improvements is the main factor that deters people from investment. For some this might be because they over-committed themselves in purchasing a house in the first place; for others because their circumstances have deteriorated, for example, as a result of unemployment or because they have entered retirement without adequate savings or income to meet longer-term repair costs. Some, especially older people, may have adequate equity in their homes to support borrowing but be unable to meet repayment costs.

Money is not the only factor. Some people have other priorities for their disposable income. Some find it difficult to identify problems or organise work or are too afraid of exploitation by cowboy builders to invest. Some may be unwilling to face the disruption that is often associated with repair work.

The upshot is that certain types of owner-occupier – older people, younger people with high levels of mortgage repayment in comparison to income, unemployed people, people with disabilities or those experiencing ill-health, and women with children who have experienced divorce or relationship breakdown – are most likely to live in housing of a poor physical standard. Across all these groups those living in the older parts of the housing stock are also proportionately more likely to experience poor standards. The concentration of older housing in the inner parts of larger cities and in other localities, such as the former coalfield or mining areas or declining seaside resorts, also means that there is an important spatial dimension to the distribution of poor conditions.

Background

Measures to deal with poor housing conditions in private sector housing have a long history (Leather, 2000). Until the 1960s, most substandard private housing was owned by landlords, and compulsory acquisition of this stock at site value followed by demolition was the preferred solution. But as increasing numbers of older privately rented dwellings shifted into owner-occupation, acquisition became increasingly expensive because of demands for greater compensation and opposition from owners to rehousing in unattractive non-traditional local authority accommodation, often in peripheral or overspill locations. The late 1960s saw a shift in emphasis to the renovation of the older stock.

Grant aid had previously been available for the renovation of private sector dwellings but only for the installation of facilities (such as an indoor WC) which were not present when the dwellings were built. There was no assistance available with repair works which, it was argued, should be undertaken by owners (mainly landlords) from their own resources. Grant covered 50 per cent of the costs of eligible works, and was justified on the grounds that landlords could not recover their investment in any upgrading work through rent increases because of rent controls.

The policy shift from demolition to refurbishment led to an extension in the scope of grant aid to cover more significant improvements, such as the construction of extensions to house kitchens and bathrooms. This worked well in many older housing areas, especially those in locations that attracted more affluent households with the resources to invest. Elsewhere, for example in most inner city locations in the North and the Midlands, it soon became apparent that many owner-occupiers lacked the resources to invest in both upgrading and repairs, even with this level of grant aid. The 1970s and 1980s saw the extension of grants, both to cover repairs as well as upgrading, and to cover an increasing proportion of costs. By 1984, for example, the majority of grants provided covered only repairs and met 90 per cent of the costs of work. Later in the 1980s, some cities introduced 'enveloping' grants that covered external repairs and met 100 per cent of costs. Although there was some limited differentiation in the help available on the basis of household incomes, most grants were targeted on the basis of property condition and were not means-tested.

For the first decade of Thatcher government, the policy of grant aid to home owners had survived and indeed flourished, on a scale which, arguably, underpinned the buoyancy of the housing market in many inner city and other older housing areas. The majority of urban authorities had embarked on ambitious long-term programmes to upgrade older housing areas comprehensively. But in 1990 this was brought to a halt by the introduction of means testing for grant aid and the re-emphasis of the view that the responsibility for maintaining privately owned homes 'should rest first and foremost with the owner'. Subsequently, there was a steady and sustained decline in numbers of grants for renovation and in the level of public spending on this programme, on the grounds that only a minority of owners with incomes too low to afford repairs and improvements should qualify for state help.

The Labour government inherited and accepted this philosophy of providing help only to the poorest owners. Indeed, the Green Paper hints at more. It wants to ensure that "homeowners recognise and fulfil their responsibilities" (DETR/DSS, 2000, para 4.20). There is almost a suggestion here that owners might be *required* to keep their homes in a proper state of repair, as argued by some over-enthusiastic local authorities and academics (see Leather, 2000). But in relation to owner-occupation at least, there are no specific proposals for following up this suggestion.

Policy options

What, then, is the government suggesting it can do to help those who cannot afford to repair their homes, or to persuade those who will not to do so? In relation to the building industry something already is being done. A Quality Mark scheme is being piloted in two areas. This partnership between government and the construction industry aims to provide consumers with access to a list of competent builders and an insurance-backed warranty scheme for any work which member builders carry out. The question is whether the scheme can attract a sufficient number of competent builders into its ranks and whether consumers can be persuaded that it is worthwhile paying the premium costs that are inevitably associated with any quality assurance scheme. But the Quality Mark scheme will not stop so-called 'cowboy' builders from operating as, for example, a licensing scheme would, and indeed, may give them a further cost advantage. Nor does it do anything to increase the overall supply of good builders.

This is a neglected area. A disproportionate amount of government (and academic) attention goes into looking at the new build sector of the construction industry, yet new additions to the housing stock are marginal and the quality of repair and maintenance work is a far more important issue. If the Quality Mark scheme fails or is slow to take off, government in the longer term may be forced to look at more drastic ways of controlling the quality of operatives in the building sector, such as licensing and ways of influencing training programmes, so that better trained operatives with the skills to work in the small-scale domestic repair and maintenance sector are more readily available.

A range of other proposals in the Green Paper address the issue of providing practical help and assistance to those who find difficulty in undertaking or organising building work. One proposal is to extend funding for home improvement agencies, organisations which help older, disabled and vulnerable people to remain living independently in their own homes by identifying necessary repairs and improvements and giving practical help to carry out the work. In the past these services have been primarily targeted at older and disabled people, but other groups could benefit from less intensive assistance, for example, a free or low-cost survey to highlight key problems and put forward a plan for meeting the costs, or access to lists of reliable and competent builders to ensure that work is carried out effectively. Some local authorities have already begun to pilot initiatives of this kind, most notably the Urban Care initiative in Birmingham which provides surveys, advice, a scheme to loan people the necessary tools to carry out work themselves, a list of builders vetted by the community itself, and a handyperson service to carry out small jobs directly for older people and those on low incomes (Groves et al, 1999).

A major difficulty facing all these services is their cost. There is a general unwillingness for service recipients to pay for professional advice when alternatives are available – in this case 'advice' from a builder or from friends. Unfortunately, the Green Paper does not put forward any proposals for increasing the resources available to local authorities to fund services of this kind and it is quite likely that the majority will take the view that they are unable to fund such help.

Meeting the costs of repairs

The government's main proposals on standards relate to the *funding* of building work. The decline in grant aid to home owners charted above has accelerated in recent years with the removal of a long-standing government subsidy towards the cost, and with the inclusion of spending permission for grants within a wider 'single pot' for local authority capital expenditure – which brings grants to home owners directly into competition for resources with renovation work to councils' own stock.

The Green Paper makes no acknowledgement of this decline in funding nor any attempt to assess the overall need for public support to home owners with repairs and improvements. As in many other areas of public spending the total available is not needs-led. There *is* a recognition that more spending is needed, but the main source of this in future is to be home owners themselves. Thus the aim is "to provide better opportunities for people to maintain and repair their homes from their own resources where they are able to and help those who cannot afford to do so" (DETR/DSS, 2000, para 4.46).

This is to be achieved in two main ways: firstly, by making better use of the public resources that are available and, secondly, by using public resources to draw in more private finance. The present grant regime is relatively inflexible and gives local authorities only limited discretion in the kinds of help they can provide and the amounts they are able to pay. The Green Paper suggests that this can often lead to poor targeting of resources. The means test to determine grant eligibility does not take account of housing costs so, for example, an older household on a low income but with no mortgage might receive far more help than a younger household on a high income but with high mortgage costs. The government now proposes to give local authorities freedom to determine how to use the resources available to them most effectively to tackle poor housing conditions. Assistance might take the form of a grant, or perhaps a loan, or perhaps assistance with the costs of servicing a loan, or some combination of loan and grant. To provide this flexibility the government will use the new Regulatory Reform Act to replace the existing grant framework with a general power to assist owners living in poor conditions, including the power to help them to move elsewhere.

There are also two other proposals to make it easier for local authorities to encourage people to take out loans to fund building work. At present relatively little work is funded from loan finance. When people pay for work themselves they mostly use their savings or other resources rather than borrowing. Discussion of the reasons for this reluctance to borrow for repair and improvement has recently focused on the high costs of such borrowing, especially where individuals do not have an existing mortgage which has the potential to be increased. In these circumstances the set-up costs of a secured loan may form a substantial proportion of the overall costs of borrowing and act as a significant deterrent. The government is now proposing that local authorities' existing loan-giving powers should be amended to enable them to give preferential or even interest-free loans for home improvements to those on low incomes. Older people who may have a significant amount of unmortgaged equity tied up in their home but who may lack the income to service loan repayments would be a particular target for this form of assistance. But the Green Paper also mentions such loans for disabled people to assist them in meeting their assessed contribution towards the cost of any adaptations to their properties.

On top of this the government proposes to give local authorities a new power to make payments to third parties – home improvement agencies or other intermediary bodies – to help 'lever in' finance for home improvement. In a small number of experimental pilot projects up and down the country such intermediaries have helped to smooth the way towards small-scale borrowing for home improvement. They have firstly encouraged reluctant lenders to make these kinds of loans (on which profits are relatively small) and, secondly, by reducing or subsidising loan set-up costs they have attempted to stimulate demand from consumers.

These proposals, if they go through, will signal the completion of a major shift in government policy towards shrugging off responsibility for the financing of owner-occupiers' repairs and improvements. The provision of grant aid to home owners has been a feature of policy since 1949 and its main plank since 1969, with the introduction of means testing in 1990 being the only significant modification. In the last two decades the rising number of older home owners primarily dependent on state pension and without adequate savings to meet repair costs has been supplemented by increasing numbers who bought in late middle age under the Right to Buy and who have now entered retirement. Many would question the fairness or long-term wisdom of attracting millions of low-income households into home ownership (often into that segment of the stock which carries the highest ongoing repair and maintenance costs) without providing them with help in meeting these costs.

Undoubtedly there were many problems with the provision of grant aid. The original principle of providing grants for the installation of a basic set of amenities that all households might reasonably expect was swept aside long ago, and the introduction of 90 per cent or 100 per cent grants was tantamount to an acceptance that owners could benefit from the capital gains associated with ownership without taking on the responsibility for the associated costs. There was never any prospect that the state would continue to support this on any significant scale in a context of pressures to minimise public expenditure, and it was easy for successive governments to reduce the budget for grant aid to its present residual level.

A proposal that owners should give up some share of the equity in their homes to the state in return for help with repair and maintenance costs was floated in the mid-1980s but rejected as ungenerous and impractical. Even now there are still many who refuse to consider the replacement of grant aid by any alternative and who argue for a return to the resource levels available in the mid-1980s. Proposals for alternatives to grant aid which would give the state some return for its investment and enable resources to be recycled are at last on the agenda, but the resources to implement them on the scale that is required are no longer available as they were at that time. It is doubtful whether spending can now recover to the level that would be necessary. Looking across the whole Green Paper at the relative weight given to public and private sector renovation, or to public and private sectors in relation to broader issues such as social exclusion, it is clear that the public sector is well to the front in the government's thinking and in its decisions on resources.

In the Green Paper the government is effectively washing its hands of this difficult decision by giving individual local authorities the power to choose their own course of action, whether it be the continuation of the current grant system, the development of a less generous system, or a major shift towards the provision of support and encouragement to borrowing instead of grants. By merging the resources for grant aid with other capital pots, the government also shifts the balance of responsibility for the overall level of funding going into grant activity on to the shoulders of local authorities. To some extent this is very sensible as conditions in Sevenoaks clearly differ from those in Salford. But there still needs to be some, albeit general, national strategy relating to the condition and renewal of the housing stock. Some local authorities clearly have a high proportion of their dwellings in the form of older properties that will always need high levels of renovation investment and eventual acquisition and demolition, while others have a stock that is in generally much better condition and with few such problems. Given the government's declared intention to secure an urban renaissance and to make more use of brownfield sites in cities to cater for future housing needs, it is surely unrealistic to expect those authorities with the greatest concentrations of older housing to shoulder the whole burden of renovating this housing or clearing it to provide new sites entirely by themselves.

The overall level of resources for renovation and clearance of private sector housing and its distribution across local authorities should be matters of major concern for government. At present barely 1,000 out of a total of around 17 million private sector dwellings are demolished annually because they are grossly substandard or obsolete; but there is no view in the Green Paper as to whether this level of demolition is adequate or otherwise. Similarly, we know that older people are particularly likely to experience poor conditions and their propensity to do so is increasing with greater longevity, but there is no recognition of this trend in the Green Paper and no specific plan to take any action to do something about it. Although sustainable home ownership is the declared objective there is no discussion of the problem of the millions of properties acquired under Right to Buy in the last two decades by older people, who will be largely dependent on the state pension to meet the costs of repair and maintenance.

The Green Paper is to be congratulated on its willingness to address the issue of a replacement for or supplement to the present system of grants, which is in itself unsustainable at current resource levels. But there is a complete absence of any strategic thinking about the longer-term future of the housing stock, the processes which bring about poor conditions, how these might impact on the overall level of poor conditions in the future, and what government could, or should, be doing about it. To assert that individual owners are responsible for the condition of their homes is certainly a reasonable starting point, but something needs also to be said about the numbers of those who will be unable to meet this obligation and how they are to be dealt with.

Areas of market failure

A more general criticism of the Green Paper is that it has been strongly and perhaps unduly influenced by the problems of low or changing demand for housing that have emerged in recent years in the North of England and, to a lesser extent, in the Midlands (Lowe et al, 1998). This is certainly true in relation to the proposals for social rented housing. It is also true, if to a lesser extent, in relation to private sector housing. Thus the chapter on sustainable home ownership outlines the falls in market values, high levels of vacancies, and incipient abandonment experienced in some localised neighbourhoods in northern cities in the late 1990s.

The problems, as the Green Paper rightly highlights, are more those of obsolescence than of poor physical standards. To assist local authorities in responding to this problem of rapid market failure in older, private sector housing areas, the Green Paper proposes giving them more discretion over how they carry out area-based renewal. Local authorities have had powers since the 1960s to concentrate their renewal efforts in defined areas, initially called general improvement or housing action areas, but more recently known as renewal areas. The benefits of renewal area action over the provision of individual grants include powers to assist owners with the repair of blocks of houses rather than individual properties and powers to carry out improvements to the environment within areas as well as to the properties. The circumstances under which renewal area activity can be carried out are closely circumscribed by legislation and the government intends to remove many of the limitations on what local authorities can do in order to give them the powers to use area renewal as a mechanism for combating market decline.

But it is very questionable as to whether housing renewal assistance would do much to address the far more complex pattern of factors that bring about market failure and low demand in private sector housing. Some areas of significant market failure have had high levels of public investment in private sector renewal in the recent past yet are still unpopular.

The government also proposes selective or wholesale clearance as an option in some areas of chronic low demand. There has been a recent general review of compulsory purchase powers that has recommended that good practice guidance should be disseminated to local authorities to sharpen up their use of these powers. The Green Paper also proposes to broaden the scope of another existing mechanism – the relocation grant – which is available within declared clearance areas to help home owners purchase similar properties nearby. But local authorities and Registered Social Landlords (RSLs) working within areas of market failure want more than good practice guidance. More flexible and quicker compulsory purchase powers, and above all more financial resources, have been argued for (LGA, 1999). Within existing resource levels it is unlikely that individual local authorities will be able to afford to acquire properties on any significant scale and give relocation grants or other forms of assistance to a significant number of owners. None of the Green Paper's proposals are therefore likely to have much impact on problems of market failure in the private sector.

In fairness to the government, though, it is not clear that anyone else has yet come up with effective solutions. One or two individual authorities, such as Salford, which are worst affected by market failure in some of their older housing areas, have perhaps come closest with a package of proposals involving the establishment of local regeneration companies in partnership with RSLs and other organisations and drawing on resources across the board from the local authority, the Housing Corporation, and specific regeneration packages such as the Single Regeneration Budget. The debate on this issue has hardly begun.

Standards in the private rented sector

Fifteen years ago the majority view was that housing provision by private landlords was on course to decline to an irreducible minimum of tied lettings and other special cases. Since then, with the decontrol of rents and the virtual elimination of security of tenure, the fortunes of the sector have been reversed. Arguably this has been at considerable direct and indirect cost to the public purse. Higher rents impact directly on the Housing Benefit bill. The indirect costs are the impact on the demand for social rented housing, and its contribution to market collapse in older private housing areas, the costs of which are falling on both owners and the state. Yet there is little evidence to suggest that higher rents have led landlords to invest in improving standards (Crook et al, 2000). Satisfactory returns are achieved only by minimising investment or by securing state subsidy in the form of Housing Benefit.

As indicated above, the government's proposals for the private rented sector aim to increase its overall role in housing provision. But rather than accepting that the economics of privately rented housing provision dictate that many landlords will minimise their investment in the stock in order to secure a satisfactory return on investment, the Green Paper develops a distinction between 'good and well-intentioned' landlords, who need only education and support to improve their service, and 'the worst landlords' whose ill-intentioned motivation will require the use of tougher measures to improve their performance or to persuade them to leave the sector. Landlord behaviour is apparently a matter of character rather than economics.

Working with landlords

Accepting this remarkable proposition for the sake of argument, it is true that the majority of landlords in England are amateurs with only a few lettings. A quarter have only a single letting. Many are also relatively new landlords who came into the business in the early 1990s in the period after deregulation when the opportunities for purchasing properties cheaply were greater than they are at present. Although many of these landlords make use of letting agents to manage their properties, a significant number do not and many clearly need help in ensuring that they meet their obligations in terms of property condition and management. To assist these landlords the government is seeking to encourage them to organise themselves into associations and develop some form of self-regulation. There is currently no dominant, single, national landlords' association, not least because the interests of small landlords differ from those with large portfolios, but also because the rapid expansion of the sector has given rise to a plethora of representative organisations that have not yet had time to sort themselves out through natural selection. In addition to this, the government is also proposing an extension of the role of local authorities in assisting private landlords. But the exact relationship between self-regulation and local authority activity is not really thought through in the Green Paper.

The measures that local authorities should take to assist landlords, it is suggested, include private landlords' forums, occasional or regular meetings to spread awareness of landlords' legal obligations and of good practice. Many local authorities already run forums of this kind. The Green Paper also identifies a number of voluntary local landlord accreditation schemes run by authorities on their own, or in partnership with universities in cases where the schemes are linked to student housing. Accreditation schemes set and monitor standards required of members. Landlords are not obliged to join. Where they do, this is presumably because they see various advantages, such as an improvement in their competitive position in the marketplace in areas where there is a surplus of accommodation. The Green Paper additionally supports the development of the National Approved Lettings Scheme which establishes a 'kite mark' for the activities of professional letting agents.

These options represent ways of helping those landlords who feel they need help on a voluntary basis. In principle it is very hard to disagree with them, but there must be a question over whether the target landlord group recognises that it needs help or is willing to accept it, especially from local authorities. In the past, relations between private landlords and local authorities in many, if not most areas, has been one of confrontation and the use of enforcement action to require landlords to meet their legal obligations to provide housing of even a basic standard. There is a long history of hostile relations to overcome here. Furthermore, local authorities will still be taking action against problem landlords using existing legislation and perhaps significant new licensing powers (see below), so there is strong potential for further conflict.

There is also the question of what is in voluntary accreditation for landlords themselves. In addition to market advantage (which only occurs in areas of shortage) the main incentives are help with information and advice on legal responsibilities and other obligations. This could be of benefit to smaller landlords who genuinely do not want to fall foul of regulations and who are ignorant of their obligations. But this kind of advice could be provided by landlords' organisations themselves, as some currently do. Similarly, self-regulation would seem to be far more attractive to landlords than local authority regulation, even on a voluntary basis. As the Green Paper indicates, there are already many experimental initiatives in the field of landlords' forums or accreditation schemes and it remains to be seen how successful these will be.

Attracting reputable investors

The Green Paper devotes several pages to the issue of persuading reputable investors to expand the supply of private rented housing. This is a difficult section, not least because the term 'reputable' implies that current investors (mainly the small landlords who are seen as potential recipients of accreditation) are less desirable. The argument is that a large-scale expansion of private rented housing and the input of 'professional' management will not take place unless major investors (such as pension funds) can be persuaded to move into investment in residential property. These bodies it is hoped are more likely to ensure that housing provision is of a high standard because they will do the job professionally and in order to protect their reputations. They will also be able to achieve economies of scale.

There is a long history of debate on why major investors have not been attracted to the private rented sector and on appropriate measures to increase their level of interest. These include proposals for changes to the tax system. In the end the Green Paper has no real contribution to make to this debate beyond a general aspiration to attract new investment and a willingness to consider any proposals – ideas on a postcard please.

Compulsory licensing

Despite these relatively positive proposals on private renting, the longest and most enthusiastic section of the Green Paper on the private rented sector relates to 'the worst landlords'. The aim here is to ensure that these landlords improve their housing or are driven out of business. Many of the worst landlords are found in houses in multiple occupation (HMOs). Here the government is already committed to introducing a compulsory licensing system and to some simplification of the complex web of existing controls. A consultation paper issued a year ago set out a series of proposals under which it would be an offence to operate an HMO without a license. Housing professionals have been eagerly awaiting the introduction of these licensing powers (which were included in the 1997 manifesto) for several years.

One of the difficulties in relation to the control of conditions in HMOs is to identify the beast. Multi-storey Victorian properties containing bedsits with shared kitchens and bathroom facilities are easy to identify but should two-storey houses shared by groups of students (or even by grown-ups) also fall within this category? What about hostels and purpose-built student accommodation – are vice chancellors private landlords? What about rooms let to lodgers? The greater propensity of young people to leave the parental home and a variety of changes in lifestyles in the last two decades have made these questions of definition far more difficult. Yet they are, of course, very important to resolve clearly when significant measures such as compulsory licensing are involved. Although the Green Paper reaffirms the intention to introduce some form of licensing, it may well be that what eventually emerges is far more limited in scope than many housing professionals have hoped and that it concentrates on the very highest-risk properties in terms of danger to life through fire hazard and other life-threatening problems.

Since the idea of licensing was raised, some commentators have suggested that it should be extended on a compulsory basis to the whole of the private rented sector. The Green Paper rejects this on the grounds that the bureaucratic scale of the task of licensing would be enormous and expensive and that it would also be a major deterrent to many landlords, either to enter the sector or remain in it. However, it is recognised that there might be some limited circumstances under which licensing would be appropriate across the whole private rented sector.

As the problem of market failure in some areas of private sector housing has become more understood, it is argued that it has been accelerated by the involvement of speculative landlords who have bought properties cheaply and used them to make short-term returns. Criminal activities, such as Housing Benefit fraud, have also been alleged in some of these cases. In some areas it is suggested that landlords have offered homes to antisocial households on the grounds that this will further destabilise an area and encourage owner-occupiers to sell at low prices. To deal with what it calls an "unholy alliance of bad landlords and bad tenants" (DETR/ DSS, 2000, para 5.33), the government raises the possibility that local authorities could have discretionary powers to require compulsory licensing of privately rented dwellings or landlords across whole neighbourhoods. As with licensing more generally, it remains to be seen whether this proposal will be delivered.

Housing Benefit and condition

A major complaint from local authorities and agencies providing help to private rented sector tenants is that many landlords receive payments of rent funded by Housing Benefit without providing decent standards of accommodation and housing management in return. There have been a number of suggestions as to ways of linking Housing Benefit to the achievement of physical and management standards. Three approaches are discussed in the Green Paper. The first would be to restrict Housing Benefit payments on properties in poor condition in areas where there is an over-supply of private rented housing. In such areas those living in housing declared ineligible for Housing Benefit would have no difficulty in finding an alternative source of accommodation and landlords would have to invest to stay in business. A second proposal would be to refuse the direct payment of Housing Benefit to landlords in cases where they fail to provide acceptable standards of accommodation and management. A third proposal is that Housing Benefit should be limited in cases where tenants misbehave, but as the Green Paper points out, objective tests would be needed to identify circumstances under which benefit could be restricted and this might prove difficult. It is hard to resist the conclusion that the Green Paper is somewhat unenthusiastic about any of these proposals to link benefit and conditions and it would be surprising to see any of them surfacing at a later stage.

Conclusion

Quality and choice: A decent home for all is genuinely a *green* paper in relation to its proposals for standards in private sector housing in the sense that it airs a wide range of ideas. The Housing Statement that followed filtered some of these out, but many radical changes in policy towards private sector housing standards have survived this first hurdle. Looking at the balance of the paper as a whole, there is a clear feeling that questions relating to the social rented sector are of far more importance for government than the private sector despite the relative size of each. In relation to measures to improve conditions in the owner-occupied sector, the proposals set out, if enacted, would usher in a real shift in policy away from the longstanding mechanism of grant aid towards one which forced owners to make much more use of the equity tied up in their homes as security for borrowing. This remains a highly controversial area, with proponents of the current approach arguing that borrowing would not be feasible for those on low incomes. Supporters of the new approach can equally point out that the current grant framework is in reality just as damaging because it is not adequately resourced. There are also arguments on principle. Some take the view that owners should take responsibility for meeting their own repairs costs; others argue that help must be provided to those who have failed to, or been unable to, accumulate resources to meet these costs or those whose circumstances have changed so that they need help.

For the first time in a long while, a government has attempted to address these very difficult questions. It is in its failure to address the more strategic issues about private sector housing standards that the Green Paper falls down most severely. The level of resources to be devoted to private sector renewal and the distribution of these resources are argued to be matters for individual local authorities rather than for central government. But it is hard to see how government can realistically impose such burdens on individual local authorities, especially those in inner city locations that will need to shoulder a disproportionate share of the problems. Taking the right decisions on clearance or renovation will be crucial to the government's broader objectives in relation to urban regeneration, social exclusion and the containment of new development on brownfield sites. Local strategies to tackle poor conditions in the private sector are needed, but we also need a national framework to determine the overall level of investment in private sector housing by the state.

The acceptance by a Labour government that the private rented sector is here to stay and indeed that it needs to expand further is highly significant. The Green Paper also recognises that enforcement action and an adversarial approach to private landlords is no longer realistic in an expanding and vibrant private rented sector. It thus proposes a twofold approach with advice, assistance and accreditation as the new norm in relations between authorities and landlords, and compulsory licensing for the much smaller but problematic HMO sector. In many respects this is only a recognition of reality and of what is already happening in many local areas. Much of the impetus for voluntary accreditation and other informal relationships and partnerships with landlords has come from the local level; as has the recognition that compulsory action must always be limited because of its costs in terms of staffing and other resources. It may even be that there are strong second thoughts about licensing, to which Labour committed itself before the rise in voluntary working with landlords. We should not, therefore, be at all surprised to see licensing (if it comes at all) limited to a very narrow category of the highest risk multi-storey, older Victorian properties where a fire would be disastrous, or to the concentrations of student housing that have been recently making headlines in cities like Leeds and Birmingham.

Of course, the owner-occupied and private rented sectors are still poles apart in terms of their treatment by government and local authorities. It is still clear that government regards itself as having a responsibility for protecting tenants against bad landlords, but in the owner-occupied sector owners' rights remain largely sacrosanct and there is little prospect of the use of compulsion to require owners to invest in their properties even where poor conditions can be shown to have an adverse impact on health or educational attainment. But in other respects, approaches to the two sectors are converging, especially in relation to the increasing emphasis given to the role of local authorities in the provision of advice and practical assistance instead of funding owners and beating landlords. The Green Paper is full of measures to advise both groups on what they should be doing and how to do it and to smooth the path to raising finance from private sources. Whether this will generate the necessary investment or whether a new crisis of condition and standards in private sector housing lies in store in the future remains to be seen.

References

Crook, A., Henneberry, J., Hughes, J. and Kemp, P. (2000) *Repair and maintenance by private landlords*, London: DETR.

DETR (Department of the Environment, Transport and the Regions) (1998) *English Housing Condition Survey 1996*, London: The Stationery Office.

DETR/DSS (Department of Society Security) (2000) *Quality and choice: A decent home for all*, Housing Green Paper, London: DETR/DSS.

Groves, R., Morris, J., Murie, A. and Paddock, B. (1999) *Local maintenance initiatives for home owners*, York: York Publishing Services for the Joseph Rowntree Foundation.

Leather, P. (2000) 'Grants to home owners: a policy in search of objectives', *Housing Studies*, vol 15, no 2, pp 149-68.

LGA (Local Government Association) (1999) *A modern approach to private housing*, London: LGA.

Lowe, S., Spencer, S. and Keenan, P. (1998) *Housing abandonment in Britain: Studies in the causes and effects of low demand*, York: Centre for Housing Policy, University of York.

The allocation of social housing

Introduction

In many respects, chapter 9 of the Green Paper, which deals with the allocation of social housing, contains some of the most radical ideas of the whole document. To fulfil its aims, it will require not only legislative tinkering, but also a change in the ethos and culture of social housing management itself. No longer should social housing be allocated according to the mantra of bureaucratic principles, which, as Somerville points out, are seldom understood by those applying for it; rather, it should become 'customer-centred', choice-based, and such choice should be actively managed. Such a change is all the more significant because, hitherto, different types of applicants have been constructed as modern-day folk-devils, "jumping the [social] housing queue" so that they can be housed ahead of others who's housing situation is as bad. So, for example, single mothers and asylum-seekers have borne the brunt of such a discourse which, as Cowan suggests, concerns the reinforcement of the deserving:undeserving dichotomy.

Both chapters are broadly receptive to the motivations behind the proposals in the Green Paper. However, neither author holds out much hope for their success, although their reasons are rather different. One reason for this divergence is that their research questions and research base are fundamentally different.

For Cowan, other than specific problems with the choice-based policy, there are more fundamental problems within the system which must be addressed as preconditions to the success of any reform. These problems are said to be fivefold: the legislative background (by which is meant the motivations and understandings which inform the legislative process); the application process from the individual household perspective; the shift from allocations on the basis of housing need to one which incorporates principles of risk; the need for agencies and individual professionals to work together; and processes of adjudication. Drawing on socio-legal research on each of these, it is suggested that the allocations process involves the stigmatisation of a stigmatised population. This enables Cowan to provide a critique of the retention of the concept of housing need.

Somerville's approach is different, although overlapping, partly due to a different construction of the issue. Whereas Cowan focuses on the bureaucratic process and its effects on implementation, Somerville contrasts the treatment in the

Green Paper to different processes and practices – bureaucracy and managerialism; communitarianism and individual need. This critique enables Somerville to provide an alternative set of proposals, which seek to ensure "genuine social inclusion and empowerment", concentrating on increasing the choice of socially excluded households. Thus, Somerville seeks to give real meaning to the concept of housing need. From this perspective, the Green Paper's stress on active management of choice takes centre stage. The chapter concludes with a discussion of the thorny dilemma of sustainability while at the same time meeting individual needs. Arguing that the Green Paper proposals are 'essentially vague' on the issue of sustainability and 'local lettings', it remains unclear how retention of the concept of allocation according to need can be squared with the drive towards sustainable communities.

SIX

Allocating housing – or 'letting' people choose?

Peter Somerville

Introduction

The allocation of social housing has always been a contentious issue. Accusations of institutional discrimination, excessive bureaucracy and unresponsiveness to consumer demand have long bedevilled the organisations responsible for this function. It is now over 10 years since the late Valerie Karn and Bruce Stafford reported on a survey of the allocation policies and practices of local authorities in England and Wales (Karn and Stafford, 1990). This survey showed that, typically, authorities had bureaucratic allocations and lettings systems that were geared more towards administrative convenience than towards assisting customers. Since then, two major research projects on local authority housing management have been commissioned by what was then the Department of the Environment. The first of these was carried out by the University of York (Bines et al, 1993) and the second by the University of Wales (Griffiths et al, 1997). Neither of these projects, however, seems to have actually talked to any applicants on a housing waiting list or attempted to evaluate the effectiveness of the allocations process for such applicants. Consequently, until recently, with research being conducted for the Department of the Environment, Transport and the Regions by Heriot-Watt University and the London Research Centre (Pawson et al, 2000) and for Shelter by the University of Wales (Smith et al, 2000), we have had no reliable up-to-date national information on this matter.

Institutional racism is arguably one of the most sensitive aspects of institutional discrimination and, since the MacPherson Report, this issue has been very much to the fore. It is therefore sobering to recall that it was 15 years ago that Deborah Phillips concluded that: "Nearly every serious investigation of local authority housing allocations has found evidence of systematic racial disadvantage" (Phillips, 1986). Since that time, it is a virtual certainty that such institutional racial discrimination has continued in the vast majority of authorities although, of course, we cannot be absolutely certain because the necessary research just has not been done. Even now, in this brave new post-MacPherson world, there is little evidence to show that housing organisations even understand, let alone take seriously, the discriminatory implications of allocations processes (Robinson, 2001: forthcoming).

In recent years, perhaps because of the continuing criticisms of bureaucratic unresponsiveness, the emphasis in housing allocation has been increasingly on meeting consumer preferences and, even more recently, on meeting the needs of communities. The precise reasons for these changing emphases, however, have not been properly understood and the housing world has shown a lamentable lack of reflexivity on this issue. Consequently, the entirely predictable problem of low demand for social housing appears to have taken many people by surprise (Lowe, 2000). Now the government's Green Paper has wholeheartedly endorsed the established trend towards greater consumer choice and has made it the key criterion for guiding the future development of allocation policy. This chapter seeks to explore what is involved in these changing political and professional emphases and to suggest possible directions that housing allocation might usefully take in the future.

Bureaucratic allocation: the origins of the problem

The term 'bureaucratic' has unfavourable connotations but is used here in a neutral sense to refer to processes of decision making based on hierarchical authority, adherence to purportedly objective criteria, as well as action based on following clear rules and procedures. The allocation of housing in this sense began with the expansion of council housing in the 1920s. An important advantage of bureaucratic allocation over previous methods was that it eschewed forms of nepotism and corruption, as well as avoiding the moralism and paternalism of the philanthropic housing associations of the time. In those early days, however, council housing was largely restricted to families with children and was allocated on the basis of date order rather than need. It was not until after the publication of the Cullingworth Report (CHAC, 1969) that most local authorities began to allocate their housing more strictly on the basis of need. In this way, bureaucratic allocation gradually shifted from being primarily a system of administrative convenience towards one based on principles of equity and fairness. These principles, however, are open to a good deal of difference of interpretation and, arguably, have never received sufficient official clarification.

It is not clear exactly how far local authorities moved towards needs-based systems of housing allocation up until Karn and Stafford (1990). Such research as had been carried out suggested that factors other than need continued to play an important role in determining rehousing outcomes for local authority applicants. Corina (1974) looked at allocations in different northern cities going back to 1950, finding that grading and social segregation in the rehousing of applicants were widely accepted practices. English et al (1976) and Henderson and Karn (1987) similarly reported that grading on the basis of 'suitability' rather than need was normal practice in the authorities that they investigated. Power (1987) stated that almost all the hundred local authorities visited in the course of their research sifted, graded and sometimes segregated applicants. Spicker (1983) and Kay et al (1986) identified a large proportion of authorities who gave rehousing priority to factors other than housing need such as length of residence in the local authority's area, waiting time, family size and age.

There is some doubt, therefore, about the extent to which local authority housing allocation really did become based predominantly on need. It is also important to note that the definition of need typically employed was crude and narrow, based almost entirely on the physical characteristics of a dwelling deemed to be the standard required by a household of a certain size (Spicker, 1983). Unpublished research on local authorities in the North West by Somerville (1987) found that only one out of five authorities actually specified what they meant by 'social need' as something different from housing need, and this related most commonly to travel-to-work difficulties and support to or from a relative. In general, therefore, it is at least arguable that needs-based systems in practice have been overly narrow and inappropriate, failing to reflect many of the real needs of housing applicants.

The first criticisms of needs-based systems of housing allocation came from academics. Lambert et al (1978), in a study of Birmingham's allocation system, found that applicants on the housing waiting list rarely had any idea of the relevance of the number of points they were awarded, and that waiting time depended crucially on the applicant's area of choice, not on their degree of need. Even more trenchant criticisms came from

Harrison (1983), who looked at Hackney's allocation of housing. He concluded that applicants' lack of choice was very damaging, but that: "Given a great mass of needy people, and a small mass of mostly undesirable housing, there is simply no way of doing the job right" (Harrison, 1983, p 224). Clapham and Kintrea (1984) attacked the whole notion of what they called 'bureaucratic rationing' on two fundamental grounds: first, that it ignores factors which influence the allocation process but which originate from outside the organisational context of the relevant institution; and second, that it ignores the process of interaction between the allocator and the recipient, treating the recipient as a passive agent (Clapham and Kintrea, 1984, p 261). The alternative approach that Clapham and Kintrea recommended was to focus on the process by which households search for and choose their housing. They pointed out that, although it has been commonly assumed that the needs of the organisation completely overshadow individual preferences in the allocation of public housing, applicants actually start by choosing to register for such housing; that is, it is the decision by an individual consumer that marks the beginning of the allocations process (Clapham and Kintrea, 1984, p 265).

The critical approach of academics was soon followed by housing practitioners. The catalyst for change, however, was probably the 1988 Housing Bill. Cooper (1988, p 18) stated the position most clearly: "The Bill will accelerate a trend towards the interest of tenants above those of applicants waiting for council housing" and "This shift in the balance in favour of tenants is the culmination of a subtle erosion of the idea that council housing exists primarily to meet the priority housing needs on the waiting lists". Since existing tenants are on the whole less needy than housing applicants, this meant a move away from needs-based allocation. Cooper pointed out that the main justification for a system of allocation is that it is fair but "points systems are patently not viewed as 'fair' by the public at large. They are seen as bureaucratic, mechanistic and difficult to understand" (Cooper, 1988, p 18). In the housing circles of the time, Cooper's criticisms of points systems were not generally accepted: since the recommendations of the Central Housing Advisory Committee (CHAC) (1969), such systems had been widely viewed by practitioners as more appropriate for a fair system of housing allocation. Most practitioners have continued to favour needs-based systems because of their alleged objectivity and advantages in comparison with allocation based on 'merit', nepotism, corruption or political bias. They gradually ceased, however, to regard them as in any way sacrosanct.

One piece of research that had a significant impact on government thinking was Prescott-Clarke et al (1988). This research established that many local authority waiting lists grossly over-estimated the extent of housing need, with typically up to half of applicants being classifiable as 'dead wood'. At the same time, where housing need was greatest, such as in London boroughs, the proportion of lettings going to waiting list applicants had fallen to less than a third (LRC, 1988). Whether housing need was great or small, therefore, needs-based allocation systems did not appear to be working as intended. Further recognition of the problematic character of needs-based allocation came with the publication of the first national report into housing management (CHR, 1989). This report noted that needs-based systems were associated with higher refusal rates and higher administration costs. In particular, the report confirmed the judgment of Cooper (1988) that points systems were generally seen by applicants as less fair than other types of system. Even before this, Raynsford (1984) had argued, just as he has done more recently (Raynsford, 1999), that allocation systems should not be too rigid and should allow for an increasing element of applicant choice. This position has now been made more explicit in the Green Paper (DETR/DSS, 2000).

Clapham and Kintrea (1987, 1991) provided the first full-blown critique of needs-based systems of housing allocation. Their arguments were:

- in a local authority, political pressures will always, in practice, lead to departures from strict needs-based allocation;
- all housing organisations have to take account of the aspirations of their existing tenants and this inevitably runs counter to allocation purely on the basis of need;
- many people in need will ask for less popular areas, resulting in a reinforcement of social disadvantage and exclusion;
- allocation solely on the basis of need fails to take account of the housing organisation's need to manage its affairs efficiently and effectively.

None of Clapham and Kintrea's criticisms is particularly convincing as an argument for moving away from needs-based systems of housing allocation. The point about political pressures suggests a need to make the process of defining and measuring need a more democratic one. The issue of existing tenants can be represented in terms of a need to take account of the needs of communities as well as the needs of individual applicants. The third point holds true whether the allocation system is needs based or not. And the argument about the housing organisation's own needs does not resolve the question of just how far such needs should be subordinated to those of the individual and the community.

Clapham and Kintrea also provide, from their own research on Glasgow, a trenchant critique of attempts, Raynsford-style, to adapt needs-based systems by allowing for greater applicant choice within them. They point out that this approach fails to provide a realistic solution to the conflict between needs and aspirations and inevitably disadvantages those who are least able to choose (Clapham and Kintrea, 1986, 1987, p 14, 1991, p 65). In Glasgow they found that those who were better off and lived in better housing were more able to wait for what they wanted and so more able to achieve higher quality accommodation than badly housed and poorer households. Increasing applicant choice would only mean that unequal outcomes would become more likely. The Green Paper completely fails to address these criticisms.

A further report for the Department of the Environment from Prescott-Clarke et al (1994) seems to have set the seal on government thinking about needs-based allocation and housing waiting lists generally. That report found that only 43 per cent of applicants still lived at their registered address and wanted housing immediately, a percentage that was virtually unchanged from their earlier survey. From then on, the government began to consider seriously the reform of needs-based systems. At the same time, however, their concern to do something about alleged 'queue-jumping' (DoE, 1994) indicates that, in spite of the neo-liberal rhetoric of the time, they were not about to abandon rationing systems in favour of a more thoroughgoing market-oriented approach. Rather, the emphasis shifted from secondary rationing (access to housing) to primary rationing (access to the waiting list). This finally resulted in the single housing register of the 1996 Housing Act and the growth of exclusions from that register on grounds that have nothing to do with housing need (Butler, 1998). Arguably, the critique of needs-based allocation has led to a displacement and increase in bureaucratic rationing, not a reduction.

Dissatisfaction with needs-based allocation systems appears to have grown apace since New Labour came to power, among both politicians and practitioners. One reason for this is the increasing problem of low demand for social housing in many areas, which makes a rationing approach to allocation seem inappropriate. Another important factor is the new social inclusion agenda, which emphasises the role of housing allocation in meeting objectives that are wider than that of individual housing need. The first of these factors has tended to reinforce the neo-liberal, customer-centred perspective on social problems, while the latter evokes New Labour's new corporatist managerialism (Somerville, 2000). The first leads to a heightened emphasis on individual choice, and the second to allocation systems that give more priority to the needs of local communities. An example of the first type of solution is the so-called 'Delft' model being piloted by Harborough Borough Council (DETR/ DSS, 2000). And an example of the second is North British Housing Association's practice of reserving 25 per cent of its lettings on grounds other than housing need: 10 per cent on 'economic' grounds (people who will contribute to the local economy) and 15 per cent to people who can make a 'community contribution' (for example, to give or receive support from relatives or to assist community development) (Goodwin, 1999).

The Green Paper contains elements of both the individualist and the communitarian approach to criticising bureaucratic allocation but the main emphasis is clearly on the former. Discourse concerning widening the choice of individual housing 'customers' predominates over concerns with 'sustainable communities', which are mentioned in only one short section. To this end, for example, it is proposed that local authorities should be prohibited from imposing 'blanket' exclusions from their housing registers and from penalising applicants who refuse offers of accommodation. This does not mean that the government is giving up on needs-based allocation: "we believe that priority for social housing should generally continue to be given to people in the greatest housing need" (DETR/DSS, 2000, p 80). In their search for a simpler system that applicants would understand, however, they have given up on points systems and advocate a system of groups in date order. This is of course only a matter of moving from one system of bureaucratic rationing to another, and the Green Paper does not make it clear why waiting time is to be preferred to points as a form of bureaucratic currency.

The communitarian side of the government's critique of needs-based allocation is expressed in the section on local lettings policies (DETR/ DSS, 2000, p 84). Here, however, the Green Paper does no more than acknowledge what some local authorities are doing already. It may be that the government has taken on board the conclusions of the only major research project in this area (Griffiths et al, 1996) to the effect that such 'community lettings' have only a limited contribution to make to meeting community needs. This project, however, considered local lettings only as they are and not as they could be – for example, if communities were given real control over lettings in their areas. It is more plausible, therefore, that the Green Paper's dominant individualism is a reflection of the Blair government's wider capitulation to neo-liberalism (Dean, 1999, pp 222-3).

Managerialist allocation: the culmination of the problem?

It is possible to argue that the government is consciously moving away from an advocacy of bureaucratic allocation to a more managerialist position. This position accepts the reality of a diversity of approaches to defining, measuring and meeting need, and seeks essentially to ensure an efficiently managed 'market' in social housing. The framework of this managerialism has already been set out by Clarke and Newman (1997) and its application to housing has been explored by Somerville (2000): "Where 'need' was once the product of the intersection of bureaucratic categorisation and professional judgment, it is now increasingly articulated with and disciplined by a managerial calculus of resources and priorities" (Clarke and Newman, 1997, p 76). The key slogan under New Labour is 'what works', so if needs-based systems do not work they must be reformed. In relation to meeting housing need, the importance of this new ideological formation has already been signalled in the concept of ethnic managerialism (Harrison and Law, 1997), through which the highly political issue of racial inequality and institutional discrimination has been transformed into a technical problem of how to manage ethnic and cultural diversity. The government now seeks, through Best Value, to extend this approach to all housing management activities, and local authorities will be placed under increasing pressure to review their allocation schemes, consult with waiting list applicants and compare their systems with those of other local authorities. They will be evaluated not so much in terms of their fairness in meeting needs as in terms of their cost-effectiveness and customer satisfaction.

Apart from 'what works', the other slogan associated with managerialism is 'joined-up thinking'. This is put forward in opposition to the 'apartheid' thinking of what Clarke and Newman have called 'bureau-professionalism'. The managerialist perspective does not recognise the validity or even the utility of professional and organisational boundaries, and envisages the provision of seamless public services based on active 'partnerships'. In relation to the allocation of housing, therefore, a managerialist approach sees little merit in adopting narrow definitions of need that do not take account of either individual housing search processes or the needs of the communities in which individuals are housed. For this reason, the debate about housing allocation is becoming subsumed within the wider agenda of social inclusion (although, if the Green Paper is anything to go by, this is not yet reflected in government thinking). As in so many other areas of government policy, joined-up thinking remains rhetoric rather than reality.

Managerialism can be criticised, mainly for its lack of democratic accountability, but also because it is the doctrine of a new or reformed ruling class with unprecedented power in the face of a weakened trade union movement and the undermining of professional and occupational autonomy. Elite networks of politicians, senior civil servants and captains of industry conduct their affairs largely without having to explain or justify themselves to members of the public or to their subordinates. Hence the whole tone of the Green Paper is patronising to local authorities, for example in 'allowing' them to do all sorts of things that they were already free to do anyway. There is no consideration of the possibility that an element of devolution of power and resources might be necessary if local authorities are to achieve what the government says it wants them to do. There is no evidence of a commitment to any principle of subsidiarity here. Consequently, housing applicants are likely to continue to feel that they have little or no influence or control over the allocations process. At the end of the day, managerialism provides not real choice but an illusion of choice.

Fortunately, perhaps, in relation to housing allocation, managerialist prescriptions seem tentative and not well thought out. While retaining an emphasis on individual need and choice, they provide no guidance (at least not yet) as to how this emphasis is to be 'balanced' against provision for community need and the needs of the organisation (for example, in terms of economy and efficiency). For example, the Green Paper proposals on homelessness such as broadening the definition of priority need to include 16-17 year olds, vulnerable people from an institutionalised or care background and those fleeing harassment are, in themselves, to be welcomed but the implications of these changes for housing organisations and communities are not considered. It could happen, for instance, that this will result in greater priority being given to rehousing victims of racist harassment, thus reinforcing communal trends and patterns of racist residential segregation. Again, the proposal to allow homeless applicants a period of time in which to exercise choice over their settled accommodation is, in principle, admirable but the organisational need for the 'active management' of this choice will, in practice, mean that little will change for homeless people. Their 'fixed period' in temporary accommodation will be determined by the local authority, at the end of which they have to accept a single reasonable offer; in other words, business as usual.

The Green Paper appears to have given up on the issue of resource distribution. Even the term 'allocation', with its clearly distributive connotations, is to be abandoned in favour of 'lettings'. This could be argued to represent a step backwards, from bureaucratic allocation to traditional forms of patronage where the (originally feudal) landlord 'let' his liegemen use his land in return for favours such as labour, defence and, of course, rent. More realistically, perhaps, it marks a deliberate attempt to move away from a politically contested system based on principles of equity and fairness to a more technically defined one based on managerial precepts such as those embodied in Best Value. Although discrimination on grounds of sex, 'race' and disability is now outlawed, it is known that such forms of discrimination are widespread within housing organisations, but the Green Paper offers nothing new here: there is, for example, no commitment to bring an end to institutional discrimination in housing. To be fair, as mentioned above, there is some commitment to helping vulnerable young people, but other groups suffering from discrimination, such as people with mental health problems, travellers and refugees, are ignored. Finally, in the English context (as contrasted with the situation in Scotland), 'democratic participation' does not appear to extend beyond consultation, with the pinnacle of achievement being a Tenant Participation Compact, and 'shaping society' is definitely not on the agenda.

Social inclusion and housing allocation

Housing allocation, as with housing policy more generally, does not have to be tied to a managerialist agenda such as exists in embryonic form in the Green Paper. An alternative approach is through programmes for genuine social inclusion and empowerment. It is not inevitable that such programmes are subsumed within a centralising corporatist dynamic: they are capable of being radically redistributive and devolutionist.

Social inclusion covers a wide range of issues including access to a reasonable quality of life, equality of opportunity, and choice on participation in decision-making processes. The social inclusion agenda is firmly opposed to institutional discrimination of all kinds and emphasises the values of diversity and tolerance. However, discourse on social inclusion is ambivalent on the question of how individuals and groups are to be socially included. The government's commitment to 'strong communities', for example, can be interpreted as a commitment to strengthening the individuals concerned, in terms of increasing their capacity to cooperate with one another, both within and beyond their communities. On the other hand, it could be interpreted as involving an emphasis on meeting the needs of the 'community' (however this is defined) over and above the needs of its individual members. The former interpretation may be called 'individual-centred' or, in terms of housing allocation, 'applicant-centred', while the latter may be termed 'community-centred'. This chapter argues that an ambiguity between applicant-centred and community-centred social inclusion lies at the heart of the current debate on housing allocation and the Green Paper is just one expression of this.

Housing allocation can help to achieve social inclusion in a number of ways:

- meeting individual needs and aspirations in a wide sense (not just housing need in a narrow sense);
- not discriminating on grounds of 'race', religion, gender, marital status, caring responsibility, age, disability or sexuality;
- enabling socially excluded applicants to exercise greater choice over their rehousing outcomes;
- meeting community needs by housing 'key' workers (for the economic or social benefit of the community);
- being more open and democratic in the organisation of its process.

Needs-based systems of allocation can be argued to be socially inclusive because those who are more at risk of being socially excluded are also likely to be in greater housing need. The social inclusion agenda, however, requires that a broader interpretation of need should be employed, covering what has traditionally been called 'social need' as well as 'purely' housing need. Typically, this includes individual needs such as the need for education, training, employment, care or support, as well as the needs of the community such as for economic regeneration or population retention (Somerville and Spink, 2000).

The dilemma discussed earlier that increasing applicant choice tends to exacerbate discrimination is resolved within the social inclusion agenda by ensuring that allocation reforms concentrate on increasing the choice of socially excluded groups in particular. This can be done by improving the quality of information and advice given to such groups, as well as by taking greater care to ensure that offers of accommodation are as suitable as possible for meeting the applicants' needs and aspirations. To this extent, the proposals in the Green Paper to require local authorities to provide advice and assistance to homeless people to help them access relevant support services are welcome, as also is the emphasis in the 'active management' of homelessness on advising and assisting the most vulnerable households to make informed choices about their housing options. The Delft model of customer-driven housing allocation advocated by the Green Paper can be evaluated in similar terms: does it effectively give the most socially excluded households greater control over where they are housed? Its success depends on making information much more widely available to all housing applicants, and this is an area where there is considerable scope for improvement on current practice.

Meeting the needs of communities inevitably conflicts at some point with meeting the needs of individuals. For example, a key worker such as a fire-fighter may be 'adequately housed' at some distance from the community but may be given priority over an applicant who is manifestly inadequately housed. On the whole, however, the different types of need coincide to a very large degree and indeed, as Britain and Yanetta (1997, p 38) have put it: "meeting preferences is central to creating stable and effective communities". Evidence to support this claim comes from Cole et al (1996) who have shown that where applicants have more choice over where they live 'balanced' communities are more likely to be created. Difficulties arise only in determining where the balance is to be drawn between competing sets of preferences, particularly between those who are inside the community and those who fall outside of it.

The Scottish Federation of Housing Associations has recently addressed this issue (SFHA, 1999) and has recognised that the problem of striking a balance between applicant and community needs is a complex one which does not admit of any straightforward solution. Their report emphasises the importance of avoiding potential clashes of lifestyle (for example, between younger and older people) and avoiding over-concentrations of one particular household type or housing need type (such as families with children or vulnerable single people) in one area, estate, street or close (SFHA, 1999, p 41). It is not clear, however, whether these particular strictures have to do with the needs of a given community or with the needs of the housing organisation to prevent or minimise its estate management problems. It might be argued, for example, that clashes of lifestyle between young and old are part of the normality of life in any community and cannot realistically be controlled by housing organisations, unless the problem stems from poor design, construction or layout of the dwellings concerned (for example, inadequate sound insulation or lack of privacy). Again, it is not clear at what point a concentration of one type of group becomes an over-concentration. The underlying assumption appears to be that a community will be damaged if it contains more than a certain proportion of excluded people who belong to particular groups. The nature of this possible damage, however, is not specified, and neither is the proportion. It is currently fashionable to claim that such 'over-concentrations' are destructive of community life (Power, 2000) but the evidence to date is not particularly convincing (Crow and Allan, 1994). On the contrary, such evidence as there is tends to suggest that it is the actions of powerful external organisations, especially large companies and state bureaucracies, which are most likely to destroy communities (Porteous, 1989).

The final means by which housing allocation can help to achieve social inclusion is by involving socially excluded groups in the formation of allocation policies and in the monitoring of allocation practice. Britain and Yanetta (1997, p 66) argue that an open system, which is both fair and seen to be fair, promotes social inclusion; the SFHA (1999) strongly agrees; and a similar view appears to be held by the authors of the Green Paper (DETR/DSS, 2000), although they are not specifically concerned with social inclusion. Improved information and advice for housing applicants, and improved access to such information and advice, therefore seem to be priorities on which there is a general consensus in the housing world.

Whither housing allocation?

Papps et al (2000) have identified three themes in contemporary approaches to allocations policy: the widening of access, the restricting of access, and the building of more stable communities. The first two approaches appear to be in contradiction but in fact they reflect a traditional distinction between the 'deserving' and 'undeserving' poor: essentially, access is to be widened for the former and restricted for the latter, as a reaction against the moral neutrality of bureaucratic allocation. This is consistent with the wider New Labour programme for the 'remoralisation of welfare' (Burden et al, 2000). The Green Paper to some extent reflects this 'moral' dimension, for example, in its concern to ensure that people do not manipulate their circumstances to gain greater priority for rehousing and that homeless households are not favoured over those who wait patiently on the list for their turn to be rehoused. In this respect, the

Green Paper's 'modern' commitment to widening access is strictly limited by fundamentally old-fashioned assumptions about the virtues of queuing.

With regard to measures to restrict access, there is now clear evidence of a pattern emerging in terms of the types of household being excluded from the housing waiting list (see Butler, 1998; Smith et al, 2000; Somerville and Spink, 2000). Arguably, there are four such types:

1) Those who are deemed to have committed an 'offence' (for example, not paying rent due, breaching tenancy conditions, dealing in drugs, causing nuisance).
2) Those who are deemed not to be in housing need (including those who repeatedly refuse offers of rehousing).
3) Those whose need is deemed to have arisen through their own fault (for example, by giving up or losing accommodation without good reason).
4) Those for whom the organisation has nothing suitable for their needs.

Only the last of these types would be regarded as 'deserving', thus creating moral pressure on the housing organisation concerned to seek a solution for the applicant's housing problem in other ways – for example, through new developments, adaptations, nomination to a housing organisation that can meet the need, and working with other agencies that can assist the applicant. To the Green Paper's credit, as mentioned earlier, it proposes that so-called 'blanket' exclusions, that is, exclusions of classes of applicants, and exclusions of individual applicants on a permanent basis, should be outlawed. This makes it clear that, no matter how important the correction of the 'undeserving' is, it takes second place to the principle of widening access. Moralisation is firmly subordinated to managerialisation. In this respect, the Green Paper is consistent with New Labour policy more generally (Somerville, 2000; Burden et al, 2000).

Research indicates that the increasing interest in widening access may be a response to declining demand more than a genuine commitment to a customer-driven approach (Pawson et al, 2000; Smith et al, 2000). Brown et al (2000), however, suggest that it may also reflect a serious attempt by some housing organisations to take on the managerialist agenda, as reflected, for example, in Best Value. Either way, this development can be represented as one that is primarily concerned with meeting the needs of the organisation (for example, to ensure the best use of its stock or to maximise the effectiveness of its operations). Meeting the needs of individuals is only a means to this end.

What about the third theme identified by Papps et al, building sustainable communities? The Green Paper is essentially vague about what this might mean but again a pattern may be emerging from the research. From Smith et al's (2000) work in England, and Somerville and Spink's (2000) work in Scotland, the following types of policy have been identified:

- special provision and/or targets or quotas for certain socially excluded groups, for example, ethnic minorities, disabled people;
- giving priority to local residents, for example to prevent the depopulation of remote rural areas;
- allowing underoccupation of housing in order to reduce child density;
- limiting the proportion of certain household types, such as families with children or young single people or lone parents, in certain areas, to prevent 'over-concentration';
- allowing local lettings and transfers.

It can be questioned, however, how committed housing organisations are to meeting the needs of communities through their allocation policies. It is notable that, in the Scottish research, no policy actually attempted to define community need or to justify its assumptions about what this need involved, except in terms of protecting the community from potentially dangerous individuals (such as paedophiles and drug dealers). Most of the types of policy listed above could result either from attempting to meet the needs of individuals (for example, members of socially excluded groups) or from the organisation's need to ensure that its stock is let in areas where housing demand is low. The only exceptions would appear to be where the numbers of certain types of household are restricted in certain areas, and these policies have already been criticised above as not necessarily conducive to meeting community needs. Very few housing organisations have actually been found to award points directly for community needs, such as for former residents wanting to return or for young people living in the parental home (to encourage them to remain in the area). Arguably, apart from these, it should be up to communities themselves to determine what their needs are and how those needs should best be met by the allocation policy.

It may also be significant that very few housing organisations operated special 'local lettings initiatives' in particular areas where the standard allocations policy was modified to take account of local circumstances. The conclusions of the Scottish research echoed those of Griffiths et al (1996), namely that the objectives of the schemes were often not specified and their implications for promoting social inclusion consequently remained unclear. In general, the modifications to the organisation's allocation policy seemed arbitrary or trivial or both. The only exceptions appeared to be policies to give priority to local residents in certain 'designated villages' and remote rural areas that would have the effect of helping to maintain communities in those areas (Somerville and Spink, 2000).

Conclusion

Housing allocation continues to be a highly contentious issue. The rise of managerialism has been associated with a questioning of systems of bureaucratic rationing but this does not mean that such systems have ceased to dominate the delivery of public services. In relation to the allocation of housing, the replacement of such systems does not appear to be on the political agenda. Rather, what is envisaged is a reform and supplementing of such systems to allow for greater individual choice and wider conceptions of need. The issues of how increased choice is to be facilitated without increasing inequality and of how individual need is to be balanced against community need, however, have not yet been seriously addressed. The managerialist rhetoric of 'joined-up thinking' has not been matched by any joined-up practice on the ground, and the individualist and communitarian strands of New Labour thought have not been reconciled in any coherent form.

Given the undeveloped character of government thinking on this issue, it is not surprising to find that most housing organisations are not strongly committed to social inclusion in their allocation policies and are generally lacking in reflexivity on the question of the balance between individual and community need. Where mainstream organisations have moved away from allocation on the basis of narrowly-defined housing need, this has typically been in response to powerful external forces such as an escalating problem of low demand or in order to discharge their responsibilities under community care legislation. Given the decline in the status of social housing, the problem of low demand for it is likely to grow in the future, leading to further pressure to move away from systems of bureaucratic rationing. Given also the continuing problems of social exclusion associated with so many council estates, the need for 'joined-up practice' on such estates will become even more urgent than it is already. Housing organisations will need to define clearly what they mean by community need within their allocations policies, and relate this definition to the circumstances of each community in which they operate. They will need to agree their policies with partner organisations, with tenant groups and with applicants themselves, and to ensure that these policies are monitored by all these stakeholders so that they remain relevant, fair and up-to-date. Wherever possible, they should devolve the allocation function to such partnerships at local community level.

References

Bines, W., Kemp, P., Pleace, N. and Quilgars, D. (1993) *Managing social housing*, London: DoE.

Britain, A. and Yanetta, A. (1997) *Housing allocation in Scotland: A practice note*, Edinburgh: Chartered Institute of Housing in Scotland.

Brown, T., Hunt, R. and Yates, N. (2000) *Lettings: A question of choice*, Coventry: Chartered Institute of Housing.

Burden, T., Cooper, C. and Petrie, S. (2000) *Modernising social policy*, Aldershot: Arena.

Butler, S. (1998) *Access denied: The exclusion of people in need from social housing*, London: Shelter.

CHAC (Central Housing Advisory Committee) (1969) *Council housing: Purposes, procedures and priorities*, London: HMSO.

CHR (Centre for Housing Research) (1989) *The nature and effectiveness of housing management in England*, London: HMSO.

Clapham, D. and Kintrea, K. (1984) 'Allocation systems and housing choice', *Urban Studies*, vol 21, pp 261-9.

Clapham, D. and Kintrea, K. (1986) 'Rationing, choice and constraint: the allocation of public housing in Glasgow', *Journal of Social Policy*, vol 15, no 1, pp 51-67.

Clapham, D. and Kintrea, K. (1987) *Housing allocation and the role of the public rented sector*, Discussion Paper 14, Glasgow: Centre for Housing Research, University of Glasgow.

Clapham, D. and Kintrea, K. (1991) 'Housing allocation and the role of the public rented sector', in D. Donnison and D. Maclennan (eds) *The housing service of the future*, Harlow: Longman.

Clarke, J. and Newman, J. (1997) *The managerial state*, London: Sage Publications.

Cole, I. and Furbey, R. (1994) *The eclipse of council housing*, London: Routledge.

Cole, I., Gidley, G., Ritchie, C., Simpson, D. and Wishart, B. (1996) *Creating communities or welfare housing? A study of new housing association developments in Yorkshire and Humberside*, Coventry: Chartered Institute of Housing.

Cooper, P. (1988) 'Access and the market', *Housing*, June/July, pp 16-18.

Corina, L. (1974) *Housing allocation policy and its effects*, Oldham: Oldham Community Development Project.

Crow, G. and Allan, G. (1994) *Community life*, Brighton: Harvester Wheatsheaf.

Dean, H. (1999) 'Citizenship', in M. Powell (ed) *New labour, new welfare state? The 'third way' in British social policy*, Bristol: The Policy Press.

DETR (Department of the Environment, Transport and the Regions/ DSS (Department of Social Security) (2000) *Quality and choice: A decent home for all*, Housing Green Paper, London: DETR/DSS.

DoE (Department of the Environment) (1994) *Access to local authority and housing association tenancies: A consultation paper*, London: HMSO.

English, J., Madigan, R. and Norman, P. (1976) *Slum clearance: The social and administrative context in England and Wales*, London: Croom Helm.

Goodwin, J. (1999) 'Housing: who needs it?', *Roof*, May/June, pp 20-2.

Griffiths, M., Parker, J., Smith, R. and Stirling, T. (1997) *Local authority housing allocations: Systems, policies and procedures*, London: DETR.

Griffiths, M., Parker, J., Smith, R., Stirling, T. and Trott, T. (1996) *Community lettings: Local allocation policies in practice*, York: Joseph Rowntree Foundation.

Harrison, M. and Law, I. (1997) 'Needs and empowerment in minority ethnic housing: some issues of definition and local strategy', *Policy & Politics*, vol 25, no 3, pp 285-98.

Harrison, P. (1983) *Inside the inner city*, Harmondsworth: Penguin.

Henderson, J. and Karn, V. (1987) *Race, class and the allocation of state housing*, Aldershot: Gower.

Karn, V. and Stafford, B. (1990) *Housing allocations: Report of a survey of local authorities in England and Wales*, Coventry: Institute of Housing.

Kay, A., Legg, C. and Foot, J. (1986) *The 1980 tenants' rights in practice*, London: City University.

Lambert, C., Paris, C. and Blackaby, B. (1978) *Housing policy and the state: Allocation, access and control*, Basingstoke: Macmillan.

Lowe, S. (2000) 'Housing abandonment', in I. Anderson and D. Sim (eds) *Social exclusion and housing: Context and challenges*, Coventry: Chartered Institute of Housing.

LRC (London Research Centre) (1988) *Access to housing in London: A report based on the results of the London Housing Survey 1986-7*, London: LRC.

Papps, P., Rowlands, R. and Smith, R. (2000) 'Shifting the balance in social housing allocations: changing access, meeting needs, encouraging choice and promoting sustainable communities', Paper presented to ENHR conference on 'Housing in the 21st Century', Gavle, 26-30 June.

Pawson, H. et al (2000) *Local authority policy and practice on allocations, transfers and homelessness*, London: DETR.

Phillips, D. (1986) *What price equality?*, London: Greater London Council.

Porteous, J.D. (1989) *Planned to death: The annihilation of a place called Howdendyke*, Manchester: Manchester University Press.

Power, A. (1987) *Property before people*, London: Allen and Unwin.

Power, A. (2000) *Poor areas and social exclusion*, CASE Paper 35, London: Centre for the Analysis of Social Exclusion, London School of Economics and Political Science.

Prescott-Clarke, P., Allen, P. and Morrissey, C. (1988) *Queuing for housing: A study of council housing waiting lists*, London: HMSO.

Prescott-Clarke, P., Clemens, S. and Park, A. (1994) *Routes into local authority housing*, London: HMSO.

Raynsford, N. (1984) 'Allocating public housing', in *Right to a home*, London: Labour Housing Group.

Raynsford, N. (1999) quoted in J. Bright and C. Marrs, *Inside Housing*, 22 October, p 3.

Robinson, D. (2001: forthcoming) 'Missing the target? Discrimination and exclusion in the allocation of social housing', in P. Somerville and A. Steele (eds) *'Race', housing and social exclusion*, London: Jessica Kingsley.

SFHA (Scottish Federation of Housing Associations) (1999) *Raising standards in housing*, Edinburgh: SFHA/Scottish Homes.

Smith, R., Stirling, T., Papps, P., Evans, A. and Rowlands, R. (2000) *Allocations and exclusions: The impact of new approaches to allocating social housing*, London: Shelter.

Somerville, P. (1987) 'Local authority housing allocation policies in the North West', Unpublished monograph.

Somerville, P. (2000) *Social relations and social exclusion: Rethinking political economy*, London: Routledge.

Somerville, P. and Spink, B. (2000) *Written housing allocation policies and social inclusion*, Edinburgh: Scottish Homes.

Spicker, P. (1983) *The allocation of council housing*, London: Shelter.

SEVEN

From allocations to lettings: sea change or more of the same?

Dave Cowan

Introduction

Despite incessant and occasionally intense political debate about the allocation of council housing, there has been a remarkable degree of consensus between the political parties about the basic principles which should underlie it. These basic principles have been evident pretty much since the evolution of council housing in the early 20th century. These basic principles are as follows: the allocation of council housing is supposed to have been based on the concept of 'housing need'; certain pre-determined categories of households have been regarded (since the 1935 Housing Act, if not before) as being in greater housing need than others and are, therefore, entitled to 'reasonable preference' in the queue; there should be no 'perverse incentives' on households to (ab-)use the routes into council housing; certain persons are not, or should not be, entitled to council housing. These basic principles were particularly predominant in an era in which demand for council housing outstripped its supply – indeed, the principles were demanded by such an equation. During the 1990s, the principal question on which political parties disagreed was whether those households found to be statutorily homeless by local authorities should have a 'reasonable preference'. Nobody denied their housing need. Rather the concern was that there should be no 'perverse incentive' to become homeless. The rules of allocation were therefore altered, which was the subject of controversy.

By contrast with this broad political consensus, the *public* debate about council housing allocation has centred around questions of what might be termed 'morality'. This reflects a broader public debate about welfare entitlements, and the historic divide between those deserving of assistance and those undeserving of it. We have developed a series of binary divides between genuine/fraudulent, proper/abusive, appropriate/inappropriate applications for council housing. Appropriate safeguards have always been required to ensure that the 'right' people obtain the 'right' type of accommodation. This moral debate forms the undercurrent of the legislation concerned with access to council housing as well as its implementation – one cannot understand the concept of 'housing need' without relating it to these concerns.

This is one way of understanding the apparent dichotomy between, on the one hand, the generalist concept of 'housing need' but, on the other, its particularist application because certain persons are not entitled to apply. Political consensus now exists that asylum-seekers are generally 'ineligible' for council housing through the usual process; yet, one can hardly imagine a category of household with a greater form of 'housing need'. In any system which prioritises housing need – a comparative evaluation – there are always going to be those who, having applied after others, become *entitled* to 'jump the housing queue'. Despite its pejorative connotations in modern media, this should be celebrated – on this basis, the system is working. The real complaint is that the *wrong* people are accessing it.

This chapter begins by surveying the current legislative scheme and the Green Paper proposals. These proposals use the concept of 'choice' radically to shift our understanding from bureaucratic allocation to one of consumer choice lettings[1]. It is suggested that this shift may produce further injustices within the system. In the second section, a number of dilemmas in the current system are outlined drawing on, and in some cases developing, the rich socio-legal literature available to researchers in this area.

Before commencing this analysis, it should be said that consideration will not be given to the supposed dichotomy between rules and discretion: the housing selection/allocation system is riddled with discretion. It is sometimes suggested that many of the problems could be rooted out of the system by making it more rule-based – discretion is commonly "depicted as the bug in the system – a source of deviance which allowed short-term management goals to compromise the principle of social justice" (Smith and Mallinson, 1997, p 341). Early socio-legal research on housing allocation sought to address the *problem* of discretion (see, for example, Lewis, 1976) and the Thatcher government's review of the homelessness legislation sought to cure the problem by bringing extra-statutory rules to bear on the administration of that system (DoE, 1989). Current understandings, however, are rather different – the binary distinction between rules and discretion has been replaced by a more sensitive mapping of the sites of discretion. As Sainsbury (1992) shows, even heavily rule-based systems such as the then industrial disablement benefit system require continual exercises of discretion – there are "numerous holes in doughnuts, or opportunities for freedom of manoeuvre in legislative provisions which satisfy all a priori definitions of discretion ..." (p 306). It follows that this line of enquiry is, or should be, confined to a notion of *shades of discretion*; and the construction of the problem is then rather different.

The current scheme and the Green Paper proposals

The current scheme

The legislative mechanics of council housing allocation follow from the basic principles. In seeking to understand the current system, it is helpful to draw a distinction between two stages of the process: selection and allocation (Clapham and Kintrea, 1986). Households are selected, partly on the basis of the route which they choose (or are directed to take). First there is the homelessness route; second, the waiting list route; and third, other routes. In all cases, it is the council which makes the decision. Most academic and political attention has been paid to the first two routes (although arguably the third provides considerable scope for analysis).

The homelessness route first appeared in statutory form in the 1977 Housing (Homeless Persons) Act, although councils had been exhorted to adopt some prioritisation for this group for some time previously (see Hoath, 1983, pp 1-26). The household must cross a number of legislatively pre-determined 'obstacles' (Watchman and Robson, 1981) – they must be 'eligible', 'homeless', in 'priority need', and 'not intentionally homeless' (1996 Housing Act, Part VII). These obstacles are suffused with *discretion* allowing the council considerable room for manoeuvre. Homelessness, for example, is defined as not having accommodation anywhere in the world "which it would be reasonable for him to continue to occupy" (Section 175). For single people, priority need is either gained on the basis of vulnerability "as a result of old age, mental illness or handicap or physical disability or other special reason", or on the basis of emergency. As regards intentional homelessness, such a finding can occur "if [the applicant] deliberately does or fails to do anything in consequence of which he ceases to occupy accommodation which is available for his occupation and which it would have been reasonable for him to continue to occupy" (Section 191).

From its inception, the legislation was designed to ensure that applicants did not abuse its munificence. Thus, it "always required us to oppress the homeless by making *moral judgments*, not about their housing need, but about *why* the homeless become homeless in the first place" (Cowan, 1997, p 21; emphasis in original). The principal justification for such a statement lay in the intentional homelessness criterion – although comparatively few households are found intentionally homeless, it sets the ethos behind the legislation by requiring councils to be sure that the applicant has not sought to take advantage of the existence of the legislation.

The second route is the waiting list, which is similarly infused with discretion, exemplified by the fact that, until the 1996 Housing Act, there was no obligation on councils even to have such a list. Certain categories are ineligible from appearing on the list either through the statute (for example, asylum-seekers) or through council decision (for example, as a result of rent arrears or eviction for anti-social behaviour – see Butler, 1998). Once on the waiting list, councils are required to give "reasonable preference" to certain categories of household (Section 167(2)). This includes the statutory homeless, families with dependent children or including a pregnant person, those occupying insanitary or overcrowded or other unsatisfactory housing, those occupying housing on insecure terms, those who have difficulty in obtaining settled accommodation because of their "social or economic circumstances", and "households consisting of or including someone with a particular need for settled accommodation on medical or welfare grounds"[3]. Households in the latter category are entitled to "additional preference". The usual method of prioritising households has been through allocating points to applicants on the basis of pre-defined and publicised criteria. Sometimes these schemes can be extremely complex, but broadly they lead to those with the most points coming at the head of the list. Reasonable preference categories do not always head the list, a fact accepted by the Code of Guidance, to which all council are expected to have regard. The Code makes clear that other types of household could be prioritised, "such as housing key workers coming into the area, whose presence is essential for economic growth" (para 5.5). Even heading the list does not ensure automatic selection, as the Code suggests that councils "may wish to take into account the characteristics of the people they select as tenants, both individually (as potentially good tenants) and collectively" (para 5.7)[4].

The third route draws attention to the multiplicity of different arrangements which councils have with other agencies, internal or external, which guarantee to the other agency a quota of accommodation units. The other agency then selects the households which are nominated for this accommodation. Other agencies could include the council's social services department or an organisation which provides temporary accommodation (thus freeing up its units for others with immediate needs). The way these relationships operate and the households selected has been comparatively under-researched.

As regards the actual allocation of accommodation, councils once again have considerable levels of discretion, although this is often trammelled by managerial priorities. Housing allocation takes place against a backdrop of a quasi-market in which there are a number of providers of social housing in each area (sometimes the council itself has no stock, for example after a large-scale voluntary transfer [LSVT] has taken place) – Registered Social Landlords (RSLs), other housing associations, Housing Action Trusts (HATs), and even private landlords are involved in this process. Sometimes, these organisations come together to form a common housing register – a process facilitated by the Housing Corporation, which regulates RSLs – leading to the adoption of similar priority categories as exist in the 1996 Housing Act, although there are concerns about this tool (Mullins and Niner, 1998). Allegations of 'cherry-picking' the best tenants are commonly made by all providers against each other (see, for example, Jones, 1997).

The insight that council housing is allocated by matching available housing to household types, rather than vice-versa, has been the backdrop to a number of important studies. Additionally, the managerial priority is to ensure that properties are relet as soon as possible to ensure that the income stream is retained (see especially Henderson and Karn, 1987). This means that those able and willing to wait longer, tend to be able to secure the best quality housing; and those most desperate (including the homeless) are often allocated the worst quality stock (particularly, as is the case with the statutory homeless, where they are entitled to just one offer). At present, the statutory homeless are only entitled to accommodation provided by the council for two years in every three (Section 194).

The Green Paper proposals

Perhaps unsurprisingly, the Green Paper restates central government's commitment to housing need – "We want to promote a more customer-centred approach, *but without changing the fundamental role of social housing in meeting housing need*" (DETR/DSS, 2000, para 9.2; emphasis added). This commitment is, however, more wavering than before as "there may be occasions when it is necessary and desirable, for some wider community benefit, to allow exceptions to this" (para 9.12). The principal alteration is, nevertheless, potentially radical – no longer should we talk about 'allocation', with its emphasis on bureaucratic processes, rather it is suggested that we refer to 'lettings', with its emphasis on household choice. Choice is the key concept and quite amazing claims are made for it:

> Applicants for social housing who are more involved in decisions about their new homes are more likely to have a longer term commitment to the locality. This will promote more sustainable communities at village, town and city level. It will increase personal well-being, and help to reduce anti-social behaviour, crime, stress and educational under-achievement. (para 9.7)

This can only be read in the light of the reports of the Social Exclusion Unit into neighbourhood regeneration, teenage pregnancy, anti-social behaviour, and unpopular housing – all of which contained a raft of policy suggestions which are replicated in this part of the Green Paper.

This focus on choice actually means that the Green Paper has less to say about *selection* than might have been desired. Objections to permanent exclusions from the housing register have succeeded in that there is a proposal to replace this with temporary reductions in priority (para 9.13). There are suggestions that points-based systems of prioritisation might be replaced by a system which includes "people's own 'felt needs'" within a banding system (paras 9.18-9.19); and that deciding on who should have priority within bands should be done on the basis of length of time spent waiting (a principle advocated by the Cullingworth committee in 1969: CHAC, 1969, para 163, although schemes suggested were regarded as too administratively cumbersome – para 166). The Green Paper also suggests that 'housing need' includes the case where households need "to move to a particular location for some reason where, if re-housing in that area were not possible, this would lead to undue hardship" (para 9.16) – presumably this is part of the much-hyped scheme to assist the settlement of key workers – and should not include those for whom adaptations to their existing accommodation would enable them to remain where they are (para 9.16).

It is proposed that the homelessness legislation be amended so that the vulnerability criterion, through which single people have priority need, be extended to include those with "an institutionalised or care background" or fleeing domestic violence (para 9.55). Additionally, those 16 or 17 year olds with a care background will be regarded as in priority need (para 9.56 – for background, see Cowan and Dearden, 2001: forthcoming). It is suggested that the intentional homelessness provision might be jettisoned provided that there is "disincentive for people to present themselves as homeless". However, there is a proposal to enable landlords to reduce the priority of statutory homeless households on the waiting list where they have "good reason" to believe that the household has deliberately made their "housing situation worse in order to move into a higher needs band so as to gain priority for social housing (whether temporary or settled)" (para 9.51). Thus, the identification of the homelessness legislation as a "perverse incentive" (a phrase used in para 9.51) is given new life.

The real revelation of the Green Paper relates to lettings. Here, it is proposed that, within the constraints of what is available, households should be entitled to choose their accommodation without penalty if they turn it down. Successful homeless households would be time-limited as regards choice (thus reducing any "perverse incentive") but for other households "waiting time would become the 'currency' that those in the social sector could use to optimise their decisions about where to live, taking into account all their needs and aspirations" (para 9.21). The longer a household is willing to wait where they are, the better chance they would have "of securing a home which met their requirements" (para 9.22). It is suggested that choice might be facilitated by the adoption of advertising, particularly if targeted, based on schemes already existing in Holland (paras 9.24-9.28). The benefit of such an approach is said to be that it will "bring information about the entire social housing market in an area (and perhaps beyond)[1] much closer to the potential occupiers" (para 9.27). If all of this means that relet times increase, it is suggested that this "may be a price worth paying" because the benefits of choice are so significant (para 9.35). The advertising approach could also tie into 'local lettings' policies which would enable a council "to correct a significant social imbalance such as an excessive child density on certain estates" (para 9.29). Local lettings could also operate as part of the key worker policy. Related to the shift from allocations to lettings is the recognition that the role of housing officers will accordingly also have to shift from gatekeeper to "advisor and advocate" (para 9.33). In other words, then, the ethos of housing allocation will have to change to enable households to make an active choice.

The final point to make is that central government will not impose a statutory scheme on local authorities, in part because of the differences between supply and demand. However, obligations on RSLs to cooperate with councils in offering accommodation to households on the waiting list will be beefed up.

Will choice work?

The scheme outlined in this part of the Green Paper for choice is perhaps the most precocious use of this term throughout the whole document. It will require an almost total root-and-branch reworking of current housing allocation systems (although they will be carefully piloted). The boldness of this approach is probably necessary and, although there are some concerns about the new scheme, it should be welcomed as the New Labour government have sought to deal with the iniquities of the system. I suggest, however, that there are three potential pitfalls in order to avoid a different set of iniquities coming to dominate the scheme.

- First, the system quite clearly will have little or no impact in high demand areas. This much has already been conceded (para 9.36), but these are precisely the areas in which households presumably want to live and want to exercise choice. One might say, then, that choice will work in areas where people don't want to live or don't much care for; but expectations will be raised by the rhetoric of choice irrespective of location.
- Second, the principle that the longer a household waits, the more priority they will have might seem defensible but it creates a market together with the bargaining inequalities engendered by markets. The bargaining chip is waiting time, and some people can wait longer than others. A key finding in recent research is that this can produce patterns of discrimination in housing allocation:

> It also became clear to us that many applicants, particularly those living in temporary accommodation, when asked the question 'where would you like to live?', reinterpreted this question in terms of 'how long do

you wish to wait for an offer?'. This in turn related to the position of the player in the allocations game.... Given that black applicants were disproportionately represented in the homeless families channel, this put them at an initial disadvantage in the game, compared with existing tenants who were seeking a transfer. (Jeffers and Hoggett, 1996, p 336)

Certainly, it will be the case that young people who have no history of independent living will have to wait longer.

• Third, the available evidence on advertising lettings is unclear as to its success in the Netherlands (quite apart from questions about transposing a scheme to a new culture). There is a suggestion that "applicants appear to postpone a thorough evaluation of an offer until they actually turn out to be the winner" (Kullberg, 1997, p 400), at which point they can turn down the offer. If they do, this may mean readvertisement with the attendant problems of stigma and rent loss. There are also suggestions that the claims for choice in this respect may be overstated – stigmatised populations offered stigmatised homes hardly leads to sustainable communities. But there should also be concerns that the form of knowledge required by respondents to each advertisement can lead to a different set of disadvantages than currently exist.

It will be important for those putting the various choice schemes into practice, behind the rhetoric, as well as those researching them, to bear in mind these problems. What one can say is that, as households generally are going to seek to match themselves to properties rather than the other way round (which has, hitherto, been the case), much of the research concerning direct and indirect discrimination will need to be reoriented.

Current dilemmas

In this section it is argued that the development and implementation of access legislation suggests a number of dilemmas which any potential root-and-branch reform will need to tackle if it is to be successful. Broadly, what is suggested is that hitherto the operation of housing selection/ allocation has stigmatised an already stigmatised population further and that, at times, it has led to at best unfortunate results, including suggestions of institutional discrimination as well as bureaucratic injustice. I do not want to suggest that in many cases these are the *intended* results or that housing officers themselves somehow wish these results – rather, what is suggested is that a combination of contingent factors create these undesirable results. Five contingent factors are considered here[3]: legislative background; the application process; the move from need to risk; working together; adjudication. All of these influence and are part of the organisational culture of decision making at local level.

Legislative background

It is suggested that the formation and development of legislation can provide an initial driver of the bureaucratic culture (see, for example, Carson, 1970). The point which needs to be stressed is that the legislative process is a contested site in which the motivations and understandings of politicians and the media become apparent. Even though the finished product might appear value-neutral, it is nevertheless imbued with these motivations and understandings. And it is these motivations and understandings which subsequently become linked within the administrative process.

Certainly over the past 30 years or so legislative reforms to the selection process have taken place in a highly contested atmosphere. The two legislative shifts in council housing selection/allocation – 1976-77 (culminating with the 1977 Housing (Homeless Persons) Act) and 1993-96 (1996 Housing Act, Parts VI and VII) – have taken place against a backdrop of a broader societal concern about the relationship between the creation of, and response to, poverty. Parliamentary debates surrounding the 1977 Act must be read in the context of the "extensive and hysterical" media coverage of the case of Derek Deevy, the supposed 'King Con' of a broader problem of welfare scroungerphobia (Golding and Middleton, 1984, p 61). Similarly, Parliamentary debates surrounding the 1996 Housing Act, Parts VI and VII, must be read in the context of ill-founded concern that single mothers became pregnant to jump the housing queue (DoE, 1994; on this issue, see generally Cowan, 1998a; SEU, 1999). Again, this was perceived as the pinnacle of a much broader complaint about the 'problem' of welfare, in which claimants are regarded in some way as fraudulent (see DSS, 1998).

Thus, the construction of the legislation has sought to balance the 'housing need' of households against perceptions of the ways in which that legislation might be abused. Although there has been no content analysis of parliamentary debates during these periods, it might be suspected that a considerable number of sentences drew on the imagery of 'bogus', 'fraudulent', 'abusive', 'scroungers', and particularly those who seek to 'jump the housing queue'. New Labour has been quick to jump on the bandwagon. One reason why this discourse has taken hold is precisely because it is impossible to provide estimates of the numbers of fraudulent applications; a further reason is because it appeals to the media construction of welfare applicants. It is thus the easiest method of conveying broadly what people already believe to be true (Hall et al, 1978), albeit unprovable, and fits into the previously established pattern of constructing welfare claim(ant)s. Loveland (1991), for example, discusses the derivation of the intentional homelessness provision in the 1977 Act as follows:

> Conservative MPs and local authorities feared that there were innumerable idle, dishonest men and women eagerly awaiting to avail themselves of the allegedly carefree lifestyle enjoyed by welfare claimants occupying public sector accommodation. Opposition forces therefore sought to deny *any* housing entitlements to the 'self-induced homeless' – those people who would abandon, or provoke their own eviction from, current accommodation to secure immediate placement in modern, spacious council housing. (p 268; emphasis as original)

The reworking of the legislation in 1996 followed a similar path, but this time there was a link with the broader public debate generated by the 'back to basics' motif of Conservative ideology in the early 1990s. Housing need was constructed as a balance between, on the one hand, the "unmarried teenager expecting her first, probably unplanned child" (Young, 1993), and the "married couples [who] want to feel personally responsible" (DoE, 1994, para 1.2). Thus, in the 1995 White Paper, the DoE argued:

> Allocation schemes should reflect the underlying values of our society. They should balance specific housing needs against the need to support married life, so that tomorrow's generation grows up in a stable home environment. (DoE, 1995, p 36)

Even though this discourse did not find its way into the legislation in any meaningful way[4], it set the tone for public discussion.

How has the Green Paper fared against this hostile background? The limited evidence to date suggests that the media misreading of the Green Paper is negative on this issue. It draws attention to the plan to give 'priority need' to those with an institutionalised background; however, the particular concern has been that this will enable "prisoners to jump the housing queue" and that this "would reward offenders while law-abiding citizens languished at the bottom of waiting lists" (Hickley, 2000; Cracknell, 2000). The notion that somehow certain households can 'jump the queue' because they are in priority need, apart from being incorrect[5], suggests that the context of the legislation will not be changed.

The application process

The housing application process can be seen as a form of submission to the state's sovereignty, through the tool of law, which reinforces the power of the state to discipline and punish its subjects in terms of who is recognised/rewarded/disciplined (those who make the appropriate or necessary performances which enable the prevailing structure to work) and who is marginalised/punished because they cannot or will not contribute to that (re-)production. It is a sorting process through which the prevailing organisational culture and ethos can be traced.

Although this requires testing empirically, the social housing application process is the housing system's equivalent of the *confession* in which the applicant is required to confess their housing histories in the hope that absolution will be provided through rehousing. The confession is part of the "wider domain of disciplinary power" and "at the heart of the power-knowledge nexus" (Hillyard and Watson, 1996, p 329). Applying for social housing, like the sexual confession, can be seen as a "disquieting enigma" (Foucault, 1990, p 35) within a housing system which prioritises the norm of ownership (Gurney, 1999). As Hillyard and Watson put it:

> The poor, the unemployed, the sick, the immigrant, the criminal and the homeless are constantly being surveyed or monitored and asked to declare or disclose to a social researcher, police officer or social administrator something which has previously been kept secret and which is often (pre)-judicial to themselves. (1996, p 329)

The homelessness legislation, with its emphasis on fault and comparative vulnerability, and the housing waiting list, with its comparative processes, both exacerbate this confessional process. The application form and interview are two sites which have been less well-researched (or, perhaps, commented on) by those within the socio-legal tradition, but which might prove equally productive of insights into the bureaucratic processes of welfare agencies. As Foucault suggests of the one "who assimilates and records" the confession:

It was the latter's function to verify this obscure truth: the revelation of confession had to be coupled with the decipherment of what it said. The one who listened was not simply the forgiving master, the judge who condemned or acquitted; he was the master of truth. His was a hermeneutic function. With regard to the confession, his power was not only to demand it before it was made, or decide what was to follow after it, but also to constitute a discourse of truth on the basis of its decipherment. (1990, pp 66-7)

Housing officers must use the application process to construct their own version of truth against a preconceived set of criteria. Thus, in some respects, the applicant's confession might be left tantalisingly incomplete because the applicant's story does not fit. However, this way of looking at the process also enables a more sophisticated understanding of the power relationships which infuse the process – for example, does the applicant tell the story-confession which they think the officer wishes to hear? Domestic violence research has suggested that women often feel the interview to contain "excessively detailed and intrusive questioning about the violence" (because this provides important evidence as to why the person has become homeless in the first place) and that questions can be "bombarded" at them (Malos et al, 1994, pp 50-3). Halliday (1998) referred to the application process as "information bingeing" on the part of the officers, which served to justify their decision making, but which also must have some impact on the methods used to gather the information in the first place.

The pre-existing concerns about fraud and welfare dependency permeate the process so that, for example, Halliday (2000a) refers to a "culture of suspicion" operating within his case study areas. This culture of suspicion – to which other researchers have drawn attention (Loveland, 1995; Cowan, 1997) – commonly operates to deny the status of 'homeless' and deter households from making an application for housing (see Carlen, 1994). Local authority officers perceive their role as being to determine which applicants are the most deserving of assistance, against a background of actual and potential resource shortages. Applicants are constructed by housing officers as knowledgeable and strategic, able to "'change their stories' in order to circumvent the legal barriers which prevented them from being offered housing" (Halliday, 2000a). Halliday's work, in part, concerns the production of institutional racism at the selection stage of the process. He argues convincingly that this occurred in his fieldwork authorities as a result of the:

... potential interplay between structural, organisational and individual factors in the social production of institutional racism within a decision-making process.... Ethnic stereotyping emerged from the organisational schema about the nature of 'bogus' applicants, which may in turn have been informed by wider debates about the nature of the 'homeless problem' and the political context in which homelessness law had been amended [by the 1996 Act]. (p 461)

Halliday's findings chime with much of the socio-legal work concerning the implementation of welfare legislation at local level. The tools, of course, are prescribed centrally but it is their interpretation by local authority officers which has been focused on. In particular, socio-legal work has concentrated on the production of findings of intentional homelessness (see Loveland, 1992, 1994). Loveland's critique begins with the assertion that quantitative research "says very little about [its] implementation" (1995, p 193) and that closer analysis "might provide an illuminating example of the extent to which bureaucratic behaviour is effectively structured by formal legal constraints" (p 194). While there were substantive distinctions between Loveland's three case study areas, his perceptive analysis of this most judicialised obstacle concludes with the withering comment that legalism was "an intruder in the administrative arena" (1992 – discussed further below).

The Green Paper marks out a required change in administrative culture away from the housing officer as gatekeeper (or policing the system), towards a role as advocate for the client:

> Under a lettings service that puts decision-making in the hands of customers, the role of housing professionals becomes less one of gate-keeper and more one of advisor and advocate. This would help households to make informed choices about their housing options, be it with regard to meeting needs within their existing home, or the opportunities available for re-housing. (para 9.33)

It might be suspected that such a shift will be rather more difficult than is perceived by the authors of the Green Paper. The current culture of suspicion will almost certainly equally pervade the new system, more so where there is greater demand than supply because of assumptions that applicants are seeking to 'abuse the system'. Advertising simply changes the timing of the bureaucratic decision-making process (that is, once the property has been identified), not the culture of that process.

From need to risk

Much lip-service is paid across political and bureaucratic divides to the concept of housing need. It has been a unifying principle to which we can all sign up. However, it is particularly malleable and, as is continually shown through welfare restrictions, particularly contingent on the prevailing ideology. It can be argued that in the context of the selection and allocation of social housing, need has never been particularly predominant, always being sacrificed to other concepts and practices, as well as the development of newer understandings. In the past few years, some academic understandings of housing need have drawn on a particular theoretical understanding, deriving from the insights gained from the work of Giddens (1990) and Beck (1990).

Thus, it has been argued that much of the selection/allocation decision making can be deciphered through an understanding of the complexities of 'risk' (Allen and Sprigings, 1999; Cowan et al, 1999)[6]. This is more than a terminological shift – it requires a reconfiguration of our understandings of housing management – and requires us to understand the decision-making process as one which not only looks back at past housing conduct but also requires a prediction of future conduct. As assessments of risk are usually associated with the likelihood of a negative outcome (for example 'how likely is this person to re-offend?'), this implies a justification for exclusion on the basis that some households are regarded as *too* risky. As assessments of risk can go wrong there is a constant need for their review and evolution which in turn requires increased monitoring of those already housed to feed back into the housing allocation system. Drawing on their research into the rehousing of sex offenders, Cowan et al (1999) show how the internal administration of housing selection and allocation processes have shifted towards risk assessment; and they have been forced to adopt the language of risk in their communications with external agencies, most of which use that language. Thus, interagency working was both a cause and effect of this shift.

There are a number of consequences of this understanding for the Green Paper proposals. First, its reliance on the concept of 'housing need' must be regarded as problematic as, without accepting its limitations, it will cloud the development of more open decision making. Second, whilst the Green Paper suggests that there should be a scheme of time-limited penalties for 'deviant' households (for example those with rent arrears or guilty of anti-social behaviour), the reality will be that those households regarded as too risky will still be excluded in one way or another. For example, such households may not be allowed to apply to join the waiting list, or will not be given enough points on that list to obtain accommodation. Thus, on this basis, the underlying decision will not be affected one iota by the Green Paper – there will always be mechanisms which enable housing officers to exclude applicants (see, for example, Carlen, 1994).

Working together

The Green Paper rightly emphasises the need for housing services to engage in relations with other agencies and providers to inform the decision-making process and to ensure that there are fewer holes in the service offered to applicants. Research reports, government reports, and all manner of published works exhort processes of joint working and deplore the failures in providing such services. In my earlier work, I suggested that a principal reason for these failures lay in the legislation itself and the seeming inability of central government to coordinate its own efforts – there were different aims, different languages, different objectives, different working practices (advocates – gatekeepers), different organisational imperatives (see Cowan, 1995). In retrospect, this may well have overstated the case (see the analysis of Bartlett and Sandland, 1999) and been overly lego-centric but the point remains the same: bureaucratic cultures and their histories do not inspire confidence that interagency working will become a reality. There is much rhetoric but little understanding of the causes of the failure to work together.

Adjudication

The leading legal text on the council housing allocation process has 278 pages of commentary; its table of cases is 12 pages long (Arden and Hunter, 1997). In short, the housing selection/allocation process has become hemmed in by a huge body of case law, which continues to increase. Yet, at the same time, this huge body of case law rarely, it seems, seeps into decision making. When it does, the evidence suggests that unlawful decision making remains endemic but that it is sought to be made judge-proof through a formula of questioning or defensive practices; indeed, in some cases it deters those housing departments who are subjected to the judicial gaze from processes of self-scrutiny which that gaze seeks to engender (Halliday, 2000b). There is thus a systemic problem of, and caused by, adjudication – or, perhaps a better term, accountability.

Accountability for entitlement decisions seems to be a minimum basis for good administration (and this infuses the 'blue rinse' approach to administration: Harlow and Rawlings, 1999, ch 3). One method of dejudicialising this process is to prescribe a system of informal adjudication, through which the organisation effectively considers the fairness and accuracy of its own decision (Sainsbury, 1992, 1994). Such a system was put in place by the 1996 Housing Act to provide an opportunity to those persons excluded from the housing register or subjected to certain negative homelessness decisions to challenge that decision. The consultation paper on which that provision was based suggested the new arrangements for the following illogical reason: "Given the substantial number of cases in which there is an application for judicial review, it is not clear that such arrangements are working satisfactorily" (DoE, 1994, para 16.2). Such negative sentiments are no basis for reform and it appears that the new system has some holes in it (which have themselves given rise to a large number of judicial review applications) (see Atkinson et al, 1999). Furthermore, early research suggested that few unsuccessful homeless applicants actually used the internal review – in the last sixth months of 1997, only 16 local authorities, mostly in London, had dealt with more than 41 reviews; 68 per cent of the sample had conducted less than five reviews and 40 per cent none at all (Cowan and Hunter, 1998). Success rates also varied widely. A culture commonly exists within housing departments that they always make the right decisions and this may well influence the results of internal review processes (Cowan, 1998b). Other research also suggests that internal reviews as a first step on an adjudication ladder often are the only step taken by unsuccessful applicants (Sainsbury and Eardley, 1992).

No suggestions are made in the Green Paper on the subject of adjudication. But this is a burning issue which is not just a matter for lawyers and advisers – it should be positively regarded as a matter of determining good administration. The internal review's appearance as the poor relation of housing services is only exacerbated by the lack of data collected on it by the Department of the Environment, Transport and the Regions.

Conclusion

The Green Paper made some bold proposals based on the starting point of 'choice' together with a number of more technical suggestions. In this chapter I have sought to provide a critique of these proposals from a number of different perspectives. One matter which has not been discussed but is worth some thought at this pre-legislative stage is how to ensure that the objectives of the legislation will be achieved in practice. As Partington (1990, p 71) observed in a sweep of housing law "there are some who regard it as surprising that any of the prescribed objectives of legislation are ever actually achieved". In the 20th century, despite legislative and policy changes that sought to ameliorate the harsh realities of housing inequalities, it might be argued that the metaphors of housing need, and responses to it, have not altered in any substantial way, despite the invention of large-scale social housing. The worst quality housing is allocated to those with the least bargaining power – this chapter's assessment of the Green Paper's proposals is that this principle will be given legislative form.

Notes

[1] There is a suggestion that local boundaries might be crossed so that lettings could be made across regions, particularly using lower demand areas (paras 9.9-9.10).

[2] The current obligation is to "co-operate to such an extent as is reasonable in the circumstances" (Section 170, 1996 Housing Act).

[3] I do not wish to suggest that this is complete – indeed, it must be doubted whether such a list could ever be complete.

[4] The first edition of the Code of Guidance did, in fact, contain reference to these sets of preferences, but the offending paragraph was removed bty the time it reached its second edition.

[5] Quite apart from everything else, the homelessness jurisprudence suggests that many of those leaving prison are likely to be found intentionally homeless: *R v Hounslow LBC ex parte R (1997)* 29 HLR 939; *Minchin v Sheffield CC, The Times*, 26 April.

[6] There is insufficient space to do justice to these arguements here – readers are referred to the following texts: Giddens, 1990; Beck, 1990; Adam et al, 2000.

References

Adam, B., Beck, U. and van Loon, J. (2000) *The risk society and beyond*, London: Sage Publications.

Allen, C. and Sprigings, N. (1999) *Managing risk together*, Salford: Housing and Urban Studies Unit, University of Salford.

Arden, A. and Hunter, C. (1997) *Homelessness and allocations*, London: Legal Action Group.

Atkinson, R., Buck, T., Pollard, D. and Smith, N. (1999) *A regional study of local authority and court processes in homelessness cases*, London: Lord Chancellor's Department.

Bartlett, P. and Sandland, R. (1999) *Textbook on mental health law*, London: Blackstone.

Beck, U. (1990) *The risk society*, London: Sage Publications.

Butler, S. (1998) *Access denied: The exclusion of people in need from social housing*, London: Shelter.

Carlen, P. (1994) 'The governance of homelessness: legality, lore and lexicon in the agency-maintenance of youth homelessness', *Critical Social Policy*, vol 41, pp 18-42.

Carson, W. (1970) 'White collar crime and the enforcement of factory legislation', *British Journal of Criminology*, vol 10, pp 383-98.

CHAC (Central Housing Advisory Committee) (1969) *Council housing purposes, procedures and priorities*, London: HMSO.

Clapham, D. and Kintrea, K. (1986) 'Rationing choice and constraint: the allocation of public housing in Glasgow', *Journal of Social Policy*, vol 15, pp 51-66.

Cowan, D. (1995) 'Accommodating community care', *Journal of Law and Society*, vol 22, pp 212-34.

Cowan, D. (1997) *Homelessness: the (in-)appropriate applicant*, Aldershot: Dartmouth.

Cowan, D. (1998a) 'Reforming the homelessness legislation', *Critical Social Policy*, vol 57, pp 435-54.

Cowan, D. (1998b) 'Homelessness internal appeals mechanisms: serving the administrative process', *Anglo-American Law Review*, vol 27, pp 66-87.

Cowan, D. and Dearden, N. (2001: forthcoming) 'The minor as (a) subject', in J Fionda (ed) *Law and childhood*, Oxford: Hart.

Cowan, D. and Hunter, C. (1998) 'Homelessness internal reviews: a view from the sharp end', Paper for European Network of Housing Research Conference, Cardiff, September.

Cowan, D., Gilroy, R. and Pantazis, C. (1999) 'Risking housing need', *Journal of Law and Society*, vol 26, pp 403-26.

Cracknell, D. (2000) 'Prisoners will jump housing queues', *Sunday Telegraph*, 2 April.

DETR (Department of the Environment, Transport and the Regions/ DSS (Department of Social Security) (2000) *Quality and choice: A decent home for all*, Housing Green Paper, London: DETR/DSS.

DoE (Department of the Environment) (1989) *The government's review of the homelessness legislation*, London: DoE.

DoE (1994) *Access to local authority and housing association tenancies*, London: DoE.

DoE (1995) *Our future homes: Opportunity, choice and responsibility*, Cm 2901, London: DoE.

DSS (1998) *Beating fraud is everyone's business*, Cm 4012, London: DSS.

Foucault, M. (1990) *The history of sexuality*, vol 1, London: Penguin.

Giddens, A. (1990) *The consequences of modernity*, Cambridge: Polity.

Golding, P. and Middleton, S. (1984) *Images of welfare*, Oxford: Blackwell.

Gurney, C. (1999) '*Pride and Prejudice*: discourses of normalisation in public and private accounts of home ownership', *Housing Studies*, vol 14, pp 163-85.

Hall, S., Critcher, C., Jefferson, T., Clarke, J. and Roberts, B. (1978) *Policing the crisis: Mugging, the state, and law and order*, Basingstoke: Macmillan.

Halliday, S. (1998) 'Researching the "impact" of judicial review on routine administrative decision-making', in D. Cowan (ed) *Housing: Participation and exclusion*, Aldershot: Dartmouth.

Halliday, S. (2000) 'Institutional racism in bureaucratic decision-making: a case study in the administration of homelessness law', *Journal of Law and Society*, vol 27, pp 449-72.

Halliday, S. (2000b) 'The influence of judicial review on bureaucratic decision-making', *Public Law*, pp 110-22.

Harlow, C. and Rawlings, R. (1999) *Law and administration*, London: Butterworths.

Henderson, J. and Karn, V. (1987) *Race, class and state housing: Inequality and the allocation of public housing in Britain*, Aldershot: Gower.

Hickley, D. (2000) 'Prescott pushes convicts to front of housing queue', *Daily Mail*, 3 April.

Hillyard, P. and Watson, S. (1996) 'Postmodern social policy: a contradiction in terms?', *Journal of Social Policy*, vol 15, pp 321-42.

Hoath, D. (1983) *Homelessness*, London: Sweet & Maxwell.

Jeffers, S. and Hoggett, P. (1996) 'Like counting deckchairs on the Titanic: a study of institutional racism and housing allocations in Haringey and Lambeth', *Housing Studies*, vol 10, pp 325-44.

Jones, A. (1997) *Can't nominate or won't nominate?*, London: Anchor Trust.

Kullberg, J. (1997) 'From waiting lists to adverts: the allocation of social rented dwellings in the Netherlands', *Housing Studies*, vol 12, pp 393-403.

Lewis, N. (1976) 'Council housing allocation: problems of discretion and control', *Public Administration*, vol 54, pp 147-60.

Loveland, I. (1991) 'Legal rights and political realities: governmental responses to homelessness in Britain', *Law and Social Inquiry*, vol 16, pp 249-319.

Loveland, I. (1992) 'Administrative law, administrative processes, and the housing of homeless persons: a view from the sharp end', *Journal of Social Welfare Law*, vol 13, pp 4-26.

Loveland, I. (1994) 'The politics, law and practice of intentional homelessness', *Journal of Social Welfare and Family Law*, vol 15, pp 113-27.

Loveland, I., (1995) *Housing homeless persons*, Oxford: Oxford University Press.

Malos, E. and Hague, G. with Dear, W. (1994) *Domestic violence and housing: Local authority responses to women and children escaping violence in the home*, Bristol: SAUS Publications.

Mullins, D. and Niner, P. (1998) *Common housing registers: An evaluation and analysis of current practice*, London: The Housing Corporation.

Partington, M. (1990) 'Rethinking British housing law: the failure of the Housing Act 1988', in M. Freeman (ed) *Critical issues in welfare law*, London: Stevens & Sons.

Sainsbury, R. (1992) 'Administrative justice: discretion and procedure in social security decision-making', in K. Hawkins (ed) *The uses of discretion*, Oxford: Oxford University Press.

Sainsbury, R. (1994) '"Internal reviews and the weakening of social security claimants" right of appeal', in G. Richardson and H. Genn (eds) *Administrative law and government action*, Oxford: Oxford University Press.

Sainsbury, R. and Eardley, T. (1992) *Housing Benefit reviews*, London: HMSO.

SEU (Social Exclusion Unit) (1999) *Teenage pregnancies*, London: SEU.

Smith, S. and Mallinson, S. (1997) 'The problem with social housing: discretion, accountability and the welfare ideal', *Policy & Politics*, vol 24, pp 339-57.

Watchman, P. and Robson, P. (1981) 'The homeless persons obstacle race', *Journal of Social Welfare Law*, pp 1-21.

Young, G. (1993) Speech at LSE Housing, London: DoE.

Tenant participation

Introduction

In the latter part of the 20th century, the essence of tenant participation shifted away from tenant-led active protest against the state – through, for example, rent strikes and marches – towards a more politically acceptable model which sought to encourage and facilitate it. Both Conservative and New Labour governments, in power and opposition, have championed the cause (albeit for different reasons, as Robina Goodlad points out). The former introduced a Tenant's Charter in the 1980 Housing Act which gave rights to information and consultation. Those rights were increased in later legislation, culminating in the ability to set up tenant management organisations. Tenants were given voting rights on various types of transfers. New Labour has required local authorities to set up Tenant Participation Compacts, although these, as Carr et al point out, imply voluntary partnership rather than an enforceable contractual relationship. Thus, the Green Paper is able to refer to tenant participation as action already taken by New Labour to raise the quality of housing and housing management (DETR/DSS, 2000, p 9).

Despite this official interest in tenant participation, and the requirements on social housing providers to set up these compacts, both chapters note that there are differing interpretations of what it involves. Goodlad, drawing on her earlier work with colleagues, suggests that tracking the development of tenant participation structures should give way to an approach which maps what occurs across three dimensions: structures, processes, and objectives. Indeed, both chapters suggest that we should look more to process in assessing the value of tenant participation, suggesting the need for qualitative data as opposed to 'common indicators'.

However, for Helen Carr and colleagues there is a further underlying issue. Their central emphasis on the legal framework marks out their analysis: it highlights a conflict between individual and collective rights. They suggest that the Right to Buy gave local authority tenants a significant consumer right, changing the balance of power between landlord and tenant in a way in which mainstream tenant participation statutory provisions fail to do. While the Right to Buy was introduced together with a string of enforcement powers in the hands of the Secretary of State (which were used to some effect), together with individually enforceable rights (down to the minutiae) within the structure of the Act, tenant participation provisions have proved more permissive and less robust. The complexity of housing law – especially as regards tenant participation – together with the lack of housing law expertise means that any challenge is difficult to mount.

Goodlad shows how, despite a slow start, the tenant participation agenda has been adopted, funded and developed within social housing. In addition to this, however, Goodlad draws on three social theoretical perspectives which illuminate "what [tenant participation] might mean, why it might be desired and what its significance might be". These three perspectives – theories of democracy and citizenship; theories of the state; theories of power – generate considerable insight and understanding of the potential impacts of tenant participation. Tenant participation is said to meet the requirements of responsive and responsible management; the perspectives provide explanations of the state's incorporation of it; and enable broader, multi-faceted assessments to be made which incorporate processes and structural imbalances. Significantly, it may be that "apparently far-reaching forms of tenant participation or 'control' may not have enabled tenants to achieve what they want".

Carr et al's focus and analytical approach are rather different. They specifically consider whether the participation agenda does effectively empower tenants. They argue that tenants can fail to derive any benefits whatsoever and, indeed, may be further marginalised by the process. They examine two rather different schemes in London, both of which have been held out as models of good practice. Their conclusion – that both schemes developed management models and were evaluated from management, rather than tenants' perspectives – points to a need to examine critically the significance and consequences of the central role that tenant participation plays in the government's agenda.

EIGHT

Two steps forward for tenants?

Helen Carr, Dorothy Sefton-Green and Damien Tissier

> The most important outcome [of the Green Paper] should be a new
> enthusiasm for tenants to shape their own destiny and determine how
> they should be involved in controlling their homes. (Swinney, 2000, p
> 20)

This chapter attempts to go beyond the current rhetoric of tenants'
participation which assumes that it is a panacea for the problems of social
housing, empowering tenants and improving their lifestyles, acting as a
cost-saving management tool for local authorities, aiding estate
regeneration and reducing crime: "... Government seeks to empower
people as stakeholders to maximise effectiveness, efficiency and access, to
strengthen communities, create stability and sustainability" (Armstrong,
1999, p 125). We focus on the impact of the policy on tenants both
collectively and individually, and discuss whether participation does enable
them to gain a level of control over their housing.

Tenant participation is located as one possible element of 'voice',
Hirschman's (1970) intermediate means of communication, through which
tenants can articulate their concerns. It needs to be seen as an alternative
rather than a substitute for political, economic or legal rights that could
provide what Hirschman terms 'exit' in a market model. We conclude
that while tenant participation has the potential to be developed into a
more effective tool to aid efficient housing management and benefit some
stakeholders in social housing, tenants can only achieve the sort of
empowerment giving them real control over their housing consumption
by an appropriate balance between participation, protest/political action
and effective legal remedies. Other stakeholders in social housing may
have little interest in tenants having access to these alternative forms of
accountability in social housing. Indeed what we see alongside the strong
rhetoric of tenant participation is the introduction of a variety of

mechanisms which stifle protest and reduce access to legal rights. Finally, we consider the tensions between individual and collective legal rights and conclude that the dominance of consumer rights-driven initiatives means that tenant participation is a poor mechanism compared with the Right to Buy when judged by its effectiveness in enhancing the life choices of those individuals who are most vulnerable in society.

The Green Paper, but more notably the Best Value in Housing framework (BVFH), sets out the government's intention that tenant participation will achieve more efficient housing management (DETR, 2000; DETR/DSS, 2000). Local authorities seek greater legitimacy for their housing management decisions, and it is assumed tenants want their voices to be heard. The attempt to define tenants' 'voice' is a major practical weakness of tenant participation. Tenants are a diverse group with differing needs. Tenant participation initiatives can create new alliances but equally legitimise the exclusion of minorities who become further marginalised and distanced from power. The rhetoric also does not acknowledge the legitimacy of tenants disinclined to participate. We also need to consider the underlying messages within government documentation. First, tenants' participation is seen as having a moral value: by participating in the management of their housing in the manner of owner-occupiers they acquire social capital and become 'better' tenants. Second, tenant participation is a useful policy tool in combating the degeneration of local authority estates in that it recreates consent to government and to social control. By way of illustration we outline two examples of local tenant participation initiatives and attempt to assess their success beyond narrowly constructed and limited outcomes. While some explicit outcomes of tenant participation are generally to be applauded, it may be as marginalising a form of management as the old monolithic and inefficient local authorities unless robust structures are put in place to protect the rights of individual tenants.

What is tenant participation?

Tenant participation is used in a generic sense to include a wide range of participatory activities. Using the model of the ladder (see Arnstein, 1969; Burns et al, 1994) these range from tenant consultation or information-giving at the bottom – which Arnstein describes as 'degrees of tokenism' and Burns et al as cynicism – to tenant management organisations and cooperatives, the highest 'degree of power', giving tenants total control and responsibility. The hierarchical model implicitly assumes tenants want to move up the ladder, which may not be the case. It may be more useful to look at the process of participation and evaluate according to how far the outcome is a result of real deliberation. This enables us to distinguish between a representative democratic model and a managerial one. However, what all participation activities, as understood by central and local government, have in common is that they are cooperative, collaborative or holistic (McLaverty, 1999). Tenant participation is only one element of 'voice'. Local authority tenants can express their dissatisfaction through the ballot box or other political activities such as lobbying councillors, or via redress through the courts or the local government ombudsman. These alternative forms of voice are generally individual or particularistic, although collective organised protest has been a very effective tool in the past. Public participation might be designed to empower tenants collectively through the management of their housing and is distinguishable from tenant activism before the 1980s which was usually a form of protest, confrontational in approach.

Tenant participation of one sort or another has been on the political agenda for the last 20 years with the underlying assumption that it is a 'good thing', but with very little analysis of its impact on tenants (though see Cairncross et al, 1994). There are many stakeholders involved: consumers, housing and welfare professionals, local authorities, local and central government politicians as well as secondary agencies. Consumers of social housing include active participating tenants, non-active tenants, all residents of mixed housing estates and dispossessed tenants. The professionals include housing managers, tenant participation officers, social services and education officers and police. These are described by Cohen (1985) as community-control professionals who have a variety of objectives but all have an in-built tendency to system expansion through either their professional ideology or their role in information gathering and monitoring. Local authorities may be more concerned with expenditure on maintenance and management, as well as making successful bids to central government. Councillors and Members of Parliament may be more concerned with tenant satisfaction and political power while a number of professional management companies now hold vested interests in tenant participation in order to win contracts and legitimise their activities. There are of course conflicts between groups and within groups, but we take a particular view and attempt to evaluate some of the costs and benefits for tenants. This also enables us to try to understand what governments are attempting to achieve through participation policies, particularly in the light of Mullins' observation (1998) that the rhetoric of choice is being used to mask a reality of control.

The development of tenant participation

Although tenant participation was first argued for in a political and economic planning tract in 1948 and included in Labour's manifesto of 1959, it was not until 1977 that the Department of the Environment made a systematic survey and the Labour government incorporated it into proposed legislation. The proposal was watered down in the Conservative's 1980 Housing Act which imposed on local authorities the duty to 'consult' tenants on various matters. It required councils to establish mechanisms for consultation, but did not grant any collective rights. It is not clear how far the move towards participation even at its conception was actually designed to stifle tenant activity and protest. As Cole and Furbey suggest "the absorption of tenant activists into local party structures [and] the participation of tenant representatives in housing advisory committees, … can … be construed as carrying potential to contain and 'incorporate' more troublesome tenant activity" (1994, pp 160-1).

Other reforms in the 1980 Act included the granting of individual rights which later became incorporated into the Tenant's Charter. This may be regarded as the beginning of the policy shift which moved away from treating local authority tenants as passive welfare recipients and towards regarding them as autonomous empowered responsible individuals (Le Grand, 1997). The Act was also one of the first pieces of legislation during the 1980s which sought to make welfare provision more responsive to consumer wants while at the same time trying to take power away from local authorities and other monolithic providers. Consultation was the first step towards giving tenants a *voice* which can be regarded as a necessary preliminary to entering the market as a consumer, although no collective rights existed.

An embryonic collective contractual mechanism was begun in the 1988 Act giving tenants the right to exit from local authority control and to opt for an alternative landlord through Tenants' Choice or Housing Action Trusts (HATs). This was the first collective right and represented an ideological shift. However, two points are significant. First, the acquisition of collective rights reduced the tenant's individual rights since the tenant's legal status was weakened by the transfer. Second, the legislation which gave financial incentives to tenants to vote against remaining with the local authority was hardly collaborative in spirit but rather anti-participatory and perhaps an early example of the rhetoric of participation masking a specific central government agenda. Similarly the additional collective power given by the establishment of Tenant Management Organisations in 1994 also introduced a confrontational approach as it required that tenants serve a notice on the council of their intentions even before they have considered all their options (Cowan, 1999, p 183). Further it should be remembered that the Conservative measures were motivated more by a desire to weaken local government than the empowering of local authority tenants.

New Labour superimposed yet a further dimension onto existing policies, introducing compulsory Tenant Participation Compacts from April 2000 (DETR, 1999a). The government became concerned about regeneration as part of their preoccupation with social exclusion, poor educational achievement and crime, and introduced compulsory participation as "part of the Government's longer term agenda to involve local people in shaping the future of their own communities, to make Government programmes and initiatives more responsive to local needs and aspirations, and to tackle social exclusion" (DETR, 1999a, para 1.5).

This is part of a wider attempt to rebuild society, reduce alienation and strengthen local democracy, and add legitimacy through 'participative communitarianism'. The Social Exclusion Unit constantly stresses the relationship between community governance and regeneration (SEU, 1998, 2000). However, again this policy is not a replacement but is grafted on to earlier policies. We are left with an unsatisfactory quasi-contractual arrangement, with talk about empowering tenants but actually giving very little collective power. The use of the word 'Compact' is significant. It confers no legal rights as would a contract but implies voluntary partnership and collaboration: a statement of intent rather than a legally enforceable relationship. This is an example of the government being more concerned with establishing appropriate machinery to achieve their policy goals than with legal rights. It is also concerned with establishing machinery which allows tenants to participate in the implementation of government policy rather than in policy design (Khan, 1999). At the same time the centralised and authoritarian approach has been strengthened, with more tendency towards social control as illustrated by a series of legislative initiatives bringing in introductory tenancies, strengthened grounds for possession, anti-social behaviour orders and Crime and Disorder partnerships. Participation becomes a top-down policy and may be elitist and non-inclusive.

The 2000 Green Paper pays little attention to tenant participation except as it relates to the BVFH. It does continue the discourse of tenant as consumer, with eponymous 'choice' and the emphasis on the owner-occupier as the policy ideal. The BVFH gives a further impetus to tenant participation. Best Value replaces Compulsory Competitive Tendering as the mechanism for ensuring efficiency in the delivery of local government services. Instead of market discipline operating through the competitive tendering process and profit maximisation, Best Value is designed to maximise efficiency through the four Cs – challenge, compare, consult and compete. Consult is described as central to Best Value (para 6.20) and local authorities are told to "particularly bear in mind the importance of involving tenants and residents at an early stage". The emphasis here does indicate an attempt to avoid the previous failure of state provision as unresponsive, and 'efficiency' includes responding to consumer wants as well as provision at minimum cost. The former is not easy to achieve for long-term service provision, however. Whereas a repeat purchase may indicate the consumer is pleased with the commodity, consumer satisfaction surveys are a poor surrogate measure.

Rebuilding society

Participation has become a management tool stressing community rebuilding based on communitarian ideas. Communitarianism was taken up by the New Left in the 1990s at the same time as similar ideas were being articulated by the New Right under the heading of 'Civil Society'. Both were essentially ways of reforming society and represent a reaction against individualist consumerism or Thatcher's 'no such thing as society' approach. Both contain a very strong element of moral regeneration, based on personal responsibility and obligation to others, with overtones of social control and crime reduction: "Communitarians seek to rebuild community.... What is needed, is a strengthening of bonds that tie people to one another, enabling them to overcome isolation and alienation" (Etzioni, 1995, p 2). For Etzioni, strong family values of love and care for others become replicated in society so that people become motivated by collective goals. Alternative expositions (see Daly, 1994) suggest that individuals come to realise they will benefit from the formation of a Rousseau-like 'common good'. Although rebuilding communities is obviously a desirable aim, the theory does not explain how marginalised families and single-person households on an estate, many of whom may not have shared values, will coalesce into a collective which transforms individual interests into a common good.

Again the rhetoric of citizenship has been an important part of a complex policy discourse which led to the adoption of tenant involvement policies by a wide range of social landlords in Britain. One of the myriad of potential benefits claimed for tenant involvement programmes has been their potential contribution to overcoming social exclusion. Yet singling out social housing tenants for this special treatment raises important questions about the citizenship rights of a group who are depicted as oppressed and needing empowering. Moreover, the lack of account taken of tenants' views in imposing notions such as the desirability of progression towards higher levels of control and responsibility for their housing indicates that the practice of tenant involvement has, ironically, been dominated by producer interests and the state.

Tenant protest movements

Concerns about tenant protest movements have often fuelled government participation initiatives, although there is little evidence that the mechanisms of participation were designed to give legitimacy to protest movements but rather to stifle further protest. Protest as a form of voice ranges from legitimate forms through the ballot box, opposition at council meetings and creative use of the media to more confrontational forms, such as rent strikes. Its history, as Grayson (1997) outlines, can be traced from the appalling housing conditions of the early 19th century through riots, rent strikes and squatting. Protest has often achieved improvements for tenants and the experience of protesting is empowering for those involved – however embarrassing it is for those on the receiving end. Protest is a very effective method of reminding local authority landlords of their accountability. Indeed, democratic accountability is a significant factor in many tenants wishing to stay with the local authority landlord.

Ironically it was the Conservative introduction of voluntary transfers and HATs that stimulated a fresh wave of collective protest in the late 1980s (Lusk, 1997). Woodward (1991) describes how several diverse estates in Tower Hamlets were successfully mobilised into a unified collective in opposition to the imposition of a HAT. During the 1990s there has been little effective protest, possibly due to a reduction in the strength of political opposition. Increasing fragmentation and atomisation – the very thing currently causing government concern – may be another cause. Other reasons are the increasing dependence of many tenants on Housing Benefit which renders the rent strike ineffective, and the lengthy period of strong Conservative government supporting individual values (epitomised by

Thatcher's assertion that failure is using buses over the age of 30) and not dependent for political support on tenant groups (Cairncross et al, 1994). The decline of tenants' movements can be argued to arise from the tension which we have already identified, and will return to again, between the individual nature of the property relationship between landlord and tenant and any collective action by tenants (Lowe, 1997). This may well render political accountability too fragile to achieve empowerment for tenants.

Constraints on the effectiveness of tenant participation

As we have noted, tenant participation over the last 20 years has been expected to perform a variety of diverse and sometimes contradictory tasks by government, with several stakeholders having different agendas. Empowerment, even in the limited understanding of tenant participation initiatives, represented a complete change in culture in the early 1980s. It was achieved through permissive legal structures rather than as a result of an active and articulate tenants' movement. It is therefore not surprising that it was sometimes difficult and costly to convert from a culture of passivity.

The complex evolution of tenant participation has led to a series of structural weaknesses. First it evolved at a time when a growing proportion of tenants became totally dependent on the state for their income. Riseborough (1998), for example, points out the reluctance of tenants dependent on benefits to participate in tenant involvement. In assessing the potential of current participation initiatives it is critical to bear in mind the extreme levels of disempowerment experienced by many of those dependent on social housing. In response to this a great deal of education and training of tenants has been delivered, with a National Tenant Resource Centre being set up in 1995 (see Wishart and Furbey, 1997). However, particularly with the heavy burden placed on active participants, this may be creating a small band of trained empowered people who use their skills to find an alternative exit from social housing. In any case there is no way of ensuring those active are truly representative of all residents, and in fact they may be pursuing a policy of exclusion, evicting trouble makers and devolving costs elsewhere (Somerville, 1998). On the other hand there is little recognition of the legitimacy of tenants deciding not to participate (Riseborough, 1998).

Tenant participation has also evolved at a time when local authorities have been under increasing financial constraints. Tenant power and control can be used by authorities to devolve accountability and costs, by using unpaid labour instead of professionals. It may also raise tenants' expectations in excess of what is economically viable when severe constraints are placed on local authorities. For this reason tenant involvement is often enthusiastic with a new regenerative initiative accompanied by additional finance. Interest then wanes when the money is spent. The lack of trust between tenants and their landlord as regards participation initiatives (see University of North London, 1999; Riseborough, 1998) may well be exacerbated by this. We can usefully contrast local authority tenants' experience of participation with those of HATs which are much better resourced and are aided by a new culture with new legal regimes, so overcoming traditional institutional apathy (see Evans and Long, 2000).

Currently government thinks that participation will prevent local political alienation and work as part of the 'Third Way' to form partnerships. Collaboration necessarily mollifies protest and opposition through the sharing of agendas. It must be debatable which way most strengthens local democracy. In particular tenant participation appears uncritically to endorse the anti-social behaviour agenda, allowing those in authority to blame tenants for problems. Rhetoric on tenant participation also seems to slide easily into moral frameworks, as evidenced by the language in policies and notions of people becoming 'better' tenants through participation, noted by Riseborough as 'the intrusion of morality' (Riseborough, 1998). This must be viewed critically. As Sharp (1999) describes, current models tend to enfranchise those tenants who, through their personal social capital, are properly and fully enfranchised anyway. As a consequence they further marginalise those who for a variety of reasons find it difficult to express their views.

The conflict between individual and collective rights remains unsolved. As we have seen collective rights have only been granted in the past in non-collaborative initiatives and, though this may change with Best Value regimes, it will require a great deal of energy and resources from local authorities at a time when local government self-esteem is particularly low. In addition, as Lowe (1997) points out:

> [The] individual and the collective are never very clearly separated and it is not possible to understand collective rights in isolation from the dominant framework of individual rights. Moreover, at the time when tenants' rights achieved a firmer foundation in statute through the Housing Act 1980, the primacy of individual rights was asserted as against those of a collective nature. (1997, p 151)

In order to be of value to both landlord and tenant the acquisition of collective rights may mean the relinquishing of individual rights by tenants. For example, tenants in Manchester discussed whether they should waive their statutory rights to compensation for lack of repairs in order to solve the local authority's financial problem (Richardson, 1999, p 18). Furthermore, the consumerist nature of the individual rights given to local authority tenants necessarily causes repercussions for the value of the collective rights. This applies in particular to the Right to Buy.

The impact of the Right to Buy

The 1980 Housing Act gave the local authority tenant the Right to Buy – a legally enforceable right combined with stringent financial penalties against defaulting local authorities. This fundamentally altered the local authority landlord/tenant relationship by giving individual tenants an exit route, a choice of whether to remain or quit the tenure, thereby turning them into consumers. This was truly empowering for the individual with the necessary economic resources since it enabled tenants to exercise personal and individual control over their home. Owner-occupation in England has always been regarded as a superior form of tenure and much subsequent legislation impacting on the secure tenant can be regarded as an extension of property rights converting tenants into pseudo-owners (Carr and Sefton-Green, 2000). The 'tenant as consumer' was strengthened by further legislation during the 1980s and 1990s. In addition the superiority of owner-occupation has been made explicit by every policy document since the Second World War including the current government's Green Paper (DETR/DSS, 2000, p 56).

The overwhelming success of the Right to Buy meant that very little attention was paid to other extensions of tenants' rights, and in particular very little attention was paid by tenants to their potential collective voice. As Stewart (1996) points out, the Right to Buy represented a move away from political accountability to economic accountability. Whatever one's opinion about the Right to Buy, there is no doubt that it enhanced the life choices open to council tenants in a way which no other reform of tenant status has done. In contrast, the impact of tenant participation is potentially only marginal to life choices and therefore unlikely to stimulate the requisite sacrifice of personal resources by tenants for it to succeed (Bengtsson, 1998). The extent of the impact of market or economic forces in changing the role of social housing was reduced, with most of the desirable properties having been sold and the more prosperous tenants having left the tenure. The current emphasis on tenant participation can be argued to be in response to the inevitable running out of steam of the Right to Buy. Moreover when the vast majority of tenants are dependent on the state for the payment of rent via the Housing Benefit system there is not even the residue of economic or contractual accountability.

Legal rights

The legal status of the landlord/tenant relationship impacts on tenant participation in three broad ways. Firstly, as Somerville (1998, p 244) points out "The force of civil law is a uniquely strong institutional support for those seeking greater control over their lives". In Somerville's terms the ability to decide whether or not to take your landlord to court is empowering in the fullest meaning of the word. As a form of voice it is unequivocal and peculiarly validating to have a court penalise your landlord and order specific performance of its obligations towards you.

A particular and obvious strength of legal rights is that they do not discriminate between tenants, and are equally available to all, whether members of the Tenants' Association or not. Housing law grants legal rights to tenants and licensees in general and local authority occupants in particular, from security of tenure through to the Tenant's Charter and rights to particular standards of housing enforceable through civil courts. It is not appropriate here to document the development and current scope of these rights, but they are not unproblematic, and are increasingly difficult to access. Housing law is extremely complex and most tenants are unaware of the existence of their rights and/or are unaware of their relevance to them. There is a shortage of legal expertise willing to enable tenants to enforce their rights, whereas recent reforms to the legal aid system and the civil procedure system operate to increase the exclusion of the poor with low value claims from the courts. Finally, as Karn et al (1997) point out the bundle of statutory rights given to local authority tenants operates only to modify the common law and fails to change the balance of power between landlord and tenant.

The landlord/tenant relationship could be buttressed by the law to provide an effective means of support to tenant participation, and to facilitate challenges to landlord domination of the participation agenda. Unfortunately there have been very few legal moves to increase the collective rights of tenants and the little that legislation gives is not backed up with rights to enforcement (Lowe, 1997). The law is contained in Sections 104 to 106A of the 1985 Housing Act which impose obligations on landlords to provide information about their tenancies, to make explicit their legal obligations towards their tenants, and to set out their arrangements to consult tenants on housing management issues. As Somerville (1998) points out, this legal framework does not enable tenants to insist on participation. Moreover the absence of legal duties imposed on landlords means their accountability to tenants is minimal. Participation does not ensure the necessary accountability, particularly because of certain restrictions as to scope. For example, local authorities may not adopt tenants as voting members of housing committees and the right to consult does not include financial matters. The complexities of the current balance between individual rights and collective rights proves very difficult in practice, with courts generally seeming to prefer the individual rights with which they are familiar (Stewart, 1996). The right to complain both individually and collectively needs to be given a clear legal basis and simple mechanisms should be designed to enforce those rights (as suggested in Karn et al, 1997).

The final role of the law relevant here is through seeking to uphold particular standards of behaviour, generally through the criminal law. However, eviction is essentially a punitive process. The 1996 Act introduced new initiatives combining civil and criminal elements, such as measures to deal with anti-social behaviour. Introductory tenancies – a form of probationary tenancy which does not become secure until a year of satisfactory occupation has been completed – extended grounds for possession based on nuisance committed not only by the tenant, but also by visitors and members of the tenant's family, enables the social landlord to obtain free standing injunctions against the perpetrators of anti-social behaviour. More innovative are the measures moving beyond housing sanctions and into the criminal arena – for example, in the 1998 Crime and Disorder Act anti-social behaviour attracts criminal penalties which can be obtained by the local authority. This increase in social control measures, as Cowan (1999, p 504) interprets it, is simply a continuation of local authority landlords roles with new tools. He suggests that "social housing is part of the crime control system – it is there to focus our minds on inclusion and forms part of the mechanics of 'inclusionary control'". Authoritarian measures require the consent of those being policed. Tenant participation provides a forum for the creation of that consent, with nuisance neighbours and deviant adolescents often being top of the agendas of tenant meetings. Tenant participation legitimises the redefinition of social tenants into socially acceptable tenants.

This brief survey of the law suggests that the legal accountability of landlords to tenants – a major policy platform of this government – is decreasing except in the arena of social control. We suggest this mirrors the reduction in accountability and increase in control in the other relationships we have identified between landlord and tenant. There is a danger that this shift is legitimised by tenant participation.

Two examples of regeneration initiatives built on tenant participation

In this final part, we examine two recent and contrasting participation initiatives, with a view first to evaluating the gains for tenants made as a result of participation, and secondly to see if tenant participation has been at the cost of a reduction in the other forms of voice we have identified – legal rights and protest.

Holly Street, Hackney

Completed in 1971, Holly Street was one of the last – and reputedly one of the worst – system-built estates in the UK. It consisted of nineteen medium-rise 'snake' blocks and four tower blocks. From the outside, the 'snake' blocks had a forbidding, prison-like appearance; on the inside, their long internal corridors and enclosed staircases were particularly vulnerable to burglary and muggings. A catalogue of design and construction errors included leaking roofs, condensation, heavy insect infestations and poor sound/thermal insulation. The woes of the estate were compounded by deep-seated and widespread social, economic and health problems.

Hackney Council took the decision to redevelop Holly Estate in 1992 as part of its wider Comprehensive Estates Initiative (CEI). The decision was taken against the backdrop of a rapidly worsening housing crisis in the borough and after over 10 years of severe cutbacks in capital allocations. At that time, the (Conservative) government's housing policy was directed at limiting the role of local authorities to that of enablers rather than providers of social housing, attracting private finance and promoting home ownership and tenure diversification – but as we have seen it also included mechanisms for tenant empowerment. Government policy was enforced by changes to the funding arrangements for capital investment in public housing, and the introduction of competitive bidding regimes like City Challenge and the Single Regeneration Budget.

The CEI programme required substantial resources. On Holly Street alone this amounted to £97.3 million. In order to secure this scale of funding, the council had to enter into partnership arrangements with private developers and housing associations, and to compete against other local authorities to win funding from the government's Estate Action and City Challenge programmes. The formation of a partnership representing so many different and often contradictory interests was not without difficulties. One independent observer (Jacobs, 1999) suggested that underneath the public pronouncements of cooperation and collaboration the various parties involved on Holly Street were in fact engaged on a protracted and at times acrimonious struggle for power, influence and resources.

How this battle panned out in terms of eventual redevelopment is best illustrated by looking at the eventual distribution of tenure types. Originally, Holly Street consisted of 1,145 properties under council ownership. When the redevelopment is completed in 2002, the land ownership and tenure patterns will be transformed. Nearly 20 per cent of the new development will be sold to owner–occupiers; 55 per cent transferred to housing associations; and only around 20 per cent retained by Hackney Council. Only one third of the original tenants will be rehoused in the new development (London Borough of Hackney, 1999).

The reality of tenant participation on Holly Street reflects both the wider political and economic framework within which the development emerged and was a response to particular local circumstances within a context of contradictory and often competing interests. Yet tenant participation was heavily promoted by both the government and Hackney Council as being integral to the renewal of public housing. A range of motives can be identified for this: first, the emerging consensus that the problems of social housing can be put down to the fact that its tenants were not involved in either its design or management; second, the consumerist agenda which sees participation as a mechanism to extend choice in the situation where market forces do not exist and where there is a single, monopolistic service provider; third, to satisfy the criteria of funding regimes; fourth, to act as a counterweight in negotiations with government, the council, private developers and housing associations in order to secure social and political gains; and, finally, as a good in itself to foster community relations, personal achievement and civic responsibility.

An elaborate structure of tenant participation was set up on Holly Street by the council. At its head was an elected Estate Development Committee to be "a resident steering group to oversee the renewal programme" which met fortnightly. Under the Estate Development

Committee were various sub-committees: a design sub-committee; children and young persons' interest group; housing management working group; and facilities steering group. These also met fortnightly. Wider consultation with tenants has included frequent open days, community events and art exhibitions, and questionnaire surveys. The council funded an 'independent' tenant adviser to support the participation strategy.

The heavy programme of meetings was very time consuming. While council officers and other professionals attended as part of their job, tenant representatives were expected to donate their time (and expertise) for free. Not surprisingly, very few tenants took part. Out of a resident population of 2,400, only around 50 would come along to 'one-off' estate meetings, with a much smaller core group of 8-10 regularly attending the Estate Development Committee and its sub-committees. Even then the drop-out rate through 'consultation fatigue' was high.

In practice, the influence tenants could exert was quite limited. Thus on the basic principles of the redevelopment – the overall vision, the transfer of ownership and diversification of tenure, and its physical layout – tenants do not appear to have had any significant input. Their impact on the decision-making processes can be evaluated with reference to the publication published by Hackney's CEI Initiative: *Holly Street Estate – A blueprint for success*. This provides the following examples of the impact of tenant participation:

• change in the Housing Corporation's allocation guidelines that 70 per cent of new housing properties should go to homeless persons to set aside 50 per cent for existing Holly Street residents;
• overturning the decision that children would be expected to share bedrooms with their siblings;
• pre-letting agreements that allow prospective tenants to choose fittings and fixtures;
• equalisation of rents across the five housing associations;
• the building of new properties to the 'old' Parker Morris standards.

By their nature, these changes appear to be more concessions to tenant pressure from a managerialist agenda rather than evidence of real empowerment. What this points to is a need to do further research, in particular a cost benefit analysis of the time and effort that tenants have had to put in to achieve these changes. Of course, tenants who participated may have derived a range of other benefits: fostering neighbourliness and a sense of belonging, increased self-confidence and personal development.

But these benefits cannot be assumed, and there is a need for a detailed empirical analysis. A similar analysis could usefully be extended to the other 'actors' in the redevelopment of Holly Street – the profit made by the developer; the increase in the asset bases of the various housing associations; the career development of the professionals involved – to map out the benefits that accrue, and to whom, from the development process. The observation by James and Lyon (2000), made in the context of family law policy proposals, seems apposite:

> To be effective and to realise its aims, any political ideology, be it communitarian or libertarian, must be capable of finding practical expression through the provisions of social policy and law. If, however, the moral and political agendas such as those embodied in New Labour's communitarianism are based on fundamental misunderstandings of the nature of citizen's choices and decision making processes, they seem doomed to failure. (2000, p iii)

We would argue that despite the rhetoric of tenant empowerment, the participative strategy on Holly Street was a top-down approach, imposed by the council and modelled on the council's own bureaucracy. It was established for pragmatic purposes rather than to change the power structures or challenge the entrenched inequalities experienced by the Holly Street tenants. In order for the outcomes to serve tenants' interests, there is a need for there to be an exploration of what tenants would wish to achieve and for them to be fully involved in the devising of the project (Riseborough, 1998).

Coin Street

Coin Street, a well known social housing project on the South Bank of the Thames, is an example of the most extreme form of obligatory tenant participation – tenants forfeiting security of tenure for their membership of the cooperative (as tenants of cooperatives are excluded from security of tenure legislation). The regime of Coin Street is described in *Coin Street – There is another way* ... (Coin Street Community Builders, 2000):

> All the residential accommodation on the Coin Street sites is social housing, available at affordable rents to individuals and families in housing need who can show good reason to live in the area. All the housing developments are run as co-operatives. All the tenants in a

Coin Street housing co-operative become shareholders in a company that owns the lease on the building and is responsible for maintaining its properties, collecting rents and selecting new tenants. Decisions are taken democratically, and each co-op elects its own officers to represent them. This model of social housing was chosen for a number of reasons. As well as being highly democratic, residents have a greater stake in their homes and tend to take more time and effort to ensure their properties and gardens are well maintained. As the leasehold is owned jointly by all co-op members individual tenants do not have a 'right to buy' their own homes. This means that all housing will remain available at reasonable rents to those in need. Since 1984 Coin Street has opened three housing co-ops: Mulberry, Palm and Redwood, providing over 160 high quality, affordable new homes.

The most celebrated development undertaken by Coin Street Community Builders is the OXO Tower Wharf redevelopment between the London Eye and Tate Modern (described in the *Evening Standard* as the most enviable social housing in London). Its £20 million funding was raised from the Housing Corporation, English National Heritage, private borrowing and Coin Street's own equity. The OXO Tower Wharf now has on its rooftop the OXO Tower Restaurant bar and Brasserie leased by Harvey Nichols, the profits from which subsidise the rents of the social housing below. The Wharf also contains another restaurant and retail design studios. A management company runs the non-residential parts of the estate, ensuring that the parks and riverwalk are maintained as well as taking responsibility for commercial lettings so that the quality of the tenants is maintained.

There is no doubt that the Coin Street project is inspirational and has prevented the South Bank from becoming another piece of the office block and expensive residential development jigsaw that fronts the Thames. However, there are costs for the individual tenants. First, membership of the cooperative is based on obligations to participate in the running of the cooperative. Selection depends not only on an expression of interest in participating but also on the tenants' committee being convinced that the prospective tenant has the skills necessary to participate. The benefits include a stable community with a very strong identity. Prospective tenants are clear about the Coin Street ethos, and are prepared to sacrifice autonomy for the privilege of residence. However, it does mean that only those with existing reserves of social capital are selected and there is no right not to participate. Indeed failure to participate can result in eviction, although no one to date has been evicted for this reason.

Second, tenants forfeit a range of legal rights that secure tenants under the 1985 Housing Act take for granted. Security of tenure, succession rights and the Right to Buy are not available to cooperative tenants. The decision to sacrifice these rights is understandable. The benefits are affordable, high quality housing in a very attractive setting. However, we should not underestimate the inequality of bargaining power between the prospective tenant and the cooperative. There is no similar housing available to the prospective tenant at approximately £60 per week. The cooperative on the other hand has an inexhaustible supply of potential tenants. Thus the loss of legal rights is not necessarily a decision freely entered into.

Finally, the lack of security of tenure means that the individual tenant is subject to potentially arbitrary decision making with no redress – a clear example of the costs of the loss of legal rights. It is difficult to see how these tenants have been empowered as citizens, since they do not have freedom of choice, they have lost their rights as consumers of housing as they have no means of exiting from the tenure and they are legally marginalised. Coin Street is small scale and because it has an attractive site with huge commercial and tourist potential it is sustainable. But it would be difficult to replicate in areas of urban sprawl.

Conclusion

We have argued that the value of tenant participation as a method of empowering tenants cannot be separated from the contemporaneous reduction in political, economic and legal accountability. In contrast to the Right to Buy it does not affect the balance of power between the landlord and the tenant nor does it appear to impact significantly on the life choices of tenants. It fails to enhance the collective identity of tenants, which is in any case fragile, as a result of the individual nature of property relationships in English Law and the government's reluctance to embed it properly within robust legal and political structures. Here again we can see an illuminating contrast with the Right to Buy.

We have drawn attention to two examples of good practice (Holly Street, for example, is quoted as a 'key idea' in SEU, 2000) but both indicate management models have been created and that tenant participation has been evaluated from management perspectives. In Holly Street the tenants who remained obtained some concessions and a better place to live, but this does not reflect real control of their homes any better than would be achieved by strong legal rights or collective activism. It may well be the case that some of the active participating tenants became empowered, but more research needs to be done to ascertain whether they were among those who benefited. Coin Street illustrates how enviable social housing can be acquired at the cost of legal autonomy or economic freedom. Participation becomes an obligation rather than a right.

We must also recognise that not all tenants wish to participate, and that the interests of those who do not still need articulation. Moreover it cannot be assumed that remoralising and resocialising of tenants is an inevitable consequence of tenant participation.

Tenant participation may be a useful tool for the government and/or local authority in ensuring managerial accountability and in increasing its control over the provision of social housing. We would agree with Evans and Long (2000) who point out in the context of HATs that:

> ... even multi-purpose urban regeneration vehicles must work in partnership with residents, other public bodies and voluntary and private sector bodies if they are to stand a chance of permanently improving social and economic conditions in deprived estates.... All the relevant parties in estate regeneration need to be given a more equal stake in such programmes. (p 316)

What it means to be given a stake must be worked through with tenants, and real opportunities must then be given for input into the formation of policies. The agenda needs to be democratic and not managerialist. A balance needs to be drawn between participation, protest and other legal remedies.

References

Armstrong, H. (1999) 'A new vision for housing in England', in T. Brown (ed) *Stakeholder housing – A third way*, London: Pluto.

Arnstein, S. (1969) 'A ladder of citizen participation', *Journal of American Institute of Planners*, vol 35, no 4, pp 214-24.

Bengtsson, B. (1998) 'Tenants' dilemma – on collective action in housing', *Housing Studies*, vol 13, no 1, pp 99-120.

Burns, D., Hambleton, R. and Hoggett, P. (1994) *The politics of decentralisation: Revitalising local democracy*, London: Macmillan.

Cairncross, L., Clapham, D. and Goodlad, R. (1994) 'Tenant participation and tenant power in British council housing', *Public Administration*, vol 72, pp 177-200.

Carr, H. and Sefton-Green, D. (2000) 'Citizenship and local authority tenants', Paper presented at the annual conference of the Socio-Legal Studies Association, Queens University, Belfast.

Cohen, S. (1985) *Visions of social control: crime, punishment and classification*, Cambridge: Polity.

Coin Street Community Builders (2000) *Coin Street – There is another way ...*, London: Coin Street Community Builders.

Cole, I. and Furbey, R. (1994) *The eclipse of council housing*, London: Routledge.

Cowan, D. (1999) *Housing law and policy*, Basingstoke: Macmillan.

Daly, M. (ed) (1994) *Communitarianism: A new public ethics*, Belmont, CA: Wadsworth.

DETR (Department of the Environment, Transport and the Regions) (1999a) *Tenant Participation Compacts: Consultation paper*, London: DETR.

DETR (1999b) *National framework for Tenant Participation Compacts*, London: DETR.

DETR (2000) *The Best Value in housing framework*, London: DETR.

DETR/DSS (Department of Social Security) (2000) *Quality and choice: A decent home for all*, Housing Green Paper, London: DETR/DSS.

Etzioni, A. (1995) *The spirit of community: Rights, responsibilities and the communitarian age*, London: Fontana.

Evans, R. and Long, D. (2000) 'Estate based regeneration in England: lessons from housing action trusts', *Housing Studies*, vol 15, no 2, pp 301-17.

Grayson, J. (1997) 'Campaigning tenants: a pre-history of tenant involvement to 1979', in C. Cooper and M. Hawtin (eds) *Housing, community and conflict: Understanding resident involvement*, Aldershot: Arena.

Hirschman, A.O. (1970) *Exit, voice and loyalty: Responses to decline in firms*, Cambridge: Harvard University Press.

James, A. and Lyon, C. (2000) 'Editorial', *Journal of Social Welfare and Family Law*, vol 22, no 2, pp iii-iv.

Jacobs, K. (1999) *The dynamics of local housing policy: A study of council housing renewal in the London Borough of Hackney*, Aldershot: Ashgate.

Karn, V., Lickiss, R. and Hughes, D. (1997) *Tenants' complaints and the reform of housing management*, Aldershot: Dartmouth.

Khan, U. (1999) 'Some concluding thoughts', in U. Khan (ed) *Participation beyond the ballot box: European case studies in state-citizen political dialogue*, London: UCL Press.

Le Grand, J. (1997) 'From knight to knave, from pawn to queen: the state, the market and social services', *Journal of Social Policy*, vol 26, no 2, pp 149-69.

London Borough of Hackney (1999) *Holly Street Estate – A blueprint for success*, London: London Borough of Hackney.

Lowe, S. (1997) 'Tenant participation in a legal context', in C. Cooper and M. Hawtin (eds) *Housing, community and conflict: Understanding resident involvement*, Aldershot: Arena.

Lusk, P. (1997) 'Tenants' choice and tenant management: who owns and who control social housing?', in C. Cooper and M. Hawtin (eds) *Housing, community and conflict: Understanding resident involvement*, Aldershot: Arena.

McLaverty, P. (1999) 'Towards a model of public participation', in U. Khan (ed) *Participation beyond the ballot box: European case studies in state-citizen political dialogue*, London: UCL Press.

Mullins, D. (1998) 'Rhetoric and reality in housing policy', in A. Marsh and D. Mullins (eds) *Housing and public policy: Citizenship, choice and control*, Buckingham: Open University Press.

Richardson, L. (1999) *Tackling difficult estates*, CASE/Social Exclusion Unit Seminar held at the National Tenants Resource Centre, Trafford Hall, March 1998, CASE report 4, London: Centre for Analysis of Social Exclusion, London School of Economics.

Riseborough, M. (1998) 'More control and choice for users? Involving tenants in social housing management', in A. Marsh and D. Mullins (eds) *Housing and public policy: Citizenship, choice and control*, Buckingham: Open University Press.

SEU (Social Exclusion Unit) (1998) *Bringing Britain together: A national strategy for neighbourhood renewal*, London: Cabinet Office.

SEU (2000) *National strategy for neighbourhood renewal: A framework for consultation*, London: Cabinet Office.

Sharp, C. (1999) '"Getting by" or "getting ahead"? Social networks and the regeneration of Finsbury Park', *Rising East*, vol 3, no 2, pp 92-116.

Somerville, P. (1998) 'Empowerment through residence', *Housing Studies*, vol 13, no 2, pp 233-57.

Stewart, A. (1996) *Rethinking housing law*, London: Sweet and Maxwell.

Swinney, J. (2000) 'Managing direction', *Roof*, July/August, p 20.

University of North London (1999) *Tollington initiative: Towards a community-led strategy for regeneration*, A report by University of North London for London Borough of Islington and the residents of the Tollington Initiative area.

Wishart, B. and Furbey, R. (1997) 'Training for tenants', in C. Cooper and M. Hawtin (eds) *Housing, community and conflict: Understanding resident involvement*, Aldershot: Arena.

Woodward, R. (1991) 'Mobilising opposition: the campaign against housing action trusts in Tower Hamlets', *Housing Studies*, vol 6, no 1, pp 44-56.

NINE

Developments in tenant participation: accounting for growth

Robina Goodlad

Introduction

Action on tenant participation has been one of the defining features of the Labour government's housing policy since 1997. As a consequence the government's major housing policy statement, the Green Paper *Quality and choice* (DETR/DSS, 2000), treats tenant participation – in the form of Tenant Participation Compacts – largely as "action taken" (p 9). It is considered briefly in chapter 7 on 'Raising the quality of social housing', which finishes with six paragraphs on "better management and tenant empowerment" (DETR/DSS, 2000, pp 68-9). There are no new announcements or proposals for legislation, and the concept is given only a few lines. Tenant participation remains, however, an idea with strong appeal to ministers as well as tenants and housing practitioners.

This chapter considers efforts by social and political theorists to understand and account for the phenomenon of tenant participation. Social scientists have drawn particularly on theories of power, the (welfare) state, and democracy and citizenship in attempts to explain a phenomenon that they tend to agree has grown since the 1960s or 1970s. These accounts and theories are reviewed briefly then used to interrogate the development of tenant participation, including the Labour government's programme, and the questions of what it is, whether it has grown and what the nature of that growth might mean for the status and role of tenants. But first we consider what the Labour government's tenant participation programme has been.

The changing framework since 1997

The Labour government's commitment to tenant participation has been translated into a number of initiatives (DETR, 1999a, 1999b, 1999c, 1999d, 1999e; Cole et al, 2000), the foremost of which are the development of Tenant Participation Compacts and Best Value. Compacts set out "how tenants can get involved collectively in local decisions ... ; what councils and tenants want to achieve locally ... ; and how the compact will be implemented and checked to make sure it is working properly" (DETR, 1999d, p 1). From 1 April 2000, all council landlords were expected to have reached formal agreement with tenants (representatives, presumably) on how tenants are involved in local decisions (DETR, 1999e).

Best Value is a policy intended to ensure that councils "review all the services they provide for local people and improve them by the best means available". This must be done in consultation with service users and the wider community (DETR, 1999b, p 1). Compacts and Best Value will matter to an authority's reputation and resources since councils have to report each year on how well they have operated compacts and have to set improvement targets for the following year. What they say is taken into account in the allocation of resources in the annual Housing Investment Programme (HIP) process (Cole et al, 2000).

Best Value has been extended to Registered Social Landlords (RSLs), reinforcing exhortations to engage in tenant participation (Housing Corporation, 1998). Although compacts do not apply to RSLs, their introduction is bound to influence RSL debates about Best Value, and the Housing Corporation suggests that the advice available to local authorities on compacts may assist RSLs in developing their own tenant participation strategies (Housing Corporation, 1999).

There are indications that this new regime will have more leverage over social landlords than previous exhortations and legal requirements in relation to tenant participation. For example, tenants who are dissatisfied with their landlord may make their own report. The DETR (1999e) takes a firm approach to standard setting, monitoring and evaluation. 'Core standards' are set down for tenant participation, covering housing services, resources for tenant participation, and support for tenants' groups. Monitoring and measuring performance is seen as requiring regular discussions with tenants' representatives and occasional surveys of tenants. An appendix lists recommended 'good practice indicators' and 'evidence' in relation to tenant participation policy and strategy; opportunities and support for tenant participation; and tenant participation delivery, monitoring and review. The latter, however, is something on which "few local authorities had advanced very far" (Cole et al, 2000, p 22) in 1998/99.

Political science provides ways of understanding these developments: why they occur; how significant they are; and what they represent for tenants, landlords and the state.

Understanding tenant participation

Theories of democracy and citizenship

Housing and other policy areas have been affected by changing ideas about the nature of democracy since the 1960s. Indeed housing has been a rich field in which to explore the "ambiguous and inconsistent accounts" in which "key terms" such as political participation were contested (Held, 1996, p xi). The development of democracy in representative forms in the 19th and 20th centuries made the conduct of politics in nation-states both feasible and accountable but did not clarify the exact role of citizens. The restriction of citizenship to the "selection of political representatives who alone can make political decisions" (Held, 1996, p 119) became increasingly contested in the last third of the 20th century and the role of citizen-consumers was particularly contentious. Tensions between the roles of elected representatives and active citizen-consumers have featured in many accounts of public administration and citizen participation since this period (for example, Boaden et al, 1982).

In housing studies, many authors refer to this sort of theory in their accounts, stressing the way that representative democracy has been challenged by direct participation. Tenant participation can thus be seen as an attempt to provide a new answer in contemporary conditions to the question about the role of citizen-consumers (Cairncross et al, 1997). Birchall (1992) draws on a communitarian strand of political theory in promoting the idea of powerful tenants running their own housing but recognises that there are several stakeholders in housing provision in addition to tenants and councillors. He explains tenant participation as the manifestation of a struggle between interests such as private developers, direct labour organisations and local political parties in which the subservient consumer interest has been appealed to, manipulated and redefined.

Some accounts, particularly in social policy, stress the changing relationship between citizen-consumers and the state in the creation of welfare. This helps explain why participation emerged from the creation of the welfare state viewed as a set of social rights of citizenship (Cairncross et al, 1997). These rights entitled citizens to decent housing, education, health services and secure incomes irrespective of position in the labour market in the post-war period. However, the services that accompanied these rights were highly bureaucratic and dominated by professionals. This method of delivery was challenged from the Right and Left simultaneously from the late 1960s. Neo-liberal theorists saw the dominance of professional and bureaucratic power as subverting individual freedom. A different form of participation – as consumers in markets or quasi-markets – was the route to liberty and welfare. At the same time, however, "new forms of social, cultural and political movements" also emerged (Clarke and Newman, 1997, p 9). These movements have been seen as challenging "the notion of citizenship by demanding full political and civil rights to all, regardless of sex, ethnic origin or immigrant status". What is required is not just an extension of the social rights of citizenship but "an insistence that such provision is responsive and flexible to the specific expressed needs of oppressed or disadvantaged groups" (Williams, 1989, p 206). In addition, by the 1980s, writings on 'new public management' saw a coalescence of support for consumer involvement arising from the overlap between political and managerial philosophies: "managers, civil servants and politicians increasingly defined good management as management which satisfied present consumers" (Goodlad, 1999, p 248).

Theories of the state

For liberal political theory, a neutral state mediates between interest groups that might include tenants and private developers. Yet, as Hague (1990) suggests, this liberal pluralist description does not describe well the structured patterns of inequality that characterise social housing. Alternative structural theories have therefore influenced housing theorists and the role of the state in a capitalist society has posed a puzzle, particularly for analysts in the Marxist tradition. If, as Marx argued, the state cannot escape its dependence on "those who own and control the productive process" (Held, 1996, p 134), why should capitalism allow the state to make any concessions to improve the status of citizens, such as the promotion of citizen participation, unless it is in the interests of capital? This leads some theorists – and some practitioners – to distrust any state action to promote tenant participation, on the grounds it must be in the interests of capital, theorised as: "incorporation of tenant activity by the state" (Riseborough, 1998, pp 239-40). In this analysis, the more tenant participation is offered, the more it is to be distrusted.

For other theorists, however, the answer lies in the notion of a state that is relatively autonomous of capital. This can mean the state playing a role against capital during the transition to a new political-economic system. Hague, for example, argues that "it was the developing fiscal crisis in the 1970s and the particular problem of escalating public housing construction and maintenance costs which can credibly be claimed to have first persuaded the state to endorse the virtues of involving tenants in the running of their housing estates" (1990, pp 253-4). Yet he does not restrict himself to a purely economic analysis: "political and cultural structures" appear to be at least as important in the development of tenant participation and participation has "the potential to raise consciousness and to change social relations" (p 254).

Power

Hague's emphasis on social relations touches on the key social science concept of power. Few accounts of tenant participation ignore power and some, for example Somerville (1998) and Cairncross et al (1989, 1997) feature it strongly. To use it successfully in any analysis of tenant participation, social scientists have to say what they mean by this slippery concept, which remains one of the social sciences' most contested.

Several approaches to defining power exist. One view sees it as deriving from legitimate authority, including the law, so that in the democratic society of post-war Britain, tenants would accept the decisions of their landlord because of the power of the council derived from electoral politics. More recently, the changes in the law that have given tenants certain rights to information, consultation and redress can be seen as changing the balance of power slightly in favour of tenants. Yet, this is hardly adequate as an explanation of the growth of tenant participation since it does not show why this change occurred, although it helps to explain the resistance of some councillors to the idea of tenant participation.

The dominant approach understands power as someone having power over another. Power is therefore the capacity to carry out one's will regardless of resistance; or the capacity to get someone to do something they would not otherwise do. To be powerful is to get what one wants. Here we can begin to see that power may be institutionalised in the authority of councillors or officers. This would be most apparent in situations of conflict and hence much research into power and who holds it has concentrated on specific decisions, attempting to establish who was powerful from evidence about the outcome of a decision-making process: "the locus of power is determined by seeing who prevails in cases of decision-making where there is an observable conflict" (Lukes, 1974, p 1). A conflict of preferences is assumed to reflect a conflict of interests: in the field of tenant participation, for example, tenants' desire to achieve lower rents and landlords' desire to increase them shows the difference in the interests of tenants and landlords.

This – Lukes' 'one-dimensional' view of power – may serve well as an approach to detecting power in certain cases of tenant participation, but Lukes has demonstrated that it may not always suffice. The difficulty he starts with is that people may not get what they want if they are prevented from expressing their grievances in the political system. He draws on a famous paper 'The two faces of power' by Bachrach and Baratz (1962) to elaborate a "second dimensional view of power". This stresses the issue of control over the agenda of politics and the way issues are kept off the agenda or out of the political process. The "two-dimensional view of power … allows for consideration of the ways in which decisions are prevented from being taken on potential issues over which there is an observable conflict of (subjective) interests, seen as embodied in express policy preferences and sub-political grievances" (p 20). This dimension of power can be illustrated very easily in tenant participation by examples such as tenants seeking to place dampness or disrepair on the agenda for debate.

Lukes, however, is not satisfied that this is a sufficient approach to studying power. He therefore provides a third dimension of power that emphasises the capacity of some to shape the preferences of others to a false or manipulated consensus. Power may be used to shape and modify desires and beliefs in a way that is contrary to people's own interests. People may be "a product of a system that works against their own interests" (p 34) and "is it not the supreme exercise of power to get another or others to have the desires you want them to have – that is to secure their compliance by controlling their thoughts and desires?" (Lukes, 1974, p 23). This means we cannot rely on tenants, for example, always to feel or express their preferences or grievances. This makes it hard to see how power of this kind can be detected. It requires some agreed view to be taken of what *is* in people's (best) interests so that power can be traced. Yet views on that vary, as the continuing debates about stock transfer demonstrate, and ultimately a stance is taken on the basis of values or theories. Lukes has therefore been criticised for a presumptuous stance, one that would see tenants as not knowing what is in their own interests. Coincidentally, this view, if held by professionals, would be criticised for its arrogance by exponents of this Lukesian third dimension of power.

These three views or dimensions of power continue to be influential but they have been challenged by another theoretical approach. Clegg argues that instead of providing a departure from previous analysts of power, Lukes' third dimension is the latest in a 'central tradition' stemming from the work of Hobbes, which appealed to modern concerns with causality and precise measurement. From Hobbes to Lukes, power is seen as "the negation of the power of others" (Clegg, 1989, p 4). In contrast, Clegg, goes back to the earlier work of Machiavelli, whose conception of power was "imprecise, contingent, strategic and organizational" (Clegg, 1989, p 4). In this account, power is "contingent on the strategic competencies and skills of actors who would be powerful" (1989, p 33). It is inherent in relationships, not in actors, as the 'central tradition' assumes. Lukes is concerned with what power *is*; Clegg is concerned with what power *does*.

This account of power leaves more open the nature of power achieved by tenants, and stresses issues such as resources, collaboration and collective action as tactical or strategic weapons in the continuing 'game' of housing provision and management. This more fluid view of power is used by Cairncross et al (1997) to analyse the tactics and resources deployed by tenants, councillors and housing managers in the game of tenant participation in the 1980s and 1990s. This analysis acknowledges the role of actors not directly involved in the game, such as central government, who may be crucial in influencing the rules and the capacities of actors, for example through providing new legislation. Other factors, however, such as the relative exclusion of social tenants from the political and administrative system, or the sharing of responsibility for housing development with funders, may mean that apparently far-reaching forms of tenant participation or 'control' may not have enabled tenants to achieve what they want. This analysis is helpful in explaining why tenant participation may not be easily amenable to development by legislation and in showing that its development is not a simple linear process of onward and upward.

Having briefly reviewed theoretical writing about tenant participation, we now use these theories to interrogate the questions of what tenant participation is, how it has developed, whether that development constitutes growth and what that means for tenants.

The development of tenant participation

Accounts that start with what motivated tenants to participate tend to stress theories of the state. For example, Hague considers what led the state to respond to an "unprecedented level of public sector tenants' activity in the years from 1968-73" (1990, p 246). In contrast, accounts that stress local or central government action tend to rely on theories of democracy. From the early 1970s some local authorities sought new forms of engagement that extended beyond the ballot box and sporadic contact to more formal structures (Richardson, 1977). This followed developments in citizen participation in other local government services such as town planning, which revealed a tension between individual and collective interests (Boaden et al, 1982).

Tenant participation at estate level has been a feature since the 1970s, often arising from attempts by tenants or landlords to improve conditions in the worst estates (Cairncross et al, 1989; SEU, 2000). The 1993 Leasehold Reform, Housing and Urban Development Act gave tenants collectively the right to take over management of their housing from a council landlord. This followed almost 20 years after legislation in 1975, which made provision for tenant management cooperatives to be created in council housing. Cooperatives have been lauded by communitarians distrustful of state control and condemned by structuralists distrustful of states that want to divest control. In practice, however, tenant management cooperatives and estate management boards have been set up where local authorities have promoted and assisted their development (Birchall, 1992; Clapham and Kintrea, 1992; Goodlad, 2000).

Most theorists stress the potential importance of formal or legal rights and many point to the failures in turning legal rights into substantive rights. A right to consultation was a demand of the tenants' movement in the 1970s. In 1980, the Housing Act gave secure tenants in England and Wales this right in relation to housing management matters and improvement programmes, but not rent levels. The early effects were limited. Kay et al (1986) reported that only 50 per cent of authorities met the deadline for publishing their consultation schemes; a further 31 per cent met a new deadline a year later. As many as 44 per cent had failed to consult tenants over management changes. Eight years later, the rights introduced by the 1980 Act were reduced in relation to housing association tenants but the 'Tenant's Guarantee' drawn up by the Housing Corporation encouraged housing associations to replicate secure tenants' statutory rights in contract. The model tenancy agreement of the National

Federation of Housing Associations included provision for consultation (Cairncross et al, 1989).

The 1988 Housing Act also contained the Tenants' Choice legislation which gave public sector tenants the right to change their landlord. However, "Council tenants made little use in an explicit sense of the Tenants' Choice provisions, with a reported total of only 981 homes in England being transferred" (Somerville, 1998, p 245). The provision was repealed by the 1996 Housing Act. Birchall (1992) pays tribute to both main theoretical traditions of power to argue that the major effect of the 1988 legislation is that it gave tenants a lever, helping to encourage joint discussions about how to improve services and conditions. Cairncross et al (1997) see similar effects in the impending introduction of Compulsory Competitive Tendering (CCT) for housing management following the 1988 Local Government Act. Another cogent illustration of power in negotiation is the improved tenancy conditions and investment that have followed voluntary transfer by public landlords (Birchall, 1992; Mullen et al, 1997). Within identical legal frameworks, some tenants are able to achieve more than others if their landlords are weakened by external factors such as the need to wind up a new town development corporation (Goodlad and Scott, 1996).

Other rights secured by tenants in the 1980s and 1990s improved the flow of information from landlords. The 1989 Local Government and Housing Act supplemented the information requirements of the 1980 Housing Act by giving tenants the right to receive annual reports on housing management performance. The Audit Commission, following the introduction of the Citizen's Charter in 1991 (HMSO, 1991), placed additional information requirements on authorities. For housing associations the process has been similar, with the Housing Corporation's requirements converging with those for council housing (Niner, 1998). A "major stimulus" for housing associations "was provided by the Housing Corporation's *Tenant Participation Strategy* in 1992" (Riseborough, 1998, p 226). These rights have been seen as arising from consumerist developments in public management that forged a new set of expectations about the relationship between citizen–consumers and the state, but they can also be seen as consistent with changes in democratic practices (Goodlad, 1999).

Growth?

Although accounts of tenant participation over the last 20 years have claimed that it is growing, these claims are not self-evidently justified, given the general decline in the condition and status of council housing. Comparisons of the incidence of tenant participation over time are difficult because measuring the incidence requires a prior judgement about what it *is* and an assumption that it can be measured in terms that are easily quantified. In addition, legislative and institutional change muddies the picture. It is impossible to achieve directly comparable data over a 20-year period. However, researchers have addressed some issues in similar enough terms to provide an impression of change over time if interpreted carefully.

The first measure to review is local authority support for tenants' associations. This was unusual in the early 1980s, with 11 per cent of English authorities reporting that they provided grants, including 'start-up grants' to tenants' associations (Kay et al, 1986). In the late 1980s, little had changed. Cairncross et al report that, in England, Scotland and Wales, 8 per cent of authorities provided starter grants and 8 per cent provided other grants. Over three quarters (76 per cent) provided no support at all (1997). However, by 1991, Bines et al reported 50 per cent of local authorities and 66 per cent of housing associations provided some form of support to tenants' groups. Larger landlords of both types were more likely to provide support. Almost 3 in 10 local authorities (29 per cent) employed specialist staff to promote tenant participation (1993, p 73). An analysis of 1999 Department of the Environment, Transport and the Regions data shows continued growth in the proportion of authorities providing support, with 38 per cent of authorities providing starter grants and 44 per cent providing annual grants. Two thirds (65 per cent) supported external training for tenants and three quarters (77 per cent) supported access to independent advice (Cole et al, 2000).

Turning to evidence of tenant participation structures, research published in 1977 found that 12 per cent of English authorities had formal schemes for tenant participation (including tenant involvement in housing committees or sub-committees, advisory committees and regular discussion meetings between councillors or officers and tenants' representatives) (Richardson, 1977). By 1986/87, 44 per cent of authorities in Britain claimed a formal scheme for tenant participation (Cairncross et al, 1990). Comparison with the 1991 study showed that the proportion of authorities with regular discussion meetings had increased from 35 per cent in 1986/87 to 47 per cent and the proportion with joint advisory committees had increased from 23 per cent to 32 per cent (Cairncross et al, 1997; Bines et al, 1993). Bines et al also found also that housing associations in England were more likely than local authorities to have formal structures for tenant participation that involved tenant representation on committees. Data available to Cole et al does not make direct comparison possible, but their finding that half of English authorities (50 per cent) report tenants were involved on formal council committees in 1998-99 suggests that the trend continues upwards.

Significantly, the subject matter of discussions between tenants and landlords has widened to encompass issues tenants want to discuss as well as issues landlords are concerned about. In 1981, Kay et al found four local authorities – all London boroughs – that said they would consult over rent levels (1986). By 1986/87, Cairncross et al (1990) report that 45 per cent of London boroughs, 5 per cent of metropolitan districts and 9 per cent of non-metropolitan districts claimed to have consulted tenants about rent levels. By 1999, 48 per cent of authorities overall reported that tenant participation takes place on setting rent levels (Cole et al, 2000). The figure rises to 85 per cent for London boroughs and drops to 43 per cent for rural authorities, with 72 per cent of urban authorities saying that tenant participation takes place. This pattern of a higher incidence of tenant participation in more urban areas is found in successive surveys.

From 1999 data, Cole et al summarised:

> ... it seems that many local authorities have been steadily broadening their 'arena of engagement' with tenants, developing council-wide consultation processes, tenants' representation on working parties and committees, joint tenant-officer training and so on – more a part of their 'normal business' than a special accessory or set of techniques. (2000, p 2)

Cole et al's conclusions arise from qualitative as well as quantitative research, thus adding to their credibility. While it would be hard to disagree with the view that opportunities for tenant participation have grown, the question of what more structures mean for tenants is still open. To assist in answering that, the meaning of and wider context within which it has developed are examined.

Defining tenant participation

So far the term tenant participation has been used without explanation. Yet agreement on its meaning is crucial to achieving consensus about its incidence and effects. Riseborough distinguishes three approaches by social scientists to conceiving of tenant involvement. First, it is seen as a mutual partnership, as in the definition by the Tenant Participation Advisory Service for England and the Institute of Housing supplied for the first 'good practice' guide for managers: "a two-way process involving sharing of ideas, where tenants are able to influence decisions and take part in what is happening" (Cairncross et al, 1989, p 19). Implicit in this definition is a view that the views of councillors can be mediated by the involvement of tenants in debates, an approach that is more sympathetic to the notion of what power *does* than what power *is*. Second, participation is understood as a "continuum or hierarchy leading to ever greater levels of control (and responsibility) by tenants" (Riseborough, 1998, p 223). Riseborough paraphrases a number of such continua into a six-step schema: provision of information; consultation; co-option; delegated power to tenant/community groups; tenant/community action; tenant/citizen community control. This approach follows Lukes more closely than Clegg and has dominated much of the literature on tenant participation, though there are serious difficulties with its over-simplification of complex phenomena and its apparent assumption that tenants always should be suspicious of participation. This assumption, we can now see, arises at least in part from structuralist suspicions of the state. Third, tenant participation can be seen as being an accountability mechanism. This third approach borrows from recent debates about the development of public management and democracy to stress the need for special measures beyond the ballot box to ensure two-way communication between tenants and landlords.

A difficulty with these approaches is that they do not provide clarity about what actions and events constitute tenant participation. At first sight a hierarchy such as Riseborough's with "provision of information" as Step 1 and "Tenant/citizen community control" as Step 6 (1998, p 223) seems to overcome this. But this approach equally does not help us see whether techniques, such as tenants serving on committees, is to be seen as illustrating 'consultation' or 'co-option', for example, or some other 'step'.

In an attempt to overcome these difficulties, Cairncross et al (1989, 1997) favour a disaggregation into three dimensions: structures (and methods), processes and objectives. Possible processes include: providing information to tenants; seeking information from tenants; listening; consultation; dialogue; choice; control (over one or more aspects of housing). There is explicit recognition that these are not mutually exclusive categories: for example, information flows are a necessary part of all other processes. Combining different elements of each of these three dimensions will produce different types of tenant participation. In other words, specific examples of tenant participation can be placed at a specific point or points on three different dimensions. This avoids confusing the structures or techniques – such as tenants serving on committees (which can be easily measured) – with what actually takes place on committees, which cannot easily be measured without qualitative data. This suggests that common indicators of tenant participation, which usually feature structures or techniques rather than processes, should be treated with scepticism and not be taken necessarily to imply anything about the process, outcome or effect of particular methods, techniques and structures for effective tenant involvement. We should not assume that power has been exercised in line with what tenants want or even that they have had an effective voice. This approach follows Clegg in its emphasis on the fluidity of power and the tactics and resources deployed by tenants, councillors and housing managers in the game of tenant participation.

Coincidentally this approach provides a route to assessing the effects of tenant participation, understood as intended or unintended outcomes of the processes or structures. A key distinction can be made between effects of the process of participation on participants' attitudes and knowledge and the material effects on housing and housing policy. Some definitions of participation lead away from any consideration of the latter.

The context for tenant participation

Having established that tenant participation has become more common and that different definitions lead to different approaches to considering its effects, we need finally to enhance the fairly sterile picture of the relationship between tenants and social landlords provided so far. This requires reference to the recent historical context of tenant participation, as many theoretical accounts show.

The party political context for tenant participation has been broadly favourable since the 1970s. On the Left, participation was seen as a remedy for the neglect of the citizen-consumer's views in the early development of the welfare state: an extension to the rights of citizenship established in the years after 1945. On parts of the Left, however, many forms of participation were disliked – they incorporated tenants into the dilemmas and tensions involved in managing inadequate resources or they removed decisions from the only true, legitimate arbiters – elected representatives. On the Right, in the 1980s and 1990s, tenant participation, as consumerism, was part of an attempt to replicate the benefits of the market in public service delivery through market research and customer care techniques and, more radically, through the development of a quasi-market following the 1988 Act (Bramley, 1993). However, tenant participation is insufficient to satisfy some political philosophies. For example, on the Right (Henney, 1985, for example) and the Left (Clapham, 1989, for example) there were those for whom tenant participation was not the objective: tenant 'control' was the goal.

As participation grew, significant ideological differences in attitudes to the nature and role of the state in the provision of housing ran in parallel. Owner-occupation became the tenure of first choice for most. Between December 1988 and March 1999, 72 local authorities ended their landlord role in a programme of stock transfers mainly to RSLs (Wilcox, 1999). However, the size of the social rented sector declined as growth in housing association stocks in no way compensated for decline in council stocks. The characteristics of people living in the sector changed too. The proportion of 'heads of household' in full-time employment declined by more than half to 23 per cent in 1998/89 from 52 per cent in 1977/78. There is a lower incidence of people in middle age ranges. The sector is characterised by benefit dependency. The Green Paper estimates that it will require £19 billion to rectify disrepair in the council sector. The worst estates of social rented housing appear to compound the social exclusion of those outside the labour market with physical isolation and environmental degeneration. As the post-war mixed economy of housing provision became predominantly a market-based system, the social rented sector in Britain demonstrated "a much narrower social base, with a much stronger association with those on the margins of the labour market than in the past" (Murie, 1997, p 450). This part of the context is less propitious for the development of tenant participation: studies of political participation among British adults show that many of the socio-economic characteristics associated with least participation are found disproportionately among social housing tenants (Parry et al, 1992). Furthermore, the evidence about housing conditions suggests that tenant participation in council housing has not necessarily led to improved housing or environmental conditions in the face of public spending restraint and polarisation.

As well as influencing the size and character of the social rented sector, the ideology that drove restructuring of the housing system also affected the ways in which remaining social housing was managed, posing a challenge to housing managers and other public sector managers. "Managerialism" played a role "both as an ideology that legitimates the development of new organisational forms and relationships and as the *practical* ideology of being businesslike that promises to make the new arrangements work" (Clarke and Newman, 1997, p 32, emphasis in original). The 'new public management' that emerged was characterised by concepts and themes such as 'efficiency', 'downsizing and decentralisation', 'excellence' and 'public service' (Ferlie et al, 1996; Goodlad, 1999). Particularly relevant were the critiques of bureaucratic (insensitive and unresponsive) and professional (arrogant) approaches to service delivery; the belief that markets and competition would secure welfare as well as efficiency; and the use of fragmented or dispersed organisational forms in which traditional notions of accountability were challenged. Other themes include changes to accounting methods in the name of greater transparency and consumerism. This provided a favourable context for certain forms of tenant participation, sometimes as a defensive reaction by local authorities, sometimes in response to government direction. Several authors, therefore, place the policy changes that followed the 1987 General Election as particularly significant in encouraging local authorities to engage in tenant participation.

In summary, the context for the development of tenant participation has not all been favourable. Several overlapping developments have proceeded hand-in-hand or in tension with each other. These can be summarised as: the rejection of representative democracy as an adequate defence of citizens' interests; the growth of the 'new public management'; the use of market and quasi-market mechanisms to replace traditional welfare models; the redefinition of the meaning of professionalism; the development of consumerism; and the polarising effect of housing tenure and welfare restructuring which has left tenants both more involved in housing management but simultaneously less likely to be strong negotiators within contemporary welfare debates. Tenant participation therefore illustrates well the key distinction between formal and substantive citizenship rights (Goodlad, 1999).

Conclusion

This chapter has examined the development of tenant participation over the last 20 years from the perspective of social scientists who have seen it as a phenomenon in which new power relationships have developed at the intersection between welfare state restructuring and developments in citizenship and public management. Legal change is seen mainly as following from social, economic and political change but the law can also be a resource supporting the renegotiation of relationships. The evidence and theories reviewed in this chapter suggest that in social housing a new citizenship right to consultation is becoming firmly established, 20 years after the 1980 Housing Act first gave secure tenants such a statutory right. We have seen, however, that more structures may not mean more powerful tenants. Yet the growth of structures can constitute resources that those who would be powerful operate to their advantage. The changed role for tenants has not resulted in a generally improved status, confirming that caution about the potential of tenant participation alone to secure structural change is justified.

It is not clear how far the election of the Labour government in 1997 has altered the policy environment in relation to tenant participation. The context of a restructuring housing system continues with the substitution or addition of private capital to fund housing development programmes. Council housing continues to decline on a scale greater than the replacement rate achieved by RSL housing and its social base is unlikely to alter significantly. Fragmentation continues with the creation of new social landlords and stock transfers continue unabated. Consumerism is as strong a strand in the 'modernisation of local government' agenda (DETR, 1998) as it ever was for the Conservatives. There are 'important differences' between the Compulsory Competitive Tendering and BestValue regimes (Boyne, 1999, p 7), especially in relation to the conditions applying to competition, but these are unlikely to affect the arrangements for tenant participation significantly. BestValue pushes social landlords towards tenant participation with a blend of carrot and stick that is likely to be about as effective as the measures used by the previous government: that is, fairly effective. "Compacts will bring about real and lasting changes in the relationship between council landlords and tenants" (DETR, 1999e). That this is an objective of current policy is an interpretation it would be hard to draw from a bare reading of the legislation. Social theory helps us to see what it might mean, why it might be desired and what its significance might be. We will understand the development of tenant participation in the future better with the help that comes from theories of democracy and citizenship, theories of the welfare state and theories of power, just as we have done in the past.

References

Bachrach, P. and Baratz, M. (1962) 'The two faces of power', *American Political Science Review*, vol 56, pp 947-52.

Bines, W., Kemp, P., Pleace, N. and Radley, C. (1993) *Managing social housing*, London: HMSO.

Birchall, J. (1992) 'Council tenants: sovereign consumers or pawns in the game?', in J. Birchall (ed) *Housing policy in the 1990s*, London: Routledge.

Boaden, N., Goldsmith, M., Hampton, W. and Stringer, P. (1982) *Public participation in local services*, Harlow: Longman.

Boyne, G. (ed) (1999) *Managing local services: from CCT to Best Value*, London: Frank Cass.

Bramley, G. (1993) 'Quasi-markets and social housing', in J. Le Grand, and W. Bartlett, *Quasi-markets and social policy*, London: Macmillan.

Cairncross, L., Clapham, D. and Goodlad, R. (1989) *Tenant participation in housing management*, Coventry and Salford: Institute of Housing/TPAS.

Cairncross, L., Clapham, D. and Goodlad, R. (1990) *The pattern of tenant participation in council housing management*, Discussion Paper no 31, Glasgow: Centre for Housing Research.

Cairncross, L., Clapham, D. and Goodlad, R. (1997) *Housing management, consumers and citizens*, London: Routledge.

Clapham, D. (1989) *Goodbye council housing?*, London: Unwin Hyman.

Clapham, D., and Kintrea, K. (1992) *Housing co-operatives in Britain*, Harlow: Longman.

Clarke, J. and Newman, J. (1997) *The managerial state*, London: Sage Publications.

Clegg, S. (1989) *Frameworks of power*, London: Sage Publications.

Cole, I., Hickman, P., Milward, L., Reid, B., Slocombe, L. and Whittle, S. (2000) *Tenant participation in England: A stocktake*, Sheffield: Centre for Regional Economic and Social Research, Sheffield Hallam University.

DETR (Department of the Environment, Transport and the Regions) (1998) *Modern local government: In touch with the people*, London: DETR.

DETR (1999a) *Tenant Participation Compacts: Consultation paper*, London: DETR.

DETR (1999b) *Best Value in housing: A guide to tenants and residents*, London: DETR.

DETR (1999c) *Developing good practice in tenant participation*, London: DETR.

DETR (1999d) *Tenant Participation Compacts: A guide for tenants*, London: DETR.

DETR (1999e) *National framework for Tenant Participation Compacts*, London: DETR.

DETR/DSS (Department of Social Security) (2000) *Quality and choice: A decent home for all*, Housing Green Paper, London: DETR/DSS.

Ferlie, E., Ashburner, L., Fitzgerald, L. and Pettigrew, A. (1996) *The new public management in action*, Oxford: Oxford University Press.

Goodlad, R. (1999) 'Housing management matters: citizenship and managerialism in the new welfare market', *Netherlands Journal of Housing and the Built Environment*, vol 14, no 3, pp 241-56.

Goodlad, R. (2000) *From public to community housing? Scottish experiences and prospects*, London: Forum on the Future of Social Housing, IPPR.

Goodlad, R. and Scott, S. (1996) 'Housing and the Scottish new towns: a case study of policy termination and quasi-markets', *Urban Studies*, vol 33, no 2, pp 317-35.

Hague, C. (1990) 'The development and politics of tenant participation in British council housing', *Housing Studies*, vol 5, no 4, pp 242-56.

Held, D. (1996) *Models of democracy*, Oxford: Polity.

Henney, A. (1985) *Trust the tenant: Devolving municipal housing*, London: Centre for Policy Studies.

HMSO (1991) *Citizen's Charter*, London: HMSO.

Housing Corporation (1998) *Making consumers count: Tenant participation – The next five years*, London: The Housing Corporation.

Housing Corporation (1999) *Best Value for registered social landlords*, London: The Housing Corporation.

Kay, A., Legg, C. and Foot, J. (1986) *The 1980 tenants rights in practice*, London: City University.

Lukes, S. (1974) *Power: A radical view*, Basingstoke: Macmillan.

Mullen, T., Scott, S., Fitzpatrick, S. and Goodlad, R. (1997) *Tenancy rights and repossession rates in theory and practice*, Edinburgh: Scottish Homes.

Murie, A. (1997) 'The social rented sector, housing and the welfare state in the UK', *Housing Studies*, vol 12, no 4, pp 437-61.

Niner, P. (1998) 'Enhancing citizenship, promoting choice or reinforcing control', in A. Marsh and D. Mullins (eds) *Housing and public policy: Citizenship, choice and control*, Buckingham: Open University Press.

Parry, G., Moyser, G. and Day, N. (1992) *Political participation and democracy in Britain*, Cambridge: Cambridge University Press.

Richardson, A. (1977) *Tenant participation in council housing management*, London: DoE.

Riseborough, M. (1998) 'More control and choice for users? Involving tenants in social housing management', in A. Marsh and D. Mullins (eds) *Housing and public policy: Citizenship, choice and control*, Buckingham: Open University Press.

SEU (Social Exclusion Unit) (2000) *National framework for neighbourhood renewal: A framework for consultation*, London: Cabinet Office.

Somerville, P. (1998) 'Empowerment through residence', *Housing Studies*, vol 13, no 2, pp 233-57.

Wilcox, S. (1999) *Housing finance review 1999/2000*, Coventry and London: Chartered Institute of Housing and Council of Mortgage Lenders.

Williams, F. (1989) *Social policy: A critical introduction: Issues of race, gender and class*, Cambridge: Polity Press.

Anti-social behaviour

Introduction

During the 1990s the hitherto largely unrecognised phenomenon of anti-social behaviour became common currency within the media and political discourse. There were popular television programmes entitled 'Neighbours from Hell', policy documents and legislative responses. Much had already been written about anti-social behaviour by the Social Exclusion Unit and the Home Office by the time that the government published its Housing Green Paper. Partly as a consequence of the earlier activity the Green Paper has relatively little to say about anti-social behaviour. Nonetheless, anti-social behaviour has arguably become a key driver behind housing policy and innovative housing management techniques.

Yet, as both authors in this section point out, there is a lack of clarity about what actually constitutes anti-social behaviour. Nobody denies that there are real problems but, as Caroline Hunter makes clear, without an answer to such a basic question, "defining a solution seems impossible". For Pauline Card, on the other hand, this is part of a broader shift in the notion of a welfare state towards the development of a marginalised and problematised population which is required to be controlled. Thus, rather than concentrating on the nature of the acts involved, governmental responses to anti-social behaviour have concentrated on *populations*.

Such a concentration on populations neatly links in to the intersection between anti-social behaviour and housing. On one level, anti-social behaviour is no more related to housing than (say) burglary. Certainly, anti-social behaviour raises important questions about the relationship between civil and criminal law and about the importance of labelling, but it says little if anything about housing. How then has housing become implicated in this discussion? Early policy documents and media discussion linked the problems of anti-social behaviour to tenure, more particularly social housing. It became linked to a series of discourses which characterised occupants of social housing almost as anti-citizens with the tenure itself regarded as, in Card's elegant phrase, "a spatial segregation of the marginalised". Thus, 'anti-social behaviour' can be regarded as a tool through which a particular population housed in a particular tenure can be managed.

Successive governments have provided a variety of tools to manage the situation, some of which are housing- and tenure-specific, and some not. Hunter's provocative question – can law be the answer? – highlights a fundamental socio-legal issue about the role and relevance of law. The chapter shows how the law is used by social housing managers to deal with anti-social behaviour, and discusses some of the implications from the recent case law in this burgeoning area. As regards the former, research suggests that social housing managers are implementing the law differently and sometimes for extraneous reasons (such as, for example, a frustration with other agencies or the support needs of the perpetrator). For Hunter, the response to anti-social behaviour can be viewed not as a shift in housing management techniques, but rather as a continuity of social control techniques of the occupants of social housing.

Although their reasons are different, both chapters end with a discussion of alternative techniques for coping with anti-social behaviour, drawing attention particularly to the report of the Social Exclusion Unit's Policy Action Team 8. This report acknowledges that anti-social behaviour is not tenure-specific and tentatively suggests various methods of dealing with it in the private sector. Hunter is sceptical about these suggestions (noting that one is dealing with different ideological approaches to private sector tenure), while Card notes that social housing tenants are currently the only occupants who face the threat of eviction for anti-social behaviour. Discussion of alternative techniques highlights both authors' disenchantment with the use of eviction – which shifts the 'problem' on – and of other legal powers – which can criminalise.

What then should be done? Hunter favours a shift away from reliance on law towards more holistic responses which can take account of "the myriad of other social factors which must be tackled". Card suggests that the work of the Social Exclusion Unit will lead to a more coordinated interagency approach aimed at the rehabilitation or management of a cross-tenure marginalised population. Government policy seems to accept that there will need to be a mixture of therapy and zero tolerance – it is the balance between these concepts which concerns the authors.

TEN

Managing anti-social behaviour – inclusion or exclusion?

Pauline Card

Introduction

Combating anti-social behaviour, particularly among social housing tenants, has long been high on the political agenda. Since the advent of the New Labour government in 1997, the reduction of anti-social behaviour, alongside that of crime, has been seen as particularly important in relation to social exclusion (or inclusion) and low demand. Previous legislation, most importantly the 1996 Housing Act and the 1998 Crime and Disorder Act, has put in place major legal instruments to tackle acts of anti-social behaviour by both social housing tenants and non-tenants. This being the case the Housing Green Paper (DETR/DSS, 2000) gives little consideration to the issue, apart from a few speculative suggestions on the use of the Housing Benefit system as a disciplinary tool, and drawing attention to the current measures to various agencies.

Many of the measures adopted, or available for adoption, are legalistic and punitive in nature, with local authorities being given ever greater powers as both landlords and as the agency, in partnership with the police, responsible for ensuring the safety and protection of the community. This chapter places the political discourse surrounding anti-social behaviour, particularly among social housing tenants, in the wider political discourses of social welfare in general and social housing in particular. It argues that the changing nature of such discourses has allowed the identification of social housing, and those that live in it, as marginalised or excluded, labels which in turn enable more punitive and rehabilitative measures to be applied to those who fail to conform or fail to act responsibly toward the community in which they live.

Changing welfare states

During the late 19th and early 20th centuries many nation states became 'welfare' states that attempted to ensure social justice, social cohesion and economic growth through the provision of welfare services such as housing, health, education and social insurance. 'Welfare' states were not a new type of state but a new mode of government that was constituted by a 'political rationality' based on certain principles and values and a certain conception of the nature of society (Rose and Miller, 1992). By 'political rationality' Rose and Miller mean:

> ... the changing discursive fields within which the exercise of power is conceptualised, the moral justifications for particular ways of exercising power by diverse authorities, notions of the appropriate forms, objects and limits of politics, and conceptions of the proper distribution of such tasks among secular, spiritual, military and familial sectors. (1992, p 175)

Linked to the 'welfare' rationality were an array of technologies, programmes and projects which arose from the shared principles and values, for example social insurance, health care provision, education system, public housing and so on. All such 'governmental' policies and programmes, it is argued, were devised from a 'social' point of view.

By the 'social' Rose means those areas of human existence that had previously been considered part of the private domain, which, with the emergence of the disciplines of statistics and sociology and other social sciences, became knowable to governments and also became legitimate areas of governmental concern. A greater understanding of the collective experiences of certain societies at particular times gave rise to demands that the nation should be governed in the interests of social protection, social justice, social rights and social solidarity (Rose, 1996, p 329). The economic well-being of the country was seen as being inextricably linked with the health and education of the working classes. In Britain the emergence of the 'welfare' state is illustrated by the growing government involvement in the social policy arena during the 40 years spanning the 19th and 20th centuries (see Fraser, 1984). Initially public health legislation was introduced to improve the slum living conditions of the working classes, followed by the Liberal Reforms that introduced a level of social protection and basic education and eventually state subsidised local authority housing for returning First World War heroes. The culmination of the evolving 'welfare' state in Britain was the introduction of the welfare state post-1945.

During the latter half of the 20th century we have seen a retrenchment of 'welfare' states, or as Rose (1993) would argue, a mutation of the rationality of government. In today's 'advanced liberal' democracies (Rose, 1993) the notions of social protection, social rights and collective provision have been replaced by the construct of the responsible individual in the market place who insures themselves and their family against the risks that they face in society. Such a mutation means that governments no longer govern from a 'social' point of view but through individuals as members of the many and various communities to which they belong, for example family, faith community, neighbourhood, workplace, club or other affiliation. As part of the mutation from 'social' government to 'community' government there has been a redefinition of the 'subject' of government. Rather than the inclusive notions of social citizenship and social solidarity there are now new dividing practices which differentiate between the affiliated and the marginalised. The affiliated are:

> ... those who are considered 'included': the individuals and families who have the financial, educational and moral means to 'pass' in their role of active citizens in responsible communities. (Rose, 1996, p 340)

The marginal are:

> ... those who cannot be considered affiliated to such sanctioned and civilised communities. Either they are not considered affiliated to any collectivity by virtue of their incapacity to manage themselves as subjects or they are considered affiliated to some kind of 'anti-community' whose morality, lifestyle or comportment, is considered a threat or reproach to public contentment and political order. (Rose, 1996, p 340)

Government, in 'advanced liberal' democracies is seen as a 'problematising' activity whereby constant criticism of government leads to the identification of difficulties and failures which in turn gives rise to problems that need to be addressed through various 'programmes of government' (Rose and Miller, 1992). As part of this activity political discourses are developed to illuminate the way in which the state wishes to govern and who they wish to govern. 'Advanced liberal' government is concerned with the 'conduct of conduct', not just the conduct of those considered to be outside, or excluded from, society but also the conduct of the affiliated. Arising from this concern are a whole array of programmes and technologies that seek either to maintain order and obedience to law by binding individuals into shared moral norms and values, or to rehabilitate, or to minimise the risk posed by, the marginalised. Rose (2000) has divided the myriad and complex strategies of control that have been devised into two broad 'families':

> ... those that seek to regulate conduct by enmeshing individuals within *circuits of inclusion* and those that seek to act on pathologies through managing a different set of circuits, *circuits of exclusion.* (2000, p 324; author's italics)

For the purposes of this chapter attention will be given to 'circuits of exclusion' that include strategies that seek to rehabilitate or manage the risk posed by those identified as the marginalised minority. The following section identifies the political rationalities that have isolated social housing, and social housing tenants, as the legitimate subjects of control strategies that fall within the 'circuits of exclusion'.

The subjectification of social housing

Over the past two decades a number of policy objectives have had a profound effect on the role of social housing in Britain. Underpinning and informing the policies adopted has been a common political rationality, that of social exclusion, although not all discourses have been termed in such a way. The discourse of social exclusion is considered important because, as Levitas (1998, p 7) argues, "[i]t represents the primary significant division in society as one between an included majority and an excluded minority".

Despite the term not having been in general political use in Britain much before 1997, Levitas (1998) identifies three discourses of social exclusion: a redistributional discourse; a moral underclass discourse; and a social integrationist discourse. It is the latter two discourses which will be developed here as illuminating the way social housing has been made the subject of strategies of control.

The moral underclass discourse, which is concerned with the behavioural and cultural deviance of the excluded, gained prominence in Britain during the 1980s and early 1990s. Explanations of the underclass were both cultural and structural, either it is the pathology of the individual that makes them part of the underclass (Murray, 1990; Dahrendorf, 1987), or inequalities in the structure of society that have led to a growth in the underclass (Field, 1989). However, Levitas argues that both types of discourse present "the underclass or the socially excluded as culturally distinct from the mainstream" (p 21). Murray (1990) posited that an emerging underclass could be seen in Britain in the growing number of long-term unemployed young men, and the increasing numbers of never-married single mothers. In popular discourse these groups have come to be equated with social housing tenants, and in turn have been scapegoated for the many problems experienced in areas of social housing (see Campbell, 1993).

During this period there was a shift away from a concept of 'social' citizenship as envisaged by Marshall (1950) to one that came to be increasingly equated with civil rights (Dean, 1999). The provision of social rights by government was no longer seen as legitimate because it involved a call on the financial resources of the state. Those that had recourse to the safety-net welfare provision of the state, especially the non-universal provisions such as housing and income maintenance, were seen as excluded from full citizenship rights. During the 1980s the concept of 'active citizenship' was promoted whereby:

> ... such responsibilities as comfortable citizens might feel they owe to those who are less fortunate are a matter of choice and individual conscience and ought not to be collectively discharged through the payment of taxes. (Dean, 1999, p 219)

In the 1990s 'active' citizenship came to be associated with the citizen as consumer, with sovereignty vested not in social entitlements but the power to choose, complain or exit.

The identification of tenants of social housing as a morally deficient 'underclass' was exacerbated by the policies of the government. The drive for privatisation and the creation of a 'property owning democracy' underpinned the sale of council housing stock, through the introduction of the Right to Buy, throughout the 1980s and beyond. The mantras of choice, efficiency and economy and the battle against the 'dependency culture' fuelled the drive towards diversity of provision and the de-municipalisation that occurred during the final decade of the last Conservative government (1987-97). Home ownership was championed as the tenure that:

> ... ensures the wide spread of wealth through society, encourages a
> personal desire to improve and modernise one's home, enables people
> to accrue wealth for their children and stimulates the attitudes of
> independence and self-reliance that are a bedrock of a free society.
> (Michael Heseltine, Secretary of State for the Environment, 1980, cited
> in Monk and Kleinman, 1989, p 122)

Economic and social policies of the Thatcher and Major governments
accelerated, if not initiated, the process of residualisation of social housing
(Forrest and Murie, 1988). Social, and more particularly council, housing
became perceived as the safety-net tenure for those who were dependent
on welfare, the only choice of betterment available to tenants was through
exit from the tenure. Those who chose to, or had no other choice but to,
remain were labelled as an 'underclass' who through their inability or
unwillingness to enter home ownership were not contributing toward,
and were therefore outside, a free society.

During the late 1990s the social integrationist discourse has gained
credence in Britain as a counter to the underclass debate, and because of
the growing importance of the European Union. This discourse emerged
from French academic debate which defined social exclusion as the
breakdown of the structural, cultural and moral ties which bind the
individual to society, although it was later broadened to include
consideration of groups marginalised economically, socially, culturally
and spatially. However, in the hands of the EU the concept has been
narrowed to a concern with the disadvantages experienced by those
excluded from paid work (Levitas, 1998), a definition adopted by the
Blair government:

> [social exclusion is] ... a shorthand label for what can happen when
> individuals or areas suffer from a combination of linked problems such
> as unemployment, poor skills, low incomes, poor housing, high crime
> environments, bad health and family breakdown. (SEU, 2000a, p 1)

New Labour, Levitas suggests, has developed a discourse that is an
inconsistent combination of the moral underclass and social integrationist
ideal types outlined above. This is reflected in the emphasis on getting
people back into paid employment (for example the New Deal) and the
emphasis placed on not only the rights of citizenship but also the reciprocal
responsibilities the individual has to the wider community. Individuals
have a responsibility to their communities as well as themselves and their

families. By building strong communities (a term itself as contested as citizenship) social cohesion, which was lost under individualistic Thatcherism, can once again be attained. Blairite communitarianism sees social cohesion in the community as being secured by a strong commitment to common moral values (Blair, 1997; Driver and Martell, 1997), great importance is placed on family values and the duty to seek paid employment. If you are unwilling or unable to conform to these moral obligations then your claim to social rights, in particular the means with which to participate in society, is limited. Both the moral underclass and social integrationist discourses of social exclusion identify groups or locations that are outside or excluded from society. This may be because of their lack of morals and non-acceptance of society's norms, or their perceived inability or unwillingness to take up paid employment. Whatever the reason such groups are seen as not qualifying for full citizenship rights either as consumers or through the fulfilment of the responsibilities and duties concomitant with the rights of citizenship.

With the election of New Labour the rhetoric surrounding social housing has changed. Social exclusion, and its eradication, and the building of 'balanced' or sustainable communities have become the major foci of policy documents and political speeches (for example, New Deal for Communities; DETR, 1999a; Blair, 1997). Despite evidence to the contrary (Lee and Murie, 1997), social exclusion has become synonymous with large council estates where there are high levels of disadvantage, high levels of crime and anti-social behaviour and endemic low demand. Tenants are urged to become re-affiliated by improving, educating and training themselves, while being actively involved in the regeneration of their local communities. Social housing has become, in political and popular discourse, a spatial segregation of the marginalised. As residualisation has gathered pace so the perception of social housing has become that of the tenure of last resort for those people who cannot or will not participate in mainstream society. Tenants of this tenure do not have the intellectual or financial resources to act responsibly and provide protection for themselves or their families against the risks encountered in life. The changing language of citizenship and labels such as 'underclass' and 'socially excluded' compound the negative image of social housing estates, reinforcing the perception of detachment and making them amenable to differential policy making.

As areas of social housing have become identified as socially excluded, inhabited by morally deviant individuals who don't work, are involved in crime and anti-social behaviour, and behave irresponsibly as parents, for example, they have become the legitimate target of governmental control strategies. They have become enmeshed in the 'circuits of exclusion' that seek to rehabilitate them or mitigate the risk that they pose to the included. Part of the process of rehabilitation has been the identification of behaviour that needs to be controlled – such as truancy, teenage parenthood and anti-social behaviour (SEU, 2000b) – so that the individuals involved can become the subject of control strategies. The following section looks at the measures adopted and recommended for dealing with anti-social behaviour.

Managing anti-social behaviour

Despite acknowledgement that anti-social behaviour is not confined to social housing most of the work in dealing with such behaviour has concentrated on the powers, and policies, required by social landlords. Set out in this section are the many different strategies adopted by local authorities and Registered Social Landlords (RSLs), sometimes in partnership with others, to deal with anti-social behaviour among their tenants. Prior to this there is a discussion of the way in which anti-social behaviour is defined, and the importance of such a definition to the type of policies adopted and made available by legislation.

Definitions

When considering any definition of the term anti-social behaviour we must recognise that it is not in itself a behaviour but a social construction that can and does vary over time and space. Behaviour that is seen as anti-social by a group or individual in a particular setting at a particular time may be perfectly acceptable to another group or individual in another setting and/or at another time. Behaviours are categorised and labelled so that they are identifiable and can be acted on appropriately, different types of label influence the type of policies seen as appropriate and acceptable for the management or elimination of that type of behaviour.

Definitions of anti-social behaviour in both research and policy documents have changed over time. The emphasis has moved from identifying all possible types of behaviour to a concentration, especially in government documents, on criminal or near criminal acts. For example, a research team investigating the housing management function of a number of local authorities in the late 1970s recognised the wide variation in the severity of nuisance or anti-social behaviour to be found:

There are annoying but relatively minor events like children playing games in unauthorised areas; there are also the serious matters such as burglaries, muggings and racial harassment. In between these two extremes there is a wide variety of types of vandalism ... and noise is a constant source of complaints in many areas. (Legg et al, 1981, p 14)

More recently when consulting on the introduction of probationary tenancies (now called introductory tenancies) in the mid-1990s the then Conservative government concentrated on the criminal nature of many anti-social acts:

Anti-social behaviour by a small minority of tenants and others is a growing problem on council estates.... Estates can be stigmatised by the anti-social behaviour of a few. Such behaviour manifests itself in many different ways and at varying levels. It can include vandalism, noise, verbal and physical abuse, threats of violence, racial harassment, damage to property, trespass, nuisance from dogs, car repairs on the street, so-called joyriding, domestic violence, drugs and other criminal activities, such as burglary. (Welsh Office, 1995, paras 1.1-1.2)

The move toward linking anti-social behaviour with crime can also be identified in the documents produced by the present government when in opposition. In the consultation paper on the proposed measures to deal with criminal neighbours, Jack Straw, the then Shadow Home Secretary, stated that: "[s]erious anti-social behaviour by neighbours is perhaps the best example of chronic crime" (Labour Party, 1995, p 6).

Other organisations have promoted more flexible definitions that recognise that the context in which the behaviour takes place can dictate whether it is anti-social or not. The Good Practice Unit of the Chartered Institute of Housing, for example, defines anti-social behaviour as: "behaviour that opposes society's norms and accepted standards of behaviour"(CIH, 1995, p 3).

Changing definitions of anti-social behaviour clearly demonstrate the shift towards equating anti-social behaviour with criminal behaviour. Many of the definitions (for example CIH, 1995) contain implicit moral judgements about those that commit acts of anti-social behaviour. Perpetrators are seen as unaccepting of the norms of society and therefore must be outside society, excluded or marginalised. Such judgements enable governments to apply more restricted qualification criteria to services provided by them, employ stricter enforcement measures and attach tougher penalties.

Strategies for dealing with anti-social behaviour

Social landlords have long been at the forefront of tackling anti-social behaviour, partly because of its association with social housing and partly because they have available to them powers associated with the tenancy agreement. During the past decade organisations have adopted different approaches to the problem: set out below are the many tools available to local authorities and RSLs. They have been categorised into broad brush approaches but each anti-social behaviour strategy may include one, many, or all of these tools.

Housing management

One of the first tools available to social landlords is the control of access to housing through the housing register. Prevention, through exclusion of those applicants with a history of anti-social behaviour, rather than enforcement, is preferable to many social landlords and many tenants. Although some local authorities have always excluded applicants from the housing register for certain types of behaviour, many more have adopted this approach since the 1996 Housing Act. Part VI of the Act gave local authorities the discretion to identify groups that were 'non-qualifying' (Cowan, 1996) and therefore excluded. Recent research undertaken for Shelter, the homeless charity, found that 46 per cent of local authorities and RSLs surveyed had changed their exclusions policy since the 1996 Act: 47.7 per cent of respondents excluded on the basis of ex-tenant behaviour and 40 per cent for tenant behaviour (Smith et al, 2001: forthcoming).

The tenancy agreement has been seen as the most powerful tool available to landlords in dealing with the behaviour of tenants. In good practice literature it is seen as important that tenancy agreements should clearly set out the rights and responsibilities of both tenants and landlord, including those relating to anti-social or nuisance behaviour. Many local authorities and RSLs have revised their tenancy agreements since 1996 to reflect the widened ground for possession introduced by the 1996 Housing Act (see below). However, the detail and clarity of clauses relating to anti-social behaviour varies widely (Nixon et al, 1999).

The 1996 Housing Act introduced introductory tenancies for the use of local authorities. If introductory tenancies are adopted all new tenancies become shorthold tenancies of 12 months duration. If during the 12-month period a tenant causes a nuisance then the local authority could gain possession without going through the normal possession proceedings. Although the legislation did not apply to RSLs starter tenancies can be granted on the same basis with the agreement of the regulatory body (the Housing Corporation in England and the National Assembly for Wales in Wales). By 1999, 30 per cent of local authorities and 13 per cent of RSLs in England have adopted introductory tenancies or starter tenancies. Of the local authorities that had adopted introductory tenancies nearly 50 per cent had evicted introductory tenants during the first 12 months, however, 68 per cent of the evictions were for rent arrears and only 19 per cent for neighbour nuisance (Nixon et al, 1999, pp 53, 55). This may reflect a situation where tenants that have behavioural problems may also be experiencing other difficulties including non-payment of rent and it is easier to take action for rent arrears.

Since the early 1990s a number of local authorities have introduced various types of neighbourhood warden schemes, not all of which are part of the housing function of local authorities, to tackle problems of anti-social behaviour. Many are extensions of existing caretaker, concierge or intensive housing management schemes while others have been introduced with the main objective of tackling anti-social behaviour either in particular areas, across all council estates or across the whole authority (see, for example, Papps, 1998). The role of the wardens differ greatly but some can be seen to have taken over the 'low level policing' role that was once provided by the local 'bobby on the beat' (Papps, 1998), where surveillance and monitoring are a major part of their function.

Legal tools

A number of legal tools are available to social landlords to deal with anti-social behaviour among their tenants (see Hunter et al, 1998; SEU, 2000c for further details). Legislative changes introduced by the 1996 Housing Act have enhanced their ability to do so. Part V of the 1996 Act strengthened and expanded the ground for possession for nuisance behaviour. Tenants are now responsible for their own behaviour and that of those living or visiting them, and within the vicinity of the property not just the property itself. This enables landlords to seek possession, for example, on the grounds of nuisance caused by the children of the tenant or the anti-social behaviour of a partner who is not a tenant.

During the early 1990s the London Borough of Hackney began using injunctions in an attempt to stop anti-social behaviour on the Kingsmead Estate (NACRO, 1997), with positive results. Many local authorities have followed this example and adopted injunctions as part of their anti-social behaviour strategy. They can be used either to prohibit certain behaviour or to ban individuals from certain areas. The 1996 Act introduced housing injunctions which can have the power of arrest attached. A breach of a housing injunction can be punished either by a fine or a prison term.

Anti-social behaviour orders (ASBOs) were introduced by the 1998 Crime and Disorder Act. These are civil orders obtained by local authorities or the police through the Magistrate Courts when a person, over the age of 10, has been acting in an anti-social manner. Orders may last at least 2 years and any breach is a criminal offence which may result in a prison sentence. Take-up of the use of ASBOs by local authorities and the police has been slow, and over recent months the government has undertaken a re-launch with seminars taking place across England and Wales. There have been a number of concerns raised about ASBOs not least that they may breach the Human Rights Act (Rowan, 1999, p 20), and that a criminal conviction can result from an initial civil action.

Further legal responses to anti-social behaviour are available to local authorities using legislation that is not connected to their role as landlord. The 1990 Environmental Protection Act and the 1996 Noise Act can be used to tackle problems of persistent noise and other legislation addresses environmental hazards such as unkempt houses and gardens. Bylaws can also be adopted to prohibit certain behaviour in defined areas, for example the public consumption of alcohol. However, recent research found that few local authorities had adopted such an approach, despite the success of those that had in enforcing the bylaws (Nixon et al, 1999).

Other approaches to anti-social behaviour

Beyond the managerial and legal approaches available to social landlords to deal with anti-social behaviour there have been a myriad of initiatives and policies adopted by them, often in conjunction with other agencies (see SEU, 2000c for examples of good practice). In general terms these include:

• working with communities to building community capacity;
• mediation;

- case conferences;
- family support; and
- information sharing protocols.

Many of the projects or strategies are aimed at preventing anti-social behaviour rather than punishing those that have committed anti-social acts. Although there are examples of good practice, the penetration of alternative strategies is not deep among local authorities. Coverage of multiagency working, working with communities and working with individuals or families to prevent anti-social behaviour is patchy and the initiatives are of variable quality (SEU, 2000c).

The 1998 Crime and Disorder Act introduced further tools for tackling anti-social behaviour. Crime and Disorder Partnerships are to be established by local authorities, the police and other key agencies to develop and implement strategies for reducing crime and disorder in each area (Home Office, 1998). Strategies should reflect the issues and problems of each particular area, which are identified through a crime and disorder audit. This was one of the first moves, along with ASBOs, to extend the responsibility for reducing anti-social behaviour beyond social housing managers. Anti-social behaviour is slowly being recognised as a cross-tenure issue rather than a problem for social housing estates, tenants and landlords.

The future

Anti-social behaviour, or the tackling of anti-social behaviour, has been a major theme of many of the consultation and policy documents that have been produced over the past 12 months by the Policy Action Teams (PATs) set up by the Social Exclusion Unit. Hence, although the Housing Green Paper has very little to say on the subject of anti-social behaviour, other than drawing attention to the available tools, action is being taken by central government which impacts directly on housing.

The Social Exclusion Unit was created by the Prime Minister in 1997 with the remit to "develop integrated and sustainable approaches to the problems of the worst housing estates, including crime, drugs, unemployment, community breakdown, and bad schools etc" (SEU, 1998, p iv). One of the first reports produced by the unit was on the renewal of the most disadvantaged neighbourhoods in Britain (SEU, 1998). As part of the development of a national strategy for tackling poor neighbourhoods 18 PATs were set up to look at specific issues, working on a fast-track to tackle remaining policy problems and gaps. Under a theme of 'getting the place to work' the report argued that:

> ... if housing is poorly managed or unlettable, or crime and anti-social behaviour are not tackled, community support systems can easily crumble. We need to get to grips with what drives area abandonment, make good neighbourhood and housing management the norm, develop a watertight framework for tackling anti-social neighbours, and clarify how community wardens can best complement the police in combating crime. (SEU, 1998, p 11)

A number of PATs have considered the impact of anti-social behaviour on disadvantaged areas. PAT 5, *Unpopular housing* (DETR, 1999b), identified anti-social behaviour as a factor which contributes to the cycle of decline associated with the development of areas of low demand housing. PAT 6 (Home Office, 2000) looked at the role of neighbourhood wardens, in various forms, in improving areas of problem housing and reducing anti-social behaviour. However, it was PAT 8 that was given the remit of looking at ways in which anti-social behaviour was being tackled and producing recommendations for the future.

PAT 8 suggested that despite examples of good practice and 'promising initiatives', there were a number of underlying factors that were undermining the success of strategies for tackling anti-social behaviour (SEU, 2000b). These factors included:

- lack of priority given to tackling anti-social behaviour by agencies concerned;
- no government department having clear responsibility for reducing anti-social behaviour and coordinating all departments' efforts to combat it;
- a lack of joint working, with many agencies working with the same families on an individual basis rather in a coordinated way;
- a lack of information about the level, causes and effects of anti-social behaviour, without such information anti-social behaviour cannot be given the appropriate priority;
- a lack of information on the initiatives and policies being used to combat anti-social behaviour, little dissemination of information on promising approaches, and a lack of information on perpetrators of anti-social behaviour being shared between agencies.

From this analysis of the current situation PAT 8 made recommendations for the future that would ensure, it was claimed, that tackling anti-social behaviour would be given a high priority and involve all agencies in the "fight against anti-social behaviour" (SEU, 2000c, p 10). Broadly the recommendations were:

- assigning responsibility for reducing anti-social behaviour to the Home Office, chosen because action is to be based around the Crime and Disorder Partnerships;
- promoting prevention, with mainstream services of all agencies engaging in the process of prevention;
- greater enforcement using the current powers to deliver rapid and tough action;
- resettlement, changing the behaviour of a small number of perpetrators by rehousing them in appropriate settings with the necessary levels of oversight and support;
- combating racial harassment placed at the centre of any anti-social behaviour strategy;
- information sharing between agencies dealing with anti-social behaviour.

Prior to the 1998 Crime and Disorder Act measures dealing with anti-social behaviour had been firmly related to the powers that local authorities possessed, or required, as landlords. Attempts were made at rehabilitation of both individuals and/or estates by local authorities, sometimes in partnership with other agencies: families were provided with support and advice, while community development work, in its many guises, encouraged tenants to take responsibility for making improvements to the environment in which they lived, including dealing with anti-social behaviour. Individuals or families who were considered beyond rehabilitation were made subject to the legal system. Either they were evicted or some aspect of their behaviour was restricted by the use of injunctions. The possibility of future anti-social behaviour was managed through the exclusion of those judged to be a high risk.

These strategies have continued since the 1998 Act but anti-social behaviour has, at least superficially, become a non-tenure specific issue. Legal action across all tenures has been made easier with the introduction of ASBOs, and the new Crime and Disorder Partnerships have widened the responsibility of local authorities to cover all residents of their area rather than just their tenants. The work of the PATs suggest that the future approach may be more coordinated and have less of a legal focus but strategies are still aimed at the rehabilitation or management of marginalised, excluded or deviant individuals.

Conclusion

As Britain's 'advanced liberal' government seeks to control the conduct of individuals through their membership of interwoven communities the discourse of social exclusion has labelled social housing and social housing tenants as non-affiliated or marginalised. Such a label has made them the subject of governmental control strategies that seek to rehabilitate (or re-affiliate) the excluded, or to manage the risk that they pose to the affiliated. The management of anti-social behaviour is a manifestation of the 'circuits of exclusion' used by government to control the conduct of marginalised individuals and communities. Perpetrators of anti-social behaviour must either accept support, advice, re-education and training in the hope of being rehabilitated, or be faced with legal action that can result in the loss of their home or restrictions on their behaviour.

The implementation of ASBOs, Crime and Disorder Partnerships and the promotion of strategies that involve residents in the renewal of many different types of neighbourhood suggest a move away from associating anti-social behaviour solely with areas of social housing. However, the map of disadvantage continues to be drawn so that social housing estates figure prominently: this sets them apart and compounds the negative effects of the social exclusion discourse which resulted in differential policy treatment. Social landlords still have the greatest powers to deal with anti-social behaviour and currently only social housing tenants face the threat of eviction from their homes for behaviour that is considered anti-social.

References

Blair, T. (1997) 'The will to win', Speech given on 2 June at the Aylesbury Estate, Southwark.

Campbell, B. (1993) *Goliath: Britain's dangerous places*, London: Methuen.

CIH (Chartered Institute of Housing) (1995) *Housing management standards manual*, Coventry: CIH.

Cowan, D. (ed) (1996) *The Housing Act 1996: A practical guide*, Bristol: Jordans.

Dahrendorf, R. (1987) 'The erosion of citizenship and its consequences for us all', *New Statesman*, 12 June.

Dean, H. (1999) 'Citizenship', in M. Powell (ed) *New labour, new welfare state? The 'third way' in British social policy*, Bristol: The Policy Press.

DETR (Department of the Environment, Transport and the Regions) (1999a) *Code of guidance for local authorities on allocation of accommodation and homelessness: A consultation draft*, London: DETR.

DETR (1999b) *Unpopular housing, report of Policy Action Team 5*, London: DETR.

DETR/DSS (Department of Social Security) (2000) *Quality and choice: A decent home for all*, Housing Green Paper, London: DETR/DSS.

Driver, W. and Martell, D. (1997) 'New Labour's communitarianisms', *Critical Social Policy*, vol 17, no 3, pp 27-44.

Field, F. (1989) *Losing out: The emergence of Britain's underclass*, Oxford: Basil Blackwell.

Forrest, R. and Murie, A. (1988) *Selling the welfare state: The privatisation of public housing*, London: Routledge.

Fraser, D. (1984) *The evolution of the British welfare state*, Basingstoke: Macmillan.

Home Office (1998) *Crime and Disorder Act: An introductory guide*, London: Home Office.

Home Office (2000) *Neighbourhood wardens, report of Policy Action Team 6*, London: Home Office.

Hunter, C., Mullen, T. and Scott, S. (1998) *Legal remedies for neighbour nuisance: Comparing Scottish and English approaches*, York: Joseph Rowntree Foundation.

Labour Party (1995) *A quiet life: Tough action on criminal neighbours*, London: The Labour Party.

Lee, P. and Murie, A. (1997) *Poverty, housing tenure and social exclusion*, Bristol/York: The Policy Press/Joseph Rowntree Foundation.

Legg, C., Kay, A., Masdon, J. and Nicholas, K. (1981) *Could local authorities be better landlords?*, London: Housing Research Group, City University.

Levitas, R. (1998) *The inclusive society? Social exclusion and New Labour*, Basingstoke: Macmillan.

Marshall, T. (1950) *Citizenship and social class*, Cambridge: Cambridge University Press.

Monk, S. and Kleinman, M. (1989) 'Housing', in P. Brown and R. Sparks (eds) *Beyond Thatcherism: Social policy, politics and society*, Milton Keynes: Open University Press.

Murray, C. (1990) *The emerging British underclass*, London: IEA Health and Welfare Unit.

NACRO (National Association for the Care and Resettlement of Offenders) (1997) *Crime, community and change: Taking action on the Kingsmead Estate in Hackney*, London: NACRO.

Nixon, J., Hunter, C. and Shayer, S. (1999) *The use of legal remedies by social landlords to deal with neighbour nuisance*, Sheffield: Centre for Regional Economic and Social Research Paper No H8, Sheffield Hallam University

Papps, P. (1998) 'Anti-social behaviour strategies – individualistic or holistic?', *Housing Studies*, vol 13, no 5, pp 639-56.

Rose, N. (1993) 'Government, authority and expertise in advanced liberalism', *Economy and Society*, vol 22, no 3, pp 282-99.

Rose, N. (1996) 'The death of the social? Re-figuring the territory of government', *Economy and Society*, vol 25, no 3, pp 327-56.

Rose, N. (2000) 'Government and control', *British Journal of Criminology*, vol 40, pp 321-39.

Rose, N. and Miller, P. (1992) 'Political power beyond the state: problematics of government', *British Journal of Sociology*, vol 43, no 2, pp 173-205.

Rowan, M. (1999) 'See you in court?', *Housing*, September.

SEU (Social Exclusion Unit) (1998) *Bringing Britain together: A national strategy for neighbourhood renewal*, Cm 4045, London: The Stationery Office.

SEU (2000a) *The Social Exclusion Unit Leaflet*, London: Cabinet Office.

SEU (2000b) *National Strategy for Neighbourhood Renewal: A framework for consultation*, London: SEU.

SEU (2000c) *Report of Policy Action Team 8: Anti-social behaviour*, London: SEU.

Smith, R., Stirling, T., Papps, P., Evans, A. and Rowlands, R. (2001: forthcoming) *Allocations and exclusions: The impact of new approaches to allocating social housing*, London: Shelter.

Welsh Office (1995) *Anti-social behaviour on council estates: A consultation paper on probationary tenancies for council tenants in Wales*, Cardiff: Welsh Office.

ELEVEN

Anti-social behaviour and housing – can law be the answer?[1]

Caroline Hunter

Introduction

Given the government's apparent obsession with anti–social behaviour, it came as rather a surprise that the Green Paper (DETR/DSS, 2000) did not have a chapter dedicated to the issue. On reflection, perhaps this should not be such a surprise since there has been a surfeit of legislation designed to deal with the problem (see, in particular, the 1996 Housing Act, Part V and the 1998 Crime and Disorder Act). Furthermore, as the Green Paper points out, there is already a lengthy document on the subject produced by Policy Action Team (PAT) 8 of the Social Exclusion Unit (SEU, 2000). Thus, apart from the particular measure relating to Housing Benefit (to which I shall return below) the Green Paper only directs four paragraphs directly to the issue. These are to be found in Chapter 12 ('Tackling other forms of housing-related social exclusion'). In this chapter I will be considering and focusing on the proposals from PAT 8 since "the Green Paper should be considered alongside the Social Exclusion Unit's Neighbourhood Renewal Strategy" (DETR/DSS, 2000, para 1.17).

Crime and anti–social behaviour: problems of definition

Although references to anti–social behaviour are limited in the Green Paper, those to crime are not. While such references are usually fleeting, they are broad in their assertions. For example the summary and key proposals include the comment that "many live on estates which have been left to deteriorate for too long, and which contribute to ill health, crime and poverty" (DETR/DSS, 2000, p 8). The key proposals for housing policy (para 1.5) include "supporting vulnerable people and tackling all forms of social exclusion, including bad housing, homelessness, poverty, crime and poor health".

Thus a clear link is made between crime and social exclusion, although who is the socially excluded in these circumstances – the victim or the criminal – is not a debate which the Green Paper begins to address. The link between housing policy, particularly that relating to social housing, and crime is perhaps a reflection of much of the literature that has emerged around 'problem estates'. There is not room here to discuss at length the relationship between crime and place, and why some areas may see higher levels of criminal activity, whether reported or not, than others. That there is a relationship would now seem to be accepted (see Cowan, 1999, Ch 18 and Burney, 1999), and indeed this may lead to a concentration of crime in areas of social housing. However, any analysis shows that this is not a problem of social housing per se. Indeed any analysis must be multi-factoral considering, among other things, issues of child densities, residential mobility, design, history of a particular estate and allocation (see Cowan, 1999). Thus Hope and Foster (1992, quoted in Cowan, 1999, p 497) conclude that their study:

> ... supports the view that the various causal influences on crime on the problem estate tend to interact with each other. This is likely to occur because their effect is mediated by the internal culture of the estate community. Changes in environmental design, management quality, and social mix appear to work together to encourage the growth of social control or of criminality.

What is perhaps unusual in the Green Paper is that the link between crime and anti-social behaviour is not so clearly made. The references to anti-social behaviour, such as there are, are not linked inextricably with crime as has been the case in many past government documents (see, for example, Labour Party, 1995 and DoE, 1995). Indeed the terms have often been used interchangeably, reflecting the view of Young (1999, p 133) that "late modernity loses the precision of both offender and offence; offenders are everywhere, offences blur together with a host of anti-social behaviours". The drafters of the Green Paper have been a little more circumspect in their use of the term anti-social.

What we do not get from the Green Paper, however, is any clear definition of what is meant by anti-social behaviour. If we turn to the PAT 8 report (SEU, 2000) we find an admission that there can be no single definition of anti-social behaviour: "it covers a wide range of behaviour from litter to serious harassment" (p 14). The report continues (p 15) that it ranges from the clearly criminal to lifestyle clashes:"Activities that are criminal are defined by law. Defining other behaviour as anti-social is more difficult. Behaviour regarded as acceptable by some can be completely unacceptable to others". Thus while criminal behaviour can be included within anti-social behaviour, it has a broader brush than this, and does include other non-criminal or, as it is sometimes referred to, 'subcriminal' behaviour. It should be acknowledged, however, that a clear dividing line between crime and non-(or sub-)crime is not always so easy to draw. Consider, for example, the provisions of the 1996 Noise Act, or the use of bylaws by local authorities, or offences such as threatening behaviour which may lead to very different perceptions of whether or not an offence has occurred. Then there is also the type of conduct which does not even come into the 'subcriminal' category, which might be perfectly acceptable to a different neighbour, but in a particular instance will lead to a neighbour dispute.

Surveys undertaken with householders tend to show that the most common form of complaints are at the non-criminal end of the spectrum (see, for example, Karn et al, 1993; Swinden, 1996; Dignan et al, 1996; and Liddle et al, 1997) with the most commonly cited being that of noise. Thus there immediately emerges a mismatch between the rhetoric of (earlier) government policy which talks of dealing with anti-social behaviour as a means of dealing with essentially (serious) criminal behaviour, and the type of problems to which the majority of complainants are seeking some form of solution.

Problems of definition clearly lead to problems of solution; if the nature of the problem has not been defined then defining a solution seems impossible. The legal response to anti-social behaviour has been two-fold. First, there is the response that sees anti-social behaviour as a problem of social housing, and more particularly the inhabitants of social housing. The provisions of the 1996 Housing Act, Part V are clearly this type of response. Second, the 1998 Crime and Disorder Act illustrates a response which does not link the problem to housing (social or otherwise) and is not linked to any particular type of tenure or place. Here it is more closely allied to a response based in criminal law, with criminal punishment against the individual perpetrator. In both cases, the response is to take action against the individual or his or her family, a response that is founded on a view that once anti-social behaviour has occurred there is an individual who is responsible for it and who should accordingly be punished for it.

The 1996 Housing Act

The provisions of Part V of the 1996 Housing Act relating to anti-social behaviour were three-fold.

Provision of introductory tenancies

These allow local authorities to adopt a scheme under which all new tenants of the authority are granted an introductory tenancy rather than a secure tenancy. The effect of this is that if the authority wishes to evict, there is no requirement to prove any ground for possession, nor is there any discretion on the part of the judge. Certain procedural requirements, including offering an internal review of the decision to evict, must be completed before possession can be sought in the court. The introductory tenancy lasts for 12 months and, providing possession proceedings have not been commenced, converts automatically to a secure tenancy after 12 months.

It should be noted that such tenancies are not available to Registered Social Landlords (RSLs). The Housing Corporation has, however, developed guidelines when dealing with 'problem' estates, for the use of assured shorthold tenancies (which similarly give minimal security), known colloquially as 'starter tenancies' (Housing Corporation, 1999).

Extended grounds for possession

Tenants of social landlords are generally either secure or assured and accordingly subject to the provisions of either the 1985 Housing Act or the 1988 Housing Act. To obtain possession on the basis of neighbour nuisance the landlord has to rely on a ground for possession. Both Acts contain two relevant grounds: breach of a term of the tenancy and a specific ground relating to nuisance and illegal behaviour. The specific grounds (2 in the 1985 Act, 14 in the 1988 Act) were extended by the 1996 Housing Act. The amendments made four main changes:

• including visitors to the dwelling among those whose conduct was to be considered;

- including conduct "likely to be a nuisance", so that it was not necessary to prove that anyone had actually suffered a nuisance or an annoyance and accordingly intended to make it easier to use 'professional' witnesses;
- extending those who were suffering the nuisance from 'neighbours' to any persons "residing, visiting or otherwise engaging in a lawful activity in the locality";
- adding to relevant convictions those of an arrestable offence committed in, or in the locality of, the dwelling house.

New forms of injunction

Injunctions may be used by landlords to order tenants to desist from particular behaviour. One of the perceived problems with injunctions was that while tenants could be injuncted on the basis of a breach of the tenancy agreement, it was very difficult for landlords to take action against non-tenants. The 1996 Act introduced a new basis for injunctions which could be sought by local authorities against both tenants and non-tenants where the person against whom it was sought had committed or threatened to commit violence. However, the threat had to be against someone residing in, visiting or otherwise engaging is a lawful activity in or in the locality of local authority housing. In certain circumstances, a power of arrest could also be attached to such injunctions.

In addition, the courts were given the power to add a power of arrest to injunctions based on breach of both local authorities' and RSLs' tenancy agreements, again in cases of violence or threatened violence. This means that the police can arrest immediately for breach of the injunction without having first to obtain a warrant for arrest from the courts.

Responses to the 1996 Act

The responses of social landlords to these powers is difficult to measure because of a lack of accurate recording among landlords (Nixon et al, 1999). However, it is clear that there has been an increasing use of legal powers among both local authorities and RSLs, with almost the same rate of service of notices of seeking possession (NSPs, the first step to possession proceedings) and conversion of these notices to actual proceedings (Nixon et al, 1999, ch 9). However, between landlords there were wide differentiations in the use of NSPs. Because of the lack of proper recording it was impossible to gauge how much the use of possession proceedings had increased among RSLs, but for local authorities there had been an increase of 127 per cent in the number of court actions commenced per 1,000 tenancies in the period 1996/97 to 1997/98 (Nixon et al, 1999, p 42).

In the use of injunctions there was a marked difference between local authorities and RSLs. The majority of local authorities stated that they sometimes or always used injunctions, which the majority of RSLs rarely or never used injunctions (Nixon et al, 1999, pp 47-8). In practice neither type of landlord made great use of injunctions, with very few being able to cite any instances where they had sought one.

The use of introductory/starter tenancy has had a mixed take-up, with 30 per cent of local authorities having adopted introductory tenancies and a further 12 per cent intending to in the next 12 months. Among RSLs 13 per cent had adopted starter tenancies and a further 18 per cent intended to over the next 12 months (Nixon et al, 1999, p 53). Where introductory tenancies were being used to evict tenants it was generally not for anti-social behaviour, but rather for rent arrears (68 per cent of cases) (p 55; see also Ruggieri and Levison, 1998).

The response of the courts to the increased powers has generally been to back up local authorities. For those landlords who could provide figures, 65 per cent of cases resulted in an outright order for possession (a higher rate than for rent arrears cases – see Nixon et al, 1999, pp 43-4). At the Court of Appeal whether in granting possession (see Manning, 1998), imprisoning for breach of injunction, or making challenges to introductory tenancies more difficult[2] the response has almost uniformly been one of victory for the landlord.

It is the eviction cases which have been most numerous in the Court of Appeal. Here the Court has emphasised that the needs of the victim must be weighed in the balance. The fact that the nuisance has been caused not by the tenant, but by the tenant's children does not prevent eviction. This is well illustrated by the case of *Newcastle CC v Morrison (2000) 33 HLR forthcoming, CA* where May LJ referred to the conduct of the tenant's sons as a "reign of terror". On the tenant's side there were matters which the court should take into account:

> "She has lived in the Newcastle upon Tyne area all her life and in the premises for about 10 years. She is a single parent with a small son to house and provide for and one sympathises at a personal level with a mother who is unable to control one or both of two rampaging, destructive, intimidating and, at times, dangerous teenage sons. She

gave evidence that she had made attempts to control her sons, and had at one stage in 1999 turned [one of them] out of her home, only to receive him back again when it was necessary for him to have an address for the purposes of bail conditions."

Notwithstanding this, the balance in this case "so obviously falls on the side which says that it was indeed reasonable to made an order for possession" that the judge below was "plainly wrong to conclude otherwise".

That such responses, particularly eviction, can have a devastating effect on families is undeniable. In our research (Hunter et al, 2000) we interviewed a number of tenants who had had eviction proceedings taken against them. They highlighted that some landlords did not carry out sufficient investigation. A number concerned evictions based on previous criminal convictions and seemed purely punitive in nature. In two cases there had been no complaints from the neighbours about the criminal activity – indeed they turned up in court to support the tenants. The evictions seemed to serve no purpose in housing management terms, but seemed more like a further punishment for the criminal offences. In the *Morrison* case above the sons had already been punished through the criminal system for their behaviour. Further steps could have been taken against the sons, such as an anti-social behaviour order (see below), and yet the fact that other remedies were available was not a reason not to evict the mother.

Such an approach to those convicted of criminal offences or indeed to their families, reflects a social disciplinary model of policing where

> ... its initial and primary purpose is to remind an individual or a community that they are under constant surveillance: the objective is to punish or humiliate the individual, or to communicate police contempt for a particular community or family, or to demonstrate that the police have absolute control over those who challenge the right of the police to define and enforce 'normality'. (Choongh, 1998, p 626)

The difference in these cases is that it is not the police asserting this control but the social landlord, taking their cue from criminal conviction as a reason to commence action.

Two caveats must, however, be acknowledged. First, housing officers interviewed for the purposes of our research (Hunter et al, 2000) did not express any views which chimed with this model. Second, in some cases 'due process', the requirement of the landlord to obtain a court order before evicting, meant that the landlord was unable to evict. The families concerned were, however, extremely frightened and humiliated by the process, even if they were able to stave off the ultimate sanction.

Social control of those in social housing

The approach of the 1996 Act can be said to be one which targets those living in social housing, reduces and limits the rights of such people, and ultimately takes away one of their most basic rights – the right to live in their home. It is accordingly essentially punitive. That such an approach can be taken against those residing in social housing should not come as such a great surprise to those familiar with the history of social housing.

Burney (1999) identifies two approaches to housing management which emerged at the end of the Victorian era, as social landlordism first began. These were "control of access, and control of tenants' conduct". Both, she concludes, have "been practised widely by council landlords for the greater part of their existence". It is this control of tenants' conduct which seems to have become a dominant concern of the last 20 years. As Clapham (1997) has suggested, an emphasis on surveillance of tenants has become an accepted part of housing management work. Haworth and Manzi (1999) also identify that this social control approach has emerged more forcefully in recent years and is strongly influenced by the specific policy discourse of 'residualisation', 'social exclusion' and 'underclass' theories.

Haworth and Manzi (1999) go on to examine how this discourse has come to dominate in housing management:

> A dominant deontological theme permeates the practice of housing management, underpinned by strong moralistic perspectives, reinforcing a disjuncture with the discourse of empowerment. Resource constraints and the stigma attached to public rented housing are inexorably connected to the kind of restrictive housing policies operating in contemporary housing management. (p 163)

Thus this approach to dealing with anti-social behaviour can be seen to fall within the historical pattern of housing management as an instrument of social control. Indeed, as illustrated above, social control may slip into an even more forceful form than social discipline. The legal powers given to landlords simply strengthen their hand. Some landlords have taken more readily to using the powers than others, but where they have the courts have provided them with strong support.

The 1998 Crime and Disorder Act

The 1998 Act contained a number of disparate provisions. In relation to anti-social behaviour, the primary focus must be the anti social behaviour order (ASBO), which can be sought by the police or a local authority (acting in partnership with each other) where a person over the age of ten has been behaving in an anti-social manner and the order is necessary to protect others from further anti-social behaviour. The orders are made by the Magistrates Court, and any breach is a criminal offence.

The relevant provisions only came into effect in April 1999, and it is still too early to find any detailed research on their use. Comments from the Home Office indicate, however, disappointment that greater use has not been made of them (see, for example, Home Office, 2000). In the first 14 months 'only' 80 ASBOs had been imposed in England and Wales. In order to "encourage greater use" the Home Office has produced a guidance booklet. Policy Action Team 8 identifies some reasons for the low number of applications. Among these (SEU, 2000, p 40) was "discussions and disagreement about *who* is actually responsible for the application and administration of procedures within partnerships". Thus a problem emerges where the focus for dealing with it is taken away from the landlord. Locating the problem as a housing issue provides a clear responsibility for action, which is lost when it ceases to be constructed in this way.

ASBOs do not appear to have been primarily used as a tool against tenants of social landlords. The reported cases show use in a large number of cases against children. The conduct relates to both that in and around the home and in other public spaces such as shopping centres. Indeed there is some evidence to suggest that they are being used to deal with other criminal problems, such as to remove repeat offenders from a particular area, or to deal with prostitution. What it is impossible to say at this stage is whether they have had any effect in reducing anti-social behaviour.

Directions from PAT 8

Two distinct themes emerge from the PAT 8 report. First, the purely 'legal' approach is not sufficient. While they acknowledge that using the existing powers more effectively is important in some areas, much more work needs to be done on the underlying causes of anti-social behaviour and promoting prevention. Second, they acknowledge that it is a problem which is not confined to social housing. Sanctions are necessary against perpetrators who are living in privately rented accommodation or are owner-occupiers.

Tackling the underlying causes

In our research we examined 67 case files where some form of action had been taken against the tenant in the past three years for anti-social behaviour. The files came from a variety of landlords in a range of geographical locations. The files confirmed the views of housing officers that those tenants with support needs were most frequently the subject of complaints (Hunter et al, 2000). Thus 18 per cent of perpetrators had themselves been subject to physical or sexual abuse; 18 per cent had a mental disability; 15 per cent had out of control children; 12 per cent had a drugs problem; 11 per cent an alcohol problem and 9 per cent a physical disability (Hunter et al, 2000, p 19). It is likely that these figures were an underestimate, as they were taken from what had been recorded on the tenancy or legal files, and there may have been information unknown to or unrecorded by the relevant officers. It is also worth considering the cases which have reached the Court of Appeal, where there is also a preponderance of single mothers with children with severe behavioural problems and single men with mental health difficulties.

What these figures suggest is that PAT 8 is correct in calling for much greater preventative work which tackles the underlying causes of anti-social behaviour. After all:

> Evicting anti-social people does not mean that the problem will go away. Some people will be deterred from future anti-social behaviour by the experience of eviction or exclusion from the housing register. Some people will not. If their problems are not addressed, the pattern of behaviour will repeat itself. (SEU, 2000, para 4.35)

How is this to be achieved? As ever there are calls for better multiagency working. Yet the difficulties of this are well documented (see, for example, Crawford, 1997; Wilson and Charlton, 1997; Coles et al, 1998). Our own research revealed enormous frustration among housing officers towards social services, so that it was not uncommon for possession action to be initiated in order to gain a response from social services:

> There is a reluctance of the social services to become involved in nuisance cases. To a certain extent the housing department is left to take inappropriate action ... but sometimes we have to do it to actually bring social services on board. (Hunter et al, 2000, p 32)

For any progress to be made there needs to be an enormous effort to break down what we have characterised as the problems "arising from different organisational cultures, agendas, and lack of understood and agreed communication channels" (Hunter et al, 2000, p 38). But it must remain the case that the taking of punitive action such as possession proceedings, merely in order to obtain access to a support service, cannot be an appropriate use of legal proceedings.

Other housing tenures

The concern expressed by various governments during the mid-1990s focused almost exclusively on the problems of the anti-social behaviour in and around social housing. However, in more recent months the concern has widened to embrace the private sector. One recent study (Genn, 1999) suggests that problems of neighbour disputes are more prevalent among owner-occupiers than tenants (the study does now, however, seek to define what is meant by neighbour disputes).

The Social Exclusion Unit PAT 7 report (SEU, 1999) identified a cycle of decline that can encompass areas of private sector housing. In such areas demand falls, leaving properties impossible to sell to owner-occupiers. Landlords purchase the properties for very low prices. They then let to tenants in receipt of Housing Benefit. Such landlords are unconcerned about the behaviour of their tenants and "just one anti-social tenant can clear a street, and so the spiral of decline accelerates, as the owner-occupiers and good landlords are forced out" (SEU, 1999, para 1.26). The Green Paper (DETR/DSS, 2000, para 5.33) refers to an unholy alliance between bad landlords and bad tenants.

The PAT 8 report (SEU, 2000, p 95) notes that practitioners on the ground have concerns that "victims living next to perpetrators in private rented or owner-occupier accommodation are less protected from anti-social behaviour than social tenants". Our own research (Hunter et al, 2000), shows a problem of displacement of social tenants evicted for anti-social behaviour into the private sector. The new concern emerging therefore is how to control anti-social behaviour perpetrated by people living in private sector housing.

The focus of the PAT 8 report in relation to other tenures is very much on the legal differences which make it difficult to control behaviour. It is suggested that there are legal anomalies in that private tenants are less likely to be subject to specific anti-social behaviour clauses in their tenancy agreement and there can be no power of arrest applied to any breach of their tenancy agreement. Given the lack of rights that private tenants have, it might be thought that this would not make a great deal of difference to their position (it is this form of tenure that the Housing Corporation have introduced as a measure to deal with anti-social behaviour!). The PAT 8 report goes on to suggest a much more important difference at para 4.31: "it appears that private landlords are much less prepared to take action". This is not surprising, given the evidence above of differential use by social landlords of the remedies available.

The PAT 8 report tentatively sets out some options to deal with the problem. These include empowering local authorities to take action against private tenants through injunctions and evictions and charging the private landlord for the costs incurred.

For owner-occupiers there is a similar analysis of the legal problems. Owner-occupiers generally have no landlord to whom they can look to protect them if they are victims of anti-social behaviour. On the other hand, if they are perpetrators, the victim cannot look to a landlord to take action to stem the behaviour through eviction or injunction. The range of legal options is more limited. For owner-occupiers, two are canvassed by PAT 8. The first is that local authorities include covenants in the freehold conveyances or leases of properties they sell and enforce them. The second option from PAT 8 is to encourage local authorities and community groups to support individuals to take out injunctions against perpetrators. The option does not set out the basis for any such injunctions but it may perhaps be assumed that they would primarily be based on nuisance.

The focus of these suggestions is on tackling anti-social behaviour as a 'housing' problem through an attack on property rights. This is essentially the same approach as that of the 1996 Housing Act, outlined above. In legal terms it proves much more difficult to achieve because of the very different legal structures controlling these modes of occupation, which are themselves a reflection of the very different ideological approaches to these forms of tenure over the past 20 years (see Hunter and Nixon, 2000).

The only new suggestion relating to anti-social behaviour in the Green Paper is similarly directed at using housing as the focus to control individual behaviour. It is suggested that:

> Local authorities could be given the powers to reduce Housing Benefit for unruly tenants as an alternative, or as part of the process of pursuing an Anti-Social Behaviour Order. Full benefit would be restored once the tenant's behaviour had improved. (DETR/DSS, 2000, para 5.47)

It is recognised that this would "mark a fundamental shift in the nature of Housing Benefit" and that great care would be needed in proceeding with such a policy. "Above all we would need to ensure that the innocent families of unruly tenants did not suffer" (a factor that does not always seem to matter during eviction proceedings). Thus rather than reducing property rights, it is the welfare rights of tenants which would diminish.

Conclusion

There is always a tension in dealing with (and indeed writing on) anti-social behaviour. For victims it is indeed most disturbing, particularly where this takes place in and around their home. Even where the complaint is of a non-criminal matter such as noise it is clear that it can have profound effects on the victim. For victims punitive action, the removal of the perpetrator from the neighbourhood does indeed solve their problem and provide peace of mind. The courts have been very mindful of this in explicitly referring to balancing the needs of the victim against the potential homelessness of the perpetrator. On the other hand, the evidence suggests that many of the perpetrators will continue with the behaviour wherever they live. Eviction will just move the behaviour elsewhere.

What then is the way forward? The work of PAT 8 provides some indication that a more measured approach is at last emerging from the government. The punitive individualistic responses of both the 1996 Housing Act and the 1998 Crime and Disorder Act are giving way to a more holistic response which will encompass the physical environment, allocation policies, youth services, neighbourhood wardens, mediation services and intensive work with perpetrators.

This does not mean, however, complete abandonment of punitive strategies. These will undoubtedly continue, and have become embedded in government responses to issues of crime and disorder (see Rose, 2000 and Young, 1999 for possible explanations of the broader changes in society which give rise to this phenomenon). Enforcement is a key message in PAT 8. Yet we have to ask ourselves what forms of enforcement are appropriate. And, as the 1998 Human Rights Act comes into force and incorporates the European Convention on Human Rights into domestic law, we have to ask what forms of action are proportionate. This will clearly have an impact on individual cases. Already the issue has been raised in asking the question as to whether it is proportionate to evict an elderly tenant of many years standing from her home for the conduct of her errant teenage grandsons[3].

But it should also have an impact in considering what should be done in relation to those in other tenures. It seems inconceivable that an owner-occupier whose teenage son is convicted of burglary in the surrounding area should be evicted from his home. Yet, this is what happens to tenants in social housing. In exploring the way forward in tackling problems arising in other tenures we must begin to examine how rights to housing may be distributed more equitably.

Furthermore in focusing on the fact that anti-social behaviour is not confined to those living in social housing, PAT 8 has drawn attention to a fundamental point. In dealing with it as a housing issue we lost sight of the fact that it arises not from people's housing circumstances but rather from a myriad of other social factors which must be tackled. If we can break the link between housing and anti-social behaviour and see it as a wider problem of society (not one to be dealt with by social landlords) then these broader approaches will be more readily acceptable.

But this is not to say we should move to a view where the way forward is the ASBO and to criminalise every errant teenager. The ASBO itself is a very punitive response, creating an individualised criminal offence in its very terms. Again alternative strategies need to be developed to avoid their use, particularly against young people.

Nor is it to say that housing policy cannot have a role to play, particularly in helping to build and maintain communities. It is rather to argue that legal measures in this area, whether housing or criminal, all focus on punishing the individual. We must also not lose sight of the fact that the legal process tends to focus on those cases at the criminal end of the anti-social spectrum. To improve the lives of the majority affected by anti-social behaviour – be it litter or noise – it is unlikely that punishment of individuals will be a way forward.

Notes

[1] The writing of this chapter would have not been possible without my previous work and writing with other colleagues on this subject, in particular Judy Nixon and Sigrid Shayer (at Sheffield Hallam University) and Suzie Scott and Tom Mullen (at Glasgow Univeristy). The views expressed here though are my own, and I remain responsible for them.

[2] Space precludes a discussion of all these cases but see: on eviction *Kensington & Chelsea RLBC v Simmonds (1996) 29 HLR 507; Darlington BC v Sterling (1996) 29 HLR 309; Bristol CC v Mousah (1997) 30 HLR 32; Northampton LBC v Lovatt (1997) 30 HLR 875; West Kent HA v Davies (1998) 30 HLR 416; Newcastle upon Tyne CC v Morrison (2000) 32 HLR forthcoming; Bryant v Portsmouth CC (2000) 33 HLR forthcoming;* on injunctions *Manchester CC v Lawler (1998) 31 HLR 119; Tower Hamlets LBC v Long (1998) 32 HLR 219;* on introductory tenancies *Manchester CC v Cochrane (1998) 31 HLR 810.*

[3] See *Bryant v Portsmouth CC (2000) 33 HLR forthcoming,* per Sedley LJ, but which did not affect the ultimate decision upholding a suspended order for possession.

References

Burney, E. (1999) *Crime and banishment: Nuisance and exclusion in social housing,* Winchester: Waterside Press.

Choongh, S. (1998) 'Policing the dross: a social disciplinary model of policing', *British Journal of Criminology,* vol 38, no 4, pp 623-34.

Clapham, D. (1997) 'The social construction of housing management', *Urban Studies,* vol 34, pp 761-74.

Coles, B., England, J. and Rugg, J. (1998) *Working with young people on estates: The role of housing professionals in multi-agency work,* Coventry: Chartered Institute of Housing.

Cowan, D. (1999) *Housing law and policy,* Basingstoke: Macmillan.

Crawford, A. (1997) *The local governance of crime: Appeals to community and partnership,* Oxford: Clarendon Press.

DETR (Department of the Environment, Transport and the Regions)/ DSS (Department of Social Security) (2000) *Quality and choice: A decent home for all*, Housing Green Paper, London: DETR/DSS.

Dignan, J., Sorsby, A. and Hibbert, J. (1996) *Neighbour disputes: Comparing the cost-effectiveness of mediation and alternative approaches*, Sheffield: Centre for Criminological and Legal Research, University of Sheffield.

DoE (Department of the Environment) (1995) *Anti-social behaviour on housing estates: Consultation paper on probationary tenancies*, London: DoE.

Genn, H. with National Centre for Social Research (1999) *Paths to justice*, Oxford: Hart Publishing.

Haworth, A. and Manzi, T. (1999) 'Managing the "underclass": interpreting the moral discourse of housing management', *Urban Studies*, vol 36, pp 153-65.

Home Office (2000) *New guide to help crack down on anti-social behaviour*, News Release June 26 (www.homeoffice.gov.uk).

Hope, T. and Foster, J. (1992) 'Conflicting forces: changing the dynamics of crime and community on a "problem" estate', *British Journal of Criminology*, vol 32, pp 488-504.

Housing Corporation (1999) *Performance standards, addendum 4 to the social housing standards for general and supported housing: Anti-social behaviour*, London: The Housing Corporation.

Hunter, C. and Nixon, J. (2000) 'Controlling anti-social behaviour through property rights', Paper to European Network for Housing Research Conference, Gävle, Sweden, June.

Hunter, C., Nixon, J. and Shayer, S. (2000) *Neighbour nuisance, social landlords and the law*, Coventry: Chartered Institute of Housing.

Karn, V., Lickiss, R., Hughes, D. and Crawley, J. (1993) *Neighbour disputes: Responses by social landlords*, Coventry: Institute of Housing.

Labour Party (1995) *A quiet life: Tough action on criminal neighbours*, London: Labour Party.

Liddle, M., Warburton, F. and Feloy, M. (1997) *Nuisance problems in Brixton: Describing local experiences, designing effective solutions*, London: NACRO.

Manning, J. (1998) 'Reasonableness: a new approach', *Journal of Housing Law*, vol 1, no 4, pp 59-61.

Nixon, J., Hunter, C. and Shayer, S. (1999) *The use of legal remedies by social landlords to deal with neighbour nuisance*, Sheffield: CRESR, Sheffield Hallam University.

Rose, N. (2000) 'Government and control', *British Journal of Criminology*, vol 40, no 2, pp 321-39.

Ruggieri, S. and Levison, D. (1998) *Starter tenancies and introductory tenancies: An evaluation*, London: The Housing Corporation.

SEU (Social Exclusion Unit) (1999) *Report of Policy Action Team 7: Unpopular housing*, London: SEU.

SEU (2000) *Report of Policy Action Team 8: Anti-social behaviour*, London: SEU.

Swinden, T. (1996) 'Neighbour nuisance: the Camden experience', Unpublished report for Joseph Rowntree Foundation, York.

Wilson, A. and Charlton, K. (1997) *Making partnerships work: A practical guide for the public, private and voluntary and community sectors*, York: Joseph Rowntree Foundation.

Young, J. (1999) *The exclusive society*, London: Sage Publications.

Housing management in the era of Best Value

Introduction

Before coming to power New Labour committed to replacing Compulsory Competitive Tendering for local authority services with a regime of Best Value. The first few years of government were spent attempting to construct a framework to attach to the 'Best Value' label. The result was embodied in the 1999 Local Government Act. All local authorities in England were placed under a duty of Best Value from April 2000. This has implications for all services – including all aspects of the housing service – provided by local authorities. The Housing Corporation – the regulator for Registered Social Landlords (RSLs) – administers a comparable voluntary regime to which RSLs are expected to adhere. Best Value will undoubtedly reshape the way in which social housing is provided and managed: precisely how substantial the effect will be is as yet unclear.

The two authors asked to reflect on housing management in the era of Best Value address the issue from very different angles and with a different focus. Yet, while approached from different disciplinary perspectives, a shared concern with the relationship between regulator and regulatee, regulatory strategies, and the impact of regulation on the behaviour of the regulatee are apparent.

Peter Vincent-Jones locates Best Value within a broad current of change which, he argues, is resulting in a move from housing management to "the management of housing" as local authority provision declines. He identifies the range of regulatory mechanisms that are available to central government before focusing on central commands and financial incentives. A contrast is drawn between the rigid prescriptions of the competitive tendering regime and the seemingly more flexible approach to regulation under Best Value. Nonetheless, taken alongside other policy changes impacting on local authority housing, Vincent-Jones argues that Best Value contributes to the 'responsibilisation' of local government and could have potentially far-reaching consequences. Responsibilisation entails the (re)orientation of local government thinking and strategy so that local government actions align with central government policy objectives. As Vincent-Jones summarises, this occurs through "inculcation of common calculative technologies, forms of evaluation, and norms and values" in such a way that local authorities follow the course that government wishes them to take without the need for crude 'command and control' regulation.

In contrast, Bruce Walker focuses on the Best Value framework that is emerging in the RSL sector. The perspective adopted is that of economics. He opens by reviewing the arguments against public sector provision before reviewing the possible sources of comparative advantage accruing to RSLs, drawing on the literature on the economics of not-for-profit organisations. Walker examines how regulators can try to ensure the efficient performance of RSLs and how the role and approach of the regulator is changing in the light of changes in the nature of RSL operations, RSL performance and the advent of Best Value. The focus is squarely on incentives: the incentives set up by systems of performance measurement and the effect that regulation can have on the profile of the activities of the regulatees. Walker identifies tensions between the regulatory style that has been favoured by the Housing Corporation in the past and the requirements of the Best Value regime. He argues that regulation has tended to favour compliance approaches, but the increased emphasis on performance indicators and comparison, audit and inspection gives the Best Value regime a stronger 'deterrence' and 'enforcement' dimension. He closes by reflecting on whether any attempt at enforcement will be successful given that the regime has no statutory basis in the RSL sector. Even if enforcement is possible, as Walker observes, this may not necessarily be beneficial.

Much of the attention in the literature around Best Value has, quite rightly, been on local authorities. With social housing provision moving rapidly away from local authorities, the uncertainties over the operation and impacts of Best Value in the RSL sector, and the way the system develops over the coming years, are going to be of the utmost significance to the consumers of social housing.

TWELVE

From housing management to the management of housing: the challenge of Best Value

Peter Vincent–Jones

Introduction

This chapter analyses the transformation in the housing management role of local authorities in recent government policy and legislation, drawing on theoretical perspectives on governmentality and regulation. The general change in the form of regulation of local by central government over the past 20 years has been well documented (Loughlin, 1996). From 1979 the traditional emphasis on facilitation, collaboration and negotiation was replaced by a climate of antagonism and confrontation, with legislation being used increasingly as an instrument to curtail the autonomy of local councils. The resolution of problems through bargaining and administrative processes gave way to central control and prescription, and to juridification expressed in legal disputes, litigation and resort to the courts on an unprecedented scale. In the 1990s the regulatory grip of central government was further tightened, with more explicit legal rules and powers, more central oversight, supervision and monitoring, and the increasingly routine use of punitive sanctions to discipline wayward local authorities (Hood et al, 1999). Such developments, typified by the 19-year regime of compulsory competitive tendering (CCT), involved a relatively crude 'command and control' approach to regulation. Many of the failures of CCT were arguably associated with legal formalism – the highly specific nature of rules and regulations inviting their manipulation and subversion through 'creative compliance', leading ultimately to the defeat of legal policy (McBarnet and Whelan, 1991).

While New Labour is continuing and extending the fundamental policy objectives of the Conservatives in the field of housing, the regulatory means to the attainment of these ends are significantly different[1]. This chapter considers housing management aspects of the 'Best Value in Housing' (BVH) framework (DETR, 2000) and the Green Paper *Quality and choice: A decent home for all* (DETR/DSS, 2000), against the background of the regulatory failures of CCT[2]. In the first section, the general duties on housing authorities under BVH are outlined, followed in the second section by an overview of the variety of mechanisms (central commands, financial incentives, competition, information and regulatory fragmentation) involved in the regulation of social housing. The third section examines in depth the regulatory techniques being deployed in the pursuit of three key housing policy objectives: (1) the encouragement of a more strategic local authority role in managing housing, in place of the traditional function of housing management of council-owned property; (2) the separation (where the council retains housing stock) of local authority ownership and housing management functions, aimed at improving the management of council-owned properties; and (3), the encouragement of both greater diversity of social housing provision and increased choice on the part of housing 'consumers' among different types of social landlord. In the concluding section, current changes in housing management are considered in the broader context of the government's attempt to 'steer' local authorities in certain directions through 'responsibilisation' strategies aimed at aligning their organisational thinking and strategy with centrally determined housing policy objectives.

Best Value in housing framework

CCT mandated that local authorities could carry out certain housing management functions by direct labour only where the work had been put out to tender and won by the council workforce in open competition[3], prescribing in detail the competitive processes, accounting requirements, and penalties to which authorities were subject in the event of default. Under BVH the duties and sanctions are more generally defined. The principal duty – to make arrangements to secure continuous improvement, having regard to economy, efficiency and effectiveness – is deliberately vaguely worded to minimise the possibility of legal challenge. Additional duties may be individually imposed on authorities through powers of the

Secretary of State to make different orders for different authorities, applying at different times. The relative success of authorities in achieving Best Value will be judged with reference to a central framework of performance indicators and standards. National performance indicators for housing, including tenant satisfaction, are expected to be supplemented by local performance indicators, reflecting local needs and priorities (DETR, 2000, Annex C and para 6.52).

Not only are the duties more general under Best Value, but the scope of the new framework is much wider. Whereas housing management CCT applied to a limited range of council landlord responsibilities, all local authority housing functions must be reviewed within a five-year period and within consecutive five-year cycles thereafter (DETR, 1999a). These functions include (in addition to the management of council stock owned by the authority) responsibilities for the environment and sustainability, investment through renovation grants, home adaptations for disabled people, energy efficiency, and housing needs assessment and advice. Furthermore, the duty to secure continuous improvement is owed to all local householders, whether council tenants, leaseholders, housing association tenants, owner-occupiers or private tenants. The general duty to consult with representatives of council tax payers, non-domestic ratepayers, service users and other persons applies to housing in the same way as to other functions, reflecting the strategic importance of the local authority role in addressing wider 'cross-cutting' social issues that are connected with housing (DETR, 2000, para 2.13).

The BVH regulatory framework is complicated, however, by the imposition of specific duties regarding tenant participation, in recognition of the 'special relationship' between local authorities and tenants. Under the *National Framework for Tenant Participation Compacts* (DETR, 1999b), Tenant Participation Compacts (TPCs)[4] must have been introduced for all council tenants and leaseholders by 1 April 2000. The purpose of Compacts is to define a clear role for tenants in the decision-making process, in particular those tenants who have traditionally been hard to reach. By specifying tenants' rights and roles in consultation and participation, the government hopes that councils will become more responsive to local needs and better able to develop policies tackling social exclusion. Compacts are regarded as an integral part of the Best Value regime, complementing and underpinning the consultation function in BVH. *Neighbourhood Compacts* governing day-to-day management may be agreed covering particular areas, estates or communities, while *council-wide Compacts* involving strategic housing issues may have a wider and more general application.

The National Framework sets out core standards which the government believes are the necessary foundation for successful tenant participation (DETR, 2000, para 4.19). Existing participation fora and processes of decision making must satisfy these minimum standards, thus forming an integral part of the Best Value duty. The standards concern minimum levels of support/resources to enable participation to work (ie, facilities, officer support, training, advice), standards for tenant meetings and tenants' groups (ie, constitutions, equal opportunities, regular elections, open financial records, publicity, action plans, regular newsletters), and performance monitoring (ie, regular reviews, remedial action taken, assessment of compacts' efficacy through surveys and samples). To ensure continuous improvement, TPC standards will be subject to a national performance indicator target forming part of the Best Value annual service reviews.

Techniques of regulation

Regulation may be defined for present purposes as a process of social ordering in which public welfare goals, either explicitly articulated in the political sphere or implicit in the operation of state and non-state bodies, are promoted through regulatory arrangements or frameworks establishing in greater or lesser detail policy ends and means to those ends. The elements common to virtually all types of regulation include the specification of rules or standards, the monitoring of compliance, and the existence of some form of enforcement mechanism. Regulation may occur through legal compulsion, the deployment of wealth or the control of information. It may involve the devolution of regulatory tasks to regulated bodies themselves ('self-regulation'), may take the form of private law rules or public standards, may apply to populations generally or be specifically addressed to particular regulatees, may involve state or non-state bodies, and may give rise to obligations and liabilities under private or public law (Vincent-Jones, 2000a).

A variety of theoretical approaches may be used in analysing bureaucratic or public sector regulation (Hood and Scott, 1996). This section considers the BVH and related initiatives principally with reference to Daintith's categorisation of regulatory techniques of *imperium* and *dominium*. According to this analysis *imperium* is characterised by commands backed by force – by duties or rules whose breach is accompanied by negative sanctions (but compliance may be rewarded through the relaxation of rules). *Dominium*, on the other hand, refers to the employment of wealth, usually in the form of government grants or contracts, as incentives to comply with central policy (but withdrawal of such benefits may serve a sanctioning purpose) (Daintith, 1994, p 212). Dominium is able to operate effectively as a regulatory technique in the housing context due to the increasing dependence of local councils on central government funding following decades of erosion of their financial autonomy. This perspective will be supplemented by consideration of competition and information as regulatory resources and the increasingly wide dispersal of regulatory functions (in contrast to simple hierarchical command of the state) among a range of parties and bodies occupying the 'regulatory space' around local authorities.

Imperium

Best Value represents a significant shift in the form of *imperium* control by comparison with its predecessor. The formalistic regulatory schema of CCT, with its rigid definition of duties in terms of inputs, processes and financial outputs, encouraged many local authorities in the 1990s to divert their energies from the improvement of services into undermining the process of CCT. The attempt to close loopholes by tightening the rules through secondary legislation led to further avoidance, confusion and the constant revision of implementation timetables. As McBarnet and Whelan commented in a different but analogous regulatory context, "How do you control those playing by the rules? New rules simply mean new games" (1991, p 873)[5]. Other defects of formal 'input' regulation may also be said to have accompanied the attempt under CCT to prescribe methods, rules and sanctions in exhaustive detail. Best Value, by contrast, represents a more 'anti-formalist' type of regulation, which is relatively flexible, open-ended and policy-oriented, relying on general principles and broad standards, and attaching greatest weight to Best Value *outcomes*. Just as the level of performance that will satisfy Best Value is difficult to know in advance, so the sanctions that may accompany Best Value 'failures' are hard to predict, given the general nature of default powers and the wide discretion left to the Secretary of State in their exercise[6].

The *specific requirement* on the part of housing authorities to draw up TPCs with council tenants is in contrast to the generally facilitative and non-prescriptive Best Value framework. Here the government considers that additional regulation is necessary to improve the responsiveness of the management of council-owned properties, other landlords being free from such regulation because they are presumed to be exposed to other pressures for improvement, or to be more likely to be better managers. But regulation (albeit 'self-regulation') applies to the voluntary sector, and the aim to achieve comparability and 'read-across' between sectors may limit the significance of the formal distinction, as will be shown below.

Dominium

The increasing dependence of local authorities on central government finance has been secured through the imposition of a range of public borrowing and expenditure controls. In the 1980s the introduction of the 'block grant' mechanism enabled central government to withhold grants from local authorities that overspent centrally imposed targets, so that the burden of additional expenditure had to be borne by local ratepayers. From 1984 'rate capping' then restricted the ability of councils to raise funds through local taxation, with maximum figures for increases being imposed by central government. The financial autonomy of local authorities was further curtailed after 1992 by stringent controls on spending based on Standard Spending Assessments (SSAs). While 'crude and universal' capping was abolished under the 1999 Local Government Act, it was replaced with more 'discriminating and flexible' reserve powers to limit council tax increases deemed excessive by central government. The powers will enable the Secretary of State to examine an authority's budget requirements over a period of years, and take into account such factors as the authority's performance in the delivery of Best Value and the support of the local electorate for the proposed budget. From 1 April 1999 local authorities were also made responsible for meeting part of the cost of council tax benefit subsidy as a further spur to increasing local responsibility for council tax increases. Under this system council tax benefit may be partially withdrawn where authorities set their council tax above guidelines set by the Secretary of State. Councils are also prevented by Treasury rules from using assets or future income from rents as security to borrow on the open market, although capital receipts from council house sales may now be used for designated purposes such as the repair of existing council stock.

The clearest example of the exercise of *dominium* regulation of local authorities' housing functions is in relation to the housing investment programme (HIP). The HIP process requires local authorities to produce a housing strategy, plans and priorities for tackling housing needs in the area, and to draw up annual plans for the housing capital programme. In producing their housing strategy, the authorities must consult widely with tenants, residents, Registered Social Landlords (RSLs) and other housing providers, taking account of related interests involving health and social services (DETR, 1999c, para 6.68). The annual HIP round is conducted by Government Offices for the Regions (GOs) in close collaboration with regional offices of the Housing Corporation. Financial allocations by GOs are based on indices of relative need and on assessments of the quality of authorities' housing strategies (40 per cent), programme delivery (20 per cent), housing management (20 per cent) and tenant participation (including TPCs and tenant involvement in strategy, monitoring and decision making) (20 per cent). These assessments are used in the allocation of half housing capital resources, with higher shares going to better performers (DETR, 1999c, para 6.68). Allocations could be reduced by as much as one fifth where local authorities fail to meet targets. Performance on TPCs is likely to be particularly important in the determination of future funding levels. Councils will be required to report annually on how Compacts have operated and to set improvement targets for the following year as part of their Best Value performance plans. GOs will be closely involved in the monitoring of progress with TPCs. The government has acknowledged that it will be necessary for HIP assessments and Best Value housing inspection processes in particular to complement one another, and to avoid the duplication of regulatory burdens (DETR, 1999b, section 5). An additional £12 million was made available to councils in England over the two financial years beginning in April 2000 to help with the administrative costs of setting up TPCs.

Competition, information and regulatory fragmentation

The idea of regulation as the imposition and enforcement of formal rules and commands emanating from identifiable points in the state hierarchy is deficient in a number of respects. As the analysis of imperium and dominium has already suggested, regulation is the product of the interaction of a variety of forces (including rules, standards, wealth, competition, information and financial incentives) which are fragmented and dispersed among a number of public agencies, private firms, pressure and interest groups, national and international organisations, and other state and non-state bodies. While this insight has been developed primarily in relation to the privatised utilities and telecommunications industries

(Hancher and Moran, 1989; Scott et al, 1997), it is just as relevant to the 'bureaucratic regulation' of government by other state bodies (Hood and Scott, 1996).

First, regulation may be said to occur in markets and quasi-markets through the incentives and pressures accompanying competition and their capacity for generating efficiency. The point that market forces may themselves constitute a form of regulation has led Sir Stephen Sedley to inquire whether the market needs the rule of law or is itself a novel form of law (Sedley, 1997, p viii). Efficient and effective service-providing outcomes are likely to depend on contestability and on the nature and degree of competition[7]. The role of competition as a technique for modifying the behaviour of local authorities has increased in recent years (Hood et al, 1999). The difference between CCT and Best Value is that while in the former case competition was compulsorily imposed, in the latter it is being encouraged in a more subtle and less coercive manner.

Second, many agencies are currently at work in the regulatory space around local authority housing functions, including the Audit Commission, the Central GOs, the Housing Inspectorate, the Housing Corporation, housing associations, the Local Government Association, the Improvement and Development Agency, and the specialised housing units within the Department of the Environment, Transport and the Regions. Local authorities themselves play an important self-regulatory role in conducting performance reviews and drawing up plans, in setting and monitoring improvement targets, and in determining local standards and Compacts. Citizens and residents in the local community have opportunities to participate in BVH at various stages, particularly council tenants under the TPC initiative. Participation will be encouraged generally by regulatory provisions governing the availability and circulation of information (which also serves to enhance competition). Local people will be informed of progress on targets in published performance plans. The reports of auditors and the Audit Commission will similarly be published. Authorities subject to intervention powers will receive information at various stages of the enforcement process. The general publication of information is intended to encourage authorities to learn from one another and to spread good practice. The availability of information will enable councillors, officials, contractors and other authorities and agencies to become involved in the implementation of Best Value. Problems of coordination of regulatory processes (for example inspections) and factionalism among different constituencies competing for influence may from this perspective be regarded as natural and even welcome consequences of the widening of participation (Vincent-Jones, 2000b).

From 'housing management' to the management of housing

The changing role of local authorities in housing management is the inevitable consequence of policies – inherited from the Conservatives and given added impetus by New Labour – aimed at reducing public sector service provision. While large-scale voluntary transfer (LSVT) had a relatively modest impact following its introduction in the 1980s in comparison with the Right to Buy, the programme has recently expanded beyond recognition. The number of units transferred in 1996/97 was 25,000; in 1998 and 1999 the numbers were 80,000 and 140,000 respectively. According to one estimate the size of the housing association sector could be 2.3 million units by 2008 (Cooke, 1999), while stories about the government's plans to 'abolish' council housing have made newspaper headlines[8]. The attitude of Labour councils has changed dramatically from stout opposition in the mid-1990s to positive enthusiasm in 2000, with authorities queuing up to transfer homes in record numbers. The present position is in stark contrast to the belief of many Labour and Liberal-Democrat councils at the time of the General Election in 1997 that the new government would return power to local councils to build homes.

Given increasing restrictions on the financial autonomy of local authorities and the estimated £22 billion cost of repairing and renovating crumbling council housing stock, the attractiveness of voluntary transfer as a means of off-loading housing responsibilities and liabilities to other social landlords, who enjoy relative freedom from public borrowing constraints, is understandable. The LSVT programme provides indirectly a financial inducement, distinct from the direct financial incentives normally associated with *dominium*. The success of this technique is evident in the current competition in applications for LSVT, with some of the biggest social landlords in Britain, such as Glasgow and Birmingham, heading the queue. Reports following the General Election that the Labour government might have to *force* councils to switch 100,000 homes a year now seem far-fetched. More homes have been *voluntarily* bid for transfer this year than in the last six years put together.

Against this general background, three specific 'housing management' objectives may be discerned in recent legislation and policy documents, each analysed here with reference to the regulatory techniques introduced in the foregoing section.

1.A more strategic local authority role in the coordination of local social housing provision

The government wants to see a change in the local authority housing role from owning and managing stock ('housing management' as traditionally conceived), to 'managing housing' in the sense of overseeing provision by a variety of social landlords and different tenures. As their direct landlord function is being reduced, councils are being encouraged to "bring themselves back into the heart of their communities" by taking a more strategic view of their responsibilities (DETR, 2000, Foreword), for example with respect to the environment and sustainability, integrating standards across the increasingly varied and fragmented range of housing providers, and dealing with 'cross-cutting' challenges (DETR, 1999d). Local authorities and their elected members are regarded as well placed to coordinate local partnerships and deliver sustainable improvements in their communities, beyond traditional 'service-providing' boundaries (DETR, 2000, para 5.2). Partnership is now at the centre of the local government modernisation agenda, rather than being championed just as a means to an end: "Where the relationship between the council and its essential local partners is neither strong nor effective, that council cannot hope to lead its community successfully"(DETR, 1998). According to this vision, housing managers for an estate will be coordinators, responsible for deciding "who should do the joining-up", rather than providers of services (DETR 1999d, para 17). Councils are 'managing' the provision of housing by a variety of providers as part of their broader responsibility for the sustainability, health and well-being of their communities. One of the express benefits of the transfer programme, according to the Green Paper, is that it helps to separate out local authorities' strategic responsibilities from their landlord functions (DETR/ DSS, 2000, para 7.15).

The essential purpose of the Best Value framework, together with the panoply of audit, inspection and other regulatory processes accompanying it, is to encourage local authorities radically to rethink their traditional roles and functions. The abstract nature of the principal Best Value duty and its associated pressures is intended to bring about such critical self-reflection. The point to emphasise here is that while under CCT housing management was narrowly defined in terms of the council's landlord responsibilities, the broader Best Value duty to secure continuous improvement in housing functions is owed to *all* local householders, whether council tenants, leaseholders, housing association tenants, owner-occupiers or private tenants. The fundamental change in the local authority housing role is being pursued, therefore, through very general imperium commands combined with greater self-regulation and fragmentation of regulatory inputs, and with all local residents having greater involvement in decision making on housing issues.

2. The separation (where the council retains housing stock) of local authority ownership and housing management roles

Where local authorities *retain* housing stock, they are being encouraged to improve the quality of housing services by separating the management and ownership roles. The obvious and preferred way of achieving this separation is through outsourcing of management services to the private sector, with increased quality and efficiency supposedly being ensured by the competitive conditions of the market. While on the face of it authorities have the freedom to provide housing services by whatever means they choose, they are unlikely in practice to be able to demonstrate Best Value just by 'traditional' in-house delivery. The separation of ownership and management functions might still be achieved to the satisfaction of auditors and inspectors, however, where the service continues to be provided by direct labour. The expectation here is that some form of competition involving open tendering or market testing will be necessary (rather than just benchmarking), resulting in internal client-contractor arrangements similar to those that operated under CCT where contracts were won by Direct Service Organisations (DSOs) (Vincent-Jones and Harries, 1996). Government pronouncements and policy documents have given explicit priority to competition and to other market arrangements involving private–public partnerships as methods for securing Best Value. While the government's preferences are nowhere legislatively prescribed, the whole philosophy of Best Value encourages authorities to adopt innovative solutions with competition at their heart: "Competition will be a key management tool for delivering Best Value and driving up standards, but, unlike CCT, it will be fair competition and it will be a means to an end, rather than an end in itself"[9]. In addition to these pressures, the specific requirement on the part of councils to agree

TPCs with their tenants provides further impetus to improvement of local authority housing management services.

Beyond these obvious alternatives, two novel 'hybrid' forms of separation are envisaged in the Green Paper, both involving inducements through the relaxation of financial restrictions that otherwise apply to the management of homes remaining in local authority ownership. First, as long as councils can demonstrate an appropriate transfer of risk to the private sector, Private Finance Initiative (PFI) schemes allow access to private finance unencumbered by public expenditure controls, without having to transfer ownership of stock as under LSVT. In this type of PFI arrangement, the local authority will specify its requirements (for example, refurbishment works, continuing management, repairs and maintenance services) in terms of outcomes rather than inputs, and potential private providers will compete for the contract. The winning bidder will be responsible for raising the funds to do the work, with payment by the authority on a performance basis and in the form of annual service fees under a long-term contract rather than initial capital expenditure. Tenants will remain tenants of the local authority, and be encouraged to play their part in defining and monitoring performance standards of the PFI contractor in a similar manner to CCT. The PFI approach is being piloted in eight pathfinder schemes. "We expect PFI to establish itself as an option that many authorities will want to consider as part of their investment strategy, and we will be considering future levels of support for it during the current Spending Review" (DETR/DSS, 2000, para 7.44).

Second, the Green Paper envisages the setting up of arm's-length companies for local authority-owned housing, requiring the relaxation of current rules on local authority companies which specify that, unless the ownership of housing is being transferred to a local housing company (effectively creating a new RSL), then the company is subject to the controls on capital expenditure that apply to local authorities (treated as part of the local authority). New regulations will permit the setting up of a company, *controlled* or *influenced* by the local authority itself, to perform the specific function of housing management (para 7.37).

The key regulatory technique involved in improving the management of council homes, whether this function is performed by the council or some other provider, is competition. In the case of both arm's-length companies and the PFI, the relaxation of prohibitive public financing rules operates (through a combination of imperium and dominium regulation) as a fine-tuning mechanism, increasing the freedom of local authorities to explore options for improving housing management, but within a framework of constraints dictated by central government policy.

3. The encouragement of greater diversity of social housing provision and increased choice on the part of housing 'consumers' among different types of social landlord

The government is seeking to stimulate competition between social landlords and increase sensitivity to consumer choice through mechanisms allowing easier comparability and read-across between different providers. The objective is not to prescribe the exact mix of forms of social housing, but to create the conditions that will allow this balance to be locally determined by market forces in particular areas. The principal regulatory techniques in this instance are competition and information.

First, on the supply side, a fundamental purpose of developing common BestValue standards and performance indicators is to promote competition between local authority and other social landlords as providers of rented housing. Complementing the growing momentum of LSVT is a range of initiatives designed to expand the role of the non-profit sector in housing provision. Housing associations and RSLs are now being viewed by the government as 'social businesses', requiring a loosening of borrowing and other restrictions to enable them to play a more entrepreneurial role in regeneration and combating social exclusion. The 'permissible purposes' of RSLs are being widened to enable them to deliver services to people who are not their own tenants, and generally to choose whether to consolidate their role as social landlords, to specialise in particular areas, or to broaden their field of operations to provide a range of products (Cahill, 1999). The Green Paper makes clear that the goal is diversity of provision rather than the replacement of one monopoly landlord with another: "Transfer will not achieve the government's objectives if it entails replacing a large monolithic local authority landlord with a large monolithic registered social landlord" (DETR/DSS, 2000, para 7.23). Hence the Transfer Guidelines specify that ministers do not expect more than 12,000 dwellings to be transferred to one new landlord.

Increased comparability and read-across between the more fragmented and diverse providers of landlord and housing management functions is to be achieved by subjecting housing associations and RSLs to a form of regulation comparable to the statutory framework applying to local authorities (Weaver, 1999). Although non-profit providers are not formally subject to the Best Value framework, a voluntary regime adopting similar standards has been administered by the Housing Corporation since 1998 (Foreshaw, 1999). There is an expectation that there will be convergence between council and RSL approaches to Best Value over the next five years (NHF, 1999). Performance indicators and targets are thus not just drivers of improvement, providing a measure against which authorities, service users, external auditors, the Housing Inspectorate and GOs can judge how well a service is performing, but are the basis on which the different sectors can be made to compete with one another. Competition is an accepted management technique in the RSL sector, where an interesting recent development is the growth of outsourcing of housing management to other non-profit or private organisations (NHF, 1999)[10].

Second, on the demand side, the corollary of competition between housing providers is choice of tenure by housing consumers, the aim being to increase the sensitivity of the social housing sector to consumer demand by increasing the range of opportunities for access to social housing:

> We want to promote a more customer-centred approach, but without changing the fundamental role of social housing in meeting need.... In particular, we wish to encourage social landlords to see themselves more as providers of a lettings service which is responsive to the needs and wishes of individuals, rather than purely as housing 'allocators'. (DETR/DSS, 2000, paras 9.2-9.3)

The overall shape of the 'economy' of housing provision may be influenced by the differential application of prohibitive rules creating incentives favouring some tenures against others, involving a blurring of the distinction between imperium and dominium, as in the different constraints on public borrowing for council and non-profit landlords. Within the council housing sector prohibitions may be relaxed to reward compliance on the part of some authorities and to encourage others to follow the good example, as in the exempting of 'Beacon' councils from reserve capping controls, reflecting the philosophy that central government interference should vary inversely with the demonstrable ability of authorities to manage their own affairs.

Conclusion: Best Value, regulation and governmentality

The underlying argument of this chapter has been that the changing local authority role in housing management needs to be seen against the background of trends in the regulation of central–local relations. The evident decline in the ability and willingness of local authorities to provide and manage social housing is just part of a more general and far-reaching transformation, in which councils are increasingly being regarded as vehicles for the promotion of innovation and partnership in the performance of public functions, in competition with other such agencies in the public and private sectors (Loughlin, 1996, p 108). One interpretation of the Best Value and subsequent legislation is that "it goes further than the wildest dreams ... of Nicholas Ridley in his view of how local government should evolve into annual meetings to let contracts"[11]; another that the measures "could lead to the complete demise of local government, to be succeeded by local administration" (*Local Government Chronicle*, 28 May 1999, p 1). Beyond the general requirement on the part of local authorities to question whether a service is necessary and how it is being provided, the 'challenge' of Best Value is to the existence of local government as traditionally conceived, and in the case of housing to the landlord role of local councils. The major difference between Labour and Conservative policy, following widespread acknowledgement of the failures of CCT, lies not in policy ends but in the regulatory means being deployed for their attainment.

Since the 1997 General Election there has been a significant shift in housing regulation away from command and control towards more subtle forms of *imperium*, combined with increasingly varied *dominium* pressures and incentives[12]. Specific restrictions on how services should be provided are being lifted, but pressures favouring certain types of competitive practice and encouraging financial responsibility continue, backed by powerful central powers to deal with public authorities perceived as 'failing.' From a governmentality perspective[13], the interplay of regulatory forces – involving the imposition of general duties, increased competition, the dissemination of certain types of information, greater self-regulation, and the measurement of quality according to performance indicators and standards – is expressed in (and synonymous with) the 'responsibilisation' of local government. This concept refers in the present context to the ways in which the organisational thinking and strategic orientation of local authorities are being brought into alignment with central policy objectives through the inculcation of common calculative technologies, forms of evaluation, and norms and values whose combined effect is the 'self-steering' of these corporate bodies in directions the government wishes them to move (Miller and Rose, 1990, p 18). Augmenting the regulatory analysis provided in the previous sections, the governmentality perspective helps explain the apparent paradox of continuing centralisation involving erosion of the traditional powers and autonomy of local government, on the one hand, combined with less prescriptive regulation and even increased powers in certain fields (for example in respect of arm's-length companies and PFI schemes), on the other (Vincent-Jones, 2000b). Greater freedom on the part of local authorities is not inconsistent with increased central government control, since the parameters of this freedom are in reality closely circumscribed by the central regulatory framework. The shift in the local authority role from housing management to the management of housing is thus being achieved through 'responsibilised autonomy' rather than by the crude methods of command and control typified by CCT.

While the metaphor of a 'game' played by regulator and regulatees may have been appropriate in analysing the attempt of central government to control local councils in the era of CCT, the present regime of Best Value requires a far subtler conceptualisation of the central–local regulatory relationship. The key question is how a situation has been created in which the 'game' has ceased to be adversarial and conflictual in nature, and to have become governed instead by common objectives supported by a renewed commitment to partnership and cooperation. The most fundamental factor in securing the alignment of local authority strategy with central government policies, and the pre-requisite for successful dominium regulation, has been the imposition of public borrowing regulations and expenditure controls that have restricted the financial autonomy of councils. This has prepared the ground for the assimilation within the operations of local authorities – as necessary means to their survival as organisations – of common vocabularies of financial calculation and techniques of measurement, evaluation and monitoring, without the need for direct central government intervention. Best Value benchmarks, standards and performance indicators are playing a major part in this process. An environment has been created for councils in which outcomes desired by central government are being produced by the rational self-interested calculations of these regulated bodies, on the basis of shared technologies and accepted management practices (performance plans, reviews and targets), rather than being specifically required or dictated. Under such conditions, substantive and particularistic interventions become both unnecessary and counter-productive, being replaced by mechanisms of the 'government of government', described by Dean as "the trajectory by which government through processes comes to be displaced by a government of governmental mechanisms themselves" (Dean, 1999, p 210).

Certainly this form of regulation is more likely to be 'successful' than CCT in achieving the government's immediate policy objectives. Best Value is also likely to be relatively successful in the sense of reducing the economic costs of stipulating rules in detail and monitoring and adjudicating disputes, and avoiding numerous cultural costs associated with the command and control style of regulation. The lack of precision in Best Value rules undermines the basis of strategies of avoidance by local authorities (even assuming they had the will to oppose regulation) since there is nothing concrete with which they can 'creatively comply'. At this point, however, the limitations of theories of governmentality and 'reflexive' regulation become apparent. In moving beyond the crude antithesis of state and civil society, and in producing insights into the exercise of power in modern societies, these perspectives cast light on how regulatory processes work and help specify the conditions under which regulation is likely to prove technically effective. What they lack is an adequate critical dimension. It is far from clear whether present housing policy is legitimate in the sense of there having been proper opportunity for debate over policy ends (at least as these have been identified in this paper). Participation as a fundamental constitutional value needs to apply to policy formation as well as implementation; the 'participation' that central government is keen for local citizens to enjoy may not be the type of participation they either need or want. These perspectives also appear incapable of overall policy evaluation[14] – of taking into account the negative impact of regulatory systems on constituencies or interests that are 'externalities' from the viewpoint of the principal objectives being pursued. On this criterion, present housing policies might be judged severely deficient if their effect is to perpetuate social disadvantage by further marginalising an 'underclass' of citizens (Cotterrell, 1996, p 460) in poor quality council housing.

Notes

[1] Best Value duties are broad in scope and expressed in terms of outcomes to be measured and evaluated according to a combination of centrally and locally determined standards. There is a strong element of self-regulation in provisions

for the setting of targets and the making and revision of local performance plans. While 'command' is being relaxed, ultimate 'control' is being enhanced through the Secretary of State's wider discretion in the use of capping, enabling and default powers. Where conflicts occur, resort to judicial adjudication will not normally be possible.

² But for an account of the positive effects of contracting for housing management services in one metropolitan local authority, see Vincent-Jones and Harries (1996).

³ That is, housing applications and allocations, terms and enforcement of tenancies, rents and service charges, inspecting and re-letting vacant properties, arrears and removal of unlawful occupiers, repairs and surveys, disturbances and neighbour disputes.

⁴ Defined as "locally negotiated binding agreements between tenants and local authority setting out how tenants will participate in decisions which affect their home and community" (DETR, 2000, para 4.18).

⁵ For example, inhibition of innovation, rapid obsolescence and a variety of social welfare losses (Ogus, 1994, p 167).

⁶ Where imperium sanctions take the form of penalties, financial investments might be said to exist for *not* breaching the rules.

⁷ According to economic theory market organisations may produce efficiencies, despite the absence of direct competition, where markets are 'contestable' – in other words where entry barriers are low so that there exists the threat of new competition from new entrants.

⁸ For example, 'Prescott plans to abolish council housing', *The Guardian*, 24 January 2000.

⁹ *HC Deb vol 323 col 127 12 January 1999, Ms Armstrong.*

¹⁰ In a different context, as he has seen, councils are now competing with one another for the right to transfer homes to the private sector.

¹¹ *HC Deb vol 323 col 154 12 January 1999, Mr Burstow.*

/

[12] Daintith argues that *dominium* displays considerable advantages over *imperium* "in reconciling the information problems faced by government in policy implementation with the rather limited demands posed by constitutional principle" (1994, p 229) and that this form of regulation is overall less costly than *imperium* as a means of influencing behaviour. Nevertheless, he detects a shift towards *imperium* in the early 1990s, associated with the privatising policies of the Thatcher government, restrictions imposed by the EU, and the increasingly interventionist attitude of the UK courts.

[13] The term 'governmentality' is defined simply by Dean as "how we think about governing others and ourselves in a wide variety of contexts" (Dean, 1999, p 209). For an overview of Foucault's later work on governmentality and its development by other scholars, and an interesting application to 'compacts' between the government and voluntary sector, see Morison (2000).

[14] Miller and Rose are explicit on this point: "Policy studies tend to be concerned with evaluating policies, uncovering the factors that led to their success in achieving their objectives or, more usually ... their failure. We, on the other hand, are not concerned with evaluations of this type, with making judgements as to whether and why this or that policy succeeded or failed ..." (1990, p 4).

References

Cahill, A. (1999) 'Helping to make a start', *Housing Today*, Issue 144, 29 July.

Cooke, M. (1999) 'RSLs may outstrip LAs as landlords within 10 years', *Housing Today*, Issue 136, 3 June.

Cotterrell, R. (1996) 'The rule of law in transition: revisiting Franz Neumann's sociology of legality', *Social and Legal Studies*, vol 5, pp 451-74.

Daintith, T. (1994) 'The techniques of government', in J. Jowell and D. Oliver (eds) *The changing constitution*, Oxford: Clarendon Press.

Dean, M. (1999) *Governmentality: Power and rule in modern society*, London: Sage Publications.

DETR (Department of the Environment, Transport and the Regions) (1998) *Modern local government: In touch with the people*, Cm 4014, London: DETR.

DETR (1999a) *Local Government Act 1999: Part I – Best Value*, Circular 10/99 and SI 1999/3251, London: DETR.

DETR (1999b) *National Framework for Tenant Participation Compacts*, June, London: DETR.

DETR (1999c) *Housing Investment Programme 1999, Guidance Notes for Local Authorities*, June, London: DETR.

DETR (1999d) *National Strategy for Neighbourhood Renewal Report of Policy Action Team 5 on housing management*, London: DETR.

DETR (2000) *Best Value in housing framework*, London: DETR.

DETR/DSS (Department of Social Security) (2000) *Quality and choice: A decent home for all*, Housing Green Paper, London: DETR/DSS.

Foreshaw, R. (1999) 'RSLs are ahead on Best Value regulation', *Housing Today*, Issue 117, 21 January.

Hancher, L. and Moran, M. (1989) 'Organizing regulatory space', in L. Hancher and M. Moran (eds) *Capitalism, culture and economic regulation*, Oxford: Oxford University Press.

Hood, C. and Scott, C. (1996) 'Bureaucratic regulation and new public management in the United Kingdom: mirror-image developments?', *Journal of Law and Society*, vol 23, pp 321-45.

Hood, C., James, O., Jones, G., Scott, C. and Travers, T. (1999) *Regulation inside government*, Oxford: Oxford University Press.

Loughlin, M. (1996) *Legality and locality: The role of law in central-local government relations*, Oxford: Clarendon Press.

McBarnet, D. and Whelan, C. (1991) 'The elusive spirit of the law; formalism and the struggle for legal control', *Modern Law Review*, vol 54, pp 848-73.

Miller, P. and Rose, N. (1990) 'Governing economic life', *Economy and Society*, vol 19, pp 1-31.

Morison, J. (2000) 'The government-voluntary sector compacts: governance, governmentality, and civil society', *Journal of Law and Society*, 27, pp 98-132.

NHF (National Housing Federation) (1999) *Survey of RSL Best Value activity*, NHF Briefing, 20 July.

Ogus, A. (1994) *Regulation: Legal form and economic theory*, Oxford: Clarendon Press.

Sedley, S. (1997) 'Foreword', in M. Taggart (ed) *The province of administrative law*, Oxford: Hart Publishing.

Scott, C., Hall, C. and Hood, C. (1997) 'Regulatory space and institutional reform: the case of telecommunications', in P. Vass (ed) *Regulatory review of 1997*, London: CIPFA.

Vincent-Jones, P. (2000a) 'Contractual governance: institutional and organizational analysis', *Oxford Journal of Legal Studies*, vol 20, pp 317-51.

Vincent-Jones, P. (2000b) 'Central-local relations under the Local Government Act 1999: a new consensus?', *Modern Law Review*, vol 63, pp 84-104.

Vincent-Jones, P. and Harries, A. (1996) 'Conflict and cooperation in local authority quasi-markets: the hybrid organisation of internal contracting under CCT', *Local Government Studies*, vol 22, pp 187-209.

Weaver, M. (1999) 'Councils and RSLs to share PIs', *Housing Today*, Issue 152, September.

THIRTEEN

Registered Social Landlords, Best Value and the changing organisation and provision of social housing: a perspective from housing studies

Bruce Walker

Introduction

In this chapter we examine a number of aspects of the changing provision of social housing services. We first briefly consider why the management of such housing by local authorities was perceived to be no longer appropriate and why registered social landlords (RSLs) were deemed to be a more suitable organisational form through which to provide such housing. The significance of RSLs in the future provision of social housing was underlined by the Housing Green Paper (DETR/DSS, 2000), a significance demonstrated by the expectation that they will be the major providers of such housing within five years. Therefore, after outlining the nature of the Best Value (BV) regime as it is being implemented in the two sectors, we examine two issues of particular significance for the RSL sector under BV. First, we examine some difficulties in both principle and practice in ensuring the efficient performance of RSLs. Second, we discuss the changing role and approach of the regulator in the light of both recent sectoral performance and the requirements of BV. We conclude with some observations on what the future might hold for the sector under BV.

The transformation of social housing management

The policy of, initially, transferring from local authorities to RSLs the supply and management of new social housing and, subsequently, the ownership and management of existing social housing has its basis in the same reasoning that brought about the introduction of Compulsory Competitive Tendering (CCT) for local authority services more generally. The requirement that local public services, including housing management, be subjected to competition stemmed from the position of local authorities as, in the Green Paper's terminology, "large monopoly providers" (DETR/ DSS, 2000, para 7.14) of such services. In the housing field, these large public monopolies had been created, in the main, through local government reorganisation in the early 1970s. As monopoly providers of public services, local governments appeared to provide a clear example of the sort of large, inefficient, bureaucratic government organisation that had been subject to intellectual attack in the work of writers such as Niskanen (1971). This critique suggests that, by being insulated from the market, such organisations would enable bureaucrats to exploit their monopoly position in pursuit of their own objectives, such as status, power or perks. Such objectives could be achieved by maximising the bureau's size or budget and would tend to result in the market being inefficiently supplied. Asymmetries of information in the bureaucrat's favour would limit the ability of taxpayers or their representatives to constrain effectively the actions of bureaucracies. The result for consumers would be an unresponsive, x–inefficient and more costly service. This was the gloomy picture of public housing management and provision as painted by, for example, Minford et al (1987).

The economic prescription for reforming such institutional arrangements, advanced since at least the work of Tullock (1965), was to make the markets for public services contestable by introducing competition. The CCT regime reflected this in its requirement for local authorities to put out to tender those services designated by the Secretary of State. The services so designated were initially the manual, blue-collar activities of which building maintenance was the function most closely concerned with the public housing service. The regime was subsequently extended to white-collar services, including housing management.

At the same time as the management of public housing was being subjected to market principles through CCT, competition in the 'market' for social housing was being further extended. This was achieved through the redirection of public resources for new social housing supply from local authorities to RSLs. Unconstrained by the requirements of CCT and initially heavily funded through supply side capital and revenue subsidies, RSLs rapidly became the main supplier of new social housing in the late 1980s and 1990s (see, Hills, 1991, ch 8). Existing tenants of local authorities were also encouraged to consider changing to the RSL sector, first through the Choose a Landlord scheme and subsequently through the rapidly expanding large-scale voluntary transfer (LSVT) programme examined elsewhere in this volume (see Chapters Two and Three). The sector expanded from about half a million dwellings in 1988 to just over a million in 1997 (Wilcox, 1999), with about half of the increase resulting from the transfer of local authority dwellings to housing associations (Mullins, 1999, p 8). RSLs have now clearly become central government's favoured suppliers of social housing in the UK.

The position of RSLs as the main supplier of social housing at present and in the recent past is, therefore, clear. Further, the continued enhancement of the sector's role in such provision in the future is a clear policy objective as can be seen from, for example, the continued enthusiastic endorsement of LSVT in the Green Paper (DETR/DSS, 2000, ch 7). This implies, then, that RSLs are seen, by previous and current central government administrations, as the most appropriate organisations through which to provide social housing. This in turn suggests that RSLs are perceived to have a comparative advantage over state provision in the supply of such housing. If the perceived disadvantages of local authorities as providers, as outlined above, have been well rehearsed, the advantages of RSLs also require consideration. We attempt this in the next section.

The comparative advantage of RSLs in social housing provision and management

We can begin by observing that there is relatively little empirical evidence available to demonstrate that RSLs are in practice more efficient or effective housing providers than local authorities. Indeed, it could be argued that local authorities have a stronger claim to having demonstrated their efficiency. Approximately 56.5 per cent of all contracts for local authority services for which in-house providers competed under CCT and over 70 per cent of such contracts by value were won by local authority providers (LGMB, 1997).

Nevertheless, in seeking an alternative form of organisation to the state in the provision of social housing, RSLs are prima facie the obvious solution. First, self evidently, but non-trivially, the RSL sector already exists. RSLs have, as a sector, experience in the provision of housing for the social groups for whom local authorities traditionally provided housing and the sector operates under a regulatory regime intended to ensure that RSLs fulfil social housing objectives. This saves government and taxpayers the significant set up, support and promotional costs that would be incurred if alternative institutions were to be created.

Further, in being outside of the public sector financial regime, RSLs have enabled public funded capital expenditure to be reduced to an average of 54 per cent of the costs of new housing development through RSLs' ability to access private sector finance. Indeed, in the case of most LSVTs, the capital costs to the state in the absence of overhanging debt on transfer are effectively zero. This, and the absence of any supply side revenue subsidy for RSLs under the current regime, implies considerable savings to the public sector compared to the alternative of publicly funding new development and capital improvements to the social housing stock through local authorities.

In adopting a not-for-profit objective, it is possible to argue, as does Krashinsky (1986), that not-for-profit organisations such as RSLs might provide a cheaper form of provision than government. Cost savings can arise from the reduction in the negotiating and logrolling costs involved in ensuring state provision for minority interests. Further, where subsidies are given to social housing suppliers, using nfp rather than profit making providers is likely to result in cost savings for taxpayers by ensuring that organisations targeting the 'right' consumers receive the subsidy and, as a result, reducing the costs of monitoring the policy's implementation (Schill, 1994; Walker, 1998). There may also be efficiency gains from using not-for-profit organisations where, as in the UK housing context, they are subject to competition from other not-for-profit organisations, from private suppliers, and from the government itself through continuing local authority provision (Schill, 1994).

In addition, the raison d'être for the RSL sector is the provision of social housing and the diversity of the sector enables the provision of social housing services to be tailored to the needs of different groups. Rose-Ackerman (1996) also suggests that such organisations are, by their nature, likely to be more experimental and innovative in the provision of the services in which they specialise, and are less subject to the competing demands that face government departments. This view of the benefits of such specialism in the field of housing provision and management is clearly endorsed by the Green Paper in its desire to "...enable local authorities to concentrate on their *strategic* responsibilities for housing" (DETR/DSS, 2000, para 7.11, italics added) by relinquishing their role as direct providers.

One of the explicit aims of the reforms proposed in the Green Paper is "... the greater empowerment of tenants" (DETR/DSS, 2000, para 1.10). Such empowerment is to be achieved not only by offering a greater choice within the housing system but also through the management of provision itself. In particular:

> Meeting tenant priorities requires organisational cultures that actively seek tenants' views through a variety of channels and build these into decision-making processes. (DETR/DSS, 2000, para 7.49)

RSLs' regulatory body, the Housing Corporation, certainly places emphasis on consumer involvement. Its regulatory Performance Standards require RSLs to "provide information for residents, consult them and offer them reasonable opportunities to participate in and influence the management of their homes" (Housing Corporation, 1997, para 2.2). It cannot be doubted that the sector as a whole has cultivated an image that suggests it is more responsive and participatory in its approach to tenants than the stereotypical monopoly landlords in the public sector that they are increasingly displacing. In particular, RSLs formed as local housing companies (LHCs) normally have a significant representation of tenants on their governing boards so that: "...there is a pluralism to decision making which is not always apparent in other models of social housing" (Nevin, nd, para 5.2).

Arguably the final advantage to government of increasing further the significance of RSLs in the management and provision of social housing is, as noted above, the existence of a regulatory framework for the sector. Mullins (1999), in the course of a valuable summary of the Housing Corporation's regulatory role, points out that: "RSLs are subject to fairly intensive regulation by Housing Corporation Regional Offices" (p 13). We discuss this further below but can note here that, for the tenants of RSLs, such regulation, in principle, replaces the set of safeguards offered by the democratic accountability of local government with those of participation and 'objective' regulatory activity.

One of the key regulatory policies of the Housing Corporation since 1995 has been the limitation of RSL rents and rent increases. The significance and implications of this are discussed elsewhere in this volume (see Chapter Fourteen). For our purposes, the importance of such rent and rent increase ceilings is that they are in the nature of a 'price (increase) cap' and as such should provide high powered incentives to RSLs to monitor costs closely and to reduce them where possible. The efficiency properties of such an incentive scheme are well known (see, for example, Laffont and Tirole, 1993 and Barrow, 1996, for a discussion). They have the potential to ensure that current and previous public and private investment in the sector is deployed efficiently, with benefits to taxpayers, private investors and tenants alike.

In summary, then, compared to local authorities, RSLs appear to offer clear advantages in terms of public sector savings, increased investment and an improved consumer orientation, under a regulatory regime intended to ensure that the RSLs adhere to the core values of social housing management and provision. These advantages lie at the heart of central government's decision to choose these organisations as the vehicle for the delivery of social housing services.

The nature of the Best Value regime

The stated reasons for the Labour government replacing the CCT regime with that of BV, which came into force for local authorities in April 2000, was CCT's: "...drive to bland uniformity ... by legalistic rules and regulations drawn up by the centre". Further, it was regarded as:

> ... anachronistic, failing to reflect the modern relationships which have been developed by forward thinking councils and forward thinking companies. (Hilary Armstrong, MP, *Progress*, Spring 1997, p 12)

For local authorities, the regime emphasises performance planning and review and external audit and inspection. Geddes and Martin (2000) argue that:

> [Best Value] emphasis on efficiency, value for money, inspection and quantitative performance indicators means that, in a number of important respects, the Best Value regime intensifies previous local government 'reforms'. (p 380)

The Housing Corporation has introduced a parallel regime of BV for RSLs (Housing Corporation, 1999). Unlike BV for local authorities, which is mandatory, the requirements for RSLs to achieve BV are not regulatory as such (Housing Corporation, 1999, para 4.1). However, RSLs are clearly expected to respond to the regime's imperatives.

The area where BV has, arguably, the most congruence with the previous CCT regime is in respect of the role of competition in promoting efficiency. However, for local authorities competition in the form of market testing and contracting out is only one of four Cs which are aimed at ensuring efficiency and effectiveness of service provision (DETR, 1998). Indeed, explicitly, this 'C' is not seen as "... a requirement to put everything out to tender" (DETR, 1998, para 7.29). Rather, local authorities are expected to:

> ... approach competition positively, taking full account of the opportunities for innovation and genuine partnership which are available from working with others in the public, private and voluntary sectors. (DETR, 1999, para 36)

In contrast, for RSLs, this 'C' arguably represents a new, rather than a modified, set of expectations. However, there is no requirement embodied in the Housing Corporation's Performance Standards that market testing or its variants should be undertaken by RSLs nor is it given significant emphasis in the Corporation's guidance on BV (see Housing Corporation, 1999, paras 2.14 and 2.15).

For local authorities, alongside the four Cs are the government's 12 principles of Best Value which summarise the broad thrust of the policy regime. These principles cover inter alia the regime's scope, the mechanisms by which improvements in economy and efficiency will be achieved, the audit requirements placed on authorities and the actions available if a local authority fails in its duty to secure Best Value. Thus, in the case of local authorities, BV shifts the emphasis away from competition as the mechanism to curb inefficiency and towards an emphasis on providing consistent and transparent performance information, including that provided through the BV Performance Indicators (PIs) (DETR, 2000, Annex C).

For RSLs, performance information under BV is similarly being emphasised (Housing Corporation, 2000a) and the proposed performance measures mirror those for local authority housing (Housing Corporation, 2000b). In both cases this will allow greater external monitoring and user choice and provide the basis for performance comparison and benchmarking activities. For local authorities, the setting of explicit performance expectations, coupled with the prospect of a strong audit and inspection regime, provides incentives to enhance efficiency. In contrast, the BV 'inspection' regime for RSLs is still being clarified, although, as we discuss below, the monitoring of both BV plans and outputs are to be a part of what we might call BV 'enforcement' by the Corporation (Housing Corporation, 2000a)

There is little doubt that the BV regime may allow local authorities and RSLs the scope to assess the relative merits of different ways of arranging and delivering their housing and other services and to make choices accordingly. This certainly appears to be how local authorities are interpreting BV at this early stage (see Geddes and Martin, 2000, for a discussion). In having such choices, which were effectively proscribed under CCT, the regime could be seen as more likely to lead to forms of public service delivery that are structured so as to maximise efficiency. Further, it might be argued, the emphasis on consultation – and hence, potentially, the effectiveness of service delivery – represents a departure from the CCT regime.

These and the other benefits that can potentially flow from the adoption of the BV regime are only likely to be generated in practice if the organisations themselves are concerned with efficiency, or their inspectors and regulators can ensure it. Whether this is likely to occur in the RSL sector we consider next.

RSLs under BV: some emerging issues

BV and the performance of the RSL sector

While organisations with a profit making objective are able to judge their efficiency by the level of and changes in their profitability, housing and other not-for-profit organisations face the difficulty of ensuring efficient operation in the absence of a profit making objective. As Duizendstraal and Nentjes (1994) have argued, the absence of such an objective may encourage x-inefficiency and a diversion of resources into activities or managerial perks that are at odds with the not-for-profit organisation's primary objectives. This suggests then that the inefficiencies deemed to be associated with bureaucratic state provision might be replicated in not-for-profit organisations outside of the public sector. In respect of housing specifically, Nentjes and Schopp (2000) have shown that where the not-for-profit organisation has market power and x-inefficiency is present, the output of a state-subsidised housing not-for-profit organisation may be lower, and the price higher, than it would be in a perfectly competitive private market. This is a result of the not-for-profit organisation's resources being diverted into managerial slack. Nentjes and Schopp (2000) argue that these effects may be reduced where the not-for-profit organisation's housing output is subject to a price cap and, where the private market is also subject to price regulation, the output from the not-for-profit organisation will normally be higher than that of the competitive market. The effect of price capping in terms of increased efficiency may justify the rent and rent increase controls placed on RSL housing, noted above.

The not-for-profit objectives of RSLs in respect of their social housing activities mean that other indicators of whether the organisation is achieving its objectives and operating efficiently are required. In the RSL sector a range of standard setting and comparative activities occur, with the objective of increasing the efficiency of the RSL sector either through the RSL's own remedial action or through the regulatory responses from the Housing Corporation. In many ways, the Housing Corporation's activities in this respect are similar to the 'yardstick competition' criterion used by regulators in other fields. Where asymmetries of information concerning the performance of individual organisations favour the organisations rather than the regulator:

> ... the regulator ought to use all available information to reduce these asymmetries. One way ... is to compare the [organisation's] performance to that of other [organisations] facing a similar ... environment. (Laffont and Tirole, 1993, p 84)

As part of its regulatory role the Housing Corporation employs Performance Standards and associated PIs to measure RSL performance. The Social Housing Standards cover RSLs' subsidised housing and/or that which is used for social housing purposes, and concern the "housing and related services that the Corporation expect RSLs to provide to their residents and communities" (Housing Corporation, 1997, para 9). These include rents and service charges, lettings and repairs and maintenance.

Associated with the Social Housing Standards are five PIs defining quantitative standards that RSLs are expected to meet and which relate to RSLs' 'core' business as social landlords. These particular PIs will continue to be calculated and published under the BV PI regime (see Housing Corporation, 2000b). Data for these indicators are provided through the annual statistical returns that the RSLs complete for the Housing Corporation. In addition to informing the regulatory process, the main 'public' use of these PIs to date has been in providing information to tenants, allowing comparisons of relative RSL performance within RSL peer groups and in enabling the presentation of sector wide, year-on-year comparisons of performance.

The significance of PIs to the Housing Corporation in its role as regulator becomes apparent when the performance of the RSL sector from 1996/97 through 1998/99 on the five Social Housing PIs is considered. This is shown in Table 7.1 below.

The table indicates a clear decline in performance on these measures. This decline is of sufficient concern for the Housing Corporation to propose changes in the use of these measures. In particular, it is proposed to publish rankings of RSLs' relative performance in relation to current Performance Standards and to the BV PIs when introduced. This represents

Table 13.1: RSL sector performance against Housing Corporation performance standards (1996/97-1998/99)

Performance standard	1996/97	1997/98	1998/99
Average % of rent collected (Standard ≥ 97%)	**98.3%**	**98.31%**	**97.38%**
RSLs not meeting target	9.1%	17.7%	37.6%
RSLs where performance has declined	n/a	61%	67.9%
Average rent arrears as % of income (Standard ≤ 5%)	**4.67%**	**5.71%**	**6.29%**
RSLs not meeting target	40.1%	52.7%	57.7%
RSLs where performance has declined	n/a	70.1%	64.2%
Average rent losses as % of income (Standard ≤ 5%)	**2.90%**	**3.05%**	**3.22%**
RSLs not meeting target	22.6%	22.8%	26.3%
RSLs where performance has declined	n/a	56.4%	55.9%
Average vacancies as % of stock (Standard ≤ 2%)	**1.49%**	**1.53%**	**1.57%**
RSLs not meeting target	19.2%	21.1%	23.4%
RSLs where performance has declined	n/a	47.4%	51.5%
Average re-let time in weeks (Standard ≤ 4 weeks)	**3.9**	**4.2**	**4.3**
RSLs not meeting target	40.1%	43.8%	47.5%
RSLs where performance has declined	n/a	55.5%	58.5%

Source: Housing Corporation (2000a, para 3.8)

a significant departure from the Housing Corporation's previous use of such measures and could be seen to suggest the adoption of a more explicit performance measurement culture comparable to that which is being introduced in the local authority sector.

The use of performance measures such as those shown in Table 7.1 is, of course, subject to a number of criticisms. The first set of criticism concerns the principle of attempting to measure organisational performance using relatively simple – and therefore potentially misleading – indicators. In particular, the context of performance, such as whether the RSL is operating in a low demand area, is omitted from such measures. This is recognised by the Housing Corporation (2000a, para 3.10) who argue, nevertheless, that such measures provide a benchmark against which the achievement of the BV 'continuous improvement' imperative can be assessed (Housing Corporation, 2000a, para 3.12).

The second set of criticisms relates to the possible distortionary effect of measuring only certain aspects of RSL performance. This is an area of concern which has been given increased attention in the literature over the recent past (for example, Holmstrom and Milgrom, 1991; Milgrom and Roberts, 1992, ch 7; Whynes, 1993; Walker, 2000). If the incentives for scoring highly – as offered through the regulatory system – are sufficiently strong, including the negative incentives of the effects on an RSL's reputation of being 'named and shamed' for poor measured performance, then managerial effort and other resources are likely to be diverted into achieving high scores. This may be at the expense of performance, unmeasured by PIs, on aspects of service delivery that are of more significance to residents, RSL board members and funders. The benefits of innovation and diversity which it is suggested that nfps offer, as noted above, could be diminished by the reallocation of resources required to achieve approved scores on standard indicators that are set for the sector as a whole.

Almost irrespective of these arguments, the apparent decline in the sector's performance can be argued to be something of an embarrassment given RSLs' expanding role in the provision and management of social housing. It provides an additional argument for the extension of BV to the sector and reinforces the important role that the Housing Corporation ascribes to performance measurement in its attempts to ensure that BV is adopted by the RSL sector. The issues that arise for the Housing Corporation as regulator in ensuring BV compliance requires an examination of the Corporation's regulatory role. This we undertake in the next section.

Regulating RSL performance under BV

Under the plans for BV in local authority housing, central government has created a significant array of incentives and possible sanctions to encourage local authorities to adhere to the regime's requirements. A dedicated Housing Inspectorate, under the Audit Commission, has been set up which will singly or jointly with other Inspectorates examine BV performance and report nationally and locally on it. Failure to act on the recommendations of such reports could lead to government interventions: "... which range from requiring a local authority to amend its BV [Performance Plan] to taking away the authority's responsibility for a function" (DETR, 2000, para 10.4).

An 'excellent' rating from the Housing Inspectorate will be one of the necessary requirements for an authority to set up an arm's-length housing management company, with its attendant financial advantages (DETR/DSS, 2000, para 7.40). It is also intended that: "... performance against the national BestValue performance indicators specified for housing [will] be incorporated into the HIP assessment framework" (DETR, 2000, para 6.69).

Hence there are a number of clear incentives built into the BV framework for public housing authorities to respond positively to the requirements of the regime.

The Green Paper makes it clear that central government expects that:

> Registered social landlords ... should be subject to an inspection regime as rigorous and testing as that operated for local authorities by the Housing Inspectorate. The Housing Corporation will need to adapt its regulatory framework to promote further efficiencies in management and responsiveness to tenants by registered social landlords. (DETR/DSS, 2000, para 7.50)

It is known that changes to the Housing Corporation's regulatory approach are planned, but these are unpublished at the time of writing. It has already been announced that these changes will encompass not only performance in relation to PIs but also the content and outcomes of the BV Performance Plans that RSLs are expected to submit (Housing Corporation, 2000a, para 7.2). Further, the Corporation is considering the external auditing of BV PIs (Housing Corporation, 2000b, para 2.11) and "... developing inspection arrangements and thus our regulatory role" (Housing Corporation, 2000a, para 7.4). It would appear that an inspection function will indeed be created with the objective, among others, of ensuring that RSLs are working for continuous improvement. Their efforts in this respect will be judged in relation to the outputs and outcomes of their service provision rather than the process of that provision. It is also intended that the inspection reports will be more comprehensive and more widely available than is usual under current regulatory arrangements (Housing Corporation, Personal Communication).

Certainly the set of regulatory and other instruments that the Housing Corporation has open to it at present to promote BV appears to be significantly smaller than that available to central government. This is perhaps inevitable, given that BV in local authority housing has the force of law, as we have noted. In contrast, the Housing Corporation, as a regulatory rather than a legislative body, appears to have to rely currently to a greater extent on exhortation in its attempts to ensure that the BV regime is adopted in the RSL sector. For example, in respect of the sort of performance indicators shown in Table 7.1, there does not appear to be an implication under current (or planned) arrangements that a better performance as judged by a higher rank will increase the probability of receiving public funding for investment. Clearly, the Housing Corporation's approach appears to differ in this respect from that proposed for local authority housing functions through the HIP under BV. It could be argued that the Housing Corporation could similarly incentivise efficient performance in respect of the BV PIs. Possibly, the decreasing significance of public subsidies noted above provides some explanation for why such incentives have not been introduced to date.

Since it seems that the new inspection regime will not, at least initially, involve 'star ratings' of RSLs, unlike that for local authorities, the 'negative' incentives (sanctions) for RSLs will presumably be primarily that of potential action, as now, under the regulatory regime. Currently, regulation involves the Regional Offices in reviewing annually RSLs' statistical returns, identifying and investigating apparent non-compliance with Performance Standards, and visiting a sample of all RSLs. In 1998/99 the returns of all 2,047 RSLs subject to review were examined, 255 received 'validation' visits and 365 were subject to investigatory review. Non-compliance with standards that can be remedied in the short term renders an RSL liable to 'observation' by Housing Corporation staff. More serious non-compliance involves direct intervention in the RSL's affairs in the form of 'supervision', the cessation of public subsidy and possible transfer of the RSL's activities to another RSL. At the end of 1998/99, 181 RSLs were under observation and 99 were under supervision (Mullins, 1999, p 13).

How action under the regulatory regime as a result of a perceived failure to achieve BV will square with the current non-regulatory nature of BV for RSLs is unclear. As we noted above, one of the key regulatory instruments – or at least triggers for regulatory intervention – that is available to the Housing Corporation is the limitation of rents and rent increases by RSLs. The regulatory response to a failure to keep within these guidelines is one of 'naming and shaming' those RSLs that fail to comply, with more direct intervention in the more serious cases. It is not clear how the rent guidelines themselves, as a regulatory requirement, could be used to enforce BV unless breaching these guidelines were ipso facto seen as a failure to achieve BV. However, the activity of naming and shaming in itself may be a significant sanction in the context of the increasing reliance of RSLs on private finance. The reputation of the sector for efficiency generally, and financial probity in particular, is clearly important, given the significance of private lending to new development and for LSVTs.

If the reputation effects of ranking and publishing RSL performance, and the implicit or explicit naming and shaming that this entails, are significant for an individual RSL, then this may prove a sufficient incentive to comply with BV. However, this is clearly a policy that, from a regulatory perspective, needs to be employed sparingly. First, the more RSLs that are so identified, the greater the implications for the reputation of the sector as a whole, including BV-compliant RSLs. Second, the more RSLs that are identified as failing to achieve BV, the greater the impact on the reputation of the Housing Corporation as the regulator of the sector.

If a steady stream of RSLs were to be labelled as BV failures, the competence of the Housing Corporation as the body responsible for the implementation of the regime is likely to be questioned. This would add to the current competency debate in the sector that has arisen in the context of the diversification of RSLs. Such diversification takes the form of the increasing use of private rather than public finance and from RSLs extending their activities into such areas as regeneration, private renting, housing for sale, community development and social care.

This diversification has raised the issues of the right of the regulator to investigate non-core activities and the competency of the regulator to do so. Concentrating on the second of these issues here, in a poll of RSLs discussed in *Housing Today* (30 March, 2000, Issue 177, p 7), over 56 per cent of RSL respondents disagreed or strongly disagreed that the Housing Corporation had the right experience to regulate them. Less favourable attitudes were expressed by the larger RSLs. Regulatory 'non-competence', in this context generated by asymmetries in information and expertise in favour of the regulated organisations, can lead to the capture of the regulator by those organisations and thus fewer constraints on their activities. Mullins has argued further (for example, 2000) that the close interaction of RSLs with the regulator has led to at least some elements of regulatory capture. This has resulted in, for example, the exclusion of for-profit providers from the Housing Corporation's funding remit and the adoption of value based norms (such as housing need and equal opportunities) as part of the regulatory process. Further, he reports research that indicates that:

> [RSL] chief executives were actively seeking to influence the policy environment, lobby individually and collectively and to build relationships with politicians and civil servants. (Mullins, 2000, p 20)

An interesting analytical issue arises here in distinguishing regulatory capture – which implies some sort of failure on the part of the regulator – from what could be perceived as a more informal approach to regulation. Many of the characteristics of capture can appear similar to those of such an informal approach since the latter involves collaboration between regulator and regulatee, particularly in respect of information sharing and pooling. Writers such as Mackintosh (1999) have suggested that a regulatory framework which encourages such cooperation between the regulated and the regulator, based on more relational rather than adversarial approach by the latter, is more appropriate in social provision. To use the distinction employed by, for example, Ogus (1994), this suggests that the regulator should seek *compliance* from the regulatee: "... as a result of persuasion and negotiation before the event" rather than regulating through *deterrence* which involves: "... penalizing offenders for offences already committed and thus deterring further violations" (p 95). Further, a compliance approach may also reduce the costs that the extension of regulation would have imposed on both the funders of the regulatory body (the taxpayer) and RSLs themselves.

To date the Housing Corporation's approach to regulation can be argued to have been more in the nature of compliance seeking rather than deterrence. For example, 'lead regulators' from Regional Offices now maintain regular, rather than annual and arm's-length contact with larger, diversified providers, an approach that is likely to be reinforced under the planned regulatory reforms (Housing Corporation, Personal

Communication). If an RSL fails to comply with Performance Standards, the Housing Corporation's "... strong preference would be to work with it to remedy matters" (Housing Corporation, 1997, para 8). The Corporation has also attempted to ease the regulatory burden on RSLs by increasing the amount of self-certification by RSLs in assessing compliance with Performance Standards (Housing Corporation, 1997, para 6).

Consider in this light, then, central government's expectation, noted above, that the Housing Corporation will employ a more 'rigorous and testing' inspection regime under BV and the proposed introduction of an inspection function. Despite the emphasis laid on a 'compliance culture' in the Housing Corporation's public pronouncements on the regulatory reforms, this could be seen as a change in the Housing Corporation's approach to regulation from one of seeking compliance to one of applying deterrence. Such a change is certainly consistent with the Housing Corporation's move to the sort of ranking, naming and shaming and investigatory exercises that are being proposed under the BV regime. If, irrespective of the willingness of the sector as a whole to sign up to BV, these changes prove costly or otherwise unacceptable to RSLs, then this may have significant implications for the ability of central government to regulate the sector in the longer term. We discuss this in the final section.

Summary and conclusion

It is clear in the light of both recent history and the Green Paper's proposals that the RSL sector will be responsible for the delivery of the majority of social housing services in the near future. This is despite the fact that although there are strong arguments in theory for suggesting that RSLs are more efficient housing providers than local authorities there is relatively little empirical evidence to this effect. On the contrary, there are indications that the performance of the RSL sector as a whole has recently declined. Given this, and the application of the BV regime to the public provision of housing (and other) services, it is quite reasonable that central government should require the RSL sector to deliver social housing services in accordance with the principles of BV. The two questions that arise are whether BV can be 'enforced' in the sector and what the longer-term impacts of that enforcement might be.

As to the first of these questions, we have argued that the regulatory system which is charged with the responsibility of ensuring BV may exhibit elements of regulatory capture and, in any event, has experienced some difficulties in attempting to regulate a diverse and diversifying set of organisations. The requirements to ensure BV represent an additional set of responsibilities for the Housing Corporation, although these cannot be argued to conflict with existing regulatory responsibilities. However, in planning for the future regulation of BV the Housing Corporation, responding to the requirement that RSLs' BV performance be rigorously tested, appears to be moving much further towards a 'performance measurement' culture than previously. Ultimately, this may mirror the extensive inspection and classification regime introduced for local authority housing. In any event, it represents a significant change of approach for the Housing Corporation. If the previous approach to regulation could be classified as one of seeking 'compliance', then the proposed approach could be argued to be based to a much greater extent on 'deterrence'. Whether this proves to be successful – indeed, whether in the end it proves to be necessary if it transpires that RSLs are willing to embrace BV principles in any event – is a matter for speculation. However, the possibility arises that the new regulatory regime itself may affect RSLs' decision as to their role and future in the sector.

This brings us to the second question as to impacts of the BV regulation regime. Suppose that the costs to RSLs of such regulation, particularly in the context of the diversification of their activities are indeed significant, while the benefits of 'signing up' to the regime requiring such costs to be incurred are relatively low. In this case a strategy of leaving the sector – an exit strategy – may be one that some RSLs may wish to consider. Mullins points out that: "[s]mall RSLs who have not recently been in receipt of public subsidy have been able to de-register and thus escape the regulatory burden altogether" (Mullins, 1999, p 13). Fifty-seven small RSLs de-registered in this way in 1998/99.

We recognise that a change in the law (albeit a relatively minor one) would probably be required for RSLs that have received public funding to implement an exit strategy. However, if direct public funding finances a relatively small part of an RSL's activities, but the RSL can still demonstrate its efficiency and effectiveness under less costly, less onerous, or more suitable regulatory regimes, then the pressure to allow exit as an option may increase. This could be facilitated by, for example, registering social housing activities with other nfp regulators such as the Charity Commissioners. Further, if the alternative forms of regulation have less distortionary effects on an RSL's choice of activities and on its ability to fulfil its objectives than the 'BV enhanced' Housing Corporation regime, then additional benefits may flow from such a decision.

In our view, such a course of action is unlikely to be followed by many

RSLs in the short term, even given the legislation required for it to be allowed. This is primarily because the signal that registration and successful regulatory compliance provides for other public and semi-public funders, such as health trusts, universities and Regional Development Agencies, and for private finance sources is likely to remain important. However, it is possible that the balance may be tipped in favour of de-registration if the Housing Corporation's inspection activities do indeed transpire to be as, or even more, demanding than those of the Housing Inspectorate.

Thus, both the RSL sector and the regulatory regime to which it is subject are facing a number of difficulties. BV, though laudable in itself, has added to these and increased the uncertainties to which these difficulties have given rise. How these are finally resolved is likely to be of great significance for the social housing sector and, not least, to the consumers of social housing themselves.

References

Barrow, M. (1996) 'Public services and the theory of regulation', *Policy & Politics*, vol 24, no 3, pp 263-76.

DETR (Department of the Environment, Transport and the Regions) (1998) *Modern local government: In touch with the people*, Cmd 4014, London: The Stationery Office.

DETR (1999) *Local Government Act 1999: Part 1. Best Value*, DETR Circular 10/99, London: DETR.

DETR (2000) *Best Value in Housing framework*, London: DETR.

DETR/DSS (Department of Social Security) (2000) *Quality and choice: A decent home for all*, Housing Green Paper, London: DETR/DSS.

Duizendstraal, A. and Nentjes, A. (1994) 'Organizational slack in subsidised non-profit institutions', *Public Choice*, vol 81, nos 3-4, pp 297-321.

Geddes, M. and Martin, S. (2000) 'The policy and politics of Best Value: currents, crosscurrents and undercurrents in the new regime', *Policy & Politics*, vol 28, no 3, pp 379-95.

Hills, J. (1991) *Unravelling housing finance: Subsidies, benefits and taxation*, Oxford: Clarendon Press.

Holmstrom, B. and Milgrom, P. (1991) 'Multi-task principal-agent analyses: incentive contracts, asset ownership, and job design', *Journal of Law, Economics and Organisation*, vol 7, Spring, pp 24-52.

Housing Corporation (1997) *Performance standards for registered social landlords*, London: The Housing Corporation.

Housing Corporation (1999) *Best Value for registered social landlords: Guidance from the Housing Corporation*, London: The Housing Corporation.

Housing Corporation (2000a) *RSLs – Next steps in Best Value and performance reporting*, Discussion Paper, London: The Housing Corporation.

Housing Corporation (2000b) *Performance indicators for registered social landlords 2000/2001*, London: The Housing Corporation.

Krashinsky, M. (1986) 'Transaction costs and a theory of the non-profit organisation', in S. Rose-Ackerman (ed) *The economics of nonprofit institutions: Studies in structure and policy*, Oxford: Oxford University Press.

Laffont, J.-J. and Tirole, J. (1993) *A theory of incentives in procurement and regulation*, Cambridge, MA: MIT Press.

LGMB (Local Government Management Board) (1997) *Service delivery and competition information service: Survey Report No 15*, Luton: LGMB.

Mackintosh, M. (1999) 'Informal regulation: a conceptual framework and application to decentralized mixed health care systems', in M. Mackintosh and R. Roy (eds) *Economic decentralization and public management reform*, Cheltenham: Edward Elgar.

Milgrom, P. and Roberts, J. (1992) *Economics, organisation and management*, New Jersey, NJ: Prentice-Hall.

Minford, P., Peel, M. and Ashton, P. (1987) *The housing morass*, London: Institute of Economic Affairs.

Mullins, D. (1999) *Non-profit housing at the millennium in England, Scotland and Wales*, Working Paper, Birmingham: Centre for Urban and Regional Studies, University of Birmingham (mimeo).

Mullins, D. (2000) *Social origins and transformations: The changing role of English housing associations*, Birmingham: Centre for Urban and Regional Studies, University of Birmingham (mimeo).

Nentjes, A. and Schopp, W. (2000) 'Discretionary profit in subsidised housing markets', *Urban Studies*, vol 37, no 1, pp 181-94.

Nevin, B. (nd) 'Local housing companies: progress and problems', Birmingham: Centre for Urban and Regional, University of Birmingham (mimeo).

Niskanen, W. (1971) *Bureaucracy and representative government*, Chicago, IL: Aldine-Atherton.

Ogus, A.I. (1994) *Regulation: Legal form and economic theory*, Oxford: Clarendon Press.

Rose-Ackerman, S. (1996) 'Altruism, non-profits and economic theory', *Journal of Economic Literature*, vol 34, pp 701-28.

Schill, M.H. (1994) 'The role of the non-profit sector in low-income housing production: a comparative perspective', *Urban Affairs Quarterly*, vol 30, no 1, pp 74-101.

Tullock, G. (1965) *The politics of bureaucracy*, Washington, DC: Public Affairs Press.

Walker, B. (1998) 'Incentives, choice and control in the finance of council housing', in A. Marsh and D. Mullins (eds) *Housing and public policy: Citizenship, choice and control*, Buckingham: Open University Press.

Walker, B. (2000) 'Monitoring and motivation in principal–agent relationships: some issues in the case of local authority services', *Scottish Journal of Political Economy*, vol 47, no 5, pp 525-49.

Whynes, D.K. (1993) 'Can performance monitoring solve the public services' principal–agent problem?', *Scottish Journal of Political Economy*, vol 40, no 4, pp 434-46.

Wilcox, S. (1999) *Housing Finance Review 1999/2000*, York: Joseph Rowntree Foundation.

Rent policy in the social rented sector

Introduction

The level of rents in the social rented sector has changed dramatically over the last two decades. Successive Conservative governments manipulated the subsidy system as a means of pursuing a policy of raising rents and subsidising low-income households through Housing Benefit. Rent policy has thus been a source of tension between central government and local housing providers. While central control has been exerted, there are important areas of discretion in how rents are set at local level.

New Labour proposes a substantial reform of the way rents are set. It will result in a single national system of rent setting being imposed on both Registered Social Landlords (RSLs) and local authorities. All social landlords will be expected to follow this system, except in very specific circumstances. The government sets out a number of aims for rent policy which motivate this reform. In her contribution Barbara Mauthe summarises these aims as: "simplification, choice, affordability, equality and efficiency". One of the points raised by Alex Marsh in his chapter is whether these aims are compatible. This is something that is yet to be explored fully.

The discussions of rent policy provided by the following two chapters have different preoccupations. Yet they share a number of common concerns, albeit expressed in somewhat different terms. Marsh seeks to develop the argument that while the New Labour "reform agenda has evolved from preceding rounds of policy change it also represents a significant shift in focus". In particular there is a shift from concern with average rent levels to a concern with both how rents are distributed across dwellings and with local convergence of rent levels between landlords. Marsh uses a review of the options for reform currently being discussed as a means to highlight some of the fundamental issues surrounding the functions we can expect rents to fulfil. His chapter suggests that current policy debate has not yet engaged with these issues. He concludes that "the debate over social housing rents needs to be located more clearly within the wider context of a clear vision of the purpose of social housing and supported by a better understanding of the way in which housing consumers will respond to changes in policy".

Mauthe focuses much more specifically on central–local relations. She examines current changes using the socio-legal concepts of juridification and governance but argues that neither is adequate for the job. Her favoured approach is that of 'politicalisation': decisions over rent policy are simultaneously being politicalised and depoliticalised. At the local level, rent policy is being depoliticalised as decisions about rent structures and levels are largely removed from the hands of local actors. At the same time, they are being politicalised because central government is seeking to impose its own particular vision of the principles on which the system should be based.

Mauthe notes that much of the discussion about the strategic role of local authorities has focused on the local authority rather than on the impact that the change has on RSLs. As a consequence of change RSLs are being drawn further into the delivery of social welfare. This presents problems for a government seeking to impose its vision on local actors. How these changes are best analysed is one of Mauthe's key concerns. She notes that law is not always an adequate control mechanism and argues that ideology is possibly more effective: hence the lengths to which government is going to establish a vision of the purpose of social housing rents.

Common themes to emerge from the two contributions are the issue of centralisation, on the one hand, and the question of the levers that central government has over RSLs as independent bodies, on the other. Mauthe points to the way in which central government has constructed the rent issue so as to justify a strong central intervention to correct the perceived 'problem'. Marsh notes that the centralising impulse behind the policy has, in contrast to earlier attempts to exert central control, met with relatively muted resistance so far. Marsh considers the problem of influencing the activities of RSLs to be an implementation issue and an issue in the operation of the subsidy system. However, Mauthe seeks to make the point at a more fundamental level with the – not uncontroversial – view that RSLs are private law bodies that the government wishes to see execute public law functions. Government attempts to influence the activities of such private law bodies are seen as problematic, if only because it undermines the very rationale for their involvement in housing provision in the first place.

Rent restructuring is likely to be a key area in which debates about the role of the state and the purposes of social housing will be played out. Our two contributions seek to pinpoint some of important issues that need addressing. This is clearly only the start of a process of analysis and debate.

FOURTEEN

Restructuring social housing rents

Alex Marsh

Time for a change

The system of finance and subsidy for social housing in the UK has been a recurrent source of concern and not a little exasperation among politicians, commentators and practitioners. In 1974 Anthony Crosland famously described the system as a 'dog's breakfast'. Subsequent policy directions and legislative changes have transformed the way the system operates, but have not set the system on clearer, more coherent or more widely accepted foundations.

At a more detailed level, the methods that individual social landlords use to set the rents for their properties change over time. Two decades ago, the majority of local authorities used a method based on the gross values of each property[1]. By the mid-1990s the most popular systems were points-based and the use of such systems continued to spread during the late 1990s (Walker and Marsh, 1995, 2000). The use of points systems is also seen as good practice in the Registered Social Landlord (RSL) sector, although some smaller RSLs operate relatively ad hoc systems. A small number of local authorities still use systems based on 1973 Fair Rents, while others base their rents on capital values or use a formula-based method. In some authorities current staff are unable to articulate the rationale underpinning long-standing methods of setting rents.

The need for change in rent setting method is typically justified with reference to the anomalies in pricing generated by existing systems. Anomalies can arise because existing methods become increasingly out of step with contemporary perceptions of the desirability or 'value' of different types of dwelling or different locations. But anomalies are also generated by processes of local government reorganisation. The absorption of New Town stock or the amalgamation of authorities following the

Local Government Review of the late 1990s placed under the management of a single organisation stock which has previously been subject to divergent, and possibly conflicting, rent policies. Some local authorities still operate systems which perpetuate anomalies arising from local government reorganisation in 1974.

RSLs operate under a different and changing financial regime. Apparent anomalies in the rents set by different landlords for similar dwellings can arise because the landlords developed their schemes under different financial frameworks or with a different package of funding. Current rents can also differ between RSLs because of differences in past or current policies towards rent pooling, provisions for major repairs or rent surpluses.

The patchwork of rents that arise at regional and local level as a result of these different systems operating in tandem is typically considered to be undesirable. Wilcox (1997) captured the sentiment of many commentators when he characterised the situation as 'incoherent'. The grounds for criticism are considered in more detail below. The system has been considered ripe for reform for some considerable time. In discussing reform it is typical to link the reform of rent structures to the reform of the Housing Benefit system (for example Kemp, 1998). Reforming one without reforming the other is seen as having either limited impact or perverse consequences. However, in this chapter the focus is restricted to rent policy. This is in part because the issue of personal subsidy is picked up again in Chapters Sixteen and Seventeen, but also because the current government has sought to break the link between these two reform agendas. It argues that a two stage reform process is needed: more appropriate rent structures need to be put in place and only then, in the medium term, does it make sense to implement fundamental changes to the structure of Housing Benefit. While this is plausible, it is a rather timid agenda and, even within this broad two-stage approach, commentators have suggested that there is more that could be done to reform Housing Benefit in the short term (Wilcox, 2000). It is accepted by those on all sides of the debate that the full benefits that are argued to flow from rent restructuring will not be realised until the reform of both rents and Housing Benefit has occurred.

Before considering the current government's proposals for rent restructuring, the next section provides an overview of the nature of, and motivation behind, the rent reforms that have been implemented over the last two decades. This contextualises the New Labour proposals and leads to the view that while the government's reform agenda has evolved from preceding rounds of policy change, it also represents a significant shift in focus. This point is developed further in section three through a more detailed discussion of the proposals presented in the Housing Green Paper. The reform agenda raises a host of issues that should be addressed and questions that need to be answered before it would be wise to proceed further with the sort of options for change currently being contemplated. Some of the issues that seem particularly pertinent are discussed in section four. The final section of the chapter reflects briefly on the whole exercise of rent reform.

The Thatcher–Major reforms of social housing finance

The 18 years of Conservative government that followed the election of the first Thatcher government in 1979 were an active period of reform in social housing finance. The changes are reasonably well-rehearsed (see Malpass, 1990; Hills, 1991; Malpass et al, 1993; Walker, 1998; and, for a brief overview, Gibb et al, 1999) and for current purposes a summary will suffice.

The 1980 Housing Act set local authority revenue finance on a new footing. The key innovation was the use of the subsidy system as a lever to raise the average rents charged by individual authorities. The system was a victim of its own success: by the late 1980s the lever the government was using – the withdrawal of subsidy – had become ineffective because many authorities were no longer receiving any subsidy. The 1989 Local Government and Housing Act restructured the system by combining general subsidy and central government contributions to the cost of personal subsidies. This had the effect of bringing all authorities back into the subsidy system because all authorities paid personal subsidies to tenants. Central government could again exert upward pressure on average rents by withdrawing subsidy. The rationale for this policy was the belief that, first, rents should be higher in areas of relatively high capital values: subsidy was withdrawn in a way that led to greater rent increases in higher capital value areas. Second, it was felt that support for low-income households is better delivered through a system of means-tested personal subsidy than through general bricks-and-mortar subsidies. The reliance on personal subsidy allows assistance to be more closely targeted. The removal of general subsidy and the consequent increase in local authority rents towards market levels creates a more tenure-neutral pricing structure for housing. It means that, in theory, households will choose local authority housing not because it is subsidised but because it is preferable to other tenures. In practice, however, local authority rents increased over time but they never reached the level of rents in other tenures.

The housing association sector has long worked on a system dominated by capital rather than revenue subsidy. The major change with respect to finance was the introduction of mixed funding for new construction in the 1988 Housing Act. Whereas housing association development had been funded through a combination of public sector grants and loans, from 1989 it was to be funded by a mixture of public sector grants and private sector loans. Moreover, the proportion of funding accounted for by public sector grants was progressively reduced. The net effect of this policy was for the average rent of new housing association developments – and of existing properties as housing associations attempted to spread the burden of increasingly costly capital financing – increased substantially over the early 1990s. The primary motivation for this policy was to attempt to maximise the output generated by a given amount of public expenditure. It had the side-effect of raising housing association rents towards – and in some localities, above – market levels.

While these legislative changes were part of a political agenda "aimed at curtailing council provision, pluralising social housing and reviving private investment in rented housing" (Maclennan and More, 1991, p 164), the thrust of policy was broadly in accord with mainstream economic thinking on the need for greater housing market efficiency through reducing price distortions and the use of personal subsidies to assist low-income households. Yet, in the face of critique offered by, for example, Wilcox and Meen (1995) and Treasury concerns about the level of public spending, the policy of raising local authority rents was suspended, if not thrown into reverse, in 1995. This was not because the price distortions had been removed – local authority rents were still considerably below market levels – but because of concern about the Housing Benefit bill, the impact of raising rents on inflation and index-linked social security benefits, and the work disincentive effects of the deepening poverty and benefit traps. These may be good political reasons for changing tack, but there was nothing particularly notable about the average rent levels at which the policy paused.

Similarly, the rapid increases in housing association rents over the early 1990s led to concerns about the deep poverty trap that low-income working households were facing (see for example Ford and Wilcox, 1994). The notion of housing 'affordability' and of an affordability crisis entered the lexicon of housing debate as the question of how much low-income households should be expected to contribute to their housing costs became a preoccupation (see Whitehead, 1991, for an early discussion). As with the local authority sector, the policy was thrown into reverse in the mid-1990s. The 1995 Housing White Paper indicated that henceforth affordability and the rent that a housing association was proposing to charge would become a consideration in providing further grant funding (see Malpass, 2000, for a discussion).

The focus of all these policy changes was the level of *average* rents charged by social landlords. Central government has, in general, been much less concerned with the way in which social landlords distribute their rents around the average: setting rents on individual dwellings has been a key area of discretion for local authorities (see Walker, 1998) and RSLs. Until the end of the 1980s the main exception to this was the 1972 Housing Finance Act which stipulated that rents for individual dwellings should be set on the basis of the Fair Rent system. The 1972 Act was a disputed and disliked piece of housing legislation: the refusal by the councillors of Clay Cross to implement the legislation because it interfered with their right to pursue rent setting policy locally illustrates the vehemence of opposition to the Act (see Malpass, 1992). The Act was repealed shortly afterwards.

It was not until 1989 that central government again sought to influence the way local authorities set *relative* rents – that is, the rents on one type of property relative to those of another – through Section 162 of the 1989 Local Government and Housing Act. This Section stated that local authorities were to "have regard in particular to the principle that the rents of houses of any class or description should bear broadly the same proportion to private sector rents as the rents of any other class or description" (Section 162(3)). The main motivation behind this policy was a concern to replicate market-like differentials in the public sector and thereby to present tenants with incentives to consider their housing costs and to optimise their housing consumption. This would make more efficient use of the housing stock and bring benefits in addressing long-standing government concerns about the under-occupation of local authority housing.

In practice, very few local authorities acted on this subsection or made the comparisons with the private sector that it implies (see Walker and Marsh, 1995, 2000). Even where comparisons were made the vagueness of the phrase 'have regard in particular' means that there appeared no compulsion to act on comparisons that indicated differences between public and private rents. This policy raised a range of problems of both practice and principle (see Walker and Marsh, 1998) which suggest that, on balance, the apparent failure of many local authorities to implement it may in fact be the optimal outcome for the coherence of social rent setting.

Many of the reforms to social housing finance and rent setting policy since 1980 can find a rationale in mainstream economic thinking, which highlights the benefits of tenure-neutral pricing and of presenting tenants with financial incentives encouraging them to adjust their housing consumption towards optimality. The belief that personal subsidies such as Housing Benefit are preferable to general (price) subsidies is strongly held among academic commentators, although unequivocal endorsement of personal subsidies has recently been questioned (Yates and Whitehead, 1998). Also, a greater appreciation of the long-term public expenditure implications of personal versus capital subsidies (eg Holmans and Whitehead, 1997) should perhaps moderate enthusiasm for personal subsidies. But the benefits of removing anomalies from rent setting systems and removing unjustifiable cross-tenure disparities remain. Gibb et al (1999, p 211) suggest that "[i]deally, one would have a national rent scheme, transparent, fair and differentiated according to a tenant's true perceptions of the rental value of a property". They go on to observe that: "Of course, for the present, this is unrealistic" (p 211) because social landlords value their independence in rent setting. Consequently some lack of coherence across landlords will have to be tolerated. Yet, as we now turn to consider the current government's proposals, it is clear that a scheme of precisely this nature seems to be the goal of current policy.

'Moving to a fairer system of affordable rents': New Labour rent proposals

The proposals to alter the way in which social landlords set their rents is one of the most high profile and fundamental changes suggested by the Housing Green Paper (DETR/DSS, 2000a, ch 10). It is also an area in which the government acted relatively quickly: following consultation the government decided not to pursue any of the options as presented in the Green Paper but to adopt a modified scheme (see DETR/DSS, 2000b). Guidance on its implementation was issued by the end of 2000 (DETR, 2000b).

In seeking change the government has a number of aims, including: holding rents at affordable below-market levels, making rents fairer and less confusing to tenants, providing a closer link between rents and the qualities which tenants value in properties, giving tenants the opportunity to take more responsibility for their choice of housing, and reducing unjustifiable differences between the rents set by different social landlords (DETR/DSS, 2000a, para 10.1). There is also the desire to improve the way that landlords manage their stock by precluding them from using rent increases simply to soak up inefficiencies. The Green Paper offers no discussion or reflection on whether these objectives are compatible.

Perhaps the most striking thing about the government's proposals is the balance struck between concern with average and relative rents. Unlike previous rounds of change, much more emphasis is placed on the issue of relativities than on average rent levels. Moreover, the proposals address directly the coherence of rent structures across tenures.

The government notes that in judging the appropriate level for average rents questions of affordability have to be set alongside concerns about the impact of rents on work incentives, the efficiency of below-market rents in targeting help, the impact of any rent policy on public expenditure, and the impact of different policies on the finances of social landlords (DETR/DSS, 2000a, para 10.3). It is welcome to see this enumeration of the range of factors that are to be considered. The previous government was somewhat less forthcoming regarding the full range of factors that were driving policy.

The broad conclusion that the government draws is that there is no convincing case for either increasing or decreasing the level of average rents (DETR, 2000a, para 10.11). One interpretation of this is that we have apparently serendipitously arrived at precisely the average rent level that meets the government's objectives. Given the route by which the current distribution of average rents was reached, it seems unlikely that this is the case in terms of housing market coherence or efficient assistance to low-income households. It perhaps tells us more about the incompatibility of the objectives that are being pursued. Moving rents up or down comes into conflict with one or other of the government's aims and hence paralysis prevails unless one of the self-imposed policy constraints is relaxed.

Yet, the early discussion in Chapter 10 of the Green Paper which implies no change in average rent levels is somewhat misleading. Later in the relevant chapter the government articulates its desire to see the rents of local authority and RSL landlords converge at a local level. The mechanism for realising this goal is manipulation of the permissible rate of increase in average rents. Hence, the structure of average rents would change over the 10-year period that the policy of rent convergence is implemented.

The Green Paper discussion of average rents suggests continuity with previous policy directions, and the government will continue to use existing mechanisms (the RPI+X formula) to restrain average rent increases. Indeed, in order to realise the goal of convergence between local authority and RSL rents, the government is proposing to restrain rent increases in the RSL sector even more severely that they are at present. In contrast, the discussion of rent structures indicates not so much a change of direction, but more vigorous pursuit of policy directions initiated by the previous government relatively half-heartedly through Section 162. To do so the government is proposing a complete overhaul of the way social housing rents are set. It is proposing that, for the first time since 1972, the government will set out the method by which it expects social landlords to set their rents. All the options set out in the Green Paper, and the scheme finally adopted, can most plausibly be read as closely circumscribing – if not determining precisely – the rents on individual properties. Hence, if these proposals are implemented they will effectively remove local discretion in rent setting. In the context of the broader thrust of the Green Paper towards an enhanced strategic role for local authorities and policy which is more sensitive to local circumstances, the rent setting proposals have an intriguingly different flavour.

The justification for this centralisation of control is the perceived need to establish a structure of social housing rents that is "fair and which complements choice-based lettings schemes" (DETR/DSS, 2000a, para 10.12). The key principle underlying the government's proposals is that rents should more closely reflect property attributes: properties that are larger, in more desirable areas or a better state of repair should have higher rents. There should also not be arbitrary or unjustifiable differences between the rents for similar properties in a particular locality, whether they are owned by one landlord or several. In implementation terms the important word here would seem to be *unjustifiable*. Removing anomalies is seen as a positive move because it would reduce the confusion that tenants and landlords are said to suffer from under the current system and would increase fairness (DETR/DSS, 2000a, para 10.14). Restructuring rents would also in principle facilitate choice – by removing perverse incentives – and encourage tenants to take more responsibility for their housing decisions.

Given these objectives, how should rents be set? There is a range of possible rent setting methods available and the Green Paper considers six. While these six options operate in different ways, they are underpinned by a narrower set of principles. It is possible to set rents in relation to the income of tenants and some notion of what proportion of income tenants should devote to housing (option 1: affordability). It is possible to set rents based on identified attributes of dwellings (option 2: points systems). Alternatively rents can be set with reference to market valuations, either of properties or the rental streams that could be obtained in the private sector (option 3: discount on market rents; option 4: property values). Market valuations may generate disparities between rents that are considered to be in some sense 'too big' and hence a system can be based on market valuations but those values are damped in some way (option 5: following the current local authority subsidy system, which is based on capital values and regional earnings). Finally, alongside capital values, rents could be set in direct relation to some measure of running costs, an approach championed by Hills (2000) (option 6: running costs).

The government considers that none of these options meets its objectives entirely, but nonetheless sees options 5 and 6 as the most plausible. The first four options are looked on unfavourably for a number of more or less plausible reasons. It is worth considering each in a little more detail because they highlight some fundamental issues regarding the purpose of rents and rent policy.

The affordability option requires tenants to make a contribution that depends on their available resources. However, it is not considered appropriate because it breaks with the government's objectives of aligning rents with the attributes of properties. Nor could it easily form the basis of a system which forced tenants and potential tenants to make their housing choices in the light of financial incentives to ration/optimise their consumption: a household could pay the same rent regardless of the type of property they occupied.

Points systems are currently the most popular method for setting social sector rents. While the Green Paper is positive about the fact that they "provide the sort of clear and sensible link between rents and the quality of rented homes that we are looking for", it highlights the drawback that they are "inflexible and can take account only of features that can be easily measured". As a consequence they may not "take into account some factors which tenants see as important, in particular popularity of location" (DETR/DSS, 2000a, para 10.19).

Yet, dismissing points systems on this basis seems not only premature but inappropriate. While it is clear that they can only operate on the basis of factors that can easily be measured, it is not the case that they are limited to a small number of such factors. They may not be infinitely flexible but they are certainly extremely flexible. If the concern is to approximate the valuation of attributes implicit in market rents then that is certainly possible (see Walker and Marsh, 1995; also Maclennan and More, 1991). Some points systems take into account measures of popularity (such as transfer requests or waiting lists) and where such factors are not included it is more likely to be because it is considered inappropriate or unacceptable than because it is not feasible. As discussed further below, it is also not clear that 'tenants' as a whole see it as appropriate to include measures of popularity. In addition, points systems are the method that can most easily form the basis of tenant consultation and participation in determining priorities.

Finally, market-based approaches are dismissed because they generate undesirably high rents and large differentials between types of properties in areas of high house prices (paras 10.22-10.24). Whether basing rents on property values generates rents that are too high presumably depends on the multipliers that are applied to the property values (if annual rents are set as a 2 per cent return on capital then they will be very much lower than if they are set at 10 per cent). That is in turn related to the levels of subsidy that government intends to make available to underpin the system. The concern that the rents of large properties would be too high relative to the rents on other properties and in relation to incomes goes to the heart of the rent setting question: what function do we expect rents to perform and what is it that we are expecting rents to achieve? The property values for large properties are, crudely speaking, a reflection of the valuations people place on the extra attributes available in large but not small properties. As such, if we want tenants to make housing choices in the light of appropriate financial incentives then the differentials embodied in property values may be the correct ones to use. Reducing the differentials because they are 'too big' will, if sub-market pricing generates excess demand, mean that there will be excess demand for larger properties. If we find those differentials unacceptable then we need to question whether we expect rents in the social sector to provide the sort of incentives that they do in the private sector and, if not, to articulate clearly the precise function we are expecting them to fulfil.

The Green Paper suggests that the remaining options are to be given serious consideration. It proposes two versions of option 5, alongside option 6. That is, social rents could be determined using one of the following schemes:

• 50 per cent set in relation to property value and 50 per cent in relation to the level of regional earnings;

- 30 per cent set in relation to property value and 70 per cent in relation to the level of regional earnings;
- running costs determined by allowances and a small percentage set in relation to property value.

Research examining the impact that these options would have on the rents of RSLs at regional level indicates that they would each affect the pattern of rents in different ways and that in some regions average rents would change dramatically (HACAS Consulting, 2000). Clearly, changes in regional averages are likely to mask more complex, and potentially more dramatic, changes at a more local level. Taking a longer-term view, the pattern of rents generated by each option is likely to carry different implications for the revenue streams of individual landlords and therefore for their financial viability and the subsidy central government will need to make available if landlords are to continue operating.

As noted above, in the end the government did not adopt any of the options as presented in the Green Paper. The approach taken was a variant of the 30/70 option above which made further adjustments for property size (DETR/DSS, 2000b, paras 9.11 and 9.12).

The final component of the government's proposals considers the issue of convergence between the local authority and RSL sectors. As noted above, the government is looking for rents to be restructured and to converge over a decade. There is a concern to ensure that restructuring does not impose undue year-on-year burdens on tenants and so it is proposed that rent changes in pursuit of a new pattern of rents are to be restricted to no more than £2 per week per year. There is currently some vagueness regarding precisely what the 'converged' situation will look like. There is a range of reasons – such as, that the RSL stock is typically newer – that will mean that there will continue to be *justifiable* differentials between the rents of the RSL and local authority stock in a locality: it is unlikely that rent equality between the sectors will be appropriate.

The final dimension to the government's approach to rents that is worth noting is the recurrent reference to the importance of ensuring that RSLs remain financially viable. The mixed funding policies pursued since 1988 mean that many associations are tied into a range of long-term financing deals with banks, building societies and the capital markets. It is quite conceivable that compelling an RSL with relatively high rents operating in a low capital value area to restructure their rents downwards would result in revenues insufficient to meet their commitments. The government appears to make it clear that such commitments will take precedence over rent convergence. This is one reason why, even if the restructuring programme were to be implemented as fully as is compatible with RSL viability, there would remain anomalies in the rents set by different landlords in many localities.

The government's proposals: a move towards a fairer system of affordable rents?

In laying out the proposed direction for rent policy a number of issues and questions have already been identified. This section develops some of these points further and examines a number of the more apparent possible objections to the proposals and some of the obstacles that need to be overcome if the government's agenda is to be implemented successfully.

Issues of principle

At least two separate concerns are driving the Green Paper proposals. The first is a concern with the fairness of the structure of social rents. The second is a concern with presenting tenants with incentives to make efficient choices. The former is an ethical question, while the latter is clearly inspired by economic arguments around perverse incentives and the possibility that tenants are over-consuming housing because they are not being asked to face the cost of additional amenity. Importantly, the former is largely a static issue: rents should be restructured so that tenants are paying a more appropriate rent for their current dwelling. In contrast, the second is dynamic and concerned with choices and behaviour: in the face of a more 'appropriate' pricing some tenants will be discouraged from over-consuming and decide to relocate to smaller properties and hence free up larger properties. Similarly, once the rents of social landlords in a locality are harmonised, tenants may wish to readjust their consumption by transferring between landlords, without facing an arbitrary financial penalty.

Notions of fairness, like related ethical principles such as equity or equality, are contested. Yet, the Green Paper implicitly assumes that the version of fairness it advances is self-evident. In contrast, it is not implausible to argue that a 'fair' system could be based on, for example, the requirement that all households contribute a fixed proportion of their income towards the cost of their accommodation. This is effectively the Green Paper's rejected option 1. Furthermore, to argue, as the Green Paper does, that 'tenants' in general want popularity reflected in rent setting is by no means clear. As Gibb et al (1999) note, and as expressed strongly by tenants interviewed by Walker et al (2000), it is typically the social environment – the people rather than the properties – that make areas popular. Hence, if rents are set reflecting popularity it means that people are effectively being financially penalised for being pleasant neighbours. Tenants feel this to be 'unfair'. This argument, taken to its limit, could be used to justify moving in the opposite direction to current policy. If we treat tenants' behaviour as generating external effects that should be internalised in the price, then the external benefit of good behaviour should lead to a rent reduction. Conversely, the external cost of anti-social behaviour should lead to a rent increase. Hence, a rent structure apparently insensitive to popularity could be the most appropriate. At least an element of this type of thinking appears to underlie government proposals to use Housing Benefit as a tool to discipline anti-social behaviour by private tenants (DETR/DSS, 2000a, ch 5).

Pricing to influence tenants' housing choices

The second principle underlying the rent restructuring proposals is the desire to influence tenants' housing choices through pricing. Leaving aside the important question of the choices of households entering the sector, we will concentrate on existing tenants' responses to changing rents. We also assume that rent restructuring to reflect property values more clearly will result in increasing rents for larger, better quality or better located properties and reductions in rent on properties that are smaller, in worse repair or less desirable locations. Will this affect tenants' consumption decisions and, if so, will the result be positive?

Answering the first of these questions is complicated by the way that the Housing Benefit system shields tenants from rent changes. Recent research with local authority tenants by Walker et al (2000), however, suggests that there is considerable inertia in the system. When offered a range of options representing different mixes of rent, amenity and quality tenants showed a marked reluctance to move from their existing dwelling. They showed some inclination to move to better quality properties at higher rents, if such properties were available. Yet, the research suggests that only a very small proportion are inclined to move to a less desirable property simply for a lower rent. This result was largely invariant to the tenants' Housing Benefit status.

Even if this research understates the behavioural response to rent restructuring and, for example, under-occupying tenants moved from larger to smaller properties in order to save money, would this be desirable? Structuring rents to elicit this type of response is a fundamental shift in the basis for resource allocation from bureaucratic allocation on the basis of need to a more market-like willingness to pay. The implications of this have been rehearsed in the literature (see, for example, Maclennan and More, 1991; Walker and Marsh, 1998). There is no guarantee that the desired behavioural response will occur: if 'under-occupying' small households (eg, single older people) have a relatively high willingness to pay then they will not move. Even if they do, the properties they vacate will not be occupied by the 'more appropriate' larger families unless such families place a high enough valuation on housing consumption. Even if the desired reallocation were to occur and the small (typically older) households choose to move to the smaller properties and the larger (typically working age) households choose the larger properties, in the absence of a restructured system of housing allowances the consequence will be to increase the depth of the poverty or benefit trap for the (potentially) working households. Allocation on the basis of willingness to pay is not compatible with a policy goal of meeting households' 'objective' needs (whether bureaucratic alternatives can do so is an important, but separate, question). And, unless choices are constrained in some way, it represents a departure from treating housing as a merit good for which there are socially sanctioned minimum standards of consumption.

Joined-up thinking

The possibility that the desired behavioural response by tenants could worsen the poverty/benefit trap raises the broader question of how the rent restructuring proposals mesh with other policy proposals advanced by government. Most straightforwardly there is the question of how it will interact with the Right to Buy. As has been noted with respect to previous policies (Walker and Marsh, 1998; Gibb et al, 1999), if the rents on the more desirable properties increase faster than those on less desirable properties then it increases the probability that those living in the better properties will exercise their Right to Buy. This will reinforce the selective take-up of the Right to Buy that has been evident since the policy was introduced (Forrest and Murie, 1991). Given that much of the most desirable stock has already been sold, this effect may be less pronounced than during the 1980s. Nonetheless, there is no evidence, from the published documents at least, that government has considered the issue. Given that Right to Buy erodes the asset base of the landlord, in the context of the broader stock transfer agenda it is surely of continuing relevance.

Where rents are linked to property values it may, for example, generate considerable disparities in rent within local authority areas. It is not the case that larger properties will necessarily command higher rents than small properties. It depends on the spatial distribution of properties and capital values. There are undoubtedly social landlords who will find their small properties in high capital value areas commanding higher rents than large properties in low capital value areas. If the government has the desire to see mixed communities and lower-income households being able to reside in high demand, high capital value areas – as is suggested by policies such as the Key Worker and Starter Homes initiatives – then rent policy clearly needs to avoid pricing social tenants out of high priced areas. Unless, that is, policy takes the view that the mixing of communities only goes so far and that there are some areas in which it is inappropriate for low-income households to live. This is an old debate, but is of central importance to the future direction of rent policy within the broader context of the drive to foster social inclusion.

Finally, there is a tension between the government's policies on tenant participation and the proposals for rent setting, in the local authority sector at least. The Tenant Participation Compacts (TPCs) that all local authorities were required to have in place by April 2000 cover a range of topics including rent setting policy. The implication of this would appear to be that tenants should have some input into the process of deciding the shape of rent setting policy. As noted above, perhaps the easiest rent setting method on which to have this type of dialogue is a points system. The government's rent proposals centralise control of rent setting policy such that the landlord – let alone the tenants – has almost no discretion or input into the process.

Implementation

The Green Paper is, appropriately, not a document directed at questions of implementation (but see DETR, 2000a, 2000b). Yet the obstacles facing any attempt to implement the type of national rent setting scheme envisaged appear to be considerable. Many of these problems flow from the fact that the government has broadened its vision of rent setting policy to include RSLs, which are independent organisations. The government does not possess the same sort of levers to influence RSL performance that it does to influence local authorities. A simple example is the question of capital values. The early guidance issued by the government (DETR, 2000a) indicates that the capital values that are being considered as the basis for the system are the beacon values that are being established by local authorities for resource accounting purposes. Hence, local authorities are obliged to establish these values regardless of the rent setting proposals. If rent convergence is to be meaningful then presumably RSLs will also need to have beacon values on which to set their rents. Yet, they are under no obligation to establish such values and the process of valuing the stock is costly and time-consuming.

A second example relates to the question of how rent restructuring will interact with the subsidy system. Subsidy is not addressed in the Green Paper, but it would be reasonable to assume that the subsidy system will be used to ensure that local authorities who see their rent roll reduced as a result of rent restructuring will be compensated through subsidy. Conversely, in high capital value areas local authorities may generate surpluses and these will presumably be clawed back through the subsidy system. In contrast, the government has no obvious lever by which to make these sort of financial adjustments in the RSL sector. The Green Paper makes clear that restructuring rents downwards will not be allowed to affect viability, so this is perhaps not an issue. However, where an RSL sees its restructured rents generating an increased surplus then there appears little the government can do within existing systems to claw that money back. Also, if this remains the case then it would appear to give local authorities in high capital value areas a strong financial incentive to transfer their stock to the RSL sector as fast as possible.

Concluding discussion

Rent setting has been an active area of policy for the last two decades. While current policy proposals display considerable continuity with policy directions established by previous administrations, the government appears to be contemplating far-reaching changes to the system. The most obvious consequence of these changes appears to be increasing central government control over the process. It is notable that, in contrast to the 1972 Housing Finance Act, opposition to the proposals on the grounds that they erode long-established local discretion has been relatively muted. The rent setting scheme finally adopted by government makes some small concessions to requests for more local discretion, but the thrust of policy remains the same. It retains the strong centralising flavour that is somewhat at odds with much of the remainder of the current policy agenda.

While the government has apparently now decided the direction rent policy is going to take, we still lack a more fundamental discussion about the principles that should underlie rent setting. Current government thinking accords with much contemporary thinking on the appropriate direction for rent restructuring, but it embodies a set of implicit assumptions and value positions that need to be scrutinised and debated more extensively. For the majority of its history, social rented housing in the UK has been about breaking the link between income and housing consumption: it is fundamentally about (partially) decommodifying housing consumption (Harloe, 1995). Yet, current discussions seem to be predicated on the view that more market-like pricing could be grafted onto the system without compromising the objectives of social housing provision or, alternatively, that there is an implicit acceptance that the objectives of social housing will change. Over the last decade, the impact of the quasi-market reforms of the late 1980s (for example, Le Grand and Bartlett, 1993; Bartlett et al, 1998) and the introduction of fees and charges into local public service provision (eg Walsh, 1995) have been debated at this precisely this level of principle. It is interesting that at the same time as there is an increased concern with pricing and incentives in social housing, the government has, in the health sector at least, moved away from the quasi-market approach because it was perceived to have failed to deliver.

There is no doubt a case for examining the way social housing rents are set. There is good reason to think that reform is necessary. Yet, the debate over social housing rents needs to be located more clearly within the wider context of a clear vision of the purpose of social housing and supported by a better understanding of the way in which housing consumers will respond to changes in policy. The current government is only just beginning to articulate its vision for social housing (DETR/DSS, 2000a, ch 3) and the role it could play in building and sustaining communities. There is a distance to go before future directions for social housing are clearly perceived and widely agreed. The constraints that government faces in realising its vision as a result of the increased reliance on independent organisations need to be recognised more fully. It is essential that the reform of rent setting policy is set on a firm and coherent foundation and that rent structures are reformed in ways which accord with, rather than frustrate, this broader vision. Changing rent setting

---

policy at local level is a very costly and time-consuming exercise (Walker and Marsh, 1995): the worst case scenario would be to reform rents over the next couple of years only to have to reopen the issue in the medium term because the reforms do not fit into the bigger picture.

Acknowledgements

In preparing this chapter I have benefited from discussions with, and comments from, Dave Cowan, John Hills, Alan Murie, Pat Niner, and, as ever, Bruce Walker. They may not agree with the chapter that was informed by those discussions, but the chapter certainly benefited from their willingness to discuss the issue of rents, sometimes at length. All the views expressed are those of the author. Any errors of fact or interpretation are my responsibility.

Note

[1] Gross values were determined by the Inland Revenue. The values were used as the basis for calculating owner-occupiers' liabilities for imputed rental income tax until the tax was abolished in 1961. Gross values were intended to reflect the annual market rent of a dwelling when the landlord is responsible for repairs and maintenance. The most recent valuation of the whole housing stock took place in 1973. After that date, properties added to the local authority stock were valued using comparisons with the gross values of other similar properties.

References

Bartlett, W., Roberts, J. and Le Grand, J. (1998) *A revolution in social policy: Quasi-market reforms in the 1990s*, Bristol: The Policy Press.

DETR (Department of the Environment, Transport and the Regions) (2000a) *Calculating prospective rents according to the formulae outlined in the Housing Green Paper*, Housing Research Summary No 119, London: DETR.

DETR (2000b) *Guide to social rent reforms*, London: DETR, December.

DETR/DSS (Department of Social Security) (2000a) *Quality and choice: A decent home for all*, Housing Green Paper, London: DETR/DSS.

DETR/DSS (2000b) *Quality and choice: A decent home for all – The way forward for housing*, London: DETR/DSS.

Ford, J. and Wilcox, S. (1994) *Affordable housing, low incomes and the flexible labour market*, Research Report no 22, London: National Federation of Housing Associations.

Forrest, R. and Murie, A. (1991) *Selling the welfare state*, London: Routledge.

Gibb, K., Munro, M. and Satsangi, M. (1999) *Housing finance in the UK* (2nd edn), Basingstoke: Macmillan.

HACAS Consulting (2000) *Impact and implications of restructuring rents in the registered social landlord sector: Summary*, London: DETR.

Harloe, M. (1995) *The people's home*, Oxford: Blackwells.

Hills, J. (1991) *Unravelling housing finance*, Oxford: Clarendon Press.

Hills, J. (2000) *Reinventing social housing finance*, London: Institute for Public Policy Research.

Holmans, A. and Whitehead, C. (1997) *Funding affordable social housing: Capital grants, revenue subsidies and subsidies to tenants*, London: National Housing Federation.

Kemp, P. (1998) *Housing Benefit: Time for reform*, York: Joseph Rowntree Foundation.

Le Grand, J. and Bartlett, W. (eds) (1993) *Quasi-markets and social policy*, Basingstoke: Macmillan.

Maclennan, D. and More, A. (1991) 'What price? Social housing', in D. Donnison and D. Maclennan (eds) *The housing service of the future*, Harlow/Coventry: Longman/Institute of Housing.

Malpass, P. (1990) *Reshaping housing policy: Subsidies rents and residualisation*, London: Routledge.

Malpass, P. (1992) 'The road from Clay Cross', in C. Grant (ed) *Built to last*, London: Shelter.

Malpass, P. (2000) *Housing associations and housing policy*, Basingstoke: Macmillan.

Malpass, P., Warburton, M., Bramley, G. and Smart, G. (1993) *Housing policy in action: The new financial regime for council housing*, Bristol: SAUS Publications.

Walker, B. (1998) 'Incentives, choice and control in the finance of council housing', in A. Marsh and D. Mullins (eds) *Housing and public policy*, Buckingham: Open University Press.

Walker, B. and Marsh, A. (1995) *Rent setting policies in English local authorities*, DoE Housing Research Report, London: HMSO.

Walker, B. and Marsh, A. (1998) 'Pricing public housing services in the UK: mirroring the market?', *Housing Studies*, vol 13, no 4, pp 549-66.

Walker, B. and Marsh, A. (2000) *Rent setting policies in English local authorities 1999*, DETR Housing Research Report, London: DETR.

Walker, B., Niner, P., Marsh, A. and Wardman, M. (2000) *Social housing tenants' attitudes and reactions to rent levels and rent differentials*, London: DETR.

Walsh, K. (1995) *Public services and market mechanisms*, Basingstoke: Macmillan.

Whitehead, C. (1991) 'From need to affordability: an analysis of UK housing objectives', *Urban Studies*, vol 28, no 6, pp 871-87.

Wilcox, S. (1997) 'Incoherent rents', *Housing Finance Review 1997/98*, York: Joseph Rowntree Foundation.

Wilcox, S. (2000) 'Contrasting ambitions', *Housing Finance Review 2000/ 2001*, Coventry: Joseph Rowntree Foundation/Chartered Institute of Housing/Council of Mortgage Lenders.

Wilcox, S. and Meen, G. (1995) *The cost of higher rents*, London: National Federation of Housing Associations.

Yates, J. and Whitehead, C. (1998) 'In defence of greater agnosticism: a response to Galster's "Comparing demand-side and supply-side housing policies"', *Housing Studies*, vol 13, no 3, pp 415-24.

FIFTEEN

The politicalisation of social rents

Barbara Mauthe

Introduction

This chapter will commence by outlining the proposals in the Housing Green Paper (DETR/DSS, 2000) relating to the setting of social rents. It will argue that the proposals will create a structure that could fundamentally alter the normative foundations for the distribution of 'housing' within society. The chapter will consider how these changes could be evaluated using theories selected from current legal and non-legal analysis of local government and the central–local relationship, in particular 'juridification' and 'governance'. It will be argued that each of the theories cannot adequately evaluate the proposals. The chapter will then consider an alternative evaluative approach – that of 'politicalisation' – and offer a number of conclusions relating to the setting of social rents.

A fairer system of affordable rents: the Green Paper proposals

In the context of the existing structure of social rents, the aims of the Green Paper are simplification, choice, affordability, equality and efficiency (DETR/DSS, 2000, para 10.1). However, it acknowledges that the achievement of these goals is influenced by social and economic factors and by the legacy of policies inherited from the previous government. These factors have to largely be taken as given: the level of control which central government can exercise over them is limited. These factors can, however, be influenced in part by policies such as altering public expenditure or by targeting support through specific policies, such as the national minimum wage or the Working Families Tax Credit. Yet ultimately such policies can only force rents either upwards or downwards. In other words, such policies are limited in that they impact only on the *external* notion of social rents. The proposals in the Green Paper are arguably directed at a somewhat different goal.

The Green Paper argues that there is no case for substantial reform of rent levels but that there is a case for reform of rent structures, that is, "how rents vary between the registered social landlord and local authority sectors, between different landlords and between individual homes" (DETR/DSS, 2000, para 10.11). What the government is seeking to do is to shift the focus of the debate on social rents away from the objective and external – the relationship between rent and issues such as housing finance and Housing Benefits – towards the subjective nature of social rents and how they are internally conceived. The government is concerned with the framework of rules that form the basic structure of social rents. In other words, rent is to be perceived as a social good that is distinct from housing. The distinction is difficult to identify at an objective level since both housing and rents possess similar attributes and draw on common values and norms. It is only at the subjective level that any divergence can be identified, such as, the differing factors that Registered Social Landlords (RSLs) and local authority landlords may take into consideration when setting rents. RSLs, for example, conventionally focus on capital rather than revenue subsidy.

The Green Paper argues that there are problems with the current structure of rents in terms of fairness. There are anomalies and arbitrary differences between local authority owned properties and RSL properties (DETR/DSS, 2000, para 10.13) and these differences result in confusion to tenants and landlords alike. A number of suggestions are made to bring about coherence to the structure of social rents, such as, setting rents on the basis of their affordability to individual tenants, a points system, basing rents on property values, following the Housing Revenue Account (HRA) Guideline Rent system, and setting rents so that they cover landlords costs with an additional element based on property values. The Green Paper continues that none of the suggested options meets the government's objectives, although the options which are represented as the most promising are the schemes based on the existing HRA subsidy system and the *meeting running costs* option. However, the ultimate goal is that, whichever scheme is chosen, rents between the two sectors should be based on the same principles. In addition, there should be some convergence or a reduction in the gap between the average rents of the two sectors. These proposals raise issues for local authorities, social landlords and their tenants. Significant issues include the timetabling of the rent restructuring, the amount of the changes and their impact on vulnerable groups.

At least two justifications can be identified from within the Green Paper for the convergence of social rents. First, it will be beneficial for tenants because they will be better able to understand the rent system and the rent structures it generates. Convergence will also offer tenants wider choices and be more equitable. Second, convergence would make it easier for the transfer of housing stock from local authorities to registered social landlords (DETR/DSS, 2000, para 10.36). The Green Paper does not provide much by way of historical explanation of why existing patterns of divergence came about. The absence of such an explanation means policy proposals can be portrayed as corrective and therefore paramount, even if they result in the merging of smaller RSLs (DETR/DSS, 2000, para 10.40).

Rent restructuring, the enabling local authority and housing providers

As is discussed elsewhere in this book (see especially Chapter Twelve), the broader agenda of the Green Paper is one of creating 'enabling' local authorities concerned with strategic issues and largely relinquishing their role as direct providers of rented housing. Although the Green Paper focuses on the implications of enabling for local authorities, it is suggested that altering this role also impacts on RSLs as the providers of social housing. Diminishing the status of local authorities as landlords enhances the status of RSLs within the housing policy arena and should focus concern on their wider role within the housing policy process. The possession of an enlarged share of social housing will also impact on how RSLs are financed, regulated, and relate to central government.

One view of the Green Paper could be that it is about finding methods for central government to become involved in the decision making of RSLs. Given that the Green Paper argues for a revision of the housing policy process and that finance, as opposed to need, is to be the primary consideration within the revised process, it will be the issue of finance which will provide the basis for that involvement. In seeking to use finance as the lever to influence RSLs the government is following the well-established strategy for shaping the behaviour of local actors. Perhaps most notably, the changes embodied in the 1980 Housing Act and the 1989 Local Government and Housing Act focused on financial mechanisms which resulted in the relatively rapid reduction in local authorities' role as housing providers.

There is, however, an important difference in the manner in which central government is attempting to achieve greater involvement with RSL decision making. The difference has its roots in the nature of the bodies concerned. It is, for example, easier for central government to interfere with local authority decision making since local authorities are public law bodies performing public law functions, such as the distribution of social welfare. They also possess an inferior constitutional status: local authorities can be represented as being 'beneath' central government in the central–local hierarchy. Local authorities are also financially dependent on central government for their primary source of income. In contrast, although RSLs perform a public law function they are essentially private law bodies. Differences in constitutional status are not an issue, although RSLs could possibly be described as sub-central government agencies because of their social welfare role (Rhodes, 1999).

Should central government use the social welfare role as the basis for intervention this would entail using a public law issue to strike at the very justification for the involvement of RSLs in housing, that is, their private law status. This could heighten the potential for conflict, possibly damage the relationship and ultimately inhibit the provision of the desired social good of housing. This means that central government cannot use its status and legal powers to control RSLs in the same manner that it can control local authorities. It must instead identify alternative mechanisms to facilitate control. What provides that basis is the issue of finance. While RSLs will receive funds from the private sector they also receive income in the form of social rents. By placing finance at the centre of housing policy and representing rents as a social good, separate and distinct from housing, this provides central government with the necessary mechanism. Furthermore, as a distinctive and subjective social good it will be central government rather than RSLs or even local authorities that will become the key body in devising the "principles that are to govern rent-setting in the future" (DETR/DSS, 2000, para 10.32).

Social rent policy in the context of the central–local relationship

It is possible to argue that the proposed division in the role of local authorities along with the potential impact on RSLs represents a continuation of central government's use of law to alter the manner in which social resources are defined and allocated within the central–local and sub-central government relationship. Socio-legal analysis of this use of law and its outcomes has developed along two avenues: 'juridification' and 'governance'. Accordingly, the Green Paper proposals are examined using each concept in turn in order to determine whether the theories will provide an adequate explanation or whether an alternative approach may be required.

Juridification

Juridification can be defined as a theoretical representation of the processes by which the state intervenes in areas of social life in ways that limit the autonomy of individuals or groups to determine their own affairs (Teubner, 1987, p 3). Inherent within the processes of juridification are the concepts of 'formalisation' – the increased use of law and reliance on law – and the 'de-politicalisation' of social conflict. As conflicts emerge concerning the distribution of social goods, law rather than politics becomes the chosen mechanism for resolution.

In the context of the central–local government relationship it has been argued that a process of juridification occurred in the 1980s when central government used its superior constitutional position to pass legislation in order to achieve specific political and economic goals (Loughlin, 1989, p 21, 1994, p 261, 1996a). Central government created a 'command and control' regime when its views on social welfare and the mechanisms for its distribution predominated over the views of local authorities. Local authorities effectively became 'rule bound' agencies, no longer the 'providers' of social welfare. The growth in RSLs during the 1980s and into the 1990s complemented the juridification process which diminished the provision and funding of local authority housing. Clear examples of the juridification process are legislation such as the 1980 Housing Act which introduced the Right to Buy for council tenants and the 1989 Local Government and Housing Act – together with the extensive specification of housing revenue finance in quasi-legislation – which 'ring-fenced' HRAs.

It is possible to argue that the proposals contained within the Green Paper represent an extension of the processes of 'juridification'. In order to implement the social goals contained within the Green Paper, but defined within the political arena, central government will need to exercise its regulatory powers. Furthermore, the proposals represent central government further redefining the role of local authorities and RSLs within the housing policy arena. The role of local authorities as a direct provider of social housing is limited while central government will direct the development of the principles regarding the setting of social rents. In the context of Loughlin's definition, the Green Paper represents central government imposing its normative beliefs on local authorities. Local authorities will become increasingly 'rule bound'. Even the discretion available through the strategic role is limited because local authorities are not the sole decision makers but must consult with other agencies. In other words, the Green Paper proposals do, in some respects, appear to reinforce a 'command and control' regime. However, instead of using the courts there may be greater reliance on the flexibility inherent in the administrative decision-making networks to resolve 'normative' differences between central government and local government.

In the RSL sector central government could never create a pure 'command and control' regime because the private finance which many RSLs have drawn on means they are required to be accountable to their investors. Central government has to rely on action by the regulators, the Housing Corporation. Furthermore, central government will not want to engage in conflict with RSLs as this could jeopardise the availability of the private finance and thereby undermine its wider vision for social housing. This would suggest that the Green Paper proposals do not accord completely with Loughlin's definition since Loughlin specifically sought to examine legal decision making and exclude administrative decision making from his analysis (Loughlin, 1989, p 21).

Governance

Governance has been defined as "governing without government" (Rhodes, 1996, p 653). In one respect governance can be described as the converse of juridification. While juridification is about control as command by government through the operation of hierarchy, governance is about control without the presence of hierarchy. There are a number of forms of governance (Rhodes, 2000, p 55; see also Pierre, 2000). A specific feature that is particularly relevant in the context of the Green Paper is the operation of disparate, but interdependent agencies through networks in relation to a social welfare system. Within the networks, agencies will regulate themselves and develop their own rules and sanctions. The focus of the analysis is not the narrow concern of the government per se but the wider coordination and interactions, both formal and informal, in the context of a policy arena.

Legal analysis of self-governing systems draws on autopoiesis (Teubner, 1993). The concept of autopoiesis originates from biology and characterises systems as 'living'. 'Living' refers to the reproduction which occurs within each system as the system generates its own network of processes. Each system is, however, operationally closed in that other external systems – such as law, economics or politics – are unable to impact on the internal operation of the system once it has been created. This operational closure is central to the analysis. A further characteristic of the closed social system is that it can only interpret interactions which the system can 'see'. This includes both internal and external communications and furthermore the interpretation of these communications occurs within the terms of reference of the receiving system. Autopoietic systems can only be governed by their own internal self-referencing modes of operation and organisation.

Autopoiesis has been deployed in the context of local government (Vincent-Jones, 1998, 1999) and housing (Cowan, 1999). It is possible to argue that should the Green Paper proposals be implemented the concept could be applied to the new social housing system. However, the proposals do not result in the creation of one single decision-making system but several disparate systems each with its own specific objectives. Thus, autopoiesis may not be applicable unless a single basis for the operation of a system can be identified. One approach could be to represent housing as a 'mega-system' with various sub-systems, such as housing strategy (the role of local authorities) and social rents (RSLs). Alternatively, it may be possible to represent finance as the primary system and strategy as a secondary system. However, such approaches do not accord with the parameters of autopoiesis, which views systems as autonomous rather than hierarchical in nature.

There would also be the issue of communications between the various systems. Within autopoietic analysis a system may receive communications from other systems but the decision to award hierarchy or status to a particular communication can only be made by the system which receives the communication. In other words, one system, for example housing strategy, cannot tell another system, such as social rents, that its communications are important or possess command. Furthermore, autopoietic systems may exaggerate, even corrupt, a particular communication or possibly ignore or minimise it. This would suggest that autopoiesis is not a suitable analytical tool for evaluation of the Green Paper proposals since the government is specifically seeking to centralise the structure of social housing rents and impose its vision of 'fairness'.

An alternative approach would be to draw on the analysis of networks. Networks, however, like hierarchies and markets also possess limitations. As a mechanism for the allocation of resources networks are perceived to work where the commodity concerned is difficult to price and expertise/ professional discretion are regarded as core values. Conversely, networks can be unrepresentative and may not be accountable to the state. As networks are at least partly self-organising the state does not occupy a privileged or sovereign status. This means that ultimately the state can never command a network, only steer.

The strong tradition of state-led welfare provision in the UK, whether directly through hierarchies or indirectly as the regulator of welfare markets, remains relatively robust. It would therefore be unlikely that the intention behind the Green Paper proposals is to create a system of networks for housing. Such a system would present the state with problems in exercising control, even if only to ensure that the objectives contained within the Green Paper are met. Nor does the Green Paper seek to exclude the state. Rather it is concerned with shaping, channelling and guiding the conduct of others. Accordingly, it is possible to argue that the Green Paper proposals in relation to social rents represent an alternative dimension to the notion of 'control'.

The control of social rents in the context of the central–local relationship

If it is accepted that current socio-legal analysis of the central–local government relationship is unable to accommodate fully the impact that the Green Paper rent restructuring proposals could have on the role of local authorities and RSLs then perhaps an alternative approach should be applied. The basis for an alternative approach can be identified from further examination of the implications that flow from the proposals rather than the proposals themselves.

The role of the local authority

One possible – and fundamental – consequence of the revised role of local authorities within the housing policy process is the de-politicalisation of local authority decision making. There will be 'political' activity within the local policy arena in the sense that there will be conflict and disagreement between the various agencies as local authorities negotiate with other organisations in order to influence outcomes. But key decisions will be removed from this local arena.

Traditionally there has been a strong link between the provision of housing and ideology (Kemp, 1997). The link was part of the notion of 'service content' (Sheldrake, 1989, p 61) which was a key feature of local government. The provision of services was allied to a set of philosophical or political preferences which viewed local government as the most appropriate means of delivering public services generally. The notion of 'service content' has, however, been redefined over the years as services have been given to and taken away from local authorities and as central government has altered its attitude to welfare. In respect of housing, the preference had been for a statist approach with a heavy reliance on local authorities rather than the privately rented sector. Even with the marginalisation of local authorities in the provision of housing and the growth of the 'voluntary housing movement', the link between housing and ideology has generally remained unscathed, albeit diluted, largely because housing stock was transferred to bodies which shared the same 'ideology' as local authorities. In other words, housing has always had its own belief system based on its self-perception as a merit good.

However, it is possible to argue that the proposals contained within the Green Paper represent the demise of ideology or the de-politicalisation of local authority involvement in the housing policy process. This de-politicalisation is a consequence of redefining the strategic role of local authorities and the demise of the landlord function. This removal of ideology, or de-politicalisation, is distinct from the process of juridification. Juridification entails the use of law to impose specific values and norms. The problem with juridification is that while it can alter the legal framework for the delivery of social welfare it leaves untouched the political-administrative networks which must implement the changes. These networks may be influenced by the changes, such as the introduction of markets, but unless the changes are extremely fundamental and radical the belief systems within the networks can remain intact and operational (Mauthe, 2000). It is a matter of the communication of values and norms. Law can be expressive of a particular set of values and norms but its communication of these values and norms to those within the political-administrative networks who implement the law can be ignored, corrupted and even exaggerated.

An example of the flaws which can accompany the legislative communication of beliefs is the Compulsory Competitive Tendering

(CCT) system. The introduction of CCT for housing management resulted in diversity because local authorities interpreted and implemented the policy at an individual level. Autopoietic analysis highlights this problem of communication. However, it does not seek to resolve it, merely to incorporate the flaw within its analysis. It is able to do this by representing systems as closed and distinct. Communication failures then become a feature rather than a flaw and regulation is then designed on this basis as a set of incentives.

Since it is unrealistic, possibly ineffective and even inefficient for central government to legislate to remove political-administrative networks, the alternative is to alter the ideological basis for their operation. This the Green Paper does, not by imposing a particular set of beliefs, but by broadening the strategic role of local authorities and linking decision making to other policy areas such as crime and health. Ultimately, this should result in the decline of the single ideology which has operated in the wider context of housing where rent was linked to the notion of need. The existing belief system may instead become subsumed or corrupted through interaction with other policy areas. The result could be a shift to a distinct and new set of core values and norms in the context of housing strategy. Furthermore, the demise of the local authority landlord function largely removes the potential for conflict, influence and even communication between housing strategy and housing finance. Central government is seeking to use the inevitable failures which appear to follow from the communication of beliefs to undermine the existing belief system.

The role of RSLs

Just as the revision of the role of local authorities results in the de-politicalisation of decision making the same process can be identified in the context of RSLs. The politicalisation is the result of separating and elevating the role of finance and in particular the notion of a social rent. By representing rent as a distinct but separate and subjective social good central government opens up the notion that 'social rent' constitutes something which is separate and distinct from 'need' or 'merit'. As a distinct notion rent can then be perceived as containing discretionary elements which will require defining before it can be controlled. The discretionary elements can be represented as the principles on which the notion will rest. Within the Green Paper the government identifies a number of key principles that it wished to be deployed, such as fairness and choice. The government further compounds this redefining of the notion of social rent by suggesting that the context within which the discretion will operate is the strategic arena.

The Green Paper does not attempt to establish or identify an objective notion of what constitutes a 'social rent'. Instead, the Paper seeks to create a decision-making framework which isolates and separates the various forms of discretion which are inherent within any social welfare system. As the innovator of the new decision-making framework central government will act as the manager. Each sector may possess its own 'ideological baggage' but as the innovators of the new housing strategy arena the government will be able to define the principles and goals to ensure that the new emerging ideology within the de-politicalised housing system accords with its preferred subjective values and beliefs.

The 'politicalisation' of housing

So far it has been argued that the Green Paper has the potential to alter the ideological basis in housing. It has also been suggested that this shift represents a form of control as the 'politicalisation' of housing. However, in order to explain how 'politicalisation' can exercise 'control', it is necessary to identify the concepts which underpin the argument. This will entail defining what is meant by the terms 'power' and 'control'.

The essence of the central–local government relationship is the allocation of power. Power can be defined as the ability to control by means of the exercise of formal capabilities, such as law, politics, economics and administration (Smith, 1999). In the context of housing central government in the 1980s and 1990s used RSLs to break up the near monopoly that local authorities had. Central government exercised a number of powers, in particular law and economics, to 'control' the provision of social housing.

Control can be defined as the directing of decision makers to do that which is required of them, limiting or defining the parameters of their decision making and structuring decision making in order to ensure that the correct values have been applied (Feldman, 1988). There are flaws in using the exercise of formal powers – such as law – as a mechanism for control. Law can require local authorities to limit, define and structure their decision making but it does not necessarily remove or alter the fundamental ideological beliefs which underpin decision making. This has been particularly evident in the context of social housing. The large-scale transfer of housing stock from the public to the private sector has altered the nature of service delivery and resulted in the limitation of the role of local authorities and the restructuring of housing provision. But the setting of rents, in both sectors, has always been largely a matter of shared ideology.

It is suggested that central government has become aware that focusing exclusively on legal techniques for the distribution of social welfare will always be flawed, even when legislation expressly directs local authorities towards specific economic and political goals. In the Green Paper discussion of social rents this recognition is particularly apparent when it argues for the creation of principles, rather than rules or standards, for the setting of social rents (DETR/DSS, 2000, para 10.32).

Principles and the setting of social rents

Rules can be defined as concrete guides which address themselves to specific fact situations. Therefore their application can be mechanistic. Standards also involve identifying a fact but are more general and contain an element of flexibility which can be absent from the notion of a rule. The problem with standards is that there may be an absence of consensus concerning the particular fact by which the standard is to be measured. In contrast, principles involve judgements by which rules and standards can be evaluated (Jowell, 1973, p 201). Principles do not address themselves to specific facts but relate to norms and values.

The particular principles which the Green Paper seeks to apply in the context of social rents are those of fairness and affordability. The preferred rent setting options – using principles underlying the existing HRA system or the *meeting of running* costs – are the most open-textured. They involve a comparative element which is absent from the alternatives, such as setting rents on the basis of their affordability to individual tenants, the points system, the offering of discounts or basing rents on property values alone. These options are more restrictive in that they focus on a specific set of facts. In other words, for principles such as affordability and fairness to emerge there must be a comparative element. The process of comparison, and therefore ultimately deciding what constitutes fair and affordable, could be conducted by means of law or economics. This would, however, entail central government involving another party along with their accompanying values and norms. The Green Paper also argues that the flaws in the current system are a consequence of the influence of social and economic factors along with the policies inherited from previous governments (factors which it argues are objective and beyond its control).

In other words, the only way that central government can ensure that its vision of housing policy is implemented is to exercise control through politics.

Politics as a form of control

One view of politics is to equate it with some particular organisation such as the state. An alternative approach is to view politics as a set of social acts which are reflected and expressed in varied organisational contexts such as the central–local government relationship. Here, politics is about the exercise of power and one basis on which power can be exercised is that of 'ideology'.

The notion of ideology is complex and varied. Rather than define 'ideology' it is proposed to deploy a number of its features in order to explain how politics can act as a controlling mechanism similar to law. Ideologies perform a number of functions.

First, ideology can act as a form of restraint on individuals and agencies. The beliefs and norms within a particular ideology will define what is and is not acceptable. In other words, ideology can limit decision making. In the context of social rents ideology can therefore exclude the notion of need and facilitate finance as the primary consideration.

Second, an important but latent function of ideology is to provide a common set of beliefs. Given that the Green Paper proposes to alter the structure for the provision of housing by separating the strategic and landlord roles of local authorities and elevating the role of finance, such fundamental alterations could create uncertainty. One way to create certainty and provide sense to the changes is to explain them at a 'belief level'. As a 'belief' the ideology will also provide in more or less detail the desired goals to be achieved and the mechanisms to achieve them. The Green Paper certainly specifies its goals in the context of influencing the structure of social rents and housing generally and identifies its preferred options for achieving them (DETR/DSS, 2000, para 10.15). If one of these options – or some variant of it – were implemented it will be these goals and mechanisms that will provide the focus for the activities of administrators, although it may not necessarily explain their activities. Thus, ideology can direct decision making.

Third, ideology can provide rational justification for decision making. Rational decision making occurs when decision makers apply the correct ideology because failure to apply the correct ideology is irrational. Decision making that is irrational circumvents accepted values and goals.

In other words, ideology can require decision makers to structure their decision making in order to demonstrate the application of ideology. The Green Paper provides the justifications for its proposals. The justification for the centralisation of control is the need to establish a structure of social housing rents that is "fair and which complements choice based letting schemes" (DETR/DSS, 2000, para 10.12). Should the proposals be implemented these justifications – fairness and choice – will provide the basis for rationality.

Finally, ideology can provide legitimacy for decision making. This is in many respects the most significant role. Legitimacy can only be achieved when both the correct values and procedures have been deployed as part of the decision-making procedures. Whether or not a decision is legitimate can only be determined from a historical examination of the decision-making procedures. Legitimacy would also find expression through the choices exercised by tenants.

As a form of control, ideology as politicalisation shares many of the qualities of law. It can require administrators to limit, confine and structure their decision making. If administrators fail then there is justification for the intervention by central government on the basis that the decision lacks legitimacy. Furthermore, this absence of legitimacy, while rooted in a political context, could ultimately provide the basis for intervention by means of law.

Conclusion

The initial focus of this chapter was the Green Paper proposals for the setting of social rents. However, examination of the proposals, particularly the changes to the role of local authorities and their impact on the role of RSLs revealed a number of phenomena which would impact beyond merely altering the existing framework for the provision of housing. It was argued that the proposed changes have the potential to act as an alternative to law as a mechanism to control decision making and the defining of key notions such as 'social rent'. This control would be exercised through the construction of an alternative ideology which would accompany the revised framework. The construction of this ideology would be led by the government. Of course such a task will take time and ultimately it may only be the government who understands the basic principles and the vision that it seeks to create. The real test will be in communicating the beliefs to local authorities, RSLs and ultimately tenants.

References

Cowan, D. (1999) *Housing law and policy*, Basingstoke: Macmillan

DETR (Department of the Environment, Transport and the Regions)/ DSS (Department of Social Security) (2000) *Quality and choice: A decent home for all*, Housing Green Paper, London: DETR/DSS.

Feldman, D. (1988) 'Judicial review: a way of controlling government', *Public Administration*, vol 66, no 1, pp 21-34.

Jowell, J. (1973) 'The legal control of administrative discretion', *Public Law*, pp 178-220.

Kemp, P. (1997) 'Ideology, public policy and private rental housing since the War', in P. Williams (ed) *Directions in housing policy*, London: PCP.

Loughlin, M. (1989) 'Law, ideologies and the political-administrative system', *Journal of Law and Society*, vol 16, pp 21-42.

Loughlin, M. (1994) 'The restructuring of central-local relations', in J. Jowell and D. Oliver (eds) *The changing constitution*, Oxford: Oxford University Press.

Loughlin, M. (1996) *Legality and locality: The role of law in central-local government*, Oxford: Oxford University Press.

Mauthe, B. (2000) 'The notion of rules and rule making in the central-local government relationship', *Anglo-American Law Review*, vol 29, pp 315-42.

Pierre, J. (ed) (2000) *Debating governance*, Oxford: Oxford University Press.

Rhodes, R.A.W. (1996) 'The new governance: governing without government', *Political Studies*, vol 44, pp 653-67.

Rhodes, R.A.W. (1999) *Control and power in central-local government relations*, Aldershot: Ashgate.

Rhodes, R.A.W. (2000) 'Governance and public administration', in J. Pierre (ed) *Debating governance*, Oxford: Oxford University Press.

Sheldrake, J. (1989) *Municipal socialism*, Aldershot: Avebury.

Smith, M.J. (1999) *The core executive in Britain*, Basingstoke: Macmillan.

Teubner, G. (1987) 'Juridification – concepts, aspects, limits and solutions', in G. Teubner (ed) *The juridification of social spheres*, Berlin: de Gruyter.

Teubner, G. (1993) *Law as an autopoietic system*, Oxford: Blackwells.

Vincent-Jones, P. (1998) 'Responsive law and governance in public service provision: a future for the local contracting state', *Modern Law Review*, vol 61, pp 362-81.

Vincent-Jones, P. (1999) 'The regulation of contractualisation of quasi-markets for public services', *Public Law*, pp 304-27.

Housing Benefit and personal subsidy

Introduction

Personal subsidies – that is, subsidies tied to people rather than to property – have assumed increased importance in the British housing system over the last two decades. Personal subsidy in the form of Housing Benefit is now the key mechanism for meeting the housing costs of low-income renters. The subsidies available to owners and renters are different and there are groups of housing consumers – low-income households who own their home outright, for example – who are largely excluded from state assistance with the costs of running their home.

While personal subsidies are an important element of the British housing system, the form that the subsidies take has attracted considerable criticism and repeated calls for reform. Early in its administration the New Labour government suggested that substantial reform was being considered, but when it finally outlined its plans it was apparent that proposals were relatively modest, at least in the short term.

The two contributions that follow examine the current state of policy in this area from strikingly different perspectives. Peter Robson focuses on Housing Benefit and seeks to locate debates about the reform of Housing Benefit in the context of development and change in the nature of welfare policies more broadly. In charting the development of assistance to low-income households in Britain it is possible to draw parallels between contemporary debates and the preoccupations of policy in the mid-19th century. Robson argues that, while the current reform agenda may make a modest contribution to improving the system, it is only if the basic system of income redistribution is altered that the housing circumstances of the poor will improve markedly. This suggests that current discussions focus on refining the detail and fail to address the major questions.

Robson develops a distinctively socio-legal dimension to his contribution when he briefly reviews the literature on the way in which administrative practices impact on the way that Housing Benefit operates and the literature on the impact of the adjudication process. He points up some of the contrasts between the administration of Housing Benefit and of other benefits. He makes the important point that if we are unhappy about the way subsidy systems are being implemented then this is only partly related to the formal rules of the system.

If government wishes to improve the system it needs also to consider the 'administrative culture'.

The second contribution, by Kenneth Gibb, encompasses assistance to low-income owner-occupiers alongside Housing Benefit. He takes an explicitly economic approach and reviews the in-principle benefits that economists believe personal subsidies offer. He then relates this discussion to current subsidy systems and their problems. He considers both the desirability of a tenure-neutral and/or unified system of personal subsidy and the alternative systems that have been proposed. Importantly, he briefly reflects on why the New Labour government has backed away from major reforms in this area. There is a range of factors which could be identified as constraining the government's room for manoeuvre.

Gibb has been very much at the centre of the discussion of personal subsidies within the housing finance community. Much of his contribution is concerned with the technicalities of alternative systems and, equally importantly, how housing subsidies interface with other social security systems and with market provision. Such discussions are of fundamental importance and while reading them it is worth bearing in mind Robson's observation that "behind technical terms like 'tapers' and 'earnings disregards' choices about levels of inequality and social division are being made".

SIXTEEN

Housing Benefit

Peter Robson

In calling general attention to the PARISH ROLL for the current year, the HERITORS and KIRK SESSION flatter themselves, that from the great diminution of expenditure, since the publication of last year's Lists, the inhabitants will be disposed to view with approbation, the measures that have been pursued, and are still in progress, to mitigate the pressure of Assessment: and ameliorate the condition of the Poor, by throwing them more on their own resources, and the kind attention of their neighbours and relatives. The Ministers of Religion are loudly called on, to urge the obligations of private and public Benevolence: seeing the effects that have resulted from the salutary exertions of those entrusted with the Parochial Funds. The public may rest satisfied, that the determination of the Heritors and Session, to persevere in their present efforts, shall undergo no relaxation, till the sum, raised by Assessment from Town and Parish, shall be reduced to a mere trifle.

Kilmarnock, 10 January 1829

Background

The Full Report of those charged with supporting the poor by way of 'outdoor relief' goes on to indicate a desire to save money and to root out false claims. There is a concern to address welfare dependency and the culture of living off benefit. Somewhere around 10 per cent of the Poor Law relief budget was spent on direct subsidy of the necessity for the poor of paying house rent[1]. It is seldom unhelpful to examine how an issue facing contemporary society has been dealt with in earlier epochs. Again, although the example provided above is from Scotland it nonetheless sheds light on the chronic issue of how a relatively expensive commodity like housing can come within the reach of those in society with limited financial resources. The level of what is considered poverty may have altered and so have our expectations about what is required for property to be regarded as fit for human habitation. The mismatch, however, between resources and societal expectations persists. The underlying motif behind policy in the early 19th century – a time when the private market economy was relatively unregulated – may provide some kind of clue to what realistic expectations the poor may have today. Then as now the clarion call was for welfare reduction. Then as now the concern was abuse of the system of financial support. Then the response was to set up institutions to incarcerate the poor. Our current response can be seen as some sort of indicator as to whether we have made progress in social policy.

This chapter looks at what changes have taken place in relation to financial support for housing the poor in the intervening 170 years in order to locate the concerns of the April 2000 Green Paper in a broader context. Housing Benefit is payable to some 4.5 million households in Great Britain. Nearly 60 per cent of those who claim it live in council housing, with the figure rising to 75 per cent in Scotland where the proportion of housing built by local authorities has traditionally been higher. The cost for Great Britain of Housing Benefit rose from £2.3 billion in 1978/79 to £11.1 billion in 1998/99. This was part of a deliberate shift away from bricks and mortar subsidy to personal subsidy pursued during the 18 years of Conservative administration. £12 billion was spent in 1978/79 on bricks and mortar housing subsidies which had fallen to £4 billion by 1998/99. In percentage terms the shifts were from 84 per cent bricks and mortar and 16 per cent personal subsidy to 27 per cent bricks and mortar and 73 per cent personal subsidy.

While Housing Benefit is clearly central to the existing subsidy system, it is not seen as unproblematic. The Green Paper identifies a number of interrelated problems which it suggests need to be addressed. Some are administrative and others more clearly involve policy issues. The former include the fact that delivery of Housing Benefit is complex and confusing and that the rules of entitlement are complex. Actual administration of the benefit by local authorities was inefficient with claimants left with the worry of arrears and the risk of eviction due to administrative delay. Policy issues included the suggestion that Housing Benefit deters people of working age from getting jobs and that the existence of the benefit allows landlords to charge high rents for poor quality housing. In addition tenants have little interest in their rent levels because these costs are met by Housing Benefit. Finally, at the intersection between policy and administration is the estimate that fraud and error cost an estimated £840 million per year – money which could be used more equitably on disadvantaged groups in the community. Before looking at the range of remedies that are proposed it should, of course, be stressed that parts of the foregoing analysis are themselves highly contentious.

The response to the problems identified

The Housing Green Paper (DETR/DSS, 2000) suggests in the short term no major structural changes to the system established almost 20 years ago and refined in the interim. A number of areas for relatively minor adjustment are offered. The general tone of the Green Paper makes it clear that no alternative approach to dealing with the issue of poor people's housing costs is envisaged. The purpose of this chapter is to explore why Housing Benefit policy is in a state of stasis with no clear way forward. No significant alternative for enhancing the financing of poor people's housing options appears to enjoy extensive political support. The paradoxical conclusion is that an unpopular and hugely complex system of financial support for which few have a good word to say appears likely to limp on for want of any other option being offered. The alternatives all involve different forms of radical thinking which is alien to the emergent consensus politics of the new millennium. After all this is not the principal area of financial expenditure. Potential savings are comparatively modest. While it has increased in expenditure in the past 10 years from £2.3 billion to £11.1 billion, Housing Benefit still only accounts for 12 per cent of the welfare budget. This compares with such areas as retirement pensions (44 per cent) and child benefit (19 per cent) (*Social Trends*, 1999; McKay and Rowlingson, 1999).

As the Green Paper makes clear, any decisions to reform and re-evaluate the role and nature of Housing Benefit depend on how other elements of housing policy are addressed and the political solutions which find favour. Thus the future extent and nature of Housing Benefit depend on what rent policy government opts for as well as how housing is dealt with as a commodity. It also depends crucially on the future shape of the welfare system and what decisions are taken as to how this might best be financed and how comprehensive it is expected to be. These are, of course questions of political choices. Increasingly welfare and housing policy debates assume a complex labyrinthine discourse dominated by experts. This should not disguise the fact that behind technical terms like 'tapers' and 'earnings disregards' choices about levels of inequality and social division are being made.

Housing Benefit in context

At the start of the 20th century there were limited solutions available for those unable to afford housing in the market place. In addition to the very real threat of virtual incarceration in the workhouse (Mackay, 1904, p 236) there were two market solutions – the working poor could rent short-term and trade down at times of particular economic hardship (Gauldie, 1973). Subsequently there was a temporary suspension of the market in the face of industrial unrest and the encouragement of the public provision of housing to meet local housing need.

At much the same time a related, but quite separate, set of debates took place in relation to income poverty and the solutions for those unable to work through sickness, age, or absence of work. The result was a modest old age pension for the destitute in 1908 and unemployment and sickness insurance in 1911 in a limited range of industries. These initiatives provided the start of an effective modern alternative to the workhouse.

The temporary indirect subsidy through the impact of the Rent Acts involved initially freezing rents and, from 1965, the rather more sophisticated concept of the 'fair rent'. Both these approaches involve fixing rents for properties at below market rent. There is a direct benefit to those with low incomes from this process. Being a property subsidy, it also, of course, benefits those who are well off disproportionately.

Providing housing whose costs were subsidised by local and national taxation was the core of the experiment with municipal housing which expanded considerably after 1919 when local authorities came under a legal duty to consider housing needs in their area and provide housing accordingly (Gilbert, 1970). The shortfall between the costs of providing housing was met in two ways. The level of rents was supplemented by charges on the local tax base and national tax payers. A return to personal subsidy rather than subsidy for buildings occurred at a relatively late stage in 20th-century Britain. It became a feature of a hotch-potch of local authorities' discretionary schemes and was extended to private rented sector and local authority housing on a national scale during the Heath government in the 1972 Housing Finance Act. Interestingly, this first national system of rent allowance used as its rent fixing mechanism the private sector fair rent scheme, introduced by the 1965 Rent Act. The rents, thus, were set by Rent Officers using objective criteria such as the age, character, locality and state of repair. Assistance to tenants was available for those with incomes below a specified level.

Housing Benefit in the context of the modern welfare state

This shift in welfare benefits policy has to be seen in the context of the developments in the Beveridge welfare system. The key aspect of the approach to welfare provision in the post-War era was the concept of universal insurance against common risks. This meant that all workers were covered against a range of financial calamities which might affect their lives. Thus sickness, unemployment, widowhood, old age and children all resulted in payments to all those covered by the compulsory National Insurance system.

What occurred in the ensuing twenty five years was the exposure of the limited coverage of the apparently universal system together with a reappraisal of the meaning of poverty. Beveridge's vision, as a Liberal, was that individuals should be saved from penury but not that the system would stifle initiative. Given the flat rate system of financing adopted for the British welfare system the structural weaknesses of the system were exposed when inflation seriously started to erode the original benefit rates (Kincaid, 1975).

In addition, the insurance system did not address such questions as long-term unemployment, disabled workers and female-headed households. The limitations of the insurance system in failing to cover all risks may seem clear in hindsight but the expectation was that it would be unnecessary for anyone to claim against the means-tested National Assistance benefit which had superseded the Poor Law (Beveridge, 1942)[2].

The result of these limitations on the Beveridge scheme has been that, instead of the mean-tested sector withering away and being replaced solely by insurance based benefits, reliance on means-tested benefits grew appreciably during the 1950s and 1960s. This occurred also for reasons of benign neglect as such benefits as Family Allowance (subsequently Family Credit), introduced to provide financial support for families with children, were uprated in a very limited way (Dean, 1996).

The active espousal of means-tested benefits as a way of targeting financial assistance to the poorest in society started seriously under the Conservative administration of Edward Heath. In 1971 they introduced a benefit – Family Income Supplement – for families receiving low wages. In addition the benefit to assist with the housing costs of those on low wages was introduced in 1972. The pattern of benefits introduced during the next twenty five years shows, however, a use of both financially targeted benefits as well as the emergence of non-insurance benefits aimed at gaps in the insurance scheme. At the same time as Family Income Supplement (FIS) and Rent Allowances came into existence the Mobility Allowance and Attendance Allowance were introduced as neither means–tested nor contributory. In fact they harked back to the singular example of Family Allowance. After the two means–tested experiments in the early 1970s the gaps in the insurance scheme were filled by benefits which are non–contributory, non means–tested and non taxable. This has produced a set of welfare interventions which scarcely merit the name of a system (McKay and Rowlingson, 1999).

It is in this confusing context that we find the future of Housing Benefit being discussed. Partly for financial as well as political reasons support for targeting benefits has been touted as an alternative way of seeking to deliver welfare benefits. The abolition of Child Benefit, the successor to Family Allowance, has been suggested on a number of occasions. While this might be regarded as something of sacred totem, immune from attack, it should be noted that one-parent benefit was abolished during the early days of the Blair administration. The same concerns about paying benefits to rich recipients have been voiced in connection with the first ever welfare intervention, the retirement pension. Its future as a universal insurance benefit is far from assured. The failure to re-link its level to that of wages rather than prices casts doubt on its role in the future, as its value shrinks.

In terms of long-term trends, of course, these choices can be seen in a post-Fordist world as determined by economic globalisation, developing labour market flexibility, more complex patterns of family life and the dissolution of the traditional class structure (Taylor–Gooby, 1997). As far as poor people are concerned in the last quarter of the 20th century there has been a focus on specific social groups within the disadvantaged. Questions of gender, race, sexuality and age have come to the fore (Williams, 1999). Issues like health care and the role of carers have tended to direct attention from the social democratic agenda of redistribution in favour of the 'active welfare subject' (DSS, 1998). In this context consideration of the role of Housing Benefit has become highly specialised and threatened with disjuncture from the wider debate about the politics of welfare (cf Kemp, 2000a).

Debates on Housing Benefit

There has been a continuous flow of case comments on the case law which has developed in relation to Housing Benefit in a range of practitioner journals[3]. These have included the operation of the discretionary elements within the decision-making process as well as the meaning of specific statutory provisions like 'eligible rent' (Partington, 1998). The areas of dispute include how decision makers determine alternative cheaper accommodation and what amounts to unreasonably high rent[4]. Disputes have also encompassed such issues as the distinction between cohabitation and sharing accommodation on a commercial footing[5] and the adequacy of review board decision letters[6]. Again these have been the subject of case comments but have not been subject to study from a policy perspective[7].

Within the specialist policy-centred literature over the past 20 years the issues which have dominated the discussions on financing poor people's housing costs can be divided into two principal area of interest. Within socio-legal literature there have been limited but stimulating contributions on the way administrative practices impact on the operation of Housing Benefit and the impact of the adjudication process. Both these areas are directly addressed in the Green Paper.

Housing Benefit adjudication

Looking to the actual method of adjudication for the resolution of disputes, the internal review approach was examined by Sainsbury and Eardley in their work in the late 1980s. What they came across was poor conduct of hearings, inconsistency in the law's application and inadequate training for members (Sainsbury and Eardley, 1991). At first glance the Housing Benefit Review Board method of challenging discretionary decisions might seem to have little to do with other adjudication models available in the tribunal or court system. This system of internal review has always been favoured by decision makers. It retains the possibility of predictability and does not run the risk of sudden unexpected expense. It promotes predictability in a Weberian technical-rational sense. It was favoured in the 1930s in the early days of the successor to poor law outdoor relief, national assistance (Lynes, 1975) and was resuscitated in 1988 with the introduction of the Social Fund in place of the regulation-bound Single Payments regime (Ogus et al, 1995). Appeals against Benefit Agency decisions to refuse applicants loans to buy long-term necessities were not assigned to Social Security Appeal Tribunals. Instead the full range of non-enforceable rules and applications was put in place with no appeal mechanism (Baldwin et al, 1992).

In fact the use of this kind of internal review was seriously considered in the mid-1990s when the government of the day was addressing the future of the welfare tribunal system. The decision at that time of rationalisation in pursuit of efficient predictability was to remove as much detail from the legislative system as possible. Regulations were altered to remove as many tests involving such notions as 'reasonableness' as possible and to introduce blanket restrictions on such issues as backdated claims. This work has borne fruit in the decision to alter the nature of appeals against Housing Benefit. In addition separate legislation is being introduced which will replace Housing Benefit Review Boards with a new appeals structure using the Appeals Service in line with the rest of the benefit system.

Complementing this work there has also been an issue relating to unaccountable power stemming from the detail of the legal rules governing Housing Benefit. These concerns, made explicitly legal by the framework of the legislation, centre on the availability of housing and whether the accommodation for which support is sought is excessive. Although this was framed as a question of discretion for local authorities it serves to illustrate one of the perennial issues where total subsidy for the costs of a good is involved. In a range of judicial review cases during the 1990s[8] we can see how this crucial policy issue was played out on a legal stage. The limited amount of the litigation in relation to Housing Benefit compared, for instance, with homelessness, as well as its disparate nature, has militated against extensive writing in this area (Partington, 1998). None of the judicial review studies shed light on the effectiveness of judicial review as a remedy in relation to Housing Benefit (Mullen et al, 1996; Bridges et al, 1995; Hadfield and Weaver, 1994). With the replacement of Housing Benefit Review Boards, part at least of this work will pass to the more accessible Appeals Service.

Other socio-legal issues

The location of Housing Benefit administration within the scattered and varied world of local government has produced two specific impacts which any policy review would expect to address. Firstly, the actual process of administering the benefit and reaching the estimated likely beneficiaries has produced a considerable accumulation of both anecdotal as well as formal evidence. The process has, in stark operational terms, been an arcane disaster. Less visible than the poll tax and less emotive than child support, nonetheless, the legislation has been an object lesson in how not to operate a benefit. Concerns were evident after the early version of the system came into effect in 1982 (Hill, 1984; Kemp, 1984) and have been further documented during the intervening period (Hill, 1989; Kemp, 1992). The picture which emerged from these studies is of a complex system malfunctioning and under stress. The Housing Green Paper effectively takes up the series of critiques which have been made in relation to administration and the changes mooted in this area are the most radical, involving as they do the possibility of fining recalcitrant local authorities or having the work carried out privately. It does not, however, take account of the work on bureaucratic culture which suggests that what determines policy implementation is only partly related to formal rules.

Thus, Loveland's work on fraud related matters made clear that in addressing this issue it was misleading to assume that rules were central. Instead the 'administrative culture' needed to be considered (Loveland, 1989). This is an issue which the Green Paper has not directly addressed. The notion of a distinctive working environment developing its own rules is a theme which is echoed in other areas of housing practice. It has been explored in the context of another area of rule-centred discretion, the operation of homelessness legislation (Loveland, 1995; Halliday, 2000).

Finally, the role of the rent officer has been raised in the context of setting maximum rent levels (Partington, 1997). The Green Paper shies away from the question of how best this issue should be addressed and concentrates most of its comments on rent on the public sector. Given the highly political notion of the rent officer concept and its threat to market forces this is perhaps not surprising.

Housing studies

This attention to the detail of the decision making process is complemented by more technical economic concerns within housing studies and how these feed into the broader policy (see Chapter Seventeen in this volume). In the 1980s the concerns which emerged from research into the operation of the newly introduced Housing Benefit system focused on a range of questions including the problem of introducing a nationwide scheme (Kemp, 1984; Walker and Hedges, 1985) and the detail of the unified scheme (Kemp, 1986). These included the impact of this choice of delivery system on claimants (McLaverty and Kemp, 1994) as well as the impact on income distribution (Gibbs and Kemp, 1993). In addition the relationship between notions of benefit retrenchment and Housing Benefits has been explored (Kemp, 2000a). The issues raised in the academic literature stemmed, of course, in many instances from research commissioned by the relevant departments (Sainsbury and Eardley, 1991; Oldman et al, 1996; Sainsbury et al, 1998, Sainsbury, 1999). It is no surprise, therefore, to find many of these concerns reflected in the Green Paper. Housing Benefit, after all, as indicated, flows from broader housing policy goals rather than providing such direction.

The Green Paper

The Green Paper devotes Chapter 11 specifically to the issue of Housing Benefit. This is linked to the chapters on rent policy (Chapter 10) and the section on the private rented sector (Chapter 5). The link with rent policies is of course crucial. The government's continued commitment to a personal subsidy such as Housing Benefit as a core feature of support for low-income citizens where a significant proportion of the poor are located in social housing depends on some kind of guarantee that social sector rents address the issue of affordability. The previous administration seemed to belatedly come to accept this point. Influencing rent levels in the area of social housing involves no change in direction merely one of extent (see Chapter Fourteen of this volume).

As for the private rented sector, here the discussion continues to be dominated by the concern that personal subsidy should guarantee that tenants have an interest in rent levels and value for money. This had its basis in the 1965 fair rent concept which allowed some kind of public-orientated 'value for money' yardstick to be applied to rental housing allowances. In the Green Paper there is a commitment to a healthy private rented sector. The future does not include a return to rent control but includes assured and shorthold assured tenancies which are described as working well. This involves a recognition that the two previous approaches to coping with private renting have been abandoned. Making a profit out of renting is no longer seen as improper[9]. Municipalisation only briefly found favour as Labour policy in the early 1960s. The more recent attachment to housing associations does not seem to go beyond using this as the vehicle for the dismembering of socially owned housing. The possibilities for expanding the social rental sector from this quarter are not mentioned and have to be taken to be outwith consideration.

The notion of managed decline of the private rented sector once discreetly pursued in the 1960s and 1970s has been replaced by a more positive attitude towards this as a form of tenure. So far have things altered that tax measures to make the private rented sector yield bigger profits are regarded as a possibility. The role of financial support to low-income tenants is of crucial importance for the future.

Short-term options

The Green Paper deals with a number of modest matters in relation to Housing Benefit on which there is a clear way forward. It identifies three specific changes:

* improving customer service
* reducing fraud and error
* improving work incentives.

Improving customer service

The proposals for making the system more efficient will be welcomed by all. As far as reduction of complexity is concerned consolidating regulations can only be a good thing. In addition, there can be little complaint at the replacement of the internally staffed Housing Benefit Review Boards by an independent appeals structure, given the general satisfaction with how the system has worked in the past (Baldwin et al, 1992). More recently the revamped Appeals Service has drastically reduced waiting times for most areas of their work. The lay element regarded as crucial in the setting up of these alternatives to remote and inaccessible courts has already been removed from the system. The rationale involved the costs of the unpaid lay members. In addition there were delays resulting from seeking to convene three person Tribunals with both genders present.

Speeding up the administration of benefits will depend on authorities seeking to meet the Best Value standards operating from April 2000. While the Green Paper merely exhorts authorities to better practice it does point out that where the authority fails to provide a satisfactory service legal powers already exist for imposition of a financial penalty or for contracting out the administration of Housing Benefit.

Other areas which involve quicker and more efficient processing of applications are perhaps more contentious. For instance, details of changes of circumstances will be sent electronically rather than by post. The ability for data transfer with on-line access for local authorities to relevant information held by the Benefits Agency on customers' Income Support and Jobseeker's Allowance claims. This may be dismissed as simply part of the encroachment of the information society into people's lives which has generated little political heat.

Tackling fraud and error

Throughout the welfare sector in the past 15 years there has been a shift in how the issue of overpayment has been dealt with. The rules about what amounts to fraud and the use of the full legal panoply have been supplemented by a concern to recover monies paid out in error. In the past claimants in national insurance claims had a defence against recovery of overpayment where they had exercised 'due care and diligence'. This offered the opportunity, for example, for a claimant to argue that in failing to disclose a partner's earnings that they had done what could reasonably be expected of them. This defence was abolished in the 1986 Social Security Act and henceforth recovery is automatically available where there is overpayment. This combined with requiring withdrawal of claims has been used as the principal weapon against fraud.

As a result perhaps of this, then, the Green Paper conjoins the two distinct items of fraud and error. Part of the text involves a description of measures which are already operative like the 1997 Social Security Administration (Fraud) Act and improving the professional standards of fraud investigators. As for the future there is the statement that a programme of inspections by the Benefits Fraud Inspectorate will help to identify weaknesses in local authority procedures. A number of other developments are mentioned, including a scheme to prevent multiple claims by getting authorities to join the Royal Mail 'Do Not Redirect' scheme as well as Department of Social Security help in the prosecution of fraudsters. In order to translate these aspirations into action, financial incentives through a performance-related subsidy regime are discussed. Local authority staff will have on-line access to trace National Insurance numbers and the national fraud hotline will assist authorities – particularly small authorities with limited resources – to deal with fraud. However, like the social security practices, policy is likely to be led by money saving rather than complex prosecution.

A related issue which the section on the private rented sector canvasses is to limit the use of payment direct so that tenants have more of a connection with the process of paying rent and seeking to ensure good standards (McLaverty and Kemp, 1998). The disadvantages for the vulnerable building up arrears are not obviously balanced by the possible psychological impact of withdrawal of such a mechanism. Similarly the notion of adapting Housing Benefit rules to be used to impact indirectly on anti-social behaviour fails to address the issue of where 'unruly' tenants end up living. Given the make up of those who are actually landlords and their limited role in active management this seems a suggestion that has little to recommend it. The anti-social behaviour order regime needs to be given an opportunity to operate before indirect stabs in the dark are given serious consideration.

Errors made by the administering authority would seem to be a completely separate issue and more appropriately located in the section dealing with the improvement of customer service. There seems little point in improving the turn-around times of benefit processing if incorrect decisions are reached. This is a problem which is more apparent than real, however. Nothing specific appears to be actually mentioned in relation to error, other than the hope that a more integrated service will help tackle error. It is worrying that the section provides no guidance as to how the level of error in the system will be addressed given its impact on people's lives. Shelter's housing advisers and housing association staff report cases in which eviction actions are taken against those in arrears where the problem stems from errors as well as delays in the processing of Housing Benefit claims.

Improving work incentives

This depends crucially on a reading of the research into the question of people's housing and work decisions (Ford et al, 1995; Kemp, 2000b). Some measures to improve work incentives are already in place such as the Working Families' Tax Credit. This involved less of a taper and a more generous threshold for low-wage families. Other matters which are not strictly to do with Housing Benefit are also mentioned. Getting people back to work and improving the support for those seeking work are mentioned. For the future, the Green Paper explains that a new agency with a clear focus on work is to be established providing a single, integrated service to benefit claimants of working age. While this will not take over responsibility for Housing Benefit the Green Paper expects it to work with local authorities to provide access to such benefits. The Housing Benefit Extended Payment Scheme was announced as coming into effect in April 2001. It will provide a better transition back into work by ensuring that in-work Housing Benefit claims are fast-tracked so that people moving into low-paid work do not face lengthy periods without Housing Benefit.

The Green Paper also addresses the question of how to increase the income difference between those in work and those out of work. This is merely stated as an obviously desirable state of affairs since it will have a knock on effect by providing work incentives. An earlier solution resulted in the building of workhouses following the Poor Law Report of 1834. The language slides neatly between the highly emotive political concept of 'incentive' into the technical discourse of 'disregards' and 'room rent restriction'. It is perhaps significant that the most recent work on the similarly unpopular and even more complex Child Support legislation casts doubt on the notion that government policy has the simple linear causal effect of the type that informs the policy frameworks of the Green Paper (Barlow and Duncan, 2000).

In an earlier part of the Green Paper it is suggested that Housing Benefit might be made conditional on landlords providing decent standards or payment in such circumstances might be restricted. A version of this operated in the old controlled tenancy regime until 1980. Landlords were denied 'repairs increases' where their houses were unfit for human habitation. It did not enjoy any degree of success as a lever to improve tenants' conditions (Cullingworth, 1963).

There is in the immediate future a prospect of more vigilance over the public purse. One of the great problems of means-tested benefits which seek to target their recipients is the costs of administering them. This comes in assessing eligibility and then distinguishing between genuine claimants and those seeking to disguise their disqualifying financial circumstances. The proposal that eligibility should be for six months would certainly address this situation. The trade-off of possible additional benefit expenditure seems worth embracing both in terms of decreasing technicality as well as saving administrative costs.

Longer-term possibilities

There are also proposals which are described as involving a fundamental reform of Housing Benefit. They are tied to extending some of the concepts discussed in the preceding 'immediate changes' section. These centre on ways to improve work incentives while at the same time giving tenants an interest in the level of their rent. A range of alternatives are canvassed from experiences in other countries. As the Green Paper acknowledges, however, there is a serious danger in attempting to simply transplant single ideas of housing policy where these are wrested from the context of housing, work, benefits and childcare availability. Hence, while there are suggestions that in other countries fixed allowances are provided for tenants to spend as they might wish, this has serious implications in terms of the chances and opportunities in the housing market which are available, particularly to those who are vulnerable. Research evidence is not encouraging (McLaverty and Kemp, 1994). The proposal fails to address questions such as family commitments which militate against individuals having as full a choice of options as they might want. Similarly the availability of only part-time work or short-term contracts affect labour mobility. The precise impact of a radically altered Housing Benefit policy seems to be uncertain (Sainsbury, 1999).

There appears to be little mileage in the notion of requiring tenants to pay a proportion of their rents so that they feel they are actually contributing towards their housing costs. Given the spending power of those on means-tested benefits this would seem to be likely to produce more risks than advantages. As the Green Paper points out, it would realistically involve an increase in the level of benefit. Interestingly, this same notion of raising the level of benefit was not in 1993 specifically factored into the requirement under the 1991 Child Support Act for claimants to pay, initially 5 per cent, but now 10 per cent of their benefit by way of child support.

The provision of some kind of income package unrelated to actual rent offers a significant change in approach and one to which the housing market seems currently ill-suited. That said, the commitment of the government in Chapter 5 of the Green Paper to a healthy private rented sector might bear dividends in the fullness of time. If it does then it could make the radical 'voucher' like proposals more viable as well as politically acceptable. The evidence from the field from Shelter does not suggest that controls over the level of poor housing conditions and the ability of tenants to secure improvements in their surroundings are functioning effectively.

The lack of commitment to any restructuring or direction in Housing Benefit policy can be seen in the absence of radical alternatives to targeted means-tested financial support measures in relation to the financing of poor people's housing costs. A combination of market solutions and targeted personal benefits are seen as the future. The details may differ. The protection may be less effective but the future will be highly recognisable. The era of broadly targeted housing subsidy for social inclusive housing has been definitively consigned to history. The much-favoured strategic interventions to meet specific local market needs – while exciting and dynamic for those involved in provision – seem likely only to be feasible and effective where the safety-net of Housing Benefit is available.

Conclusion

The prospect of a radical reappraisal of this issue has been postponed in the Green Paper. The specific policy changes are likely to be limited. There is a sense of rearranging the deckchairs in the hope that the ship will carry on steaming in reasonably calm waters without anyone noticing that the absence of any effective measures of redistribution means that the changes are unlikely to affect the housing opportunities of the poorest in our society. More effective delivery of services, a more soundly based adjudication process and a more serious concentration on detecting abuse are what is definitely offered. There may be a cautious welcome for improving the service. Some issues, like the role of the rent officer, are discreetly ignored in the absence of any very clear direction from any political source or policy writing. The broader questions like widening rights in relation to community problems like damp housing and the possibility of taking into account the question of fuel poverty do not figure and their future looks uncertain at best. While it might be thought that continued economic progress would render the role of Housing Benefit more marginal this is unlikely to occur while the basic level of income redistribution remains as it is and means-testing remains located at the core of housing welfare policies. The government does not appear to regard addressing this inequality question as a fundamental goal in its policies.

In the 1820s those concerned with supporting the poor were concerned to save money and to root out false claims. The context in which they formulated detailed policy was as part of an attack on welfare dependency and the culture of state dependency. The concerns of the April 2000 Green Paper are broadly similar and seem to suggest that the period of bold alternatives to the modified market is, for the time being at least, in suspension. In the meantime postponement of a more unfettered market solution can be taken as being a positive, if less than inspiring, response. At least a 21st century version of the workhouse is absent from the equation.

Notes

[1] £93 in house rent out of total expenditure of £1,326 16s 91/2d [down from £1,542 2s 11d previous year and £1,129 11s in rents] but by 1841 up to £145 13s 6d out of £2,198 0s 11/4d . Although the example I have chosen is based in Scotland the systems for financial support of the poor in England and Wales then and now are very similar.

[2] In fairness the problems of disabled workers were covered in the 1944 Disabled Persons (Employment) Act and women were expected to return to their primary role as unwaged homeworkers.

[3] *Journal of Social Security Law; Welfare Right Bulletin; Housing Law Monitor; Local Government and Law; Adviser; Journal of Housing Law; SCOLAG.*

[4] *R v Sefton HBRB ex p Brennan (1997) 29 HLR 735.*

[5] *R v Poole BC ex p Ross (1996) 28 HLR 351.*

[6] *R v Sutton LBC ex p Partridge (1996) 28 HLR 315*; see also Partington (1998, p 194).

[7] Partington also comments on the interesting absence of litigation on the conflict between the rules of the Housing Benefit scheme and the subsidy rules (Partington, 1998, p 194) which does not seem to have been the subject of detailed empirical enquiry.

[8] *R v City of Westminster Housing Benefit Review Board ex p Mehanne* (1999) 2 *All ER 317* and *R v Sefton Housing Benefit Review Board ex p Brennan (1997) 29 HLR 735.*

[9] "The plain fact is that rented housing is not a proper field for private profit", Harold Wilson in a speech to Leeds Labour party, 9 February 1964.

References

Baldwin, J., Wikeley, N. and Young, R. (1992) *Judging social security*, Oxford: Clarendon Press.

Barlow, A, and Duncan, S. (2000) 'Supporting families? New labour's communitarianism and the "rationality mistake"', *Journal of Social Welfare and Family Law*, vol 22, no 1, pp 23-42.

Beveridge, W. (1942) *Report of Social Insurance and Allied Services*, Cm 4606, London: HMSO.

Bridges, L., Meszaros, G. and Sunkin, M. (1995) *Judicial review in perspective*, London: Cavendish.

Cullingworth, J.B. (1963) *Housing in transition*, London: Heinemann.

Dean, H. (1996) *Social security and poverty*, Luton: Harvester Wheatsheaf.

DETR (Department of the Environment, Transport and the Regions)/ DSS (Department of Social Security) (2000) *Quality and choice: A decent home for all*, Housing Green Paper, London: DETR/DSS.

DSS (1998) *New ambitions for our country: A new contract for welfare*, London: The Stationery Office.

Ford, J., Kempson, E. and England, J. (1995) *Into work? The impact of housing costs and benefits system on people's decisions to work*, York: Joseph Rowntree Foundation.

Gauldie, E. (1973) *Cruel habitations*, London: RKP.

Gibbs, I. and Kemp, P. (1993) 'Tenure differences in income and Housing Benefit in later life', *Social Policy and Administration*, vol 27, pp 341-53.

Gilbert, B.B. (1970) *British social policy 1914-1939*, London: Batsford.

Hadfield, B. and Weaver, E. (1994) 'Trends in judicial review in Northern Ireland', *Public Law*, pp 12-16.

Halliday, S. (2000) 'The influence of judicial review on bureaucratic decision-making', *Public Law*, pp 110-22.

Hill, M. (1984) 'The implementation of Housing Benefit', *Journal of Social Policy*, vol 13, pp 297-320.

Hill, M. (1989) 'Income maintenance and local government: implementing central control?', *Critical Social Policy*, vol 8, pp 18-36.

Kemp, P. (1984) *The cost of chaos: A survey of the Housing Benefit scheme*, London: SHAC.

Kemp, P. (1986) *The future of Housing Benefits*, Glasgow: Centre for Housing Research.

Kemp, P. (1992) *Housing Benefit: An appraisal*, SSAC Research Paper, London: HMSO.

Kemp, P. (2000a) 'Housing Benefit and welfare retrenchment in Britain', *Journal of Social Policy*, vol 29, pp 263-79.

Kemp, P. (2000b) *'Shopping incentives' and Housing Benefit reform*, Coventry: Rowntree/Chartered Institute of Housing.

Kincaid, J. (1975) *Poverty and equality in Britain*, Harmondsworth: Penguin.

Loveland, I. (1989) 'Policing welfare benefits: local authority responses to claimant fraud in the Housing Benefit Scheme', *Journal of Law and Society*, vol 16, pp 187-209.

Loveland, I. (1995) *Housing homeless persons – Administrative law and processes*, Oxford: Clarendon Press.

Lynes, T. (1975) 'The development of tribunals', in M. Adler and S. Asquith (eds) *Discretion and welfare*, London: Heinemann.

MacKay, T. (1904) *A history of the English Poor Law Vol III*, London: King.

McKay, S. and Rowlingson, K. (1999) *Social security in Britain*, London: Macmillan.

McLaverty, P. and Kemp, P. (1994) *Housing Benefit, social exclusion and claimant strategies*, London: International Sociological Association.

McLaverty, P. and Kemp, P. (1998) 'Housing Benefit and tenant coping strategies in the private rental housing market', *Environment and Planning A*, vol 30, no 2, pp 355-66.

Mullen, T., Pick, K. and Prosser, T. (1996) *Judicial review in Scotland*, London: Wiley.

Ogus, A., Barnedt, E. and Wikeley, N. (1995) *Law of social security*, London: Butterworths.

Oldman, C., Quilgars, D. and Oldfield, N. (1996) *Housing Benefit and service charges: An examination of eligible housing costs*, London: HMSO.

Partington, M. (1997) 'The re-introduction of rent control?', *Journal of Housing Law*, vol 1, no 1, pp 6-8.

Partington, M. (1998) 'Judicial review and Housing Benefit', in T. Buck (ed) *Judicial review and social welfare*, London: Pinter.

Sainsbury, R. (1999) *Combating Housing Benefit fraud: Local authorities' discretionary powers*, London: The Stationery Office.

Sainsbury, R. and Eardley, T. (1991) *Housing Benefit review: An evaluation of the effectiveness of the review system in responding to claimants dissatisfied with Housing Benefit*, London: HMSO.

Sainsbury, R., Corden, A. and Carlisle, J. (1998) *Verifying Housing Benefit and council tax benefit*, London: DSS.

Social Trends (1999) no 29, London: The Stationery Office.

Taylor-Gooby, P. (1997) 'In defence of second-best theory: state, class and capital in social policy', *Journal of Social Policy*, vol 26, no 2, pp 171-92.

Walker, R. and Hedges, A. (1985) *Housing Benefit: The experience of implementation*, London: Housing Centre Trust.

Williams, F. (1999) 'Good-enough principles for welfare', *Journal of Social Policy*, vol 28, no 4, pp 667-87.

SEVENTEEN

Helping with housing costs? Unravelling the political economy of personal subsidy

Kenneth Gibb

Introduction

One of the most distinctive features of housing policy in the 1980s and 1990s has been the increasing importance of personal subsidies to low-income households. Not only has public expenditure on Housing Benefit and Income Support for Mortgage Interest payments (ISMI) risen dramatically in real terms and as a share of the wider housing budget, effectively substituting for dwelling-tied capital and revenue subsidy, but personal subsidies have also become an integral part of the way the housing system *works* for poor households. This is all the more remarkable as critics of the way Housing Benefit and ISMI work have now coalesced against the present system. This is quite apparent in the Green Paper (DETR/DSS, 2000). But there is also a reluctance to consider fundamental change. In this chapter, we examine why the UK is in this position and what might happen to move personal subsidies to a more acceptable, rational and fair position.

We start by briefly outlining some key principles of personal subsidies applied to the housing system. This acts as a framework with which to review the basis of Housing Benefit and ISMI in the UK and their wider role in the housing system. We provide a brief summary of the recent reform debate and then turn to the proposals and debates raised in the Green Paper's proposals. The chapter concludes by reflecting on the current stage of policy development.

The principles of personal subsidies

Much orthodox economic theory and the policy presumptions that accompany it are contested within the social sciences (and within parts of the economics profession). Topics on which views differ include the implications of assumptions about rationality, information requirements, market-clearing and the role of institutions. However, the traditional realm of welfare economics applied to the impacts of taxes and subsidies remains a powerful and widely recognised prescriptive taxonomy for assessing social policy. A number of these 'lessons', applied to personal housing subsidies at a fairly abstract level of generality, are reviewed below. As we will see, these ideas remain highly relevant to the contemporary reform debate.

Traditional microeconomic analysis has been used to 'demonstrate' that cash transfers (ie cash benefits or vouchers) are superior to specific price reductions (ie dwelling-tied subsidies). This alleged superiority is based on several key points. First, it presumes consumer sovereignty is superior to merit good arguments. In other words, it is better that an individual should choose how they use the resources redistributed to them than that society, as donor of those resources, should seek to guarantee minimum levels of specified consumption (housing, education, health, and so on).

Second, under standard assumptions, it can be demonstrated that it costs society less to achieve a given level of individual welfare (for the subsidy recipient) by means of cash transfer than by price subsidy. Thus, it is 'cheaper' to use cash transfers and it maximises individual freedom. Third, cash transfers, unlike price subsidies, do not change relative prices. In other words, cash transfers are argued to be less distortionary because they do not lead to shifts in consumption patterns. In contrast specific commodity subsidies reduce the prices of certain goods or services and therefore distort people's choices. This argument – that cash transfers are inherently more efficient – ignores the impact that increasing households' incomes through cash transfers has on the composition of consumer demand.

Despite the highly specific nature of the assumptions on which they are based, these conclusions have been highly influential in shaping the direction of personal subsidies in the UK. In particular, they are implicit in the case often made for the shift from bricks and mortar to personal housing subsidies, despite the fact that existing subsidy systems are far removed from the abstract subsidies of economic theory.

The other main ways in which economics has influenced these debates in the UK has concerned the twin issues of the labour-leisure choice and marginal effective tax rates, on the one hand, and, on the other, the distortions associated with personal subsidies that insulate recipients from changes in relative prices. These distortions range from creating incentives for landlords to increase rents for benefit recipients to broader problems of collusive and non-collusive fraud. From a resource allocation perspective, insulating recipients from the relative price of housing consumption can distort choices and could lead to a mismatch of households to properties because subsidy insulation restricts mobility creating log-jams and bottlenecks elsewhere in the system.

The labour-leisure choice problem arises from the fact that punitive rates of benefit withdrawal are required to keep the total benefit bill under control. Combined with other means-tested benefits and the entry into the tax and national insurance system, the overall outcome is to produce exceptionally high marginal tax rates which are believed to impact on incentives to participate in the labour market. A different variant of the problem concerns on-off subsidies that are tied up with eligibility to basic social security. Traditionally, in the UK, help with mortgage interest payments has been tied to eligibility for Income Support. Earn marginally above the threshold and one loses all of the help with mortgage payments. This creates strong incentives not to take lower paid jobs and can extend the duration of unemployment.

The progressivity of personal subsidies is governed by their specific means test but questions of access are equally important. Benefit may be differentiated according to age, employment status, family composition, housing tenure and other dimensions of horizontal equity. The American literature on the impact of the housing allowance experiment (see Gibb, 1995) identified the higher housing costs faced by all as a result of supply inelasticity. That is, if demand is increased as a result of introducing a housing allowance, supply shortages can mean that rather than seeing more housing available and consumed it simply pushes up housing costs.

Applying the principles to Housing Benefit

These abstract principles are important for two main reasons. First, they continue to exert a significant influence on the shape of policy objectives and critical discussion of personal subsidies. Second, there are important gaps between the in-principle debate and the actual practice of Housing Benefit and ISMI, which reinforce and complicate the distortions experienced by households.

Housing Benefit

Housing Benefit is an ex post subsidy to low-income tenants closely related to the income support system and based on actual housing costs. Households are assumed to have a level of general spending need (the applicable amount) which depends on household composition, age and special circumstances. If a household's measured net income is equal or less than this amount then they will qualify for Income Support and Housing Benefit will pay all of their eligible rent. For every pound that income exceeds the applicable amount, Housing Benefit is reduced by 65 pence in the pound (the taper). The taper is the main source of the labour disincentive effect associated with the income-related withdrawal of Housing Benefit. However, it should be remembered that one characteristic of the households that increasingly make up the social rented sector is that they are disproportionately cut-off from the labour market: the sector is increasingly composed of older households, the long-term unemployed, people with health problems and single-parent families.

The system is, however, much more complicated than this thumbnail outline would suggest. Significant variations are possible across the three key variables of the applicable amount, measured income and eligible housing costs. This is the result of a range of policy prescriptions that have sought to vary assistance by tenure, by age group and even to reduce the impact of the fact that marginal rent increases are fully met by Housing Benefit.

This system has developed its current structure because of its link to the Income Support system. The basic premise of Income Support is that net income (after housing costs) should not fall below a tolerable minimum. Recipients of benefit, therefore, must have their housing costs insulated. Apart from this feature, the UK is also unique in covering 100 per cent of housing costs for those on the very lowest incomes. Recipients of Housing Benefit are insulated from changes in rent, particularly in the social sector because, unlike in the private rented sector, policies to put ceilings on the rent eligible for Housing Benefit have not had an impact.

The alternative ex ante approach to assisting with housing costs would provide tenants with a fixed cash sum or a voucher which could be used as a contribution towards housing costs. This type of system implies that when rents increase low-income households pay the increase from their own pockets. Outwith the UK, this is the typical way to provide allowances. Arguably, the legacy of 'the rent problem' in the UK – that is, of significant rent differentials, a relatively modest social security payment paid to millions of households, and unaffordable housing – have combined to make it difficult in the UK to break away from an ex post approach to providing personal subsidies.

The ex post system has a number of unwelcome consequences. Perhaps the most important is the impact that it has on the behaviour of landlords and tenants. Most obviously, it can be a stimulus to fraud. Unscrupulous private landlords can charge rents at no cost to the tenant. This is one of the arguments for setting ceilings on rents in the private rented sector (although this is tantamount to reintroducing rent controls). This type of moral hazard problem has also been examined from the point of view of the tenant who can engage in up-marketing to larger, better properties: again, at no cost. Once more, the Housing Benefit system has tried to regulate this process away. While there is mixed evidence about both the extent of Housing Benefit-related fraud and about up-marketing, a much deeper concern is the interaction of an ex post system with the flat, undifferentiated rent structures found in many parts of the social sector. In such a system rents do not vary sufficiently according to quality. At the same time it is relatively costless to consume more housing than one's circumstances would dictate in the market.

The Housing Benefit system, because of its ex post status, plays an important role providing comfort for private lenders. The massive transfer of funds generated by large-scale voluntary transfers (LSVTs) and by the traditional post-1989 investment in mixed funding housing association developments has been premised on the belief that rents (ie lender cash-flow) would be underpinned by Housing Benefit. The possible future shift of Housing Benefit to a more ex ante system raises the spectre of rent arrears and an interruption to cash flow. However, in an era of low demand for social housing and competition for tenant market share, lenders are now seeking to contain and even contemplate putting downward pressure on rents.

Income Support for Mortgage Interest

There is no tenure-neutral treatment of housing costs for low-income households. We have seen that renting households are treated in different ways according to tenure. At the same time, there is no general assistance to low-income owner-occupiers. Outright owners on low incomes receive no comprehensive social security-based help with their running costs or for repairs (there will be discretionary cash-limited repair grants and Care and Repair help but this is limited and patchy geographically).

Owners with mortgages and low income (but above the Income Support threshold) receive no help with their mortgages. ISMI provides support only to long-term Income Support recipients who have mortgages. It was radically cut back in 1995 by means of postponing support for an extended period, such that, it was hoped, a private market in mortgage protection insurance would spring up.

ISMI works by providing a payment based on an average interest rate applied to a principal set at an eligibility ceiling of £100,000. However, this assistance only becomes available after nine months for most mortgages and for the next four months is only at a rate of 50 per cent of the total eligible amount. Recipients, in general, have to wait 13 months on a continuous claim before they receive the full amount. In the absence of comprehensive state support, mortgage payment insurance can be purchased privately, with the premium related to the size of monthly mortgage payments. This, however, is far from comprehensive, both because of exclusion categories (eg non-standard employment) and because of low enthusiasm from a sceptical public. Ford (2000) calculates that only 17 per cent of eligible mortgagor households have taken up mortgage protection insurance. The implication is that in a cyclical downturn, there may be serious mortgage default consequences with longer-term implications for the housing system (and Housing Benefit).

The other main structural issue associated with ISMI concerns the unemployment trap arising from the withdrawal of aid to households immediately above their relevant Income Support threshold. Because of the marketised nature of home ownership in the UK, it is recognised that there would be a major upmarketing problem were ISMI to be extended to low-income mortgagors. Nonetheless, this does mean that owner-occupiers and renters are treated inconsistently at a number of levels.

Housing Benefit, ISMI and the Exchequer

Table 16.1 and Table 16.2 summarise the expenditure and caseload trends associated with Housing Benefit and ISMI in the UK since the second half of the 1980s. Table 16.1 is in cash terms, and, for England and Wales, is in gross terms (that is, before the deduction of rental surpluses from the Housing Revenue Accounts [HRAs] for rent rebates which substantially reduces the cost to the Exchequer). It indicates that rent rebates to local authority tenants and particularly rent allowances to housing association and private tenants have grown rapidly with rebates to local authority tenants more than doubling but rent allowances increasing more than

Table 17.1: Housing Benefit and ISMI Expenditure (£m) (1986-87 to 1999-2000)

	Rent rebates	Rent allowances	ISMI	Total HB	Total social security	All HB as % of all social security
1986-87	2,419	996	351	3,766	44,913	8.3
1987-88	2,506	1,030	335	3,871	46,697	8.2
1988-89	2,718	1,055	286	4,059	47,333	8.5
1989-90	2,940	1,359	353	4,652	50,174	9.2
1990-91	3,368	1,779	539	5,686	56,509	10.0
1991-92	4,068	2,426	925	7,419	66,395	11.1
1992-93	4,593	3,284	1,141	9,018	75,313	11.9
1993-94	5,019	4,195	1,210	10,424	82,422	12.6
1994-95	5,229	4,883	1,040	11,152	84,846	13.1
1995-96	5,431	5,455	1,016	11,902	88,694	13.4
1996-97	5,569	5,810	867	12,246	92,201	13.2
1997-98	5,504	5,708	660	11,872	93,408	12.7
1998-99	5,394	5,825	648	11,867	95,847	12.3
1999-2000	5,589	6,582	600	12,771	101,243	12.6

Note: HB = Housing Benefit
Source: Derived from Wilcox (1999, table 107)

sixfold in the same period. ISMI grew four-fold by the early 1990s but has since fallen back to half of its peak levels.

Adding the different benefit items indicates that total help with housing costs for low-income households rose from £3.7 billion in 1986-87 to more than £12.7 billion planned for 1999-2000. As a percentage of a growing social security budget, these housing-related benefits grew from 8.3 per cent to 12.6 per cent – although the proportion was even higher in the mid-1990s. Of course, the table does not show the growth in *coerced* private expenditures on mortgage protection insurance in response to the changes to ISMI.

Table 16.2 indicates that over the period there has been a large reduction (more than 25 per cent) in the rebate caseload alongside a significant increase in rent allowance cases (more than 60 per cent). ISMI caseloads have moved counter-cyclically, beginning in 1990 with 310,000 cases and with 334,000 in 1998 (although it was considerably higher at half a million in the mid-1990s). Further disaggregation of the rent allowance

Table 17.2: Housing Benefit and ISMI Claimants (1986-87 to 1998-1999) (000s) (Great Britain)

Year	Rent rebates	Rent allowances	ISMI	
1986-87	3,720	1,180		
1987-88	3,665	1,195		
1988-89	3,132	965		
1989-90	2,923	1,035	1990	310
1990-91	2,944	1,044	1991	411
1991-92	2,981	1,219	1992	499
1992-93	3,023	1,315	1993	556
1993-94	3,060	1,519	1994	529
1994-95	3,007	1,660	1995	499
1995-96	2,953	1,798	1996	451
1996-97	2,887	1,875	1997	379
1997-98	2,762	1,829	1998	334
1998-99	2,664	1,811		

Source: Derived from Wilcox (1999, tables 105 and 106)

cases reveals that the numbers of housing association tenants receiving Housing Benefit more than doubled between 1992 and 1998 to 842,000 but that the number of private tenants rose and then fell, with 968,000 cases in 1998 (Wilcox, 1999, table 109a). Clearly, it has been increasing rents rather than caseloads that explain the trends in Housing Benefit in Table 16.1, although the increasing dependency of social tenants on Housing Benefit may also be having a compositional effect with higher rent properties more likely to be receiving Housing Benefit than in the mid-1980s. ISMI, on the other hand, is sensitive to interest rates levels and unemployment (as well as policy change) and has since fallen back significantly.

The reform agenda

In a recent paper, Hills (2000) looks at the social housing finance system as a whole and focuses closely on the Housing Benefit system. After identifying the sort of structural and bureaucratic problems acknowledged in the Housing Green Paper (see below), he focuses on ways to introduce an ex ante element into the system by designing a system which combines a fixed (ex ante) national element and an ex post component based on the actual rent.

This would be part of wider reforms to rents, landlord finances and subsidy, and local management of housing. As an example, Hills suggests a system wherein the flat rate amount might be set nationally in cash (and thus Income Support levels could be topped up by an equivalent amount) and the percentage contribution of local rents (that is, the amount of local rents covered by Housing Benefit – which would be less than 100%) could be adjusted according to local average rents. He gives an example of £10 per week as the national fixed element plus 80 per cent of the actual rent if it was £50 but a higher percentage, 90 per cent, if the relevant average local rent was, for example, £100. Thus, with phased reductions in these percentages, lower cost areas would move fairly quickly to a more choice-based system and higher cost areas would have deeper protection to meet affordability problems. He argues that the flat rate element should be given to all tenures (that is, including all eligible low-income owner-occupiers) and be part of the general system of benefits and tax credits.

In another recent paper Kemp (2000) reviews the failure of the new Labour government to meet its objectives of either cutting Housing Benefit and ISMI back significantly or implementing wholesale structural reform. This chimes with the incrementalist position adopted in the Green Paper, inching towards longer-term structural change (Kemp, 2000, p 271). Kemp argues that the reasons for this shift in priorities compared with the original orientation of the 1998 Comprehensive Spending Review can be attributed, not specifically to lobbies opposed to change, but to *path dependency*, wherein the political costs of reform were too great relative to the immediate benefits (p 272). Kemp identifies four reasons for this difficulty:

- *Housing Benefit and housing policy*. Both private funding for social housing stock transfers and the mixed-funding programme are underwritten by Housing Benefit. It is difficult to see how radical cuts in the system can be achieved without threatening rent arrears and other interruptions to cash flow.
- *Housing Benefit and social security*. It is difficult to move to a regionally-varied flat rate system of Housing Benefit (which would address many of the problems identified above, including fraud, the shopping incentive, and allocative issues, among others) because of the 'rent' problem – the wide variation in housing costs. This is one reason for Hills' hybrid solution. However, this has to be linked to rent structure reform and

arguably because rents are so varied across the country (and within districts), they have to be reformed prior to the Housing Benefit reform. Otherwise, there will be arbitrary winners and losers or there will have to be a punitive (to the Exchequer) increase in standard social security additions (to cover the Housing Benefit flat rate element). Transitional protection will be required.

- *Housing Benefit and work incentives.* Traditional measures to increase work incentives, by reducing the taper or extending earnings disregards, would cost the Exchequer more and push eligibility further up the income scale. However, the introduction of the Working Families' Tax Credit means that higher spending to encourage low-income working can be classified (officially) as tax foregone rather than as public spending (p 275).
- *Housing Benefit and 'responsibility'.* Policies such as Rent Direct – which allow rents to be paid directly to landlords – reduce arrears and landlord costs but are at the same time viewed as creating a context in which recipients view housing as a free good. In other words, the social security system creates rights without responsibilities. However, again, this is a situation where inertia prevents progress to the government's objectives.

These path dependency problems should be borne in mind in any discussion of the structural reform of Housing Benefit. Most importantly from a housing perspective, rent reform and some way of underpinning private funding must be achieved if a reformed Housing Benefit is going to work within the housing system, let alone if the impact on low-income households is going to be politically acceptable. As Kemp concludes, "in some cases path dependency and lock-in effects can mean that restructuring requires budgetary expansion rather than retrenchment and this may prove to be the case with Housing Benefit in Britain" (2000, p 278).

The Green Paper proposals for Housing Benefit and ISMI

In the light of the preceding discussion, we now turn to a critical analysis of the Green Paper proposals for personal subsidy, focusing on more structural questions throughout. Housing Benefit is not a formal part of the Department of the Environment, Transport and the Region's remit but is described in the Green Paper's Foreword as 'our common concern' (with the Department of Social Security). This in itself is recognition of a long-standing concern about the artificial nature of departmental boundaries and the integrative nature of housing. There is also a long-standing concern (continued in the Green Paper) about the excessive cost to the public purse implied by the Housing Benefit and ISMI systems of support. Repeatedly, efforts to change Housing Benefit in order to improve the working of the housing system or to address specific inequalities have been either constrained or prevented by the public expenditure consequences.

Chapter 1 of the Green Paper suggests that "Housing Benefit, while helping people to meet their housing costs, is complex and administered inconsistently, costing the public around £840 million per year in fraud and error and creating disincentives to work for many tenants" (p 8). At the same time, the government argues that it is presently tackling the housing problems it inherited. In particular, it is "working with lenders and insurers to ensure that more flexible mortgages and related products are available, providing stronger protection for homebuyers" (p 9) – which, in part, is about seeking to produce more acceptable mortgage protection insurance. The Green Paper also argues that proposals to improve the transition into work for Housing Benefit recipients, the adopting of measures to tackle fraud and to improve administration of Housing Benefit are all having a positive impact. Specific issues relating to Housing Benefit, ISMI and mortgage protection insurance are examined in Chapters 1, 2, 4, 5, 10 and 11. The main points are summarised and discussed below.

In Chapter 1, a distinction is made between a short run and longer run approach to Housing Benefit – tackling administration and delivery in the short run and moving towards more fundamental change in the longer run (p 17). Importantly, the Green Paper argues that "we do not envisage major structural change to Housing Benefit in the short term, not least because major changes could not be made in isolation from reforms to move towards a more coherent pattern of rents in social housing". One could go further and seek to link these changes to the discussion of choice-based allocations in the social sector and the phasing-in of reforms to rent structures. It is also indicative that the document calls for a full debate on the options for reform, after the Comprehensive Spending Review failed to come up with such fundamental reform despite extensive internal debate across key government departments in 1997-98.

Low-income owners

The Department of the Environment, Transport and the Regions express concern about 'sustainable' home ownership (DETR/DSS, 2000, ch 4). A favourable macroeconomic climate, help with mortgage interest payments through ISMI and working with lenders and insurers to produce more comprehensive insurance policies are planks of this policy (p 30). The government acknowledge that there have been "concerns about the quality and value of MPPI offered ... in the past" (p 31) and working with the industry there is a target of 55 per cent take-up by 2004. Given that, as noted above, recent estimates put the take-up figure at 17 per cent (Ford, 2000), there will have to be a major change in attitudes to mortgage protection insurance among consumers. The Green Paper also states that the promotion of flexible mortgage products such as lifestyle mortgages are an important part of the process of making income uncertainties compatible with mortgage commitments. Again, these products have emerged in generally benign market conditions – their durability needs to be tested across the entire housing market and economic cycle.

A number of specific proposals and suggestions are advanced in the Green Paper with reference to ISMI. The design of ISMI – in particular, the nine-month waiting period and the interest only nature of support – is defended because of alleged positive work incentive effects and its role in encouraging the take-up of private insurance (which is questionable). It is recognised, however, that the reformed design of ISMI may be a source of accumulated mortgage arrears. It is also acknowledged that there is a disincentive associated with the withdrawal of ISMI: as soon as someone takes up a job and then loses it again, they have to go through another nine-month waiting period. Consequently, from April 2001, improvements will be made to the ISMI system which will mean that people losing a job within a year of ending their ISMI will not have to wait another nine months and, as with Housing Benefit, recipients who take up a job will receive four extra weeks of ISMI as transitional financial help in work.

There is limited discussion of longer-term reforms to ISMI (p 39). The aim would be to improve integration with mortgage protection insurance, covering risks and "reducing the burden on the state, and rewarding responsible behaviour". The options outlined include:

- extending the waiting period for ISMI to 14 months on the basis that "home owners could depend on two month lender forbearance" and 12 months of insurance protection and then move on to benefit;
- offering benefit help earlier (after two months) for owners with protection insurance but facing an uninsurable event;
- allowing Mortgage Payment Protection Insurance (MPPI) payments to be given a more generous treatment in assessing benefit help entitlement.

Reliance on lender forbearance for two months would appear to shift the risk on to lenders, although this should be straightforward where the lender is also the insurer (or has a clear relationship with the insurer). Such a solution would by definition generate arrears, which is a strange way to tackle the gap between insurance and ISMI periods of support. It would seem unlikely that the lenders would countenance such a move. The second option, providing benefit to owners with insurance who experience uninsurable risks appears neat in theory but how does the state satisfactorily define the entire set of uninsurable risks in such a way that is comprehensive and efficient? The government requires a large increase in MPPI take-up in order to protect the housing market against recession; yet it seems to have no way to encourage that take-up growth without extending and linking ISMI to take-up. This raises the obvious question about whether the priority of boosting the insurance element is really worthwhile if it needs to be underpinned by a more generous benefit system?

Private renting

The Green Paper discussion of the private rented sector (Chapter 5) raises some pertinent issues for Housing Benefit. First, there is discussion of the Rent Officer Service who determine reasonable market rents, which in turn determine Housing Benefit payments. It is recognised (p 50) that in areas of low demand where tenants are indifferent to the gross rent (because of the way Housing Benefit is structured) it is fundamentally difficult to determine a market rent. The government appears to be pinning (a little desperately) hopes of improvement on centralised management and quality control of the new Rent Service executive agency. Second, there is an exploration of making Housing Benefit conditional on decent standards of housing and management. One way of doing this would be to restrict Housing Benefit in respect of poor housing but only where there is ample alternative supply (that is, low demand areas) – official designation of such areas may, however, be problematic for the wider housing market, for example, lenders. Even if that were surmountable, the Green Paper acknowledges that this does nothing for bad quality provision in areas of high demand.

Another approach to the problem could be direct payments to the landlord rather than the tenant, but make them contingent on the landlord meeting standards of provision and management. The Green Paper argues that there will also be cases where the claimant might be an accomplice to the landlord. Here, benefit rules could be changed to create 'incentive compatible' behaviour on the part of both parties. For instance, local authorities could reduce Housing Benefit payments as part of an anti-social behaviour order. At the same time, direct payments could be withheld from non-cooperative landlords.

The Housing Benefit chapter

Chapter 11 of the Green paper is a substantial 80-paragraph chapter. Paragraph 11.4 (p 105) sets out what the government sees as the 'well-known' problems associated with Housing Benefit:

- delivery of Housing Benefit is complex, confusing and time-consuming;
- the benefit rules are complex;
- local authority benefit administration performance is inconsistent;
- administrative complexity has real effects on arrears and eviction threats;
- Housing Benefit fraud and error costs £840 million per annum;
- for those of working age, Housing Benefit can act as a barrier that deters people getting into work;
- Housing Benefit can be exploited by unscrupulous landlords, who charge high rents for poor quality provision;
- Housing Benefit takes away responsibility from claimants in that tenants have little interest in rents provided they are below local limits.

The government states that it seeks to improve customer service, reduce fraud and error, improve work incentives and explore other options to support housing policy (that is, that Housing Benefit should be complementary with housing policies). This involves the discussion of more fundamental reform. Here, we focus on the incremental proposals for work incentives and the longer-term debate.

The Green Paper argues that administrative improvements proposed and implemented will by definition help with work incentives (by reducing delays and uncertainties). Furthermore, there have been complementary tax and benefit changes through, for example, the Working Families'Tax Credit, which has reduced the marginal tax rates of those households formerly on Family Credit. The Green Paper emphasises the importance of the transition from unemployment to work and seeks to make a number of administrative improvements such as making it easier to get transitional payments. The government has used targeted changes to earnings disregards for carers, people with disabilities and disregards for maintenance received by lone parents. The Green Paper identifies the difficulties with reducing the basic taper but also acknowledge widespread criticism of the effect of the Single Room Rent on young people's housing choices (by restricting Housing Benefit to under-25s). One option that is discussed is the broadening of the Single Room Rent so that a range of shared accommodation rents are charged.

The Green Paper rightly points out that commentators looking at the longer-term of fundamental reform have tended to focus on work incentives and giving recipients an interest in the size of their rents (p 115). It is recognised that social sector rents will have to be restructured to be fairer and more consistent and that allocations policies would have to reflect more choice. The government argues that "there would be little point in making ... fundamental policy changes to Housing Benefit before rent restructuring". There is also the issue of the interface between devolved housing policies and a UK Housing Benefit system. In the same vein, the discussion then summarises international experience. The conclusion is that each country's system is specific to housing market context and welfare regime but that there are fundamentally two types of system (p 116):

- a flat rate contribution to an individual's housing costs;
- meets actual costs according to a wide range of socio-economic, personal and financial variables;
- a combination of the above which may involve a flat-rate element and a top-up element.

The Green Paper then examines a flat-rate option where recipients would receive a fixed sum of money, giving them more opportunity to make their housing choices. This might be varied by household type and by region. If the allowance were set at some regional average, tenants would have to pay the extra to rent above average cost rented accommodation.

The attributed advantages include simplicity and positive incentive effects. However, it is pointed out that there are risks with breaking the link between actual rents and the support provided by Housing Benefit:

- housing has high transactions costs – there are constraints that make mobility complicated relative to the continuous differentiability and instantaneous decision making of economic theory;
- it is not always possible for people to move – because of ties to an area households cannot move and thereby effectively reduce their housing costs;
- over-economising on housing may lead to little spending on other areas, jeopardising health, education, etc.

Consequently, the government does not favour a flat rate element without some account taken of actual housing costs, partly because they expect there to be arbitrary winners and losers from such a transition. They suggest a compromise option where recipients pay a fifth of their rent and four fifths comes from Housing Benefit meeting actual rents. Lower low-income households could receive an increase in Income Support to match the increase in the housing costs they have to face from their own funds.

The Green Paper argues that such proposals leave a number of issues or risks to be resolved:

- What do you do about existing claimants?
- How do you protect vulnerable people?
- What will be the housing market effects – can greater choice be buttressed by guaranteed standards of housing provision?
- Will the aforementioned changes to rents and allocations – and these are fundamental changes to social housing – actually be carried through to full implementation?

The section concludes by stating that "it would be crucial to get the right balance between giving tenants the right opportunities and practical incentives – ones they can act on – whilst also providing protection to the most vulnerable tenants, who rely on our support to give them access to housing" (DETR/DSS, 2000, p 119).

There is relatively little connection made in the Green Paper between the reform of Housing Benefit and wider welfare reform proposals or strategies. This is significant because on the one hand, Housing Benefit impinges on wider welfare reform and because it could also play a wider and more constructive role. The government seeks to transform 'welfare into work' and to pursue private–public partnerships in the delivery of welfare through, for instance, pension reform that makes better use of private pensions. We have seen that the design of Housing Benefit affects labour market and savings decisions at the margin. By penalising net income with punitive tapers it reduces work incentives and, with tariff income from savings assumed at only £3,000 (the same rate as in 1988), it serves to deter savings and the use of private pensions (Wilcox, 2000). In the debate about long-term Housing Benefit reform, several commentators have connected Working Families' Tax Credits to a hybrid flat rate/Housing Benefit reformed system. The suggestion is that those earning and receiving benefits could receive the flat rate element of a mixed reform scheme (flat rate plus a cost-related Housing Benefit scheme) in the form of a tax credit. Non-earners would receive it as either an Income Support supplement or as an allowance/voucher. Thus the benefits of the Working Families' Tax Credit – greater choice, less impact at the margin and fewer Housing Benefit claimants could help to provide a more integrated tax and benefit system. Wilcox (2000) also points out that while Working Families' Tax Credits are granted for a fixed period of six months, the Green Paper is only willing to consider such fixed periods of Housing Benefit support for pensioners, even though in the case of Working Families' Tax Credit the argument is made, officially, that the fixed period helps to overcome key labour disincentives.

Concluding discussion

This chapter has set out to, first, describe the in-principle arguments from economics that continue to hold sway about the efficacy and design of personal subsidies. Second, it described the Housing Benefit and ISMI systems and their consequences. Third, the chapter related the long-term reform proposals to those associated with John Hills and then highlighted the constraints to radical reform identified by Peter Kemp. Fourth, the chapter went through the position taken and proposals set out in the Green Paper.

As a component of Hills' proposals for the restructuring of social housing finance more generally, Housing Benefit reform is part of a wider process that moves social tenants towards a market-related but progressive system of support with housing costs, provision and management. This would involve rental reform towards capital value or target rents, more choice-based allocations, tackling low demand, more resident empowerment in terms of local management and it would involve a hybrid flat rate and actual cost Housing Benefit system wherein over time the flat rate share would increase.

It is evident that, thus far, there is no impetus to achieve tenure neutrality in support with housing costs. Support to help cash-poor outright owners with maintenance costs, or to assist those just above the Income Support level remains non-existent. Restricted or postponed eligibility to ISMI is a further major bias in the system and one that is likely to exacerbate any housing market downturn. Furthermore, the current system effectively discriminates against private tenants relative to social tenants. The housing system case for a general housing allowance based on income and needs rather than on tenure remains strong not just because of the inherent horizontal equity considerations but because it will greatly enhance the flexibility of the housing system. The long-term proposals set out by Hills and the transition route suggested do seem to be possible in-principle solutions to the path dependency problems identified by Kemp. The Green Paper, however, is fundamentally right that new rent structures and more choice in the allocations systems in the social rented sector are preconditions for change in personal subsidy. Of course, putting the tripod of reform together increases these path dependency problems geometrically. As Wilcox (2000) argues, these wider systemic constraints need not prevent worthwhile reforms that help address labour disincentives being carried out in the interim.

However, we should be clear that this is only the outline of the future design of social housing finance. It has still to overcome the risks attached to private finance, it has still to tackle the problem of transition for existing tenants and it has not substantively addressed work incentive problems. It can be argued, however, that many of the fraud and 'responsibility' issues are second order problems (but real enough) compared with these 'big' questions. It seems likely that when the next generation's Housing Green Paper is published, following 1977 and 2000, it will still be struggling with the problem of personal subsidies.

References

DETR (Department of the Environmnet, Transport and the Regions)/ DSS (Department of Social Security) (2000) *Quality and choice: A decent home for all*, Housing Green Paper, London: DETR.

Ford, J. (2000) 'MPPI take-up and retention: the current evidence', *Housing Finance*, vol 45, February, pp 45-51.

Gibb, K. (1995) 'A housing allowance for the UK: pre-conditions for a tenure-neutral income-related housing allowance', *Housing Studies*, vol 10, no 4, pp 517-32.

Hills, J. (2000) *Reinventing social housing finance*, London: IPPR.

Kemp, P. (2000) 'Housing Benefit and welfare retrenchment in Britain', *Journal of Social Policy*, vol 29, pp 263-79.

Wilcox, S. (1999) *Housing finance review, 1999-2000*, York: Joseph Rowntree Foundation/Chartered Institute of Housing/Council of Mortgage Lenders.

Wilcox, S. (2000) 'Contrasting ambitions – the English Housing Green Paper', *Housing Finance Review 2000-2001*. York: JRF/CIH/CML.

EIGHTEEN

Making connections

Dave Cowan and Alex Marsh

A key motivation behind this book was two parallel observations. On the one hand, the substance of much of housing studies is influenced by housing law, but this aspect is rarely explored by authors from the housing studies tradition. On the other hand, the substance of housing law is influenced by broader social, economic and housing policy changes, but this aspect is rarely explored by authors from the housing law tradition. Despite the considerable overlap between the interests of the two subjects, they have rarely come into contact with each other. The current re-invigoration of debate around housing policy provided an ideal opportunity to bring the two traditions together.

The primary purpose of this book was to provide a dual set of critiques of central elements of New Labour housing policy. Housing studies and socio-legal studies academics have provided their verdicts on this policy and in the process shed light on some of the key preoccupations of their subject areas. Our desire throughout this project has been to explore the possibilities for greater collaborative work in the future. In conclusion, rather than reprising the commentary on housing policy, we concentrate on this second aspect of the book. What we wish to do is reflect on the focus and approaches adopted by our contributors. In addition, we set out what we perceive to be some interesting joint futures.

Before doing so we should recognise that the contributions to this volume do not exhaust the scope of either subject area in terms of either research questions or approaches. Selecting different contributors would no doubt have led to a different degree of overlap between the two sets of contributions. For example, there is a branch of socio-legal studies which concerns itself with exploring the relevance of economic ideas to legal questions. Including a contribution from an author working in this area would have increased the apparent degree of commonality between socio-legal and housing studies. Nonetheless, we believe that the contributions demonstrate that the two areas have both a considerable commonality of interest and much to learn from each other.

We structure our discussion around three themes. We begin by looking at the research questions on which the contributors from socio-legal and housing studies focused. We suggest that there are some interesting distinctions at this basic level. Perhaps this should not surprise us because the disciplinary foundations of each set of authors would, on one level, demand this. What we should consider is the implications of these distinctions and whether there is a case for attempting to shift the terrain on which writers within the two fields operate. Should there be greater commitment on both sides to accommodate each other's research questions? It is possible to identify different routes forward. Does a recognition of the complementary contributions of the two subjects entail a commitment to greater collaborative working? Or should we simply acknowledge the difference and view the parallel paths of the two subjects as representing an appropriate division of academic labour? In this latter instance researchers in the two areas need to be 'cognitively open' to contributions from elsewhere, but not necessarily to pursue more cross-disciplinary research. Setting chapters side by side, as we have in this volume, was intended to heighten awareness of the different research questions being asked. This will, we hope, encourage readers to reflect on fruitful ways forward.

In the second section, by contrast, we identify some of the theoretical perspectives that we see as potentially making a valuable contribution to future work. Some of these perspectives have featured prominently in the contributions to this volume, while others have made a more fleeting appearance. We also draw attention to a framework – governmentality – which we believe has the potential to become a considerable boon to cross-disciplinary work, but which has, even though some chapters in this collection address some of the issues, hitherto been marginal to work concerned with housing.

In the final section, we return to questions of policy and policy development. We highlight topics that represent an agenda for future research that we would suggest can only be addressed adequately through interdisciplinary work. Included in this are aspects of New Labour housing policy which are not discussed in detail in this book but which can or will provide a focus for future policy intervention.

Research questions

The contributions to this volume demonstrate that considerable differences between the two subject areas exist at a basic level. The research questions which the authors sought to address differ significantly. Because they are starting with differing preoccupations and approach the topic from distinctive angles, the commentary and critique provided by the authors in most of the pairings illuminate different dimensions to the issue. This may not be particularly surprising; but it does support the contention that a more comprehensive understanding of the origins, substance and consequences of housing policy would result from joint approaches.

The questions of those pursuing the socio-legal agenda include changing rights and due process considerations; the gap between law and practice; the problem of discretion; the problems generated by the central–local relationship; the impact of juridification and broader questions of regulation. So, for example, the sub-title of Hunter's chapter – can law be the answer? – frames the approach which is adopted. Hunter shows how the discretion over the use of the various legal powers available to social landlords leads to different responses. Carr et al clearly link tenant participation into broader debates about collective and individual rights (using a contrast with the Right to Buy to great effect). Mullen displays similar concerns in relation to stock transfer. Several chapters – including those by Carr et al, Blandy, Cowan and Mullen – are concerned about decreasing security of tenure and due process rights. Vincent-Jones is concerned to locate the Best Value regime within the broader regulatory paradigm of *imperium, dominium*, competition, and fragmentation. Mauthe draws on literature relating to regulation and juridification of the central–local relationship to frame her analysis of social rents. Here again there is a desire to explore whether law is an effective mechanism for achieving policy objectives: in this instance the issue is the method by which central government establishes a preferred conceptualisation of social housing rents. For Cowan and Robson, in contrast, the problems of discretion, adjudication, and decision making provide the basis for their research questions.

The questions of those pursuing the housing studies agenda are perhaps more diverse because the housing studies community, as represented in this collection, has members who draw on a background in sociology, social policy, economics or politics, rather than starting with an orientation to a particular subject such as law. The contributions therefore encompass characteristically economic concerns with efficiency and incentives

(Walker and Gibb). Gibb also raises the issue of the gap between economic theory and practice. Marsh similarly seeks to question the applicability of economic ideas in the social rented sector and to link the question of rent restructuring to broader political questions. In contrast, sociological concepts such as power, democracy and citizenship are brought into considerations of participation (Goodlad), while Somerville engages with issues of managerialism, individualism and communitarianism. The concepts of social exclusion and inclusion permeate current policy discourse and a number of contributors make reference to them, with Card seeing this as a central concern in analysing anti-social behaviour. In several instances the intention is to unpick the competing influences underlying policy and its development. The contributions include attempts to highlight the unresolved tensions and conflicts in policy and the demands being placed on housing organisations. While perhaps not being as central to the analysis as for the socio-legal contributors, there were also concerns with, for example, questions of rights and the efficacy of regulation.

We can draw a further distinction between the two fields if we view them from the perspective of the policy process. In doing so we use some broad generalisations to highlight key differences.

Contributors from the field of socio-legal studies have a concern, as might be expected, with the way in which law becomes shaped, and itself shapes and reshapes social relations. There is often a greater concern with issues arising in the post-legislative phase, with problems and issues of implementation, and with micro-processes relating to bureaucratic and regulatory decision making (although this is not necessarily the case with other socio-legal work). Where proposals for legislation are being examined valuable lessons are drawn from experiences with previous and comparable legal provisions in order to identify areas of potential difficulty. The typical approach is to start from the law and broaden the analysis outwards so as to contextualise the legislative provisions being considered. This process of broadening can encompass macro-social forces or fundamental social scientific concepts, in which case the focus of the analysis can begin to shift away from the law as such. At the other extreme, authors need constantly to be alive to the danger of giving insufficient attention to these contextual factors: under-contextualised accounts can credit the law with a greater independence and greater causal power in shaping social relations than it warrants. The contributors to this volume differ in the extent to which they broadened out and contextualise their discussion of policy proposals and legislative provisions.

Yet, even where this element of the discussion is less fully developed, it is clear that there is an intention to set legal developments alongside other fundamental factors shaping the evolution of social relations in the housing field.

In contrast, those from housing studies are more likely to start from a concern with macro-level questions and with the pre-legislative phase, including consideration of the broad social forces shaping policy. There is perhaps a greater willingness to debate policy and the principles that underlie it. The law is not privileged as the starting point of the analysis. Indeed 'the law' as such does not feature prominently in many accounts. There is a view – or in some cases an implicit assumption – that legal provisions are dependent on broader social and political forces. Others credit law with some independent influence on the structure of social relations. This dichotomy is captured by Goodlad when summarising her approach to the analysis of tenant participation: "Legal change is seen mainly as following from social, economic and political change but the law can also be a resource supporting the renegotiation of relationships". Working from the housing studies perspective there can be a tendency to de-emphasise possible problems with the implementation of legal changes. There is less inclination to discuss micro-level issues of implementation.

In terms of the potential for cross-fertilisation of ideas or collaborative work between the two areas, at a minimum there is scope for each subject area to act as a counter balance to the other. An appreciation of the differing starting points and preoccupation of the 'other' discipline can help to foster an appreciation of the full range of questions and pertinent issues. For housing studies scholars it would open up questions and concerns about the way in which the legal system can act as an independent influence on social processes and outcomes. In particular it can enhance understanding of the way in which policy goals or broad social changes are mediated by legal processes that may enhance, attenuate or create inequities in the achievement of particular social outcomes. Conversely, awareness of the debates in housing studies could assist socio-legal scholars in the important task of conceptualising and contextualising their analyses of developments within the legal system.

There would appear to be a considerable return on investing time in, at a minimum, increasing the extent of information sharing between disciplines. More ambitiously, cross-disciplinary research approaches hold the promise of generating a more comprehensive understanding of questions of central concern to housing researchers. In some respects this conclusion is not novel – a number of the contributors to this volume drew on the literature from the 'other' field in order to bolster their analysis. It is noticeable, however, that this cross-disciplinary reading is largely one way, with socio-legal scholars showing a greater willingness to draw on ideas from housing studies than vice versa. This could be taken to suggest that at present socio-legal studies researchers are more 'cognitively open' than those from housing studies and to imply that it is the latter who will need more persuasion that cross-disciplinary working is of value. On the other hand, the more diverse range of interests and questions that coexist within the housing studies community means that there is likely always to be a subset of research questions and topics to which the law has more limited relevance. Complete overlap between the two fields would never be appropriate.

Finally, if it is agreed that there is merit in pursuing a joint agenda then there is the question of whether interdisciplinary or collaborative cross-disciplinary research would be the more promising route for future research. In the introduction we highlighted the danger of interdisciplinary research encountering difficulty because the researchers are 'semi-literate' in the literature of the 'other' discipline. While it is clearly possible for individual researchers to avoid this difficulty, we would suggest that research which brings together researchers from the different fields in collaboration is the most promising way of attempting to ensure that the full range of analytical resources can be brought to bear on a particular issue. More pragmatically, it is the quickest way to ensure that the relevant range of expertise is available. Much of the housing research which has attempted to forge links across the boundary of housing studies and socio-legal studies is of this collaborative type. We can see this trend continuing and developing.

Theoretical and analytical approaches

The contributors to this volume have drawn on a range of theoretical and analytical frameworks. The frameworks employed reflect the different preoccupations of each subject and largely divide across subject-based lines. Given that each framework offers some insight into the issue being analysed, the observation that frameworks largely divide across subject lines provides another reason for thinking that each subject could benefit significantly from further exchange of ideas. Inevitably those ideas we identify here represent only a subsection of those that have the potential to make a positive contribution to collaborative research.

The theoretical and analytical perspectives which we would identify as being particularly promising for future work relate to (a) the problems of juridification, (b) theories of citizenship and citizenship rights, (c) discourse analysis, and (d) the conduct and consequences of regulatory activity. The final perspective that we consider – governmentality – has been referenced by some of our contributors and we believe it has considerable potential as the foundation on which to build a more fully informed account of some important aspects of current and evolving policies that impact on housing.

(a) Perhaps the most influential social theoretical framework drawn on in the socio-legal chapters relates to the 'problems' of *juridification*. Juridification refers not so much to the quantity of regulation governing the 'social sphere' but to the nature and effects of that regulation on areas which might be better governed by other means. So, for example, one view of the problems of juridification is that "law, when used as a control medium of the welfare state, has at its disposal modes of functioning, criteria of rationality and forms of organisation which are not appropriate to the 'life world' structures of the regulated social areas and which therefore fail to achieve the desired results or do so at the cost of destroying these structures" (Teubner, 1987, p 4). Despite the influence of juridification within socio-legal studies (see further Vincent-Jones, 1999), no housing studies chapter drew on it. This suggests that there is an interesting theoretical dissonance which might usefully be explored in the future (see Goodchild, 2001).

Juridification is objectified in different ways and for different purposes in these chapters, in ways which essentially problematise it. Mullen argues that the process of juridification can be seen positively, although its 'pathological consequences' are problematic. He suggests that the large-scale voluntary transfer (LSVT) process has not been significantly affected by juridification because of the conflation of interests between the actors in the process and the lack of power of those seeking to challenge the process. By way of contrast to this approach, Blandy suggests that juridification is evident throughout the private rented sector. Mauthe draws attention to different extrapolations of the juridification thesis, but then argues that we need to go beyond them to accommodate the Green Paper's proposals on rents. Mauthe argues that a concept of *politicalisation* would be a more useful way of understanding this issue, arguing that power and control are exercised through politics and ideology. Vincent-Jones, although not explicitly addressing the questions posed by juridification, is nevertheless thinking about this concept in a different way. Rather than looking at the consequences of juridification, he specifically addresses the regulatory techniques used by central government over local government and how these are deployed in practice.

A critical engagement with the idea of juridification is clearly one of the central concerns for many of the socio-legal authors. Whether juridification is occurring, in what form, and with what consequences are core questions, especially when coupled with Teubner's observation that it refers to the inappropriate application of law and its potentially damaging consequences. For anyone looking to develop a critique of current policy directions and to articulate alternative routes to desirable social goals the debate around juridification offers a number of theoretical insights and resources.

(b) Much policy development and change is concerned with, on the one hand, reshaping or reallocating the bundle of legal rights to which individuals have access or, on the other, redrawing boundaries to circumscribe who has a right of access and on what terms. Understandings of housing policy can be enhanced by analysis that places notions of *citizenship* centre stage. The theory of citizenship offered by Turner (1993), for example, offers a dynamic account of the changing nature of citizenship. Policy is seen as the augmentation or abrogation of the rights of citizenship as a consequence of the changing balance of social forces. Yet, while citizenship theory offers a potentially fruitful analytical framework, it is important to recognise that a range of distinctive conceptions of citizenship have been advanced (see, for example, Lister, 1997; Delanty, 2000; Dwyer, 2000 for reviews). Hence the connections between citizenship and housing issues need to be theorised with care.

The most frequent point of connection between housing and the citizenship literature is to consider housing as a component of Marshall's (1950) social rights of citizenship (see discussions in Marsh and Mullins, 1998; also Clapham et al, 1996). The starting point of discussion is a focus on inadequate physical housing standards or access to housing, and corresponding questions about the responsibilities of the state to ensure standards through the provision of housing or of financial assistance such as improvement grants. Broader conceptions may include, for example, issues of tenure, choice, risk and insecure accommodation, and assistance for independent living. They also move beyond a concern with formal statements of rights and entitlements to examine whether these rights are effective in practice. Discussions of differential citizenship (for example, Lister, 1993) highlight the way in which systems of rights embody, either explicitly or implicitly, sets of cultural and political assumptions which can systematically disadvantage or fail to recognise the needs of particular groups within society (see for example Kennett, 1998, Harrison, 1995).

The changing housing policy agenda over the last two decades reflects strongly a much broader policy agenda inspired by communitarian ideas (Etzioni, 1995) and a renegotiation of the meaning of citizenship. It is encapsulated, however inadequately, in the notion of the 'Third Way', which has been subjected to extensive critical examination in the context of welfare provision (see, for example, Powell, 1999). This agenda seeks to shift the focus of citizenship away from rights and towards responsibilities. This increased emphasis on responsibility represents a significant shift in the terrain of the debate, particularly in socio-legal studies: "The responsibility thesis represents an explicit rejection of the rights–based discourse which dominated much of the legal discussions in the 1970s, 1980s and 1990s; it emphasises the *moral* responsibility that is expected of individuals, to behave in ways which accord with community and housing management values" (Cowan et al, 2000). In her contribution to this volume Blandy starts to trace out some of the implications of the rhetoric of rights and responsibilities for policy change in the private rented sector. Similarly, as Card suggests, anti-social behaviour policy is at its core a discourse of morality and the conditionality of citizenship rights. Discussions in this area are about the nature of the contract between individual and the state. The key concern is the circumstances in which state representatives interpret an individual's actions as irresponsible and thereby place them beyond the acceptable; and when this in turn leads to the suspension or removal of social rights of citizenship (by, for example, eviction from social housing).

A further distinction – between procedural rights and actual outcomes – highlights the need to look at social processes and raises questions about the extent to which citizenship offers or entails involvement and participation in decision making about housing. Where policy proposals seem to talk of rights, but these are not clearly legally enforceable, then one might be sceptical about their genuineness. For example, the contrast between policy on tenant participation and the Right to Buy is used effectively by Carr et al in their chapter to make this point.

Analysis of particular policies or policy changes from the perspective of changing citizenship rights and responsibilities exists in the literature.

However, there is much more to be done to integrate housing concerns within a broader and carefully elaborated framework of citizenship theory. Moreover, there are recent developments in citizenship theory – for example, debates about globalisation and nation states' reduced scope for or willingness to take independent policy action to guarantee social rights of citizenship – which are yet to be explored in detail in a housing context (see, for example, Delanty, 2000). There is great potential to integrate the concerns of socio-legal and housing studies at both macro- and micro-level around the notion of citizenship.

(c) *Discourse analysis* has achieved prominence in housing analyses for some time, with contributions from researchers working within both the socio-legal and housing studies fields. As a post-positivist approach it represents a fundamental break with some more traditional modes of policy analysis. Discourse analysis can cover a range of theoretical approaches and concerns, but much of the emerging literature concerns the production of regimes of truth; or, as Foucault puts it,

> It is a question of what *governs* statements, and the way in which they *govern* each other so as to constitute a set of propositions which are scientifically acceptable, and hence capable of being verified or falsified by scientific procedures.... At this level it's not so much a matter of knowing what external power imposes itself on science, as of what effects of power circulate among scientific statements, what constitutes, as it were, their internal regime of power, and how and why at certain moments that regime undergoes a global modification. (as quoted in Gordon, 1980, pp 112-13)

Blandy is the only contributor to the current volume who draws explicitly on discourse analysis as a means of illuminating the government's discussion of standards in the private rented sector. She argues that the 'three Rs' – regulation, rights and responsibility – have been "woven into government policy and legislation". This structures the argument, leading to the conclusion that greater emphasis has been placed in the Green Paper on responsibility and irresponsibility. Although not the primary node of analysis for Hunter, discourse analysis is used to suggest the predominant housing management approach of social control which ties in with some approaches to anti-social behaviour.

The broader literature contains attempts to carry out discourse analyses on a diverse range of housing issues, most with a strong policy dimension.

In housing studies, a recent issue of the journal *Urban Studies* concentrated on discourse analysis, and the work of Jacobs and Manzi has been particularly influential (1996, 1998, 2000). So, for example, specific work has used this perspective to analyse oppositional discourses about performance indicators (Jacobs and Manzi, 2000) and the moral imperatives contained in housing management (Haworth and Manzi, 1999). The ways in which housing tenure is discussed in policy documents and discussed by lay persons (including the many metaphors which exist about it) have also been analysed (Gurney, 1999a, 1999b; Marston, 2000; Watt and Jacobs, 2000).

Perhaps the major advances in our understandings of housing law have occurred (and continue to develop) through the use of this analytical tool. What one might term the 'Sheffield Hallam school' of housing law studies have drawn on discourse analysis to illustrate the languages and meaning of housing law (see Nixon and Hunter, 1998; Blandy and Goodchild, 1999; Hunter and Nixon, 1999). In particular, this has led to a greater understanding of the reproduction of myths about housing tenure within housing law. It may also explain the dissonance which exists between the different conceptualisations of housing by property law, housing law and housing discourses (Blandy and Goodchild, 1999).

Although Hastings (1998) suggests there are relatively few examples of research that take a 'fully discursive approach to policy', discourse analysis is now well established as a theoretical approach. Indeed there is arguably a danger of it becoming the bandwagon on which many are tempted to jump, without fully appreciating the significance of the shift that it requires at an epistemological level. Yet this should not detract from the view that painstaking analysis of the way in which language operates to shape perceptions can be illuminating. It can make a valuable contribution to our understanding of the way in which, for example, government seeks to construct a particular interpretation of an issue, which in turn implies its own favoured policy response.

(d) Developing satisfactory accounts of the way in which the housing system is regulated remains a major task for housing scholars. There exists a substantial body of regulatory theory on which to draw. Theories of *regulation* cross a broad compass of economic, social, legal and political ideologies and phenomena. Harlow and Rawlings (1998) have recently drawn attention to regulation theories that derive from what they term 'the blue rinse' which has swept across the political landscape. Welfare state retrenchment has led to the replacement of public provision by private provision plus regulation. The analysis of regulation and its behavioural implications has been a central preoccupation of both lawyers and social scientists with a range of disciplinary backgrounds.

The scope of application of theories of regulation is potentially vast. One can suggest, however, that particular themes have arisen in recent housing research. The regulatory issue that has been addressed most frequently, and has attracted attention from both housing and socio-legal studies, is the impact of private finance on Registered Social Landlords (RSLs) and their regulation by the Housing Corporation (Mullins, 1997; Walker, 1998; Walker and Smith, 1999; Cowan 1999). The reflexive regulation debate, which finds its foundations in socio-legal theoretical analyses of Teubner (1983), is beginning to exercise influence over our understandings of housing regulation. Reflexive regulation is a process which, rather than prescribe required behaviours (a process which may lead to regulatory failure), seeks "to work *indirectly* through 'reflexion structures' that encourage within other social systems self-reflection on the norms and values that guide their operation" (Vincent-Jones, 1999, p 310). The argument, as Vincent-Jones explains, is "not that those involved should have done better, but rather that direct control is not possible". Rather than rigid systems of command and control, regulation is required to be responsive to the regulatees.

In the current volume explicit concern with regulation has again been directed – by Vincent-Jones and Walker – at the way in which the activities of social housing providers have been regulated. Vincent-Jones' discussion, however, raises the broader issue of the way in which the whole housing system at local level is to be regulated. One component of this is the issue of housing standards in the private sector, as discussed by Leather and Blandy. There are arguably signs in this field that government is moving towards a greater emphasis on reflexive, or at least responsive, regulation in place of more legalistic enforcement-based approaches. Yet, regulation of the private sector is about more than standards of properties and management. The Green Paper raised a range of other regulatory issues – such as the performance of cowboy builders and the transparency of financial products – which have yet to be subjected to detailed, theoretically informed analysis. A key issue is the pattern of incentives that regulatory regimes present providers with, but equally important is the impact of regulatory regimes on the functioning, development or decline of markets. The government acknowledges this, for example, in its discussion of the market for mortgage protection insurance (DETR/ DSS, 2000, ch 4). More could be done to bring insights from regulatory theory to these discussions.

(e) Finally, we would suggest that the notion of *governmentality* offers considerable promise in the analysis of developments in housing policy. Despite only devoting one lecture to it, Foucault's concept of governmentality (1991) has been widely used and discussed in the socio-legal literature in recent years. Broadly, the concept refers to what Foucault described as the 'conduct of conduct'. Dean (1999) has expanded upon this to provide the following explanation of the term:

> Government is any more or less calculated and rational activity, undertaken by a multiplicity of authorities and agencies, employing a variety of techniques and forms of knowledge, that seeks to shape conduct by working through our desires, aspirations, interests and beliefs, for definite but shifting ends and with a diverse set of relatively unpredictable consequences, effects and outcomes. (p 11)

The point about this thesis is that it decentres the analysis of power, so that the focus is not necessarily on the state, but on a different set of rationalities and techniques of government (see generally, Rose, 1999; Smandych, 1999; Dean 1999). So, for example, consideration is given to the conditions which make government possible, such as the technologies of rule (like the social survey or the confession). This analytical framework is particularly useful in the current understanding of the minimal state. Rose (2000, p 324), for example, refers to an:

> ... alloy of autonomization and responsibilization [which] underpins shifts in strategies of welfare, in which substantive issues of income distribution and poverty have been displaced by a focus upon processual issues that affiliate or expel individuals from the universe of civility, choice and responsibility, best captured by the dichotomy of inclusion and exclusion.... [The politics of communitarianism, associationalism and the 'Third Way' involve] governing through the self-steering forces of honour and shame, of propriety, obligation, trust, fidelity, and commitment to others.

In this book, the governmentality thesis is drawn on explicitly by Vincent-Jones and Card, which suggests that it has potential for cross-disciplinary work. Vincent-Jones explicitly draws on the concept to illuminate the understanding of the regulatory matrix of the Best Value regime. With parallels to Rose's understandings of freedom (1999) and Stenson's configuration of sovereignty within the governmentality thesis (1999), Vincent-Jones argues that increasing freedom given to local authorities in the Best Value regime does not imply less controls on the part of the state. For Card, the problematisation of anti-social behaviour is wrapped up in the processes which make government both possible and necessary. Cowan draws on a different aspect of governmentality, analysing the housing application process through the lens of the confession. This then enables a micro-analysis of power in this context, showing how the process itself creates a 'thirst for knowledge'.

These examples illustrate the diversity of questions to which the concept can be applied but clearly they do not even begin to exhaust its potential to shed light on some of the most interesting and pressing research questions facing housing researchers.

Future agendas

We anticipate that the themes and approaches we identified above (no doubt together with others) will continue to be of importance across the terrain of housing research. In this final section, we turn to more substantive questions and seek to identify some areas that we believe would benefit from cross-disciplinary perspectives and understandings. For anyone who has research interests in housing, these are exciting times. It is not just that New Labour has produced a considerable number of policy interventions (and reasoned non-interventions) into the housing system. There is also the prospect that this will continue to be the case for the foreseeable future. In places there is a vibrant energy to housing policy, although in others there is a frustrating adherence to received wisdoms that inhibit progress.

Housing rights

Housing law is also receiving more attention from policy makers than it has done arguably since the 1970s. There is talk of a single social housing tenancy and the Law Commission now has a specific, separate programme on housing law under the auspices of Martin Partington (Law Commission,

2001). Partington's writings on housing law suggest that he favours a *consumerist* approach to housing policy. Housing rights should be easily understood, readily explainable, and there should be a regulatory body as there is for (say) fair trading. Presumably, there should be a commitment to non-traditional methods of adjudication, such as ombudsmen and internal reviews. Partington has also argued that a consumerist perspective would require the expansion of housing rights "with a view to ensuring that all citizens are guaranteed proper standards of housing service" (1993, p 133).

Within this set of futures, there lies the potential for a considerable amount of collaborative research. First, one must consider how far current housing rights and, importantly, housing advice falls short of the consumerist ideal. Research suggests that most occupants of housing are ignorant of their rights, and this is mirrored by the ignorance of some providers. As Carr et al show in their contribution to this collection, consumerisation has in the past tended to favour individualised rights, such as the Right to Buy, above collective rights. Their suggestion that this problem derives from the individual nature of property relationships in English law implies that there is a need to think beyond traditional notions of the individual as consumer. When attention is being given to the single social housing tenancy, this should be borne in mind.

Equally importantly, the consumerist ideal rests on assumptions which need to be held up to critical scrutiny. A prime example is an assumption about the relative power of the various parties. As is demonstrated in the context of harassment and unlawful eviction, it is not simply lack of information or problems with enforcing rights that lead tenants to fail to take action against harassment. There are also issues such as, for example, local market conditions that influence willingness to take action against the landlord.

More specific policy proposals raise important questions about rights. Proposals for changes to, for example, systems of allocating social housing, distributing improvement funding for low-income owner-occupiers and changing standards of housing fitness raise a multitude of questions about information, access, the use of discretion, the emergence of 'local law' and spatial inequalities. It may be a case of replacing one set of policy induced problems with another, but change which has a differential impact on households is almost inevitable. A framework structured around notions of differentiated citizenship could prove useful for examining the way in which policy develops and is implemented in these areas.

Human rights

There is important work to be done examining the development of a human rights 'culture' among housing providers. Human rights has not been uppermost in the minds of the contributors to this volume as they were not explicitly asked to address such issues. However, for the future there are a number of interesting questions such as the impact of human rights training on everyday working practices of housing organisations and the extent to which a human rights culture becomes embedded within welfare bureaucracies. Robson has identified a historical continuation in welfare policies; Cowan refers to the binary divide between deserving and undeserving as structuring legislative responses. Will the Human Rights Act have any impact on either of these?

On a broader level, policy initiatives such as the attempt to make Housing Benefit conditional on behaviour, as well as attracting a range of objections of principle and practice, may be vulnerable to challenge from a human rights perspective. Other policy interventions in recent years, such as introductory tenancies and policies towards asylum-seekers, are not entirely free from doubt in this respect. The way in which human rights concerns influence or constrain policy thinking and formulation, together with bureaucratic practice, is an issue that warrants detailed investigation.

Differentiated rights

Linking into the human rights agenda, but also going beyond it, are questions about gender and sexuality. Despite important edited collections and other work in this area which discuss housing in the context of gender and sexuality (Gilroy and Woods, 1992; Booth et al, 1996; Watson, 1999), a concern to understand the differential status of particular groups has yet to be incorporated throughout analysis of policy and the law. There is ongoing work on succession to tenancies within same sex relationships (see, for example, Sandland, 2000) and in relation to anti-social behaviour. However, it would be equally possible to re-analyse vast tracts of housing law and the writing of lawyers and academics from the perspective of gender and sexuality. For example, Collier's examination of the construction of criminology as a subject and of those involved in that process (1998, ch 2) might similarly be conducted in the housing sphere. Reading legislation and debates about legislation in terms of their construction of gender and sexuality (Bibbings, 2001: forthcoming) adds an important dimension to our understanding of the way in which policy and policy makers tackle the issues of diversity and difference, which have achieved prominence in discussions of post-modern welfare states. As noted above, analysis conducted with a clear focus on gender and rights can usefully be framed around notions of differentiated citizenship and can shed valuable light on the way in which broader socio-cultural and political assumptions shape housing policy and provision (Kennett, 1998).

The differentiated nature of the formal and effective rights of those from different ethnic backgrounds has perhaps been explored more fully within the housing studies literature and, to a lesser extent, within the socio-legal literature. Many of the key insights in housing which are largely taken for granted and some of the most sophisticated analysis of the way in which the housing system operates have been generated by scholarship in this field. A good current example is the way in which the relatively new concept of social exclusion has been analysed by those working in the field of 'race' and housing (Harrison, 1998; Ratcliffe, 1998, 1999). The overwhelming majority of this literature concerns the finding and experience of differentiated rights; in itself, therefore, this is an important area on which we should continue to focus.

The state, the individual and the community

The current government's policy rhetoric has a strong moral overtone, with considerable emphasis on responsibilities rather than rights. It also shows a desire to integrate a concern for community into policy which acts on individuals – through anti-social behaviour policy or community lettings policies, for example – at the same time as it is keen to break away from bureaucratic controls and unnecessary regulation. How these tensions will be managed – indeed whether they can be managed – and to what end is as yet unresolved. Attempting to unpick the relationship between the various themes embodied in current policy, within the traditional conception of individualised rights that operates in Britain, is a task that is likely to require the combined attention of those from both housing studies and socio-legal studies.

Public and private in the enabling state

Finally, current policy agendas have reinvigorated moves towards a strategic, enabling state that were begun under the previous administration. The transfer of responsibilities for provision from local authorities to RSLs not only brings in new stakeholders – principally the private funders – but also raises complex issues of regulation. At one level this is well known. However, the full implications of the changing structure of housing provision have arguably not been explored. Nor indeed have they yet manifested themselves.

The ability of local authorities to act strategically when they lack any particularly powerful levers to influence the behaviour of independent agents is an under-investigated topic. Equally, the impact of the involvement of lenders on the feasibility of local strategies, but also their influence on higher level discussions such as the reform of tenancy conditions, has yet to be fully understood. The path chosen for rent policy reform in the social rented sector and the reduction in ambition in the reform of Housing Benefit were both because of concerns about reduced cashflows being able to meet loan repayments. They represent two current examples of the way in which policy makers are increasingly hemmed in by the constraints that reliance on private funding imposes. As we move to an increasing reliance on privately funded voluntary sector provision these issues can only become more acute.

Were governments to become more interventionist with respect to the activities of independent providers this would raise some interesting legal questions. The dichotomy between public and private remains a crucial tool of law. Thus, all actions of public bodies are subject to the 1998 Human Rights Act; whereas only those 'functions of a public nature' of other bodies fall within the Act's ambit. The limits of the government's ability to regulate the private sphere are amply illustrated by the problems encountered with the attempt to limit increases in fair rents. A private landlord contested the government's attempts to limit by Statutory Instrument the maximum rent increases it could impose upon its properties (*R v Secretary of State for the Environment, Transport and the Regions ex parte Spath Holme Ltd*). The landlord claimed that this was beyond the powers of the enabling Statute. Although the claim succeeded in the Court of Appeal (*[2000] 1 All ER 884*) it was reversed in the House of Lords (7 December 2000).

We must wait to see precisely how this relationship between the state and RSLs will be negotiated in future, if the government decides to become more interventionist, and whether it will ever result in this sort of high profile legal dispute. Yet, the nature, scope and consequences of regulatory activity and, more urgently, the full ramifications of an increasingly privatised system of housing provision for vulnerable households are issues which will require considerable unpacking in the coming years.

References

Bibbings, L. (2001: forthcoming) *Dishonourable English men: Conscientious objection to military service in the Great War.*

Blandy, S. and Goodchild, B. (1999) 'From tenure to rights: conceptualising the changing focus of housing law in England', *Housing, Theory and Society*, vol 16, no 1, pp 31-42.

Booth, C., Darke, J. and Yeandle, S. (1996) *Changing places: Women's lives in the city*, London: Paul Chapman Publishing.

Clapham, D., Dix, J. and Griffiths, M. (1996) *Citizenship and housing: Shaping the debate*, Coventry: Chartered Institute of Housing.

Cowan, D. (1999) *Housing law and policy*, Basingstoke: Macmillan.

Cowan, D., Pantazis, C., and Gilroy, R. (2000) 'Social housing as crime control', Paper presented to the Socio-Legal Studies Association conference, Belfast.

Dean, M. (1999) *Governmentality*, London: Sage Publications.

Delanty, G. (2000) *Citizenship in a global age: Society, culture, politics*, Buckingham: Open University Press.

DETR (Department of the Environment, Transport and the Regions)/ DSS (Department of Social Security) (2000) *Quality and choice: A decent home for all*, Housing Green Paper, London: DETR/DSS

Dwyer, P. (2000) *Welfare rights and responsibilities: Contesting social citizenship*, Bristol: The Policy Press.

Etzioni, A. (1995) *The spirit of community*, London: Fontana Press.

Foucault, M. (1991) 'Governmentality', in G. Burchell, C. Gordon and P. Miller (eds) *The Foucault effect – Studies in governmentality*, Chicago, IL: University of Chicago Press.

Gilroy, R. and Woods, R. (1992) *Housing women*, London: Routledge.

Goodchild, B. (2001) 'Applying theories of social communication to housing law: towards a workable framework', *Housing Studies*, vol 16, no 1, pp 75-95.

Gordon, C. (ed) (1980) *Power/knowledge – Selected interviews and other writings 1972-1977, Michel Foucault,* London: Harvester Wheatsheaf

Gurney, C. (1999a) 'Lowering the drawbridge: a case study of analogy and metaphor in the social construction of home-ownership', *Urban Studies,* vol 36, pp 1705-22.

Gurney, C. (1999b) '*Pride and prejudice*: discourses of normalisation in public and private accounts of home ownership', *Housing Studies,* vol 14, pp 163-85.

Harlow, C. and Rawlings, R. (1998) *Law and administration,* London: Butterworths.

Harrison, M. (1995) *Housing, 'race', social policy and empowerment,* Aldershot: Avebury.

Harrison, M. (1998) 'Theorising exclusion and difference: specificity, structure and minority ethnic housing issues', *Housing Studies,* vol 13, no 4, pp 793-806.

Hastings, A. (1998) 'Connecting linguistic structures and social practices: a discursive approach to social policy analysis', *Journal of Social Policy,* vol 27, pp 191-211.

Haworth, A. and Manzi, T. (1999) 'Managing the "underclass": interpreting the moral discourse of housing management', *Urban Studies,* vol 36, pp 153-65.

Hunter, C and Nixon, J. (1999) 'The discourse of housing debt: the social construction of landlord, lenders, borrowers and tenants', *Housing, Theory and Society,* vol 16, pp 165-78.

Jacobs, K. and Manzi, T. (1996) 'Discourse and policy change: the significance of language for housing research', *Housing Studies,* vol 11, pp 543-60.

Jacobs, K. and Manzi, T. (1998) 'Urban renewal and the culture of conservatism: changing perceptions of the tower block and implications for contemporary renewal initiatives', *Critical Social Policy,* vol 19, no 2, pp 157-74.

Jacobs, K. and Manzi, T. (2000) 'Performance indicators and social constructivism: conflict and control in housing management', *Critical Social Policy,* vol 20, no 1, pp 85-103.

Kennett, P. (1998) 'Differentiated citizenship and housing experience', in A. Marsh and D. Mullins (eds) *Housing and public policy*, Buckingham: Open University Press.

Law Commission (2001) *Reform of housing law: A scoping paper*, London: The Law Commission.

Lister, R. (1993) 'Tracing the contours of women's citizenship', *Policy & Politics*, vol 21, no 1, pp 3-16.

Lister, R. (1997) *Citizenship: Feminist perspectives*, Basingstoke: Macmillan.

Marsh, A. and Mullins, D. (eds) (1998) *Housing and public policy: Citizenship, choice and control*, Buckingham: Open University Press.

Marshall, T.H. (1950) *Citizenship and social class*, Cambridge: Cambridge University Press.

Marston, G. (2000) 'Metaphor, morality and myth: a critical discourse analysis of public housing policy in Queensland', *Critical Social Policy*, vol 20, pp 349-73.

Mullins, D. (1997) 'From regulatory capture to regulated competition: an interest group analysis of the regulation of housing associations in England', *Housing Studies*, vol 12, pp 301-19.

Nixon, J. and Hunter, C. (1998) '"It was humiliating actually. I wouldn't go again": rent arrears and possession proceedings in the County Court', *Netherlands Journal of Housing and the Built Environment*, vol 11, pp 421-38.

Partington, M. (1993) 'Citizenship and housing', in R. Blackburn (ed) *Rights of citizenship*, London: Mansell.

Powell, M. (ed) (1999) *New Labour, new welfare state? The 'third way' in British social policy*, Bristol: The Policy Press.

Ratcliffe, P. (1998) ''Race', housing and social exclusion', *Housing Studies*, vol 13, no 6, pp 807-18.

Ratcliffe, P. (1999) 'Housing inequality and "race": some critical reflections on the concept of "social exclusion"', *Ethnic and Racial Studies*, vol 22, no 1, pp 1-22.

Rose, N. (1999) *Powers of freedom*, Cambridge: Cambridge University Press.

Rose, N. (2000) 'Government and control', *British Journal of Criminology*, vol 40, pp 321-39.

Sandland, R. (2000) 'Not "social justice": the housing association, the judge, the tenant and his lover', *Feminist Legal Studies*, vol 8, pp 227-39.

Smandych, R. (ed) (1999) *Governable places: Readings on governmentality and crime control*, Aldershot: Dartmouth.

Stenson, K. (1999) 'Crime control, governmentality and sovereignty', in R. Smandych (ed) *Governable places: Readings on governmentality and crime control*, Aldershot: Dartmouth.

Teubner, G. (1983) 'Substantive and reflexive elements in modern law', *Law and Society Review*, vol 17, pp 239-85.

Teubner, G. (1987) 'Juridification – concepts, aspects, limits, solutions', in G. Teubner (ed) *Juridification of social spheres*, Berlin/New York, NY: Walter de Gruyter.

Turner, B.S. (1993) 'Contemporary problems in the theory of citizenship', in B.S. Turner (ed) *Citizenship and social theory*, London: Sage Publications.

Vincent-Jones, P. (1999) 'The regulation of contractualisation in quasi-markets for public services', *Public Law*, pp 304-27.

Walker, R. and Smith, R. (1999) 'Regulatory and organisational responses to restructuring housing association finance in England and Wales', *Urban Studies*, vol 36, pp 737-54.

Watson, S. (1999) 'A home is where the heart is: engendering notions of homelessness', in P. Kennett and A. Marsh (eds) *Homelessness: Exploring the new terrain*, Bristol: The Policy Press.

Watt, P. and Jacobs, K. (2000) 'Discourses of social exclusion: an analysis of Bringing Britain together: A national strategy for neighbourhood renewal', *Housing, Theory and Society*, vol 17, pp 14-26.

Index

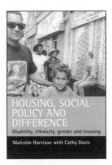